JOLLIET AND MARQUETTE

JOLLIET AND MARQUETTE

A New History of the 1673 Expedition

MARK WALCZYNSKI

3 FIELDS BOOKS
An imprint of the University of Illinois Press

3 Fields Books is an imprint of the
University of Illinois Press.

Library of Congress Cataloging-in-Publication Data
Names: Walczynski, Mark, author.
Title: Jolliet and Marquette : a new history of the 1673
    expedition / Mark Walczynski.
Other titles: New history of the 1673 expedition
Description: Champaign, IL : 3 Fields Books, an imprint
    of University of Illinois Press, [2023] | Includes
    bibliographical references and index.
Identifiers: LCCN 2022056834 (print) | LCCN 2022056835
    (ebook) | ISBN 9780252045219 (cloth) | ISBN
    9780252087356 (paperback) | ISBN 9780252054723
    (ebook)
Subjects: LCSH: Marquette, Jacques, 1637–1675. |
    Joliet, Louis, 1645–1700. | Mississippi River Valley—
    Discovery and exploration—French. | Mississippi River
    Valley—History—To 1803. | Illinois—Discovery and
    exploration—French. | Illinois—History—To 1778.
    | Explorers—Mississippi River Valley. | Explorers—
    Illinois. | Explorers—France. | Indians of North
    America—Mississippi River Valley.
Classification: LCC F352 .W185 2023 (print) | LCC F352
    (ebook) | DDC 977/.01—dc23/eng/20221130
LC record available at https://lccn.loc.gov/2022056834
LC ebook record available at https://lccn.loc.gov/2022056835

Contents

Preface   vii

Introduction: The Historical Background to 1665   1

1   Confronting the Haudenosaunee, Searching for Ore, and Allouez in the Upper Country   19

2   Copper Mines, Cavelier, and Wisconsin   35

3   St. Lusson, Marquette, Jolliet and the Sault, Adrien Jolliet, and Frontenac   56

4   St. Ignace to the Des Moines River   73

5   From the Illinois Villages to the Illinois River   84

6   From the Mississippi to Kaskaskia   101

7   Kaskaskia to Lake Michigan and Beyond   117

8   Canada, Jolliet, and Marquette   136

9   Marquette Returns to Kaskaskia   148

10 La Salle, Allouez, and Kaskaskia   159

11 Hudson Bay, La Salle in the Illinois, and the Recollects   173

12 La Salle, the Illinois Country, and the Gulf   188

Epilogue   201

Appendix: Timeline of Events   227

Notes   243

Bibliography   273

Index   279

Preface

This book is unique. It takes a fresh look at events that led to the famous 1673 voyage of Louis Jolliet and Jacques Marquette, it describes what the explorers witnessed and experienced during their journey, and it traces events that occurred in the Illinois Country and beyond that were the direct result of the expedition. It attempts to clear up mistakes and fog about the background of the voyage and the people involved in it, including claims of earlier historians that have been proven unlikely or even false that have been perpetuated down through the years. To do this, this narrative relies on sciences and techniques that were not available to earlier authors, including linguistic analysis of Native American words and terms, reports of archaeological investigations at villages that were visited by Jolliet and Marquette, knowledge of Ice Age geology that is now known to have carved and shaped specific regions of the Midwest, and the impact of climate on settlement and exploration. Moreover, this is a timely publication since 2023 will be the 350th anniversary of the famous voyage.

This narrative explores questions that earlier researchers had failed to ask. It also points out unsupported claims that have gone unchallenged for more than a half century. For example, did Jolliet and Marquette meet to plan their Mississippi voyage prior to Jolliet's arrival at Marquette's St. Ignace mission in December 1682? When did Louis Jolliet first travel to the Great Lakes country? Why was Louis, a relative newcomer to the West, chosen to participate in the

1673 expedition? Which "two Fathers of considerable intelligence" drew, or collected information for, the now famous *Lac Superieur et autres lieux ou sont les missions des peres de la Compagnie de Jesus Comprises sous le nom d'Outaouacs* map? When was the St. Ignace mission at Mackinac first established, and by whom? Was Louis Jolliet capable of drawing accurate maps in 1674–75? What kind of legal troubles did Jolliet face when he returned from the expedition? What can archaeology tell us about the sites that Jolliet, Marquette, Allouez, La Salle, and others visited? On what information did La Salle base his 1678–83 expedition to the Gulf of Mexico? Who were the largest slave owners in the Illinois Country during the French Regime? How were the Illinois and Mississippi Rivers manipulated to facilitate commerce, and how did those changes impact the environment? How did the Illinois River become a federal navigable waterway?

This book is steeped in the fabulous Native American history of the United States and Canada. It describes the customs, beliefs, and sometimes the mindset of the Indigenous people of eastern North America. It describes how the Native people understood the cycles of nature and the circle of life. It explains that, even though they had no scientific explanation for natural phenomena, their myths and spiritual beliefs offered explanatory powers that were, in fact, not much more unusual than beliefs and myths of Catholic missionaries. It explains why Native villages were established where they were, what they looked like, and why they were, at times, abandoned. It also traces Native American migrations, relocations, and resettlement that were caused by intertribal warfare, intertribal alliances, access to European trade goods, and climate. It reveals why the Illinois Indian village of Kaskaskia on the Upper Illinois River was so key to French Catholic evangelization, trade, and settlement efforts in the West and how the Native Americans who lived at the site played a vital role in French plans for development of the Mississippi Valley. It explains why intertribal warfare, including conflicts between the Haudenosaunee (Iroquois) and the Huronia tribes during the 1640s and 1650s, between the Nadouessi (Sioux) and the La Pointe tribes in the 1660s and 1670s, between the Haudenosaunee and the Illinois Indians in the 1680s, and the wars between the Chickasaw and other lower Mississippi tribes and the French during the 1730s and 1740s occurred.

This book also follows the achievements and setbacks of French and Canadian officials, explorers, traders, voyageurs, and soldiers, and explains how they directly or indirectly (or both) contributed to the political and religious environment that led to the 1673 voyage and, ultimately, to the opening of the Mississippi Valley. It introduces the reader to little-known Frenchmen, including Adrien Jolliet, Jacques Largillier, and Michel Accault, who played important roles in the exploration of Canada and Louisiana.

The manuscript follows the exploits, adventures, successes, and failures of the first Catholic missionaries to work among the tribes of the Upper Great Lakes, the Illinois Country, and the Mississippi Valley, including Fathers Jean Brébeuf, Claude-Jean Allouez, Louis Nicolas, Jacques Marquette, Claude Dablon, Louis André, Jacques Gravier, Gabriel Marest, Jean François Buisson St. Cosme, and others. It reveals the mind-set of these well-educated and sometimes worldly priests, how they viewed tribal beliefs and customs, and why they often saw themselves as lone defenders of their faith who struggled to overcome dark forces. It reveals the good-natured rivalry between Catholic religious orders, including the Jesuits and the Société des Missions Étrangères, for jurisdiction over the tribes who lived along the Mississippi. It explains why the role of French missionaries evolved from a secondary responsibility with minor importance to one of great consequence. It reveals that missionaries used essentially the same methods to instruct and convert Native Americans that evangelists did during the first years of Christianity. It also shows the challenges faced by missionaries and their *donnés* who worked to translate abstract Catholic ideas, concepts, and simple prayers into a Native American language that contains no linguistic equivalents. And it shows that the Christianization of Indigenous people did not end with France's departure from North America. It continued into the nineteenth and twentieth centuries at church-state-run schools that deprived Native children of their culture, language, and family ties and led to many deaths.

This book relies on the latest and most thorough and up-to-date reports from archaeological excavations and surveys conducted at Native American settlement sites mentioned in this manuscript. Further, it compares anthropological information gathered from Jesuit reports with bioarchaeological analysis found in archaeological reports. Linguistic analysis of Amerindian words and terms and understanding the history of how the French learned Native languages are used to clear up errors and misconceptions made by Marquette and other period missionaries that have been perpetuated for the past century. It also investigates the origins of Native American names for rivers, including today's

Mississippi, Ohio, Des Plaines, and Vermilion Rivers. In fact, recent linguistic discoveries explained in the book reveal how tribal names defined the character and culture of tribes and subtribes.

Unlike any other book written about the famous 1673 voyage of discovery, four chapters are devoted exclusively to the expedition itself—the reader will figuratively ride in the canoe with Jolliet and Marquette as they traverse the rivers and lakes of the central parts of North America. It describes potential dangers they faced from hostile tribesmen, navigational hazards, the elements, and, of course, fierce river monsters. It describes what the explorers saw during their journey by reconstructing their route from reports and memoirs of later travelers, explorers, and missionaries. It describes their contact with tribes they encountered, some of which were unknown to the French, and how by meeting with tribal chiefs and elders, the range of languages and dialects known to the group's interpreter and translator, Jacques Marquette, was delineated. The reader will also travel in canoes with Jesuits Allouez and Gravier and with explorers including La Salle as they, like the men of the Jolliet-Marquette expedition, traverse the continent's waterways.

Little time is spent with Jolliet after 1677, after he severed ties with the West and refocused his efforts on business, professional, and personal opportunities in the East, at Quebec, Anticosti Island, along the Lower St. Lawrence, and the Atlantic Coast. Jolliet's later explorations, including one to Hudson Bay, have little to nothing to do with his and Marquette's 1673 voyage and are thereby treated in a cursory manner. To detail Louis's many later exploits would go beyond the scope of this book.

Most seventeenth-century French missionaries, explorers, and administrators refer to many of the Algonquian-speaking groups of the Great Lakes as Outaouaks, Outaouac, Outaoüacs, and Ottawas. One tribal affiliation of this group includes today's Odawa, commonly known as "Ottawa." I will attempt to distinguish the Odawa from the larger combined Ottawa groups whenever possible.

I relied on the term "Indian" in certain circumstances, especially in cases where it applied to the Illinois tribe. The term "Indian," which is used today by the tribes themselves, including the Illinois, helps to differentiate between the Illinois River, the Illinois Country, the state of Illinois, the Illinois language, and the Illinois people. Furthermore, terms such as "Amerindian" or "Native American" are not compatible with the name Illinois or other tribes as it applies to their identity in a proper sentence—for example, the Illinois Amerindians or Wendat Native American tribe.

I have deferred to Raphael Hamilton's *Marquette's Explorations: The Narratives Reexamined*, one of the best sources for information pertaining to the authorship of Marquette's now-famous journal. Hamilton's study permanently lays to rest Father Francis Borgia Steck's *The Jolliet-Marquette Expedition, 1673* and other revisionist assertions that the narrative of the 1673 voyage was not Marquette's but had been written later by an anonymous author. Steck's claim can no longer be reasonably accepted. Furthermore, Steck also wrote about the "mysterious disappearance," as called it, of Jolliet's two journals that, in his mind, played into a larger conspiracy to elevate Marquette to the role of leader of the expedition.

Most distances in this book are calculated via Google Earth. Distances pertaining to river and lake travel were measured by following the courses of rivers and shorelines, as well as geographical features on the lakes such as peninsulas, as opposed to straight-line measurements, which in nearly every case are much shorter than actual distances traveled. For example, the distance between Sault Ste. Marie and the Jesuit mission at La Pointe by way of a straight line is about 475 miles, while the distance by following the shoreline of Lake Superior is about 600 miles. Some distances calculated in chapters that describe the 1673 voyage up the Illinois and Des Plaines Rivers were determined by U.S. Army Corps of Engineers maps (1867 and 1883), the Woermann Maps (published in 1905), and the Illinois Waterway Navigational Charts (1998).

During Jolliet and Marquette's ascent of the Illinois River, I used names for islands, lakes, and other geographical features that are found on nineteenth-century Army Corps of Engineers maps and the Woermann Maps, most of which were created before the reversal of the Chicago River and construction of the present lock and dam system.

Selected portions in this book have appeared in "Louis Jolliet and Jacques Marquette: Consistencies, Contradictions, and Misconceptions," *Michigan's Habitant Heritage* 38, no. 3 (2017), the publication of the French-Canadian Heritage Society of Michigan, as well as "Claude Dablon and Louis Jolliet, Constructing a Narrative from Presuppositions," *Michigan's Habitant Heritage* 40, no. 2 (2019). I also reproduced material from "La Salle vs. Jolliet: A Rivalry for Trade and Colonization in the Illinois Country," *Le Journal* (Center for French Colonial Studies) 32, no. 2 (2016). Parts of the three articles have been reproduced with the permission of both publications.

Citations from Reuben Gold Thwaites, ed., *Jesuit Relations*, are taken from the Kripke Center (creighton.edu). Quotes are taken as they appear in the sources from which they are cited.

Last, I tried to avoid dogmatic conclusions about the intentions and actions of certain individuals or groups unless they were backed by credible evidence, and I also tried to keep the scope of this study as narrow as possible to demonstrate that the Jolliet-Marquette expedition of 1673 was the key that opened the door to the American West.

JOLLIET AND MARQUETTE

INTRODUCTION

The Historical Background to 1665

The Jolliet-Marquette expedition of 1673 was an important voyage into lands and waters that were unknown to the newly arrived Europeans who lived in today's United States and Canada. Although the Spanish under Hernando de Soto were the first Europeans to have seen the Mississippi, crossing the stream in June 1541, his expedition did not establish and maintain an enduring Spanish presence along its banks. The Jolliet-Marquette expedition not only explored the central parts of the Mississippi, but also documented for the first time by way of map and journal the river, its tributaries, and the villages along its banks. Marquette's journal also described the people he and Jolliet encountered as well as their customs and socioeconomic conditions. The group also determined into which sea the Mississippi River emptied. The voyage was the single event that led to French settlement of the Mississippi Valley and the later Spanish and American occupation.

Although French explorers, missionaries, and colonial officials may not have realized it at the time, the dynamics of Native American life and settlement in parts of today's Canada and the United States by the first years of the seventeenth century were changing at a rapid pace, and much of it was caused by the arrival of Europeans themselves. Trade between Europeans and Native groups led to alliances and sometimes war. With the arrival of European manufactured goods came changes in societal and material cultures. Close contact between

Europeans and Amerindians led to the spreading of diseases that devastated tribal populations. Even though Native people had traded with other Native groups and utilized well-established trade networks for thousands of years before the arrival of Europeans, access to the new trade goods would oftentimes determine whom Native Americans allied with or fought against, how they obtained items on which they had come to rely, and even where they lived.

New France began as a cluster of base camps for fishermen and whalers. Basque mariners established whaling and fishing camps along the coast of Labrador and southeastern Canada at Hare Harbor and Red Bay.[1] French explorer Jacques Cartier encountered them in the Strait of Bell-Isle, the passage between present Newfoundland and Labrador. French, Spanish, Irish, and Portuguese fishermen trawled the Grand Banks and the Gulf of St. Lawrence for cod to satisfy Catholic Europe's demand for fish, the French alone having during this time 153 fish days per year.[2] To preserve the fish for the long voyage home, fishermen established camps where the fish flesh was dried, salted, and eventually loaded onto ships for transport. The best sites were occupied by fishermen year-round. At these camps, fishermen encountered local Indigenous people. Early relationships between fishermen and Amerindians led to small-scale, hand-to-hand, bartering for metal knives and cloth in exchange for furs.[3]

Recognizing that more wealth could be made in the fur business, administrations including those of French kings Henri IV and later Louis XIII granted trade concessions/monopolies to influential individuals such as Pierre de Chauvin de Tonnetuit, Aymar de Chaste, Troilus de La Roche de Mesgouez, and Pierre Dugua de Monts, some of whom were awarded prestigious titles such as "lieutenant-general of Canada and Acadia," fashionable but largely empty designations. Because of growing rivalries between concessionaires over jurisdiction and territory, the Company of New France, also known as the Compagnie des Cent-Associés, was formed in 1627, the brainchild of Cardinal Richelieu, Louis XIII's former chief minister and powerful Catholic ecclesiastic. The company was obligated, in exchange for full fur-trading and fishing rights, to deliver colonists to Canada, supply and maintain priests for churches, and provide for the colony's protection. They were also authorized to distribute land to settlers and to administer justice. In 1629 Canada passed into British hands after Quebec's surrender to the Kirke Brothers. By 1631, with the British in control of Canada, the company was all but ruined; only one-tenth of its original investments remained.[4] With the return of Canada to France in 1632, the company formed subsidiaries to take on some of its obligations while keeping ownership of the lands and the administration of the colony.

In 1633 Samuel de Champlain, who first arrived in Canada in 1603 as a passenger aboard a vessel under the authority of French naval officer François Gravé du Pont, was designated by Richelieu to look after the company's and the colony's interests and administration. He set sail from France with three ships loaded with settlers, a few soldiers, and supplies.[5] By 1640 Canada had become the principal source of furs for the European market. Although fur became the principal source for wealth in early Canada, fishing also remained important to the French.

Alliances between Native groups and Europeans were formed, and trade ties between Native groups were strengthened. Whether it was intentional or not, by siding with the tribes that they had first met and befriended, the French injected themselves into long-standing intertribal conflicts that would in some cases work against France's own best interests. In 1609 Samuel de Champlain's alliance with Algonquin, Wendat (Huron), and Montagnais tribesmen against the Haudenosaunee, or Iroquois, a confederation of tribes composed of the Mohawk, Cayuga, Oneida, Onondaga, and Seneca, also known at the time as the Five Nations, and his subsequent killing of two Haudenosaunee chiefs became the opening salvo in a conflict that evolved into nearly a century of war between the French and the Haudenosaunee.[6]

According to historian W. J. Eccles, the Haudenosaunee "were the most formidable military power in North America," at the time, and continued to be until the eighteenth century.[7] Besides their tribal organization that freed Haudenosaunee men to concentrate on war, the Haudenosaunee were also able to procure firearms, among many other items of European manufacture, from Dutch and British traders. Eventually, the supply of beaver and other fur-bearing animals in Haudenosaunee territory, the hides of which were needed to purchase weapons and items that they had come to rely on, began to wane, causing the tribe to seek pelts elsewhere. The Haudenosaunee also wanted to prevent rivals, including the Mahican and Algonquin groups from the Ottawa Valley, from acquiring trade goods and firearms from Dutch traders. The Mohawk, an eastern Haudenosaunee group, went on the offensive in 1624, first striking the Mahican, which, by 1628, forced the survivors to flee east to the Connecticut Valley.[8] The vacuum left by the Mahican departure was filled by the Mohawk, which, incidentally, prevented the northern Algonquin from trading with the

Dutch in modern-day New York. War also broke out between the Haudeno-saunee and the Montagnais and the Algonquin, forcing the latter tribes to abandon their fortified village at Trois Rivières.[9] The Haudenosaunee continued their raids in the Lower St. Lawrence Valley, striking not only Native groups, but also the French. To counter the raids, the French built fortified settlements, including Sorel and Montreal, both established in 1642, and strengthened existing villages, including Trois Rivières. Attempts to arm their Wendat and Algonquin allies against the Mohawk were frustrated by the Jesuits because the order convinced Canadian officials that only Christian tribesmen should be armed, believing their converts to be more "reliable."[10]

The Wendat and Haudenosaunee had sparred with each other for centuries. They fought to redress old grievances, to stop encroachment on territorial claims, to avenge past killings, to take captives, and as a means to provide young men the opportunity to prove their prowess in battle. However, during the late 1640s and early 1650s, a new and more serious motive was at play: the Haudenosaunee sought to assert dominion over the trade route between the western Great Lakes and the French, British, and Dutch in the East, territory claimed by the Wendat and other Huronian tribes, an area located roughly between Georgian Bay and the western part of northern Lake Ontario. The Wendat, weakened by the ravages of European-borne diseases and experiencing sweeping cultural transformations, were attacked and defeated by

A model of the early settlement at Montreal. Photo taken by the author at the Pointe-à-Callière Archaeology and History Complex in Montreal.

well-armed Haudenosaunee war parties manned by as many as one thousand warriors. A year or two later, the Haudenosaunee attacked Neutral and Petun villages.[11]

While some Wendat survivors of the attacks first sought refuge among the Neutral and Erie Indians, the latter tribe living along the southern shore of Lake Erie, others fled west to Georgian Bay and Lake Nipigon. About three thousand Wendat, for self-preservation, joined with their Seneca Haudenosaunee conquerors, while others fled to Christian Island in Georgian Bay. Those who survived famine on the island that winter next fled to the Île d'Orléans, near Quebec, where they established a village on Jesuit-owned property. There they were soon joined by three hundred more Wendat refugees. In 1656 a Haudenosaunee war party attacked the Wendat groups on Île d'Orléans, killing and capturing approximately sixty to seventy people. The relentless attacks by the Haudenosaunee eventually pushed most Wendat and Petun groups west to present Mackinac Island, then to an island on the Door County peninsula. Sometime later, the Wendat and Petun moved to mainland Wisconsin.[12]

◇◇◇◇◇◇◇◇◇◇◇◇◇◇◇

The ancestors of northern Europeans lived through what anthropologists have termed the Upper Paleolithic and Neolithic periods, then Copper, Bronze, and Iron Ages, a span of forty thousand years, before reaching late historical times. With the advent of European trade goods, Native American material culture, by way of comparison, changed very quickly. Trade goods such as firearms not only allowed hunters to kill game more efficiently, but also made warriors more proficient in war, increasing their effective killing range. Metal knives and hatchets made cleaning and dressing game much easier, and they could be used as weapons. Brass kettles for cooking were more durable than clay pots and were less likely to break during transport or while in use. Metal needles for sewing and for tattooing were a vast improvement over thorns and animal bones. Blankets traded by the French allowed women more time to perform other chores. Items for adornment, including beads, rings, bracelets, and even crucifixes, were also sought by the tribes. Protohistoric groups who lived in parts of today's southwestern Michigan, northwestern Indiana, and northeastern Illinois, for example, would have obtained trade items of European manufacture by way of down-the-line trade, not by direct contact with French, Dutch, or British traders.

Even though the tribes sought goods of European manufacture, not all the traditional tools and methods of crafting items for everyday use were abandoned. Women still tilled the soil with hoes and handheld spades crafted from elk and bison scapula, mussel shells, and antlers. Ears of maize were "shelled" with mussel shells to remove the kernels. As late as the early eighteenth century, some Native groups, including the PE8ARE8A, the Peoria, a subtribe of the Illinois alliance, still maintained some of their traditional ways.[13] One anonymous visitor to a Peoria village located on the Illinois River in 1718 observed that the Peoria used the bow and arrow, dressed in animal hides, and were heavily tattooed.[14]

Not only did the introduction of European goods change Amerindian material culture, but it also changed their societal culture. Trade alliances with the French led to influence in tribal politics, economics, and social affairs. Traders sometimes married Native women, thereby creating kinship bonds that gave the outsiders standing in tribal communities and influence in village matters. These associations also led to military alliances, important relationships that allowed the French to build forts and defend territory. Without Native allies, the French could have never conducted campaigns against the Haudenosaunee, Mesquakie, Natchez, and British.[15]

Not long after the French established Quebec (July 1608), missionaries of two Catholic religious orders arrived in Canada, the Jesuits at Port Royal in 1611 and the Recollects, first at Tadoussac and then eight days later at Quebec, in 1615. The Huronia tribes were of particular interest to the missionaries because they lived in large, semipermanent agricultural villages for much of the year. Not only did they sow and harvest domestic crops, but the Wendat, for example, also practiced a seasonal subsistence pattern that included hunting, fishing, and gathering assorted wild nuts, berries, and plants. Unlike for some of the first Native groups that French missionaries encountered, primarily hunter-gatherers, subsistence for the Wendat and Petun was not entirely tied to the chase. A missionary to the Wendat noted that they lived in villages and "cultivate the fields, from which they gather Indian corn,—the grain which some call Turkish,—abundance of excellent pumpkins, and also tobacco. All this region abounds in game and fish; and so the Hurons have at hand the means of supplying a living, if not luxurious, yet adequate and healthful; and they sell to others."[16]

The first Recollects to labor among the Wendat were Fathers Joseph Le Caron, Nicolas Viel, and Gabriel Sagard, who were later followed by Jesuit Jean

Brébeuf. Brébeuf remained in Wendat country until 1629, when Quebec fell to the Kirkes.[17] The surrender suspended Jesuit missionary work in Canada.

In 1634, two years after the signing of the Treaty of Saint-Germain-en-Laye, which restored Canada to the French, Brébeuf returned to Wendat country. Jesuits Antoine Daniel and Ambroise Davost also set out for Huronia. What at first appeared to be a prosperous mission field was soon seen for what it really was, in the minds of the priests, a panoply of deep-seated and time-tested cultural norms that were utterly foreign to European sensibilities. About the Catholic faith, Brébeuf wrote to Father Mutius Vitelleschi, general of the Society of Jesus, at Rome, that the Wendat "have but one answer": "Such is not our custom; your world is different from ours; the God who created yours," they say, "did not create ours."[18] But even though the missionaries were unable to change the hearts and minds of the tribesmen, a far more menacing concern for the Indians was at hand: European-borne disease.

During the late 1630s, European diseases, primarily smallpox and influenza, devastated the Huronia tribes as well as other eastern communities, including those of the Montagnais and Algonquin.[19] According to some estimates, nearly half of the Wendat population perished between 1634 and 1639. Seemingly left unscathed from the epidemic were French missionaries, some of whom after becoming sick remarkably became cured. This led tribesmen to believe that the French were witches or sorcerers who inflicted the death and misery on their people. Some Wendat took to jeering at the missionaries, while others reportedly physically abused the priests.[20] With their populations reduced by disease, the Haudenosaunee were able to more easily defeat the Huronia tribes. Caught up in the destruction were the Jesuits who, in spite of how they had been treated by the Wendat, remained at their villages. During one raid, the Haudenosaunee killed Jesuit Antoine Daniel shortly after he celebrated Mass at his mission, while fellow Jesuit Charles Garnier fell to the Haudenosaunee at a Petun village near Georgian Bay. Jesuits Brébeuf and Gabriel Lalemant were captured by Haudenosaunee warriors at their St. Louis (Taenhatentaron) mission and were later killed by their Haudenosaunee captors.

Not only did the Huronia tribes and the Erie relocate to new camps, the *aniššina·pe·k* were also on the move. According to Ojibwe tradition, the *aniššina·pe·k*, an umbrella term for the Ojibwe, Odawa, and Potawatomi, came from the east and separated at the Straits of Mackinac, likely no later than the sixteenth century.[21] From the straits, the Ojibwe journeyed north and west, into northern Wisconsin, northern Minnesota, and southern Ontario; the Odawa claimed the Mackinac region; and the Potawatomi eventually moved south into Michigan's Lower Peninsula and into the Green Bay area.[22]

The *aniššina·pe·k* then fled west to avoid Haudenosaunee war parties in the company of Wendat refugees, as well as Sauk, Mesquakie, Kickapoo, and other Native groups. Their flight took them into western Wisconsin, territory claimed by Eastern Nadouessi, Siouan groups. Believing the newcomers threatened their security, the Nadouessi struck out against them.[23] The *aniššina·pe·k* and the others fled north and east and in time settled at winter villages at Chequamegon Bay, near modern-day Ashland, Wisconsin.

The *aniššina·pe·k* eventually came to control trade in the upper Great Lakes. No forts, trading posts, or missions would have been permitted in the region during the seventeenth and eighteenth centuries had the *aniššina·pe·k* not allowed the French to do so. In the words of historian Michael A. McDonnell, "Not one canoe would have survived the trip up to the *pay d'en haut* without the help of Indian guides and translators. Not one fur would have made it to Europe without the intervention of native trappers and the consensual trade of Indians. . . . The French were there because the *Aniššinapeg* wanted them there."[24]

Nadouessi influence during the seventeenth century spread from north of the Great Lakes down the Mississippi into Illinois and Missouri.[25] During this time, and later, the Nadouessi, besides their hostilities with the *aniššina·pe·k*, also sparred with the Cree and had penetrated as far south as the Illinois River.[26] With the infiltration of the *aniššina·pe·k* into Wisconsin and Minnesota, some Nadouessi groups may have voluntarily moved west from the Mississippi Valley to that of the Missouri, their material culture changing from woodland to prairie, where bison played a more significant role in their means of survival. Historian Gary Clayton Anderson describes the Nadouessi as a "fluid society, tied more securely to the movements of game than to the land. Voluntary migration has been used to explain the movement of the western Sioux onto the prairies."[27] In the period 1669–71, Nadouessi villages, including those of the Mdewakanton, Sisseton, Wahpekute, and Wahpeton, all Eastern Nadouessi (Santee) subtribes, were located just west of Chequamegon Bay and along the Upper Mississippi and some of its tributaries. In time the Ojibwe began to slowly occupy northern and north-central Minnesota; the most western of these bands, the ones in almost near-continuous conflict with the Nadouessi, became later known as the "pillagers."[28]

The Sauk and the Mesquakie also migrated great distances during early historic times. The name Sauk, People of the Yellow Earth, and Mesquakie, People of the Red Earth, the latter known to the French as the Fox, or Renards, and to the Ojibwe as Outagami (People of the Opposite Shore, a reference to Michigan's Lower Peninsula), divide their history and migrations into legendary and historic time frames.[29]

The *known* Mesquakie historic past begins in the Detroit area in 1640. A map titled *Nouvelle France,* also known as the "Taunton Map," a chart that appears to be the work of Jean Bourdon, who according to linguist John Steckley drew other maps of the period, places the Mesquakie in the Detroit area.[30] Historians R. David Edmunds and Joseph L. Peyser have written that the tribe lived in the Detroit area until about 1650, when attacks by Ojibwe war parties forced them to flee.[31] Because of the raids, according to the "Meskwaki" tribe, the Mesquakie headed northwest from Lower Michigan to the shore of Lake Michigan, perhaps to the vicinity of Ludington. From western Michigan, they would have struck north and across the Straits of Mackinac, skirting the south shore of Lake Superior and settling briefly in northwestern Wisconsin, in the Chequamegon Bay area. From Chequamegon Bay, the Mesquakie would have moved south and established villages in east-central Wisconsin, along the Wolf and then the Fox Rivers. Their culturally and linguistically related cousins, the Sauk Indians, who lived in the Saginaw Bay area while the Mesquakie were settled at Detroit, would have fled north, first to Mackinac, and then crossing the straits into the Upper Peninsula. The Sauk's journey continued around the coast of Lake Michigan, where they would eventually settle in eastern Wisconsin, in the Green Bay–Lake Winnebago area.[32] Seeming to confirm the northern route of the Mesquakie and Sauk into central and eastern Wisconsin is a missionary's report from La Pointe that mentions the priest meeting both tribes at or near his St. Esprit mission. William Warren, who was of mixed Ojibwe and Euro-American heritage and who transcribed Ojibwe oral tradition to paper, wrote that the Mesquakie had been living along the southern shore of Lake Superior when the *aniššina·pe·k* people arrived in the region and that the Ojibwe sparred continuously with the Mesquakie while the *aniššina·pe·k* were expanding their range west.[33] Although this may have been the case, it seems unlikely that the Mesquakie would have abandoned their Detroit-area settlements and fled north and directly into Ojibwe and Odawa country, as historians have surmised.

Considering this, the best evidence indicates that the Mesquakie traveled west and around the southern end of Lake Michigan before heading north into present Wisconsin. The Mesquakie are mentioned in numerous correspondences and on maps as living in today's Lower Michigan, northwestern Ohio, Indiana, and northeastern Illinois during the seventeenth century, territory in the regions mostly south and west of Detroit. For example, as noted above, in 1665–66, a French Jesuit recorded that some Mesquakie wintered at La Pointe, a conglomeration of scattered villages located near Chequamegon Bay. It is likely that the Mesquakie the priest saw, as we will see later in this narrative, were members of a delegation from their village on the Wolf River, not the entire tribe, because the same missionary visited their village on the Wolf in 1670, a full year before the breakup of the La Pointe villages. The Jesuit also wrote in his report that in March of the same year, a Haudenosaunee war party attacked a winter village of Mesquakie located at the "foot of the Lake of the Ilinioues, which is called Machihiganing," meaning at the southern end of Lake Michigan, in the area of today's Illinois and Indiana.[34] During the attack, the Haudenosaunee killed about seventy Mesquakie and captured thirty.[35] In March 1681, two men working for the French explorer René Robert Cavelier sieur de La Salle would stumble upon a winter village of Mesquakie on or near what appears to have been the Iroquois River, not far from today's Illinois-Indiana state line.[36] In March 1684, fourteen French voyageurs who survived an attack by a Haudenosaunee war party on the Kankakee River were taken to a nearby Mesquakie village, where they were fed and protected.[37] The 1684 Jean-Baptiste Franquelin/La Salle map, the *Carte de la Louisiane*, labels today's Wabash River in northern Indiana as Agouassake, likely a corruption of Ouagoussak, the tribe known to the French during the seventeenth century as the Outagami, the Mesquakie. The name is a term that had survived since late-prehistoric times. The French engineer Minet also illustrated the name on his 1685 *Carte de la Louisiane*.[38] Then, in 1730, when the Mesquakie fled their central Wisconsin homelands to flee the French and their Native allies, the tribe traveled south into Illinois, likely by way of the Fox River of Illinois, to skirt around the lower parts of Lakes Michigan and Erie to reach lands occupied by the Seneca (Haudenosaunee), where they hoped to find refuge from their enemies. It is possible that the Mesquakie considered traveling through the upper Great Lakes and through *aniššina·pe·k*-claimed waters to reach Seneca country to be more dangerous than journeying there overland. But it is also possible that they were intimately familiar with the layout of the lands of northern Indiana and knew the passages and trails through the Great Kankakee Marsh and ultimately northern Ohio and Pennsylvania.

In late-precontact and early-contact times, the Ho-Chunk, also known as the Winnebago, journeyed to locales that spanned from the southern Lake Michigan region to the eastern parts of Lake Superior before settling in the Green Bay area. Recent scholarship indicates that during precontact times, groups later identified as Ho-Chunk lived in present northwestern Indiana, southeastern Michigan, and Illinois, including in the forest-preserve district of today's Cook County, in the Chicago area, and at a location archaeologists have identified as 11CK26, also known as the Palos site. According to Duane Esarey, writing for the Illinois Archaeological Survey's Prairie Research Institute, Huber-phase ceramics and other items unearthed at the site combined with later historical accounts identify the Ho-Chunk at the Palos site and at other sites located in today's Michigan, Indiana, and Illinois. Evidence recovered from archaeological excavations, including European trade goods, reveal that the Ho-Chunk likely abandoned the Palos site no later than between 1625 and 1630.[39]

After leaving their villages south of Lake Michigan, the Ho-Chunk are next found along the eastern end of Lake Superior, where Samuel de Champlain's 1632 map places them. Frenchman Jean Nicollet de Belleborne found them there in 1634, not at Green Bay, a hypothesis commonly held by historians, including Jean Hamelin, Charles J. Balesi, and Claiborne Skinner, as well as U.S. government agencies and state historical societies.[40] Notable researchers including linguist Michael McCafferty and historian W. J. Eccles have also concluded that the Ho-Chuck met Nicollet somewhere on the eastern end of Lake Superior.[41] In fact, the first written reference to the Ho-Chunk living at Green Bay does not appear until twenty-three years after Nicollet had found them, in 1657 at Lake Superior, and it was not until about 1665 when Nicolas Perrot actually encountered the Ho-Chunk at La Baie.[42] The Ho-Chunk remained in today's Wisconsin through the French, British, and American regimes.

Sometime during the mid-sixteenth century, the Illinois (*Inohka*) and Miami (*myaamia*), who, like the *aniššina·pe·k*, were at one time a single tribe, appear to have come from south and west of Lake Erie and settled in today's Lower Michigan, Indiana, Illinois, and Missouri, leaving their eastern settlements before the Haudenosaunee onslaught that forced other regional tribes to relocate farther west.[43] Notable Illinois villages include Kaskaskia, located on the Illinois River

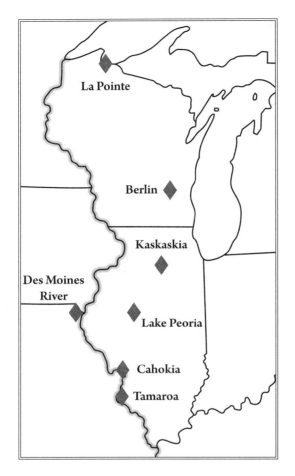

A map of historic Illinois Indian village sites.

near modern-day Utica, at Lake Peoria, at Cahokia, across the Mississippi from St. Louis, and near the Des Moines River in Missouri. Illinois groups also lived, at times, at Chequamegon Bay and along Wisconsin's Fox River. Smaller Illinois winter camps were spread throughout the region. During the 1660s and 1670s, the Miami lived along the St. Joseph River in northwestern Indiana, along Wisconsin's Fox River, and at Chequamegon Bay.

Not only did European influence, intertribal warfare, and alliances determine the movement of tribes, but so did climate. The period between the mid-fourteenth and mid-nineteenth centuries was a time of global cooling, primarily in the Northern Hemisphere, a phenomenon known to climatologists as the Little Ice Age. The coldest part of the Little Ice Age, the Maunder Minimum, occurred between 1645 and 1715, at the height of French exploration and colonization in North America.

The effects of the Little Ice Age on humans and the environment are well documented in Europe, in countries such as France, England, and the Netherlands. The French living in today's eastern Canada during the Maunder Minimum were surely unaware that they were living in a climatic anomaly since conditions in North America were like those in the Old World. Therefore, documentation of the effects of the first thirty years of the Maunder Minimum in Canada is oftentimes anecdotal. The effects of this cooling period varied. In some places, there were pockets where temperatures were much cooler than others and pockets where they were not. According to researcher Brian Fagan, author of *The Little Ice Age*, the Little Ice Age had more "extreme volatility of climate than of constant cold.... [T]he Little Ice Age was a period of very volatile climatic shifts."[44] Even during the latter years of this climatic phenomenon, temperature swings and snowfall amounts during months such as June were extraordinary. According to one Bridgeport, Connecticut, newspaper, "The remarkable change in weather, from extreme heat to cold, was as great here as the following paragraphs describes it to have been at the eastward; all kinds of vegetation has suffered, and some plants being entirely destroyed by the cold and frost."[45] As late as 1816, a year known as the "year without a summer," July, August, and September, according to one witness, "brought a contrary mix of snow, drought, and oppressive heat."[46] By the time of Jolliet and Marquette's expedition, there was little if any communication between Quebec and France during winter months. The St. Lawrence River, the channel used by mariners to reach the Atlantic from Quebec, was sometimes covered by ice for five months. The Atlantic crossing was more dangerous, too, because of the amount of sea ice that flowed into shipping lanes.

The Little Ice Age not only affected water travel, but also brought drought to parts of North America, which would have affected animal migrations, agriculture, and settlement patterns.[47] It was during this time that western bison herds expanded their range and migrated east, crossing the shallow and rocky Mississippi and arriving in present Illinois.[48] French explorers and later travelers noted that some midwestern rivers were unnavigable during summer months, even too shallow for canoes.[49] Droughts and temperature extremes may have also shortened the length of occupation at semipermanent agricultural villages and lengthened occupation at winter camps.

Together, migrations, alliances, war, trade opportunities, and climate changed how, where, and when Native Americans and Europeans settled, traveled, and lived from the sixteenth through eighteenth centuries. Although the French were witnesses to the changing dynamics of Amerindian life and culture, it is difficult to gauge how much, climate issues excluded, was the direct result of the new European presence versus what the tribes themselves controlled and allowed. Even though Frenchmen may have claimed vast territories for France, the reality was that they did not know much about who or what lay beyond their most remote trading posts or mission sites. During the early years, the fur trade, or profits from it, became the primary reason for the French occupation of Canada and parts of the United States, ahead of missionary work and settlement.

◇◇◇◇◇◇◇◇◇◇◇◇◇◇

Not only did the Haudenosaunee invade Huronia, but they also attacked French settlements along the St. Lawrence Valley. The hostilities devastated French trade, settlement, and evangelization. With France entering the Thirty Years' War in 1635, the country was preoccupied with more pressing concerns than those of a distant colony composed of only a few hundred people. The Crown was unable and unwilling to devote money or resources to Canada. Pleas to France for help seemed to go unnoticed. Canada, for now, would have to fend for itself.

During the 1650s, Montreal seemed to be virtually under siege by the Haudenosaunee. Former Jesuit superior of Canada and late procurator of the Canadian missions Paul Le Jeune wrote about the Haudenosaunee: "They would now appear at the edge of the woods, and content themselves with heaping abuse upon us; then they would steal into the very midst of our fields, to surprise the Husbandman; and again they would draw near our houses, harass us ceaselessly, and, like importunate harpies or birds of prey, pounce upon us whenever they found us off our guard, without fear of being captured themselves."[50]

The living conditions in Canada were deteriorating commensurate to the Compagnie des Cent-Associés fortunes. In 1645 the company was driven to relinquish its fur-trading monopoly to a new group, the Compagnie des Habitants, who were obliged to pay the investors of the Compagnie des Cent-Associés one thousand beaver pelts every year. Although the Compagnie des Cent-Associés retained its landholdings and its power to govern, the prospects for a solvent future were bleak. The company was unable to honor its commitments to supply the colony with settlers and to protect its citizens.[51] The company went out of business in 1663.

After decimating the Wendat and Neutral nations, the Haudenosaunee next sparred with the Susquehannock and Erie, while still conducting sporadic sorties against French settlements. Rather than fight wars on several fronts, the Haudenosaunee struck a temporary peace with the French in 1654. By 1657 the surviving Erie were absorbed into the Haudenosaunee, making a powerful French enemy even more formidable.

Travel to the Upper Country was not only hazardous for the French, but also dangerous for the tribes who traveled east to trade. Jesuit missions were also closed. Agriculture, the vital component needed to feed the diminutive colony, had nearly come to a standstill.

At Île d'Orléans, Jesuit Léonard Garreau, who had previously ministered to the Algonquian-speaking Indians who lived near the St. Matthew's mission, at a village known as Ekarenniondi, located near modern-day Collingwood, Ontario, labored among the Wendat refugees. Garreau remained at the mission until 1654, when he was sent to Trois Rivières to function as parish priest. Hoping to reestablish a mission among the Upper Country tribes at this time, Garreau left Trois Rivières in a group of Ottawa in 1656. Near Montreal his convoy was ambushed by a Haudenosaunee war party, and he was mortally wounded, ending, for the time being, any attempt to establish a Jesuit mission in the Great Lakes.[52]

One expedition that managed to run the Haudenosaunee gauntlet and reach the Upper Country was that of Pierre-Esprit Radisson and Médard Chouart des Groseilliers. Although the exact dates of their journey are uncertain, the two men reportedly traveled to Lake Superior and into today's northern Minnesota, perhaps to the headwaters of the Mississippi River. Radisson and Groseilliers retuned to Canada in a large convoy of western tribesmen whose canoes were laden with furs. Unfortunately for the two explorers, the furs were confiscated by Governor d'Argenson, who, according to Radisson, sent Groseilliers to jail. The expedition was important in that it documented the route west, into lands that no Frenchman had yet seen, and at a time when nearly all travel beyond Montreal had ceased.[53]

The flailing ship of Canada would eventually find calmer seas when in 1661, following the death of Cardinal Mazarin, Louis XIV ascended to the throne. Two years later, he declared Canada a royal colony. Despite his inheriting a country in disarray, Louis, in sync with the economic vision of his minister of finance, Jean-Baptiste Colbert, set about reorganizing the government of Canada and took steps to stabilize the colony. Louis turned Canada from a concession run by businessmen into a colony administered by the Crown, replacing private political officeholders with trusted and accomplished royal appointees. The king commissioned Alexander de Prouville de Tracy lieutenant-general of New France and Augustin de Saffray de Mézy governor, who was, not long after, succeeded by Daniel de Rémy de Courcelles. Jean Talon was appointed intendant, the colony's chief financial officer who was also entrusted with Canada's civil administration, economic development, and settlement.[54]

The king also sent troops to the colony, veteran units such as the Carignan-Salières Regiment, to supplement the meager number of Canadian fighters, mainly militiamen and volunteers, to punish the Haudenosaunee, restore the colony's viability, and allow for safe passage along the St. Lawrence. In the autumn of 1666, the French and their Indian allies marched into Mohawk territory and burned villages and food stores. When the campaign was over, the tribe agreed to a tenuous truce with the French, one that would last, in one form or another, for about eighteen years.

The Crown also established a sovereign council, a governing body like those in France composed of the colony's governor, the bishop, five councillors, an attorney general, and a clerk. It was authorized to name judges and minor officials, manage public funds, oversee commerce with France, regulate the fur trade, and formulate rules pertaining to colonial affairs.[55]

With the Haudenosaunee threat reduced, traders and missionaries could travel to the Upper Country to visit multitribal villages, including the one at La Pointe. Not knowing who or what lay beyond these remote sites, Jesuits ministering to the tribes in these lands were exhorted by their superiors to learn what they could about the lands, watercourses, and peoples of the region and beyond.[56] Do semisedentary nations, farming tribes, inhabit the distant lands? On what rivers or lakes do they reside? Are the areas rich in mines or minerals? If so, what type? Is there a water link that connects Canada to the Sea of the West or to the Orient? The Jesuits who labored in these remote posts were well suited to answer these questions. Before arriving in North America, they attended some of the finest schools in Europe where they studied philosophy, a subject that included physics, metaphysics, and mathematics, the latter being an umbrella term that included geography, astronomy, and hydrography.[57] These missionaries were trained observers of nature who recorded natural phenomena such as tides, and they drew maps based on instrument readings, personal observation, and reliable information that they received from the tribesmen. These missionaries would provide answers to some of these questions, as well as personal musings, and important anthropological information about the tribes, in their annual reports.

When compared to the Spanish and Portuguese who conquered Indigenous lands and subjugated their people, and the English whose policy excluded Indigenous peoples from their own territories after infiltrating and claiming them as their own, the French approach to relations stood in stark contrast. The occupation of Native lands by the French was possible only by fostering respectful relationships between themselves and the Indians. Amicable relations, the French understood, would promote an environment that benefited both parties. This explains why French forts, trading posts, and missions were in proximity to Native villages, what historian Joseph Zitomersky describes as a dual settlement pattern.[58] Military alliances also established ties of trust. Knowing that the French were willing to spend their sparse resources to protect Native groups from their enemies, and that the Native groups were willing to provide manpower to aid the French against theirs, was a key factor in the relationship between the two peoples.

It is into this environment that the French traders, missionaries, and explorers would find themselves fully immersed, new lands occupied by people with unfamiliar cultures and ways, where rivers, streams, and lakes meandered through dense forests and vast prairies, and where the possibility of new discoveries lay waiting to be found. With contact with the tribes of the Upper Country, the French continued to learn more about the geography of the continent and the people who lived on it. Expeditions were sent west, including one in 1673, that of Louis Jolliet and Jacques Marquette, whose crew of Frenchmen explored the waterways and viewed the lands of nine U.S. states. They were the first people of European descent to explore the central Mississippi Valley, between today's Wisconsin River to the north and the Arkansas River to the south. They were also the first Europeans to reconnoiter the present state of Illinois. During their journey, they visited Native villages and spoke with the people who lived in them. They also determined the course of rivers and learned into which sea these streams empty. The expedition opened the door to French exploration, trade, Catholic ministry, and eventually colonization in the geographically strategic Mississippi Valley. Jesuit missionaries would minister to the tribesmen at a village the French called Kaskaskia, located on the Upper Illinois near present Utica. Following the lead of the Jesuits and their *donnes*, traders and explorers including men such as La Salle would arrive in the West and build forts, one of which—Fort St. Louis at Le Rocher, a sandstone bluff known today as Starved Rock—functioned as the center for trade in the region and as headquarters for Franco-Amerindian diplomacy. There he awarded grants of land to loyal partisans, the first baby steps in the colonization of the midwestern United States. After the Upper Illinois was abandoned by the French, their focus would be the Lake Peoria area and then, beginning in the first years of the eighteenth century, the Mississippi Valley. The French would remain in the Mississippi Valley, building forts, trading posts, and settlements, until the end of the last of the French and Indian Wars. In October 1765, British officer Major Thomas Stirling assumed control of the Illinois Country, and the land east of the Mississippi became part of the British Empire. After the British, the Americans assumed control of British territory and in 1803 purchased from France what remained of their claims in today's United States, a deal known as the Louisiana Purchase, which effectively doubled the geographical size of the new country.

The 1673 voyage of discovery was the first expedition into these remote lands. As important as the Lewis and Clark Expedition was to the young United States, and the lunar landing was to mankind in 1969, the voyage of Jolliet and Marquette opened the doors for what became the future.

CHAPTER 1

Confronting the Haudenosaunee, Searching for Ore, and Allouez in the Upper Country

The circumstances that motivated the western tribesmen to brave the dangerous passage to Trois Rivières are unclear, but in August 1665 more than four hundred of them paddled east to trade with the French. Perhaps they believed safety in numbers could protect them from Haudenosaunee attacks. Maybe they sought European manufactured goods, conveniences that they had become dependent upon that had become increasingly scarce over the last two decades. Or it could have been, with the expulsion of the Wendat from Huronia, that western tribes such as the Odawa and Ojibwe hoped to establish themselves as intermediaries between the French and more distant Upper Country tribes. It may have been, too, that they learned through the intertribal grapevine that the French were preparing to strike the Haudenosaunee, which would have kept the tribe preoccupied in their homelands, perhaps planning to defend themselves and their villages instead of raiding canoe convoys.

Whatever the case, in June 1665, the first officers and soldiers of the Carignan-Salières Regiment arrived in Canada. The regiment was ordered to fortify French settlements and ultimately, with militiamen, Canadian soldiers, and Indigenous allies, invade Haudenosaunee territory. Arriving with the regiment was Alexander de Prouville de Tracy, lieutenant-general of French possessions in both North and South America. Tracy was a professional soldier, having led cavalry in 1632 and commanded a regiment of troops in Germany during the 1640s, and then was commissioned as commissary general of the king's army. In 1647 he oversaw negotiations at Ulm that concluded in a temporary truce between France and Sweden and Bavaria. In 1652 Tracy was promoted to lieutenant-general of the king's armies.[1]

Daniel de Rémy de Courcelles, Canada's new governor, arrived in the colony in September. He was a French nobleman who had been, prior to his arrival, a military officer. He also served as governor of Thionville, a city located in northeastern France. Courcelles would lead the Franco-Native American forces against the Haudenosaunee. Arriving with him was the newly appointed intendant, Jean Talon. Talon attended a Jesuit *collège* at de Clermont and at age twenty-eight joined the French military administrative services. He served as commissary during wars in Flanders, as royal administrator in the army of

Canada Jean Talon. Image courtesy of Bibliothèque et Archives Nationales, Quebec.

Henri de La Tour d'Auvergne, as *vicomte* de Turenne, and as commissary of Le Quesnoy, becoming intendant of Hainault in 1654. Talon was known in royal circles as a competent and enthusiastic administrator.[2]

Courcelles's first campaign against the Haudenosaunee, in January 1666, nearly ended in disaster for the French. The determined governor, who was itching to strike his enemy, launched an ill-timed and ill-advised winter campaign without first procuring adequate supplies, clothing, and equipment or competent guides. Cold, snow, and then rain made every step of the foray grueling. Suffering frostbite and hunger, and without the means to continue, the French abandoned their crusade and returned north.[3]

By March Courcelles and what remained of his army had returned to Canada. For days stragglers trickled into Fort St. Louis on the Richelieu, a post later known as Fort Chambly. The offensive had been a failure. More than sixty men reportedly died of hunger during and after the campaign. Humbled by the outcome, disappointing to not only Canadians but, in Courcelles's mind, to the king himself, Tracy sought divine penance by reportedly making a "general confession of his whole life" and by receiving holy communion. Two weeks later, both Tracy and Courcelles participated in a pilgrimage to the Church of St. Anne.[4]

In September Tracy and Courcelles mounted a better-organized offensive, one consisting of approximately fifteen hundred French and Native allies who marched into Mohawk (Haudenosaunee subtribe) territory.[5] After burning several villages and destroying their food caches, the Mohawk agreed to suspend their hostilities with the French. Seeing that the army was capable of marching into their homelands and destroying villages, even though the Mohawks inflicted more casualties on the French than the French had on them during the campaign, the other Haudenosaunee subtribes sent delegations to Quebec to agree to, likewise, end their attacks on the French.[6] The way west was, for now, open for explorers, traders, and missionaries. To this Jesuit superior of Canada, François-Joseph Le Mercier wrote,

> We began more than a year ago to enjoy the fruits of peace, and taste the sweets of repose, procured for us by the arms of his Majesty through the subjection of the Iroquois [Haudenosaunee]. It is pleasant to see now almost the entire extent of the shores of our River St. Lawrence settled by new colonies, which continue to spread over more than eighty leagues of territory along the shores of this great River, where new Hamlets are seen springing up here and there,

which facilitate navigation—rendering it more agreeable by the sight of numerous houses, and more convenient by frequent resting-places.[7]

The new intendant, among his many obligations, had been directed to induce Canadians to voluntarily locate copper, lead, and iron mines that had been reported in the colony.[8] These ores were essential to the French. They were the building blocks needed to manufacture war matériel and other items, at a time when the likelihood of war in Canada and Europe was ever present. Talon even took it upon himself to search for ores, as he wrote French comptroller of finance and later secretary of the navy Jean-Baptiste Colbert, the king's minister to Canada, that he had personally discovered "mines, marcassites [crystallized pyrite], and something purer" along the St. Lawrence.[9] To Talon, the prospect for finding mines must have seemed promising. Timber for shipbuilding was another important commodity to be exploited, so much so that the minister wrote to Talon that he was sending three carpenters to the colony to examine the quality of Canadian timber.

Another important matter for Talon was the integration of Indigenous people into French Canadian culture and society. This issue stemmed from the inability of French authorities to find people who were willing to relocate to Canada. Naval war on the English Channel between the English and the French stifled migration from Normandy, from which many if not most Canadians had come. Fear of being killed by Haudenosaunee and the prospects of eking out a living in a cold and inhospitable climate where settlers might spend years clearing trees and brush to provide farm ground were also disincentives. However, Colbert believed that if missionaries could convert the tribesmen to Christianity, the tribesmen might be induced to settle among the French and, in essence, become Gallicized. The French government hoped that by making the Native people French, they might not only increase the colony's population, but also contribute to its economic viability. Incorporating Native peoples into French society coincidentally made more significant the role of missions and missionaries, from a secondary role behind furs and fisheries to a primary one. Colbert hoped that missionaries might make the tribesmen Canadians. But as we will see in the last chapter, the experiment in Indian boardinghouses and schools in the United States and Canada eventually proved to be cruel, unjust, harmful, and sometimes fatal. It was into this world that Jesuit Claude-Jean Allouez was able to catch a ride to the Upper Country with tribesmen returning from a trading expedition at Montreal, to begin his ministry among the Native Americans of the Great Lakes.

Allouez was born in Haute-Loire, in south-central France.[10] After completing his Jesuit education, he sailed to Canada, arriving at Quebec in July 1658. He soon began learning Algonquian and Wendat languages, essential skills needed to communicate with the people he hoped to instruct. After two years, he served as a priest at Trois Rivières. In 1664 he was selected to begin his ministry to the Upper Country tribes but was unable to get to his new assignment because Haudenosaunee war parties had made travel between Trois Rivières and Ottawa country extremely dangerous. He was at Trois Rivières when the canoe convoy arrived in 1665. Taking advantage of the opportunity, the missionary boarded a canoe and headed west. Six other Frenchmen, one of them the trader Nicolas Perrot, also joined the convoy.

The voyage was difficult and disheartening for the priest, much more so than he had ever anticipated. He was abandoned by his Native escorts and left to fend for himself, there were times when he was so hungry that he was reduced to eating decomposing deer flesh, and during the long and arduous voyage he was scoffed, ridiculed, and humiliated by his guides. But he survived the journey and arrived on October 1, at the south shore of Lake Superior, at Chequamegon Bay, a collection of winter villages known as La Pointe, where numerous tribes had gathered.

Not long after his arrival, the priest saw that the La Pointe tribes were anxious. Their hearts were, according to Allouez, "filled with alarm at a fresh war in which they were about to engage with the Nadouessi [Sioux]—a warlike nation, using no other arms in its wars than the bow and the club."[11] The village chiefs and elders called together a general council to discuss the looming likelihood of war where Allouez was invited to speak. There the priest told the headmen that Tracy was preparing to strike the Haudenosaunee, to humble them, and by doing so open the highways between the Great Lakes and Lower Canada. He next spoke about the French king, telling the tribesmen how the monarch insisted that his deity be "acknowledged throughout his domains." The missionary finished his harangue by explaining to the chiefs the primary articles of the Catholic faith and by preaching Jesus to them.[12]

The missionary and his companions took temporary shelter under what he described as a bark roof, a structure built from bent and tied saplings, and without walls. There the tribesmen, who had never seen a European, flocked to see the priest, making it difficult for Allouez's helpers to rebuild and repair their shelter and for the priest to instruct the villagers. Therefore, Allouez decided to visit them at their cabins and speak with them individually. In time, the French completed repairs, and they built a chapel. The site was called the mission of St. Esprit.

◇◇◇◇◇◇◇◇◇◇◇◇◇◇◇

Missionary Jacques Marquette had been born into a distinguished family of Laon, France. He entered the Jesuit *collège* at Reims at age nine. He eventually earned both bachelor's and master's degrees and taught at Jesuit *collèges*, including those at Auxerre, Charleville, and Langres.[13] While Allouez was speaking to the chiefs at La Pointe, Marquette was teaching at Pont-à-Mousson.

As early as 1659, Marquette wrote to J. P. Oliva, general of the Jesuit Order, requesting to be relieved of his studies and be sent to the foreign missions, a request that the superior denied. Again, in March 1665, Marquette wrote to Oliva, asking to be sent to the mission fields. Oliva commended Marquette for his zeal for souls but reminded the young Jesuit in training that although he had completed his studies in physics (physics, metaphysics, mathematics, and so forth), he had yet to finish his theological training, a subject to which Marquette admitted he was not "so well suited."[14] Marquette also relayed to Oliva that he was concerned, too, that, because of hardships, deprivations, and dangers endemic in mission work, he should be sent to the foreign fields before he was too old or infirm to be an effective representative of the church. Oliva submitted Marquette's request to the Jesuit provincial, who later wrote back, "The Canadian Mission needs by all means a reinforcement of workers. I signify this to Your Reverence and I earnestly recommend to you as to the rest of the Provincials in France to see what subject you have in your Province sufficiently fit to set out at an early date for those shores. You have among others Master Marquette, whom you can dispatch on the first occasion."[15] Marquette sailed to Quebec in June 1666.

The Canadian missions needed help—workers, missionaries, and lay brothers to assist the overwhelmed missionaries. The Jesuits did not arrive in Canada as part of a conquering army intending to subjugate and enslave people as the Franciscans had in Mexico and Central and South America alongside their conquistador compadres. They came as individuals who lived in villages among the very people they had come to convert. It took many years to complete the requirements to become a full-fledged Jesuit, and the supply of missionaries could hardly keep up with demand.

Another Jesuit trainee who was permitted to suspend his studies and sail to Canada was Louis Nicolas, who arrived in the colony in 1664. Although Nicolas was fascinated by nature and the natural sciences, he had yet to complete his courses in theology, one of the last curricula presented to Jesuit students. Jesuit officials permitted Nicolas to sail to Canada, with the caveat that he complete his theological studies at the Jesuit house at Sillery, a settlement now part of the city of Quebec, before receiving his field assignment. However, Nicolas slipped his leash and, rather than finish his theology studies, instead, twice, fled to the Algonquin living at Trois Rivières. He eventually returned to Sillery, where he finished his studies, proclaiming his Jesuit vows in 1667.[16]

While Marquette was petitioning his superiors to be sent to the foreign missions, twenty-three-year-old Robert Cavelier was teaching grammar at the Jesuit school at Blois. Frustrated by the lengthy Jesuit preparation he was required to complete, Cavelier began to yearn for a field assignment, anyplace far away from the spartan-like Jesuit college. He was once described by his superiors as "exuberantly healthy, big-sized, lusty, proud, impressionable, stubborn, domineering, [and] hot-tempered," traits that would serve him well in the foreign missions. But feeling his creativity and talents stifled by the rigidity of Jesuit life, he began to lose interest in his studies, becoming, as one of his rectors at Tours described him, "a poor student, self-opinionated, of very middling judgment and prudence." In March 1666, he petitioned Oliva, like Marquette had done a year earlier, to be sent to a field assignment. Cavelier wrote that he desired "with the greatest eagerness" to be sent to China, explaining that even though he had not completed his studies, his "zeal for souls" more than compensated for his lack of qualifications. To sweeten his request, Cavelier offered that his family would pay his traveling expenses and donate 8,000 livres to the Chinese mission. Oliva offered to expedite Cavelier's petition by allowing him to forgo his high school teaching assignment and to begin his theological studies. But Cavelier was not satisfied. Eight days later, he wrote Oliva again, "pleading with great fervor" to be sent to Portugal, where he heard that the Jesuits had been seeking Greek and math instructors, two subjects in which he excelled. This time the Jesuit general told Cavelier to "remain quietly" and finish his studies.[17] After Cavelier's schooling was completed, the official would consider his appeals. The rebuke was more than Cavelier could bear. His impatience, his inability to accept his humble place within the society, and his internal struggle that pitted his talents against the objectives of the order finally drove him to petition his superiors to be relieved of his vows. In March 1666, Cavelier left the order to resume secular life. It seems likely that Marquette and Nicolas were permitted to leave for the missions before completing their studies because, besides the urgent demand for Jesuits in Canada, they were zealous but dedicated Catholics who understood that to try to impose their own will on the order, rather than following its policies and procedures, was futile. Cavelier, on the other hand, was too shortsighted and too impatient, *inquietus*, restless as his later mentors described him, who looked for any reason to leave for other lands. Oliva and other officials felt that Cavelier was not Jesuit material, and he was using any excuse, even bribery, to escape his obligations.

Not much is known about the first twenty-seven years of Louis Jolliet's life. Only bits and pieces appear in documents, and some of these indirectly. One of the better attempts to ferret out what we can know about young Louis was written by Jesuit historian Jean Delanglez. According to Delanglez, Louis was likely born at Beauport, in what is today part of the city of Quebec.[18] He entered the Jesuit *collège* there at about the age of eleven. As an aspiring priest in training, he received minor orders a month before his seventeenth birthday.[19] While Marquette and Cavelier were studying and teaching at Jesuit schools in France, Jolliet was a student at the Jesuit *collège* in Quebec, where he was preparing for the priesthood.

◇◇◇◇◇◇◇◇◇◇◇◇◇

At La Pointe, Allouez was receiving an eye-opening introduction into the customs and beliefs of the western tribesmen. As a student of the Catholic tradition, Allouez believed that the manitous these people respected and feared belonged to, as he wrote, a "false and abominable religion" and that they were mistaken, like the "ancient pagans" who, in his view, also worshipped false gods.[20] He saw that they believed evil spirits could inhabit snakes, that "genii [magical spirits]" can live in birds, and that the deceased "govern the fishes in the Lake."[21] He also witnessed dog sacrifices that were offered to calm rough seas. He was now living in their world and on their terms, not his. He saw how people different from him, who practiced ancient and nature-centered spirituality, viewed the universe and how their stories and myths explained the natural world to them. And, as a Jesuit, he did not like what he saw.

Allouez was a dedicated Jesuit, which meant that he held the strongest of religious convictions. He and other Jesuits were obedient to a moral code that they believed was established by the Creator of the universe himself. His Jesuit apprenticeship demanded that he submit to the authority of his superiors, that he conform to the order's rules and regulations, and that he steadfastly follow the teachings of the church and pronouncements of church councils. The priest's order, the Society of Jesus, also known as the Jesuits, began as a Catholic response to the Protestant Reformation, a way to rein in, in their view, the heresy that was consuming Europe during the sixteenth and seventeenth centuries. Members of the order swore strict allegiance to the pope and vowed to defend Catholic orthodoxy at all costs. He studied theology, learning the so-called deep things of God, including the Creator's plan for salvation, and the consequence for rejecting it. Jesuits such as Allouez were not anthropologists; they were strict partisans, defenders of a specific belief system that viewed most others as false or heretical. Seen in this light, the priest regarded Amerindian cultures as foreign, pagan, or demonic, or some combination. He made no attempt whatsoever to understand the wherefores and the whys of these people, choosing instead to judge them as uncivilized or pagan. Living in a world where the idea of science had yet to be introduced, the Indigenous people of North America understood the universe in a way that was reasonable to them. They understood the cycles of nature and the circle of life, and although they had no scientific explanation for natural phenomena, they created myths that, to their satisfaction, offered explanatory power, which were not altogether that different from some myths held by Catholics like Allouez. Considering the mind-set of Allouez and other Jesuits, is it unlikely that they would say anything constructive about Native beliefs. However, to convert the tribesmen, missionaries would often single out some of their ideas and symbols and try to make a correlation between them and Catholic ones. With other than a few coincidental similarities that they could use to attempt to convince the Indians that their beliefs were not that different from those in Catholicism, missionaries would continue to criticize and attack Native customs.

Moreover, Allouez came from a part of the world that was working its way through what historians call the "Scientific Revolution," a time when the Roman church and its authoritarian pronouncements pertaining to nature were questioned by men such as Galileo Galilei, Nicolaus Copernicus, Johannes Kepler, and Isaac Newton. New scientific discoveries such as heliocentrism, the effects of gravity, the composition of light, optics, and the fact that moons orbit planets such as Jupiter shook the foundations of the Catholic world. With these new discoveries, Englishman Francis Bacon (1561–1626) attempted to convince his colleagues that there needed to be a proper foundation for acquiring knowledge, a principle that became the "scientific method," a procedure centered on hypothesis, observation, and experiment, not a priori or deductive reasoning. Other philosophers such as Blaise Pascal (1623–62), René Descartes (1596–1650), and Gottfried Wilhelm Leibniz (1646–1716), some of whom had attended Jesuit schools, and whose minds had been steeped in the Catholic view of the universe, attempted to reconcile a faith-based world with the newly discovered scientific realities.[22] But this was not to last. By the eighteenth-century Age of Enlightenment, evidence-based reason and not church-ordained mandates guided Europe into a new world of ideas and possibilities. Even though the powerful Roman church still held sway in France during the seventeenth century, Jesuit schools taught their students some of the best, most up-to-date, and universally accepted knowledge of the time. In fact, the French aristocracy, whose children as adults would become military officers and government officials, attended Jesuit schools to acquire the necessary skills to be successful in their fields. Allouez was a product of this world, having a mathematical and philosophical understanding of reality, yet one that was overshadowed and driven by moral and theological codes of the church.

Rather than attempt to instruct the men, the warriors, and hope that they might convert to Catholicism, Jesuit missionaries often focused their efforts on the village women and children. About this Allouez wrote, "The first days of the year 1666 were spent in presenting a very acceptable new-year's gift to the little Jesus—consisting of a number of children brought to me by their mothers, through a Divine inspiration altogether extraordinary, to be baptized."[23] The women and especially the children were where the Jesuits concentrated their efforts.

The novelty of the Black Robe in their midst soon began to fade. Allouez reported that he entered the cabin of a man whom he described as a famous sorcerer, a man with six wives, who scoffed at the priest's Christianity, especially at the idea of the resurrection of the dead and hellfire judgment. As a sorcerer, he summoned and repelled, if necessary, manitous, good and evil spirits that intervened in their lives. He wielded great power among the people in the village. But what bothered the missionary more than the sorcerer was the "little army of children" in his cabin, young ones who under the influence of their father would, the priest believed, grow up to be polygamist sorcerers like him. It is unknown what Allouez said to the man, but whatever he did say seems to have led to a confrontation. The priest left the cabin thinking to himself, as he wrote, "*Ibant Apostoli gaudentes à conspectu concilii, quoniam digni habiti sunt pro nomine Jesu contumeliam pati,*" a phrase translated as "The Apostles were departing from the presence of the council, rejoicing that they were counted worthy to suffer shame for the name of the Lord Jesus." Amen.[24]

News of the incident soon spread throughout the village, inciting some people to mock the priest, while others tore down the walls of his chapel and stole some of his possessions. Not long afterward, Allouez and the French with him left the village and relocated to another. This was the missionary's introduction into what lay in store for him at La Pointe.[25]

Looking at this incident from the point of view of Allouez's alleged sorcerer, the priest was a threat to his authority, his tribe's customs, and his people's understanding of medicine, life, and the role of manitous. Like most everyone alive at the time, the tribes at La Pointe lived in a world where the idea of science, an inductive way of interpreting nature, had not developed independently, nor had it been learned from others. These people knew that things occur in nature and in their personal lives but did not know the scientific explanation for why they did. They knew well that flint for making tools is usually found in a certain geological context (rocks and soil types), that certain types of fish spawn in specific rivers and at specific times of the year, and that contact with corpses or certain people such as Black Robes could give them a fatal disease. They also believed in signs, omens, and premonitions and that guardian spirits communicated with them through dreams.[26] And living in a society with a high infant mortality rate, where most children did not live to adulthood, polygamy was both common and necessary, not, as in Allouez's view, sinful.

Allouez spent the winter visiting and preaching at several villages in the La Pointe area, including those of the Petun refugees, Kiskakon, Odawa, Potawatomi, Sauk, and Mesquakie, meeting with, in his mind, a few successes and many failures. That winter the priest baptized one hundred Petun, about eighty Odawa and Kiskakon, thirty-four Potawatomi, and five Sauk and Mesquakie, all children. It is during this time that Allouez encountered a delegation of people who would change the course of Jesuit evangelization and the French exploration of today's Mississippi Valley and midwestern United States, the Illinois Indians.

The Illinois spoke a language in the Algonquian subfamily of languages, what would later be known as "Miami-Illinois." This language was quite different from those spoken by other Algonquian-speaking tribes. Allouez admitted that he understood it "only slightly"; he had never encountered the tribe and therefore had not had the opportunity to familiarize himself with its nuances. Allouez was conversant in Wendat, an Iroquoian language, and Algonquin-Ottawa-Ojibwe, both being languages that he began learning shortly after arriving in Canada. Just as in the case of the languages of Europe in the Romance subfamily, the Algonquian languages, deriving from an ancient language that linguists call Proto-Algonquian, had spread across the North American continent from west to east and in doing so had morphed into many mutually unintelligible languages.[27] Although Allouez had spoken to the Sauk and Mesquakie at La Pointe, it was not until 1670 that he admitted that he could not converse with them without the aid of an interpreter.[28] It seems likely that Allouez had an interpreter with him when he spoke with the Illinois, or he may have relied heavily on hand gestures and other nonverbal forms of communication.

Whatever the case, Allouez reported that the Illinois whom he met at La Pointe were "affable and humane."[29] Their men used the bow and arrow and war club to hunt and for war.[30] He also learned a little about their culture, primarily their dances, manitous, and related worship, and about their prized calumet, or smoking pipe. These Illinois told him that they lived more than sixty leagues south of La Pointe, beyond a great river, where bison, deer, and bear were plentiful.[31] The Illinois also told him that their people once lived in ten large villages, but warfare with the Nadouessi had reduced them to only two. From this the priest likely understood "large villages" to mean semipermanent agricultural villages, locations where large groups of Illinois grew domestic crops and supplemented their diet with game, fish, and other wild foods and where they remained settled for much of the year. Rather than following the tribe as they chased the herds, missionaries could, after establishing amicable relations, move to a semipermanent village, build a chapel, and minister to them. Jesuit missionaries sought out people like the Illinois as they had the Wendat, Petun, and other Huronia groups twenty years earlier. Allouez also reported that "this Mission is the one where I have labored the least and accomplished the most. ... I confess that the fairest field for the Gospel appears to me to be yonder. Had I had leisure and opportunity, I would have pushed on to their country, to see with my own eyes all the good things there of which they tell me."[32]

Another important discovery was learning about the great river toward which a large and powerful tribe, the Nadouessi, lived. He wrote:

> These are people [the Nadouessi] dwelling to the West of this place [La Pointe], toward the great river named Messipi. They are forty or fifty leagues from this place, in a country of prairies, rich in all kinds of game. They cultivate fields,

sowing therein not Indian corn, but only tobacco; while Providence has furnished them a kind of marsh rye which they go and harvest toward the close of Summer in certain small Lakes that are covered with it. So well do they know how to prepare it that it is highly appetizing and very nutritious. They gave me some when I was at the head of Lake Tracy, where I saw them.[33]

This is the first unambiguous reference to the name of the river presently known as the Mississippi.

Ives Goddard, Algonquian linguist and a curator emeritus in the Department of Anthropology of the National Museum of Natural History at the Smithsonian, wrote that the name Messi-Sipi, as recorded by Allouez, and often attributed to having its origins in the Miami-Illinois lexicon, was in fact Odawa: "The Algonquian speakers that Allouez was living near when he learned the name were Ottawas, and this suggests that an Ottawa source should be sought for his form Messi-Sipi—the haplologized Messipi being simply one of the many Indian names that the editors and copyists who compiled the Jesuit Relations mistranscribed. And in fact, the name appears, and is shown in sentences, in the massive dictionary of Old Ottawa that Pierre Du Jaunay completed in 1748 and that is now at McGill University in Montreal."[34] The name first recorded by Allouez as "Messipi" is Odawa, not Miami-Illinois.

The missionary included what he learned about the western lands and waters and the people and his experiences with them in his annual report to his superior, François-Joseph Le Mercier. But even though he wrote less about the Illinois than other tribes such as the Potawatomi, his first impressions of them were unique. They were approachable and friendly, and they appeared to be the most interested in learning about Catholicism. More important, they lived in large agricultural villages near a large river. These two issues were important not only to Jesuit missionaries in the West, but also to colonial administrators in Canada and the French Court itself. As we will see later in this narrative, history will bear out the importance of this first meeting between Allouez and the Illinois, as it will eventually lead to the opening of the Mississippi Valley and the American West.

◇◇◇◇◇◇◇◇◇◇◇◇◇

In 1666 Talon was busy compiling the colony's census. Louis Jolliet, who was working quietly on his studies at the Jesuit *collège*, was listed in the register as *clercq d'esglise*, a church cleric. He also worked on honing his rhetorical skills, mastering the art of debate. In July he and Pierre Francheville participated in the school's "first disputations in Philosophy," presumably at the chapel of the Jesuit *collège* where Jolliet reportedly "presented some good arguments" and "defended the whole of logic very well."[35]

On September 20, while the army was preparing to invade the Haudeno-saunee homeland a second time, Marquette arrived in Quebec. His very first exposure to Canada's Indigenous people likely occurred at Île d'Orléans, where refugees from Huronia had settled fifteen years earlier.[36] Marquette's first impression of the Wendat he encountered there is unknown, although probably not a good one, as the Indians on the island were a defeated people who were living at the mercy of the Jesuits in an unfamiliar and unproductive environment, far away from their cherished lands, lakes, and fields.

Twenty days after arriving at Quebec, the priest set out for Trois Rivières to begin training in Amerindian languages and culture under the veteran missionary Gabriel Druillettes. Marquette reportedly had a remarkable aptitude for learning Indigenous languages. He wrote that he found "no difficulty whatever with languages that have no connection with our own."[37] Other missionaries, however, were not as linguistically gifted as Marquette. Noel Chabanel, a capable individual in other aspects of the ministry, could not even "make himself understood in Huron [Wendat]." Marquette studied Wendat for three months before beginning instruction in Montagnais, an Algonquian language spoken by some Indigenous people of the Lower St. Lawrence. Marquette also learned tribal culture and, according to Jesuit historian Joseph Donnelly, the dos and don'ts of living and working among the tribes.[38] During his apprenticeship, he likely met other Jesuits, including Henri Nouvel, Louis Nicolas, and André Richard.[39] Marquette likely visited other area villages and settlements during this time, too, including one at Cap de la Madeleine.

When spring arrived in Lake Superior country, the tribes wintering at La Pointe began breaking camp and heading to summer villages. The Illinois likely returned to their settlements near the great river, while the *aniššina·pe·k* groups headed either to the Ste. Mary's River at the Sault to participate in the annual spring whitefish run or to summer villages along the shores of the region's lakes. Where Allouez spent the summer is unknown. He may have remained at La Pointe to grow maize and prepare for the coming winter, he may have traveled to the Sault with the *aniššina·pe·k*, or perhaps he and his associates may have done some exploring.

While the tribes at La Pointe were leaving for summer camps, Louis's eldest brother, Adrien, was preparing to journey west as a voyageur, into Ottawa country. In April 1666, he signed a contract at his Cap de la Madeleine residence wherein he joined a group of voyageurs and traders that included Laurent Philippe, François Colard, Antoine Serré, Benoit Boucher, Jacques Maugras, and Jacques Largillier. Adrien would soon learn the subtleties of the fur trade and the ways of the voyageurs.[40] Soon after the paperwork was signed, Adrien's group left for Ottawa country, likely returning that autumn, while Allouez was heading back to his La Pointe mission. Adrien's activities will be a matter of interest in a later chapter of this narrative.

Allouez wrote that the Indians often found copper along the shores of Lake Superior. Copper was precious to the tribesmen. It was, as he wrote, "among their most precious possessions." Sometimes they kept copper nuggets for generations, even viewing them as "household gods." He reported that he and his companions found pieces of it at an island located along the north shore of Lake Superior while commuting between La Pointe and Lake Nipissing. They also told him about a copper boulder along the lake, one so large that tribesmen who passed it cut pieces from it. In the *Relation* of 1669–70 is a reference to a copper boulder on Lake Superior that states, "Going on to the end of the Lake [west end of Lake Superior], and coming back a day's journey along the South side, one sees at the water's edge a Rock of Copper weighing fully seven or eight hundred *livres*, so hard that steel can scarcely cut it; yet, when it is heated, it may be cut like lead."[41] Coincidentally, while exploring the south shore of Lake Superior in 1820 in a group led by then governor of Michigan Territory Lewis Cass, Henry Schoolcraft, the chronicler and naturalist of the expedition, mentioned a "remarkable mass" of pure copper that his group encountered. He reported the boulder, at its greatest length and width, measured three-foot-eight-inches by three-foot-four. Schoolcraft also wrote that travelers and passersby would oftentimes cut pieces from it, further reducing its size.[42]

Allouez discovered three things at La Pointe that would chart a new course for the French in North America. He learned that a river, the Mississippi, flowed south of Chequamegon Bay. He met the Illinois, a populous tribe of semisedentary agricultural people who were receptive to Catholic instruction. And he learned that copper, sometimes large boulders of it, could be found along Lake Superior.

In May 1667, Allouez left La Pointe for Quebec to recruit missionaries and to enlist lay helpers to till fields and to hunt and fish. He wrote that food could be so scarce that he sometimes had to subsist on ground fish bones. And he needed handymen to help build log chapels and shelters to impress the tribesmen who, according to Allouez, had only seen cabins made of bark.[43] He carried with him copper nuggets from Lake Superior, bits of ore to show colonial authorities who had been seeking mines since Talon's arrival in 1665. In addition, he brought news of the Mississippi, perhaps a passage that might link New France with the Orient. Both secular and religious authorities would, indeed, relish the news of these discoveries.

While en route to Quebec, Allouez stopped at a Nipissing village located on the lake of the same name to which the tribe had fled two decades earlier to avoid Haudenosaunee war parties. Leaving the village, his group paddled the well-known Ottawa-French River route to Montreal and then down the St. Lawrence to Quebec, arriving at the Canadian capital on August 3. There he surely met with his superior, Le Mercier, to deliver his annual reports and to give him a verbal account of his years among the tribes. The missionary also likely gave the superior the copper nuggets he carried. In addition, he requested desperately needed help for his mission, another Jesuit and perhaps also lay brothers and helpers, anyone who could assist him with his priestly duties or support his efforts in any way. Le Mercier would give the copper pieces to Talon and assign Louis Nicolas to go west with Allouez.

Allouez was anxious to return to his mission and to get there before winter. His stay at Quebec was short, only two days. Leaving Quebec, his party arrived at Montreal, where Allouez gave Nicolas orders to accompany him. From Montreal the priests fell in with a group of Indians heading back to La Pointe. However, the tribesmen were reportedly in "ill-humor" and allowed only the two missionaries and one of their men to accompany the group back to their villages. Further, their Native escorts forbade the French to carry with them food, clothing, and other necessities, items that the tribesmen believed would hinder the convoy's progress, especially while portaging around the many rapids and obstacles along their route. The French would carry only the clothes on their backs and perhaps a few personal items with them.[44] Despite the restrictions and inconveniences, Allouez and Nicolas began the long journey back to La Pointe.[45]

CHAPTER 2

Copper Mines, Cavelier, and Wisconsin

The summer of 1667 was a busy time in Lower Canada, as far as this narrative is concerned. Not only had Allouez arrived to report his discoveries, but Lieutenant-General Tracy left Canada and sailed to France. Robert Cavelier arrived in the colony and obtained a seigniory, a piece of land, from the Sulpicians near Montreal. Marquette was busy learning Native languages and customs at Trois Rivières. He returned to Quebec in September. That same year, after borrowing money from Canadian bishop François de Laval, Louis Jolliet left the priesthood and sailed for France. Although some writers claim that he "probably" studied "hydrography" there between 1667 and 1668, there is no credible evidence that he did.[1] All that is known is that he spent time in Paris and at La Rochelle.

Arriving at La Pointe, Allouez and Nicolas went right to work, likely repairing their huts and chapel and performing other tasks to prepare for the long winter. He likely also met with village chiefs to catch up with tribal affairs and to learn what he could about the deteriorating relationship between the La Pointe tribes and the Nadouessi, Nicolas following close behind him. Nicolas was a neophyte whose only experience with Indigenous peoples was limited to the Quebec and Trois Rivières area. As far as his effectiveness as a missionary at La Pointe is concerned, Nicolas may not have been, in Allouez's eyes, up to the task. Canadian historian François-Marc Gagnon wrote that Allouez was "dissatisfied with Nicholas' missionary achievements," perhaps because his true interests lay elsewhere, not ministering to the sick and dying and contending with tribesmen who had little use for what they perceived to be the priest's exhortations and meddling.[2]

In spring Allouez and Nicolas left the St. Esprit mission for the Sault. From there, Nicolas continued east, later working at Sept-Îles, Quebec, and in Haudenosaunee country. Although he may not have possessed the gumption to be an effective missionary to the Upper Country tribes, he was a keen observer of nature and student of Algonquian languages. He later authored the *Histoire naturelle des Indes occidentales*, a work that describes the plants and animals of New France, and *Grammaire algonquine*, his study of the Algonquin language.[3] Nicolas returned to France in 1675. He left the Jesuits in 1678.[4]

On May 20, 1668, Marquette left Quebec for the last time and traveled to the Sault, his first mission assignment, where upon arrival he was greeted by Allouez. That summer Allouez and Marquette conducted a survey of Lake Superior. Their goal was to document Native settlements along its shores that were dependent on the St. Esprit mission. Information they gathered from the survey became the basis for the famous Jesuit map commonly known as the map of *Lac Superieur et autres lieux ou sont les missions des peres de la Compagnie de Jesus comprises sous le nom d'Outaouacs* found in the *Relations of the Jesuits* of 1669 and 1670. Although historians disagree on who drew the map, a look at the evidence clearly demonstrates that it was Allouez and Marquette.

Claude Dablon, who became Jesuit superior of Canada in 1671, wrote that the Jesuit map was drawn by "two Fathers of considerable intelligence, much given to research, and very exact, who determined to set down nothing that they had not seen with their own eyes."[5] Who were the two fathers?

Only three Jesuits labored in the Lake Superior–Sault Ste. Marie region during the years 1667 and 1668: Allouez, Marquette, and Nicolas, the latter, whom we have seen, left La Pointe for Quebec in the spring of 1668. However, some researchers have written that Dablon not only was in the region at the time, but helped collect information for the map.[6] But this claim is contradicted by Jesuit sources. According to "The Journal of the Jesuit Fathers, January to June 1668," found in the fifty-first volume of Thwaites's *Jesuit Relations,* the entry for April 21 states, "We are going to embark to go up the river, namely: Father Dablon, Caron, Charles Panie, and myself [Le Mercier], to la Prairie de la Magdelaine, there to conclude all affairs, and to decide as to the manner of granting the concessions."[7] Dablon was at the Prairie de la Magdelaine in late April. In the fifty-second volume, covering the years 1667–69, Le Mercier wrote:

> When Father Aloez [*sic*] went down this year to Quebec [1669], to deliver to Monsieur de Courcelle the Iroquois Captives that he had ransomed in his name from the Outaouacs [Ottawas], and to ask for some aid from our Fathers, the lot happily fell on Father Claude Dablon. He has been sent to be the Superior of those upper Missions [as superior of the western missions in 1669], notwithstanding the abundant fruits he was reaping here [at la Prairie de la Magdelaine], and the pressing necessity felt for his presence here.[8]

Le Mercier is stating that Dablon was likely still at Prairie de la Magdelaine in 1669 and had not yet been sent to the western missions as superior until sometime later that year, a full year after information for the map had been compiled. Although historians have credited Dablon for assisting Allouez with the map,

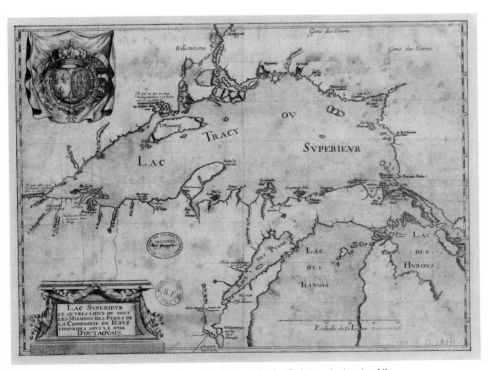

Jesuit map illustrating native villages dependent on the La Pointe mission by Allouez and Marquette. Karpinski Collection Image is in the public domain.

he was not in the region when Allouez circumnavigated the lake. Moreover, basic to Marquette's aptitude for cartography is his now famous 1673 holograph map of the Mississippi, an accurate chart for its day. Marquette's education and experience made him fully qualified to draw accurate maps, or at least able to compile accurate cartographical information to be used to produce maps. The two "intelligent Fathers" that Dablon referenced, as evidence indicates, were Allouez and Marquette.

It should also be noted that Allouez was familiar with the configuration of most of Lake Superior before he left to travel around the lake during the summer of 1668. Its shorelines were certainly no mystery to him. He viewed, and likely studied, the lake's south shore in 1665 when he first arrived at La Pointe. He surely studied the southern shore of the lake again in 1667 and part of the lake's north shore that year when he traveled to the Nipissing. And in 1668, he paddled the southern shoreline again, when he traveled from La Pointe to the Sault. He was no doubt familiar with the distances and contours of Lake Superior before ever setting out to sketch the Jesuit map with Marquette.

While Marquette was ministering to the tribes at the Sault and assisting Allouez, Louis Jolliet returned to Canada from France, where he traveled the previous year. Upon his return, Jolliet purchased a large supply of trade goods from his uncle Charles Aubert de La Chesnaye.[9] What Jolliet did with the goods is unknown.

In November Talon left Canada and returned to France. He was supposed to serve as intendant for only two years but was ordered by Minister Colbert to remain for a third. Citing health issues and family matters, he was allowed to return home. The Talon years were a time of unprecedented growth for the colony. Among his many successes were his policies that increased agricultural production and the number of livestock and horses. He supported exploration to locate mines and minerals and sought to exploit other natural resources such as timber for shipbuilding. And he championed exploration of rivers and waterways that he hoped would not only open new avenues west but might potentially uncover a route to the Orient. Succeeding Talon as intendant was Claude de Bouteroue d'Aubigny, who was reported to have been "knowledgeable and courteous" and who knew how to "make himself both feared and liked."[10] Talon's secretary, Jean-Baptiste Patoulet, remained in the colony to help guide the new official in his assignment. D'Aubigny would remain intendant for two years, until Talon returned to the colony to serve his second intendantship.

Allouez's last voyage to Quebec was in the summer of 1669 when he and his group of unknown Frenchmen delivered several Haudenosaunee prisoners that he had ransomed from the Odawa to Governor Courcelles. Leaving Quebec, the missionary traveled to the Sault. From there his party negotiated the De Tour Channel and paddled into Lake Huron, passing Mackinac Island and the present town of St. Ignace, where a Jesuit mission would be established. Continuing south his party reached what the French called La Baie, Green Bay, where he would work among the tribes living at the Lac des Ilinois, Lake Michigan, and up the Fox and Wolf Rivers of Wisconsin. On December 2, the eve of the feast of St. Xavier, he landed a short distance above the mouth of the Fox where he encountered some Frenchmen who had been trading in the area. He soon established the mission of St. Xavier at the site.

News of copper mines in the western lakes, samples of which Allouez brought to Quebec, was of great importance to the French colonial government, so much so that Talon, prior to leaving for France, approved a government-funded expedition to locate the mines. Two men were chosen for the mission, Jean Péré and Adrien Jolliet. Péré was tasked with locating the copper mines and was paid 1,000 livres in advance of the voyage. He was also responsible for compiling a report of the expedition. Jolliet's role, for which he was paid 400 livres, was to find a water route that large vessels could sail to carry the ore east. The Péré-Jolliet expedition left Montreal likely in the late spring of 1669 in four canoes full of trade goods and assorted supplies.[11]

While in the Upper Lakes, at a village called Ouinaouatoua, Adrien learned that a Haudenosaunee captive was being held by the Odawa. During this time, Canadian officials actively encouraged gestures of peace between the Haudenosaunee and the western tribes. Peace was preferable to war since intertribal conflict negatively affected the fur trade, settlement, and missionary efforts. Tribesmen, too, were less likely to leave their villages to hunt and trap for fear of being captured or killed. Since the Haudenosaunee forced the tribes farther and farther west to safer locales, traders and tribesmen had to transport their goods an extra twelve hundred miles between the Sault and La Pointe (back and forth, following the contour of the lake and conducting the portage at the Keweenaw Peninsula), for example, just to conduct business. The cessation of hostilities between the Odawa and the Haudenosaunee, even if only temporary, benefited both the tribes and the French. Adrien beseeched tribal leaders for permission to escort the prisoner back to his country, believing the act would be a good first step toward improving relations between the two tribes. Adrien knew that Haudenosaunee-claimed homelands were located south and east of Lake Ontario and likely figured that the prisoner might be able to show him a new route between Ouinaouatoua and Haudenosaunee territory, one that could, hopefully, accommodate large vessels to haul copper. If the prisoner could show Adrien such a route, he would have fulfilled his obligations to Talon. The Odawa agreed to release the captive and allow Adrien to escort the Haudenosaunee back to his village.

While Adrien traveled east, Péré continued west. The following November, in 1670, a frustrated Talon, who had since returned to Canada for his second stint as intendant, wrote to Colbert that Péré had reportedly been living with the Jesuits in the Ottawa country and he was receiving from him only "very obscurely" worded briefings. Talon believed that the Jesuits purposely interfered with Péré's assignment. While this might have been the case, it is possible, too, that Péré found trading with government-purchased goods more appealing and lucrative than searching the wilderness for mines.[12] Péré probably figured that since Talon was leaving Canada for France when he, Péré, received his commission, he might avoid all accountability for being AWOL (absent without official leave).

◇◇◇◇◇◇◇◇◇◇◇◇◇◇◇

During the autumn of 1668, two canoes of Seneca (western Haudenosaunee) who traveled to Montreal to trade reportedly spent about eight to ten months with Cavelier at his seigniory at La Chine.[13] During their stay, the Seneca reportedly told Cavelier about a large river they called "Ohio" that began three days' journey from Seneca country in present western New York. Thirty days beyond, they told him, lived many tribes, including the Shawnee, Mesquakie, Iskousogos, possibly Mascouten, and another recorded as the Honniasontkeronon, some of them having as many as fifteen to twenty of their own villages along the river.[14] The country was rich in wildlife; deer and bison herds were reportedly as "thick as the woods." Cavelier was led to believe that the Ohio was the route to the South Sea, the way to China. And it may have been, too, that Cavelier thought he should be the first Frenchman to find the route. In his mind, such a discovery might make him as famous as Cartier or Champlain. What the Haudenosaunee told Cavelier about the river, the tribes, and the resources, according to a Sulpician priest, "inflamed" him to seek out and explore the waterway.[15]

Cavelier pleaded his case to Courcelles, reportedly delivering to the governor "a great number of fine speeches," of which "he has no lack," a contemporary reported.[16] Cavelier made a compelling case, and he convinced the official to permit him to search for the Ohio. With permission secured, the future explorer soon began preparing to outfit an expedition. He enlisted a group of canoe men and perhaps a soldier or two, novices who he later learned could not survive a winter in the wilderness on their own. During the same time, another expedition was preparing to head west, that of two Sulpician missionaries, François Dollier de Casson and René de Brehant de Galinée. The priests hoped to locate, instruct, and convert the tribes that reportedly lived in the Ohio Valley. However, permission for both expeditions was contingent upon both groups traveling together and heading west as one.

Galinée knew that Cavelier was more than prone to hyperbole, a character flaw made worse by his braggadocious attitude. Although Cavelier once told the priest that he understood the Haudenosaunee language "perfectly," having a "perfect acquaintance" with it, Galinée insisted that they hire an interpreter before leaving. Evidently, the only person they could find to speak Haudenosaunee was a Dutchman who, unfortunately for the explorers, could not express himself in French. Having few options and likely figuring that Galinée could somehow make it all work, the Cavelier-Dollier party left Montreal on July 6, 1669. Ahead of the group were the same Seneca who had wintered with Cavelier. The explorers hoped to procure guides to show them the route to the Ohio at Haudenosaunee villages they would pass during their journey.[17]

Eventually, the French reached today's Irondequoit River, where the party met a group of Seneca. The next day, Cavelier, Galinée, several Frenchmen, and the Indians hiked to the Seneca village to meet tribal leaders and ask them to provide guides. Not long after they arrived, it became painfully obvious that Cavelier could not speak Haudenosaunee; he did not know the language at all. The Dutch interpreter also proved to be useless—he could not speak enough French to make himself understood. Fortunately, the French party met a lay helper of Jacques Frémin, a Jesuit missionary to the Haudenosaunee, who was living at the village, who acted as translator for Cavelier's group.[18]

The Haudenosaunee chiefs told the French that although they could provide them guides, many of their people were away trading with the Dutch and would be gone for about a week. The French would have to wait for the Seneca to return. The news frustrated Cavelier and the priests, since it was now mid-September and the season was advancing. But they had no choice other than to be patient and await the return of the tribesmen. Finally, the Haudenosaunee who had been away trading returned to the village, some of them drunk and rowdy.

Perhaps it was because the Dutch convinced the Haudenosaunee that the French were their enemies that they reversed course and refused to provide guides. The headmen claimed that if their guides escorted the Cavelier-Dollier party to the Ohio Valley, and the group was attacked by enemy tribesmen, the Haudenosaunee would be blamed for their deaths. This could threaten the fragile peace between the tribe and the French. Without guides or interpreters, Cavelier, Galinée, and their party left the village and returned to the others. Undeterred, the French reembarked and continued their trek, eventually reaching another Seneca village. There, Cavelier took to the woods to hunt but returned with a "high fever," which sidelined him for several days. No one knows for certain, but some members of the group surmised that Cavelier may have encountered rattlesnakes, some of which were reported to have been "as thick as one's arm, six or seven feet long," and the experience so unnerved him that he was unable to function. Did Cavelier use the snakes as an excuse to feign illness to rid himself of the priests and their party, or was he really sick?[19]

Time would reveal that Cavelier was prone to suffering from mysterious illnesses, symptoms of what researchers James Bruseth and Toni Turner termed a "moral malady." In their words, he may have suffered from episodes of depression and might have been today "diagnosed as manic-depressive."[20] Whether it was the rattlesnakes or depression, the group waited patiently for Cavelier to recover. Three days later, a somewhat reinvigorated Cavelier and the group boarded their canoes and continued west, eventually disembarking at a portage. Traversing the portage, the group set up camp near yet another Seneca village, a settlement known to us today as Tinawatawa, believed by historians to have been located near present Hamilton, Ontario.

◇◇◇◇◇◇◇◇◇◇◇◇◇◇◇

After navigating Lake Huron, the Haudenosaunee guided Adrien down the Ste. Claire River, through the lake of the same name, and down the Detroit River to Lake Erie, a route that was suspected by the French but had not yet been explored. Adrien and the Haudenosaunee eventually landed at Tinawatawa, where the Seneca dispatched a runner to the nearby French camp to tell them of Adrien's arrival. Surprised that Frenchmen were in the region, Dollier and Galinée walked to the village to investigate.

At the settlement, the priests met a "M. Jolliet," who they learned had been sent west to discover copper mines and to find a way to transport the ore east. Historians, including Louise Phelps Kellogg, Francis Borgia Steck, and others, have assumed that the Jolliet that Dollier and Galinée met at Tinawatawa was Louis because, viewing the incident in hindsight, Louis became a well-known explorer and was better known than any of his siblings. Talon's former secretary Patoulet identified the men sent west to find copper as "Sieurs Jolliet and Péré," not specifying whether Sieur "Jolliet" was Adrien or Louis.[21] However, the best evidence indicates that the Jolliet the priests met was Adrien, not Louis. We know that before Adrien left for the west with Péré, he gave Louis power of attorney over his affairs at Quebec on April 13, 1669, a common practice before embarking on a dangerous mission.[22] In addition, there is no evidence that Louis had ever traveled to the Upper Country before October 1670.[23]

Adrien told the priests that the Odawa permitted him to escort the Haude-nosaunee prisoner to his country. He also relayed to them that he had learned that Lakes Huron, Ste. Claire, and Erie flow into Lake Ontario, which the priests knew drained into the St. Lawrence and ultimately into the Atlantic. Adrien described the new route in detail to them, information that Galinée later con-verted to a map.[24] This new knowledge was an important step toward France's understanding of the layout of the Great Lakes, which ultimately led to the establishment of settlements such as Detroit. A decade later, men working under the authority of Cavelier would build the first bark to sail the Great Lakes, from present Buffalo, New York, west, a vessel known to history as the *Griffon*. Leaving Tinawatawa, Adrien continued on foot to avoid Andaste war parties, enemies of the Haudenosaunee, who might be patrolling the territory between Tinawatawa and the captive's village. Adrien had accomplished his part of the mission.

Adrien never saw Lake Superior country; he headed east with the Haudeno-saunee before reaching the shores of the Great Lake. Canadian historian Ray-mond Douville wrote that Adrien may have been ill when he reached Tinawa-tawa and hoped to return home to Cap de la Madeleine as quickly as possible.[25] He cites Galinée, who wrote that "time pressed him [Adrien] for his return," a vague yet possible reference to his health.[26]

After he had delivered the Haudenosaunee to his village, Adrien continued to Cap de la Madeleine. His health continued to decline. On December 1, royal notary Jean Cusson; Adrien's wife, Jeanne; Bailloquet, the local priest; and sev-eral witnesses gathered at Adrien's deathbed for the reading and signing of two wills. In them Adrien bequeathed his earthly possessions to his wife, and he gave 300 pounds to each of their two children.[27] Although Adrien was of sound mind, his body was weak, so weak that he was unable to sign the second will, a document that would be used against his brother Louis in court five years later. Adrien died early the next day.

At this point during the expedition, Galinée figured that Cavelier was having second thoughts about continuing; he wanted, for reasons unknown, to return to Montreal. Dollier and Galinée decided to strike out on their own and separate from Cavelier, taking the route Adrien had described to them to the Sault.[28] The priests arrived at the St. Mary's mission the following June and were met by the Jesuit fathers living there. Although unfounded speculation abounds about where Cavelier may have traveled after separating from the missionaries, the historical record is silent.

After spending the better part of eighteen months at the Sault, Marquette left for his next assignment, the St. Esprit mission at La Pointe, arriving there on September 13, 1669. The tribes there had been without a missionary for some time, as Marquette wrote, "because Father Allouez, who understood them thoroughly, had been unwilling to return to them for this Winter, because they did not take enough interest in Prayer,—they acknowledged that they were well deserving of this punishment."[29] Marquette would first attempt to reestablish amicable relations with the tribes and then instruct them in Catholicism.

Not long after he arrived, Marquette surveyed his mission to learn what he could about those who lived there. Where were the different villages located? With which tribes could he communicate? Where should he focus his efforts? Which tribes, if any, were receptive to Catholicism, and which ones were not? He soon learned that the "Sinagaux" (an Odawa subtribe) ridiculed prayer and seldom listened to missionaries. The Keinouché (another Odawa subtribe) told him they were not ready yet to receive instruction. Some groups, such as the Kiskakon, accepted Allouez's teachings and remained faithful to them. The priest also met members of two Siouan-speaking groups, the "Nadouessi," or eastern or Santee Sioux, and the Assiniboine.[30]

The missionary was particularly attracted to the Illinois he met at La Pointe. They told him that they traveled to Chequamegon Bay to trade with the French. To better communicate with them, Marquette was given a tutor, a young Indian slave who knew Miami-Illinois and who taught the priest the "rudiments" of the language. Although Marquette was familiar with Algonquin-Ottawa-Ojibwe, the language spoken by the Odawa, Ojibwe, Potawatomi, and Kiskakon, the priest, at first, had some difficulty learning Miami-Illinois. But with the guidance of his mentor, he soon began to comprehend and speak the Miami-Illinois tongue and was eventually able to communicate without the help of an interpreter. During their many conversations, the Illinois told Marquette about the crops they grew, the animals they hunted, and their culture and customs. He also learned that they captured many slaves, most of whom they brought to La Pointe to trade for muskets, ammunition, kettles, hatchets, and knives.[31] To get to and from La Pointe, they traveled dangerously close to Nadouessi territory with whom, as Allouez had noted, they had been at war but had since negotiated safe passage.

One important piece of information Marquette learned from the Illinois, as it applies to the 1673 voyage, was their reference to a great river, a stream they described as nearly a league in width, surely the same river the tribe mentioned to Allouez several years earlier, the Mississippi. It is possible that Allouez, who was just beginning to learn Miami-Illinois, heard the Illinois to say, as he wrote, that they lived "beyond," meaning south of the river, and therefore concluded that the stream must empty into the sea near Virginia. It must flow east, not south. Adding to the muddle, Marquette reported that a second great river was located about six or seven days' journey south of the Illinois villages. Logically, it would seem that the two rivers intersect at some point. Therefore, it would have been reasonable for Allouez to assume that the "great river," one of two that Marquette mentioned, flowed east, while Marquette surmised that the one the Illinois told him about, which flowed from north to south, might empty into the sea at California or the Sea of the South.[32]

During Marquette's first winter at La Pointe, 1669–70, he began planning to explore the Mississippi and to visit the tribes that lived along its shores. He wrote, "We [Marquette, his tutor, and a Frenchman] shall visit the Nations dwelling there, in order to open the passage to such of our Fathers as have been awaiting this good fortune for so long a time. This discovery will give us full knowledge either of the South Sea or of the Western Sea."[33]

◇◇◇◇◇◇◇◇◇◇◇◇◇◇

From the Fox River mission, Allouez set out to survey the tribes of the Green Bay region. He first visited the Sauk, where he instructed the curious and baptized the sick, primarily children. In mid-February he hiked to a Potawatomi village, where he met with tribal leaders and visited the people in their cabins. Leaving the Potawatomi, he returned to his St. Xavier mission-camp. The priest tells an interesting story about the return trip to his mission, through the snow and over the frozen waterways, which reveals that some *coureurs des bois* cared little for the priest and considered him a nuisance. Allouez wrote that during his trek, his nose had frozen, and he experienced intermittent fainting spells. Rather than help the ailing priest, his companions instead left him on the ice and continued to camp. Fortunately for Allouez, in his mind, divine Providence intervened. He wrote that he found a handkerchief that he was unaware that he carried and used it to wrap and warm his face. Protected from the wind and cold, he continued his blustery walk to the mission.[34]

Allouez remained at his mission camp until April, when he and several Frenchmen paddled up the Fox and then the Wolf River to a fortified Mesquakie village, arriving there on April 24.[35] The Mesquakie chose the remote location because they feared Haudenosaunee attacks, one of which had recently killed many of their people.

The Mesquakie village appears to correspond to an archaeological site in Waupaca County, Wisconsin, known as the Markman Site, 47-Wp-85. It is located on high ground on the east side of the Wolf River near its confluence with the Little Wolf. Archaeological surveys and test excavations at the site by a team from the University of Wisconsin–Oshkosh in 2004 uncovered occupations that date from Middle Archaic to Historic periods. A French finger ring was uncovered at the site as well as ceramics, sherds that archaeologists familiar with the site deem are consistent with a Mesquakie occupation. According to archaeologist Jeffery Behm, "The Markman site is currently the best candidate for the Meskwaki village on the Wolf River. It is sufficiently large enough to have held the more than 200 houses reported by Allouez (JR 55:219), or even the more than 600 houses reported by La Potherie (WHC [Wisconsin Historical Collections 16:39])."[36]

Allouez met with village chiefs and elders and told them the reason for his visit, to give them "the first acquaintance" with his "Mysteries." He next presented them a gift that was meant as condolences for their loss of women and children during the recent Haudenosaunee attack.

Allouez also collected demographic information at the village that included the number of men capable of bearing arms, and he learned with whom the Mesquakie were at war. He also learned about the types of foods they ate. Of particular interest to the priest were Mesquakie myths wherein, according to one tale, an ancestor of a Mesquakie tribesman had reportedly "come from Heaven, and that he had preached the Unity and the Sovereignty of a God who had made all the other Gods; that he had assured them that he would go to Heaven after his death, where he should die no more; and that his body would not be found in the place where it had been buried."[37] He also reported that one evening, four Miami arrived at the village, bringing with them three Haudenosaunee scalps and part of a human arm.

The missionary christened the new Mesquakie mission St. Marc's, whose feast day is April 24. The priest left the village on the twenty-seventh and three days later arrived at a fortified village of the Mascouten located on a hill where "beautiful Plains and Fields meet the eye as far as one can see," above the south shore of the Fox River at today's Berlin, Wisconsin.[38]

Allouez and his men were escorted to the cabin of the principal village chief where a feast was held. When formalities concluded, a village elder rose and spoke to the missionary, stating that he was glad that the priest had come to visit. He asked Allouez to take pity on his people because they were hungry, dying of disease, and fearful, living precariously close to the powerful Nadouessi

1906 photo of the Mascouten village site near Berlin, Wisconsin.
Photo courtesy of the Berlin, Wisconsin Historical Society.

and within striking range of their Haudenosaunee enemies. The elder told the priest that his people were simply too weak and too demoralized to defend themselves. Clearly, the Mascouten were suffering and hoped that the Jesuit and the French might come to their aid.[39]

Later that evening, Allouez gathered the village headmen and presented them gifts—glass beads, knives, and hatchets—items meant to curry favor with the tribesmen and to obligate them to listen to what he had to say. The missionary told them that he was not a manitou but was the manitou's representative. He then explained to them the articles of his faith.

One method he employed to garner their attention was to show them an image that portrayed the joy of the saints and "torments of the damned," the punishment for those who rejected Jesus. His audience listened attentively, silently, and respectfully to Allouez as he explained to them the image's obvious yet threatening message.[40]

He also spent one day visiting the cabins and huts of the villagers, going door to door, not only teaching but also establishing relationships that he hoped would lead to their conversion. Grateful that the priest did his best to promote friendship and goodwill, the village elders came to his cabin to thank him, asking him to visit them often to teach them how to speak to the "great Manitou."[41]

Allouez also recorded that the Indians told him that their village was located six days' travel from the Mississippi and that between their village and the river lived "populous" nations.[42] It is instructive to point out that Allouez was beginning to understand the significance of the Mississippi. The stream was more than a geographical feature; it was an elongated core of life that flowed through the North American continent. It was a primary reference used by the tribes to describe where they lived. It was also a major obstacle to cross when the Illinois and the Nadouessi, for example, traveled between La Pointe and their villages. Now, tribes such as the Mascouten who lived more than 350 miles south and east of La Pointe are referencing the location of their village in respect to the river.

Living among the Mascouten were some Miami and Illinois, primarily Kaskaskia (an Illinois subtribe). Another Illinois group, the Peoria, reportedly planned to move to the village.[43] Although Allouez would have preferred to have stayed longer, it was time for him to return to the Sault.

One of the first publications about the Mascouten village site was a paper that was read before the X-Ray Club in Berlin, Wisconsin, on February 9, 1907, by local attorney John J. Wood Jr. Wood described the likely village site as "perhaps the most beautiful spot in the valley of the Fox river." Its location, he spoke, was situated on the "crest of a fertile prairie which here falls suddenly into the valley, and which impresses one approaching from the valley as being a considerable eminence."[44] Other early articles about the Mascouten village were written by the Reverend Arthur Jones, S.J. (1907), a Jesuit historian, who also studied the Native American history of the Upper Country, and W. A. Titus (1922). In his article titled "Historic Spots in Wisconsin: The Lost Village of the Mascouten," Titus concluded, "It is not impossible that, at some future time, excavation or accidental discovery may once more fix definitely the site of this long-lost village of the Mascouten. If so, it will become a hallowed shrine for the antiquarian and the historian—an 'historic spot' indeed."[45]

Titus's words came to fruition forty-two years later in 1964, when archaeologist Dr. Warren L. Wittry of the Cranbrook Institute of Science near Detroit determined to examine the proposed Mascouten village site. Also working on the project were Robert Hall of the Illinois State Museum; Dan Shea, a student at the University of Wisconsin; and several volunteers. Work at the site uncovered features, including evidence of a stockade, residences, and fire pits. They found Native American ceramics, an important indicator to date the site's occupation, and a kaolin pipe that was manufactured in Europe.[46]

In June 1983, a team from the Wisconsin State Historical Society performed an uncontrolled, or random, survey at the possible Mascouten village, now known as the Springview Site. Because the field had been planted in soybeans, a thorough survey could not be completed; only the field margins were examined. The following June, Lynn Rusch, also from the Wisconsin State Historical Society, conducted a more thorough survey of the Springview Site, arriving just after spring planting when the ground's surface was relatively free from crops and weeds.[47] Rusch and a volunteer surveyed approximately sixty acres, where they discovered that a large village had occupied the site, the extent of which could not be determined.

During the survey, Rusch located twenty-one stone projectile points commonly called Madison points that date from 900 C.E. to the early Historic period. They also recovered stone scrapers, assorted bifaces, hammerstones, a stone wedge, and almost six hundred pieces of debitage. Nine small sherds of Native American ceramics, four of which were described as shell tempered, consistent with the types used from the Mississippian to early Historic periods, were also located. As it applies to contact with French traders, four glass trade beads were found.[48]

Although few items of European manufacture were discovered at the Springview Site, a newspaper article from January 26, 1995, reveals that a copper crucifix had been found near the site in about 1958. The article states that the crucifix was about four inches long and two inches wide, and according to "top collectors," the artifact dates to about the year 1636. The article speculates that the item may have been buried with an Amerindian convert to Catholicism.[49]

No definitive conclusions about the site have yet been reached by archaeologists. Erosion and farming and other activities have destroyed much of what remained of the proposed village site. However, the Springview Site remains the most likely candidate for the site of the Mascouten village of Allouez, and later Jolliet and Marquette.

While en route to the Sault from the Mascouten village, Allouez visited a Kickapoo village and one of another tribe he called the Kitchigamich, who, he reported, spoke the same language as the Kickapoo. Six days later, he arrived at a Menominee village along the Menominee River, at the state line between present Wisconsin and the Upper Peninsula of Michigan.[50] While among the Menominee, he established the mission of St. Michael, which he named in honor of the archangel whose feast day is May 8, according to the Tridentine Calendar. Leaving the Menominee, Allouez crossed Green Bay to visit a camp of Ho-Chunk, Winnebago, who were then living among some Potawatomi on the Door County Peninsula. War between the Ho-Chunk and the Illinois had likely driven the tribe to La Baie. Leaving the Ho-Chunk, the priest continued his journey to the Sault.[51]

Talon dispatched two more expeditions west, one led by military officer Simon F. Daumont, Sieur de St. Lusson, to locate the elusive copper mines, and one led by Cavelier southwest to find the route to Mexico and the Gulf, his second foray west.

Talon wrote to Minister Colbert:

> It is to make the first of these discoveries that m. de Courcelle and I have sent Sieur de La Salle, who is all afire for undertakings of this kind; whereas I sent Sieur de St. Lusson in another direction, ordering him [Cavelier] to push on toward the west as far as he can go while managing to find the means of subsistence. His orders are to investigate carefully whether there is some means of communication by lakes or rivers [between the St. Lawrence] and the Sea of the South which separates this continent from China.[52]

Like his 1669 misadventure, Cavelier's 1670 expedition to locate the road to the Gulf amounted to absolutely nothing. Again, speculation abounds as to where he may have traveled, but evidence of his locating anything at all of note is conspicuously absent from his correspondence, an important consideration while bearing in mind Cavelier's well-known talent for self-promotion. St. Lusson's convoy spent late summer preparing for his voyage to the Upper Country, eventually setting off from Montreal in October.

Leaving La Pointe in the spring, Marquette traveled to the Sault, where he met with Dablon, now superior of the western missions. The missionary gave the superior a verbal account of the past winter at St. Esprit. He reported that the Sinagaux were "very far from the Kingdom of God," the Keinouché were not yet ready to convert, and the Kiskakon, who had formerly refused to convert, eventually did. He recorded the habits, customs, and, in his view, the superstitions of the tribes, but also mentioned his successes converting and baptizing them. Marquette also revealed his plan to visit the Illinois in their country and to establish a mission among them during the following year, 1671, that is, if another Jesuit could replace him at St. Esprit.[53]

Marquette also updated the superior on the situation with the Nadouessi, whom he called "the Iroquois [Haudenosaunee] of this country, beyond la Pointe." He reported that Nadouessi feared the French because they brought with them iron, a strange metal, according to the priest. He also told Dablon that he planned to mediate a truce between the Nadouessi and the Illinois that autumn, and to keep the Nadouessi interested in negotiations, he gave them obligatory presents, pictures that conveyed to them tenants of the Catholic faith, likely images of Mary and perhaps Christ crucified.[54] To Marquette, the Nadouessi's fear of the French and apparent "love of God," as he wrote, indicated that Christianity would one day flourish among the tribe.

In 1670 two Jesuits were sent to the growing Great Lakes mission field to assist Allouez, Marquette, and Dablon; the aging missionary Gabriel Druillettes, who, as we have seen, introduced the newly arrived Marquette to Indigenous languages and cultures; and Louis André, who arrived in the colony the previous year. Druillettes represented the knowledge of a wide range of languages and customs that only someone who had lived among the tribes for many years could possess. He was given charge of the Ste. Marie mission at the Sault. Whereas Druillettes represented knowledge, wisdom, and experience, the younger André embodied zeal, vigor, and hope.

When Marquette returned to La Pointe in September, he found the situation there had changed considerably since spring. During his absence, Odawa and Wendat tribesmen killed several Nadouessi. The Nadouessi responded by killing several Odawa and Wendat.[55] Tensions between the tribes reached a boiling point and was about to erupt into open warfare. The La Pointe tribes now feared that they would soon be overrun by their enemies. To avoid conflict, one group of Odawa left La Pointe and resettled on Manitoulin Island.

That same fall, Allouez and Dablon left the Sault and paddled to the Fox River–La Baie area. Allouez certainly wanted to show his superior the size and scope of the new mission field. Arriving at the head of the bay, the two priests learned that several *coureurs des bois*, perhaps the ones who had left Allouez to freeze to death on the ice, had been causing quite a disturbance at local Native villages. Not only did they reportedly physically abuse tribesmen, but they also plundered their cabins and stole their property. The Indians retaliated, venting their anger on any French they encountered. Allouez and Dablon, however, successfully defused tensions and calmed the Indians. They also promised to reprimand the Frenchmen responsible for inciting the ruckus. Unfortunately, these incidents tarnished the tribesmen's image of the French, whom they had beseeched for protection from the Haudenosaunee. The tribes had been attacked and displaced, and were in some cases starving, and they hoped the French would help them. But instead, they were treated with contempt and scorn. Allouez and Dablon gave them reassurances that their God would protect them, that is, if they were obedient to him.

Leaving the village, the two missionaries paddled up the Fox, where they saw "a sort of idol," as Dablon called it, a rock that, at a distance, appeared human-like, its face painted in vivid colors. Area tribesmen reportedly honored the idol with tobacco and assorted items to thank it for protecting them from the nearby rapids. Since the idol was an affront to their Catholic sensibilities, the two priests instructed their canoe men to push it into the river.

Dablon saw the beauty and bounty of the Wisconsin countryside and described it in his report. He also, to some small extent, described the layout of the river, the rapids, and the lakes of the Lower Fox. Continuing upstream they eventually arrived at the Mascouten village that Allouez visited earlier that year. The following day, they convened an assembly of Mascouten and Miami leaders to tell them the purpose of their visit, namely, to announce that they represented the master of their lives, meaning the Christian God, and that they had come to instruct them in his ways. Allouez reviewed with them what he had taught them earlier that year, primarily about the authority and unity of his Catholic God and the salvation offered through Jesus. After the council ended, Allouez and Dablon were invited to other village feasts, not to eat, but to use their magic and power to heal the sick and bestow on them luck during the hunt and in war.

In a separate narrative, Dablon wrote that the Illinois "have already arrived with the intention of dwelling in that [this] region," in a "transplanted colony," and who, he believed, "will swell that Church."[56] This seems to imply that some Illinois were living at the Mascouten village at the time of his and Allouez's visit. He also considered the Miami, some of whom were also living at the village, to be part of the Illinois tribe. To Dablon, the friendly demeanor of the Illinois, likely the women, and their apparent interest in Catholic instruction made prospects for converting the tribe to Catholicism seem promising.

He also appeared to understand, based on what he could gather from the tribesmen and by examining the region's hydrography and topography, that the Mississippi was a drainage for the region's rivers and lakes that, he surmised, emptied into the "vermilion or Florida Sea." The river, Dablon wrote, was reported in some places to have been a league in width, and it flowed through treeless prairies where tribes used dried manure and peat to build fires, instead of wood. The Illinois, reportedly, lived along the far side of this river (the west side). His informants also told him that as one approaches the sea, the forests reappear. In these forests, men resembling Frenchmen had been seen, men who, reportedly, split trees with "long knives" and live in "houses" on the water, a possible reference to Spaniards and their sailing vessels.[57]

Dablon and his men left Allouez in Wisconsin and headed north. The best evidence indicates that he wintered somewhere in the Mackinac region, perhaps at the natural harbor and bay that would become the future site of Michilimackinac and the St. Ignace mission, located just north and east of the straits. However, Jesuit historian Joseph Donnelly wrote in his well-received book *Jacques Marquette* that after separating from Allouez, Dablon spent the winter on Mackinac Island "with the Indians already dwelling there."[58]

There are several problems with Donnelly's hypothesis. To begin, this portion of Dablon's report, chapter 3, titled "Of the Mission of Saint Ignace at Michilimackinac," describes Mackinac Island, the area's fisheries, and the island's strategic location. Dablon also mentioned the people who formerly lived near the straits but no longer did, having moved to the Green Bay area and, as he and Allouez observed, up the Fox. He wrote, "But, especially, those who bore the name of the Island and were called Missilimakinac, were so numerous that some of them still living declare that they constituted thirty Villages; and that they all had intrenched themselves in a fort a league and a half in circumference, when the Iroquois—elated at gaining a victory over three thousand men of that Nation, who had carried the war even into the very country of the Agniehron-nons—came and defeated them."[59]

The people who "bore the name of the island" is a geographic reference to people who lived in the area, not necessarily on the island, a term similar to "Chicagoans," which includes people who live in the Greater Chicago area, not necessarily within city limits. Further, it seems unlikely that Mackinac Island, which is roughly about 3.8 square miles in size, would have been large enough, considering its topography, to accommodate the camps, housing, fields, grave-yards, and spaces needed to support "thirty" villages. It is much more likely that Dablon is referring to the Mackinac area, not the island.

He also wrote, "Hence it is that many of these same tribes, seeing the appar-ent stability of the peace with the Iroquois [Haudenosaunee], are turning their eyes toward so advantageous a location as this [the region], with the intention of returning hither, each to its own country, in imitation of those who have already made such a beginning on the Islands of Lake Huron [Manitoulin, for example]."[60]

Again, Dablon is writing about the Mackinac area or region, not specifically the island. "To promote the execution of the plan announced to us by a number of Savages [from La Pointe], to settle *this country* [emphasis added] anew,—some of them having already passed the Winter here, hunting in the *neighbor-hood* [emphasis added]—*we have also wintered here* [in the neighborhood] in order to form plans for the Mission of saint Ignace [located on the mainland], whence it Will be very easy to gain access to all the Missions of Lake Huron when the Nations shall have returned each to its own district."[61] Dablon is say-ing that the tribes were planning to resettle in the Mackinac "country," where he spent the winter. Considering the above, Dablon did not spend the winter of 1670–71 on Mackinac Island.

Allouez remained on the Lower Fox. In February he began the long, cold trek through the snow and ice to St. Marc's at the Mesquakie village, where he was greeted by "jests, repulses and mockery." He learned that the Mesquakie, like the

Green Bay–area tribes, had been poorly treated by the French and responded by killing several of them. Consequently, the few French in the region, for their very safety, avoided the Mesquakie altogether. Dedicated to his mission and unafraid of death, Allouez, through his patience and style, assuaged the tribesmen and regained their respect. With relations soothed, the Mesquakie Christians planted a large cross in the center of the village.[62] However, even though Allouez repaired the relationship between himself and the tribe, their bond would continue to slowly deteriorate, leading to what would later be known as the Fox Wars (1712–35).

St. Lusson, Marquette, Jolliet and the Sault, Adrien Jolliet, and Frontenac

St. Lusson landed in Canada in August 1670 aboard the same vessel as Talon when the administrator arrived to serve his second term as intendant. Talon wrote that he dispatched St. Lusson west with instructions to locate a waterway that leads to the "Sea of the South which separates this continent from China; but only after he had given his first attention to the discovery of copper mines which is the main object of the expedition, and having ascertained the accuracy of the memoirs which have been given him."[1] St. Lusson gathered men, supplies, and arms and headed west, leaving Montreal in October in a convoy that included Nicolas Perrot.

St. Lusson's group paddled up the St. Lawrence and then ascended the Ottawa-French River route, negotiating approximate 920 miles of rapids, portages, and lakes. This route, even with its hazards, was shorter and faster than the newly discovered 1,850-mile Great Lakes route. The route veered northwest from Montreal and away from territories claimed by the Haudenosaunee. Additionally, by cutting inland and away from the Great Lakes, travelers avoided strong winds and rough seas that sidelined travelers for a week or longer, an important concern especially when traveling late in the season.[2]

By late fall the convoy arrived at Georgian Bay, located along the north side of Lake Huron. Winter was approaching. Freezing temperatures, ice along the shoreline, and strong winds typical of late autumn forced the group to suspend their voyage and establish winter quarters on Manitoulin Island next to some *aniššina·pe·k*. As spring approached, the group struck camp and resumed their voyage, arriving at the Sault on May 5, 1671.[3]

While St. Lusson's main party headed to the Sault, the Indians who had wintered on Manitoulin Island dispatched runners to tell regional tribal leaders to gather at the Sault to attend a council hosted by the French. Perrot, too, traveled to Green Bay to tell chiefs and elders there to send their influential headmen to the council. After delivering his message, Perrot resumed his journey to the Sault.[4]

Rather than locate mines as he had been instructed to do, St. Lusson, instead, held a large pageant before the representatives of fourteen Native groups, Frenchmen, and missionaries on June 4 where he claimed amid the pomp and circumstance all northern, western, and southern lands and waters for France. The French shouted in customary fashion:

> In the name of the Most High Most Mighty and Most Redoubtable Monarch, Louis the Fourteenth of the Name, Most Christian King of France and Navarre, we take possession of the said place of St. Marie of the falls as well as Lakes Huron and Superior, the island of Caientonon [Manitoulin] and all other countries, rivers, lakes, and tributaries, contiguous and adjacent thereunto, as well discovered as to be discovered, which are bounded on the one side by the Northern and Western Seas and on the other side by the South Sea including all its length and breath.[5]

Allouez and Perrot worked as translators between the French and the Natives. The priest, in addition to his role as interpreter, also took the opportunity to preach Catholicism to the assembled tribesmen. Perrot, who later wrote the official report of the pageant, noted that Frenchmen were, at the time, trading at the site and "in those quarters." The list of witnesses to the event reveals that Louis Jolliet was one of the traders and was likely the primary merchant at the Sault.[6]

In spring there was great urgency for the Odawa and Wendat at La Pointe to put distance between themselves and their Nadouessi enemies. Fearing Nadouessi wrath, the two groups fled with their families for refuge to the Mackinac area and Manitoulin Island, haunts that were not only familiar to them, but places rich in natural resources. Putting his personal and professional ambitions aside, Marquette labored tirelessly among the refugees during the long journey. After paddling about 600 miles, following the contour of the lake and along

An image of Louis Jolliet at the Starved Rock State Park Visitor Center, Utica, Illinois. Photo by the author.

the coastlines of today's Wisconsin and Michigan, Marquette and the Indians reached the Sault, likely passing the mission and Jolliet's trading post. In another 155 miles, they reached Michilimackinac, modern-day St. Ignace, Michigan, where the priest established the mission of the same name. His opportunity to visit the Illinois and open a mission among them would be delayed, as he chose to stay with the Odawa and Wendat until they were safe in their camps and were securely in the care of another Jesuit father.

At this point, two important issues having to do with Jolliet, Marquette, and the 1673 voyage need to be addressed: When did Louis Jolliet arrive at the Sault, and did he and Marquette meet to discuss their future voyage?

What should be obvious by this point is the paucity of the documentation about Jolliet's activities between 1668 and 1671. Although the historical record is by no means complete, there is more than enough information to determine what he may or may not have done as it applies to the Mississippi expedition. After Louis returned from France in the autumn of 1668, he, as we saw, obtained a large supply of trade goods from his uncle Charles Aubert de La Chesnaye. He was also mentioned in a letter to Canada bishop Laval dated November 9, 1668, wherein Adrien Jolliet agreed to "hand over" to Louis "300 livres due to me

[Adrien] of the price of the land which was sold to him [Laval]" by their mother from the Jolliet estate to help Louis pay the bishop back for loaning him the money to travel to France.[7] Louis is next mentioned in April 1669 when Adrien gave his younger brother power of attorney before he, Adrien, headed to Ottawa country. Not until June 4, 1671, does Louis appear in the surviving historical record: as a witness to St. Lusson's pageant. What happened between April 1669 and June 1671? From what we can know about Jolliet's activities during these years, it is evident that he had never been a voyageur, trader, traveler, or Upper Country woodsman. If he had been trading in the West, someone—perhaps a missionary who knew him, the historian La Potherie who several years later interviewed Jolliet, or maybe an important figure such as Perrot—would have mentioned him in correspondence. Historians agree that Louis probably first left Canada to trade at the Sault in the autumn of 1670.[8] But this raises another question: Is it not possible that Jolliet traveled to the Sault in St. Lusson's convoy?

To get to the Sault, Jolliet would have certainly traveled the Ottawa and French Rivers, not the Great Lakes route. Louis was a newcomer to the Upper Country who had, as far as can be determined, never traveled west of Cap de la Madeleine. He would not have undertaken this potentially dangerous journey in canoes laden with large amounts of trade goods and supplies this late in the year unless he had the means to defend himself and protect his valuable cargo. Coincidentally, a military escort left Montreal for the Sault in October 1670, that of St. Lusson. We also saw that St. Lusson's group was forced to winter on Manitoulin Island and that they arrived at the Sault in May.[9] It therefore seems much more likely than not that Louis arrived at the Sault in May as part of St. Lusson's group and that he did not head west for the very first time with a couple of companions. If this is the case, then Louis's first experience trading in the Upper Country was a short one, only one month or two, as he left the Sault shortly after the pageant. Moreover, in the Great Lakes country, the tribesmen often cashed in their peltry as soon as they returned to their summer villages from the winter hunt. After business was conducted, traders/voyageurs usually left for Montreal, returning to their wilderness posts the following autumn. Louis was not and could not have been the woodsman adventurer that historians and even people living at the time made him out to be.[10] He had little wilderness experience.

Jesuit historians Rafael Hamilton and Joseph Donnelly have written that Jolliet and Marquette met to discuss their future voyage while Marquette was passing through the Sault with the Odawa and Wendat in May or June 1671, or shortly thereafter. Hamilton wrote that Marquette, Jolliet, and St. Lusson met in the common room of the Jesuit mission at the Sault immediately after the pageant ceremony had ended. According to Hamilton, "De St. Lusson had decided that he need seek no further for a transcontinental passage until the possibilities of the Mississippi were explored; and he was convinced that Jolliet and Marquette were the men best equipped to explore them." St. Lusson is also alleged to have told the future explorers that Canada's governor, Courcelles, would soon resign and that he feared that he might be replaced be a Jesuit-hating Jansenist who would appoint a priest of his religious persuasion to explore the Mississippi. "On this note of uncertainty," wrote Hamilton, "the meeting ended," and soon afterward St. Lusson was off to search for copper on the Ontonagon River while Jolliet and Dablon paddled to Québec.[11]

Simply put, there is no evidence at all that Jolliet and Marquette met with St. Lusson to discuss a voyage to the Mississippi at this time, none. Hamilton's story is, indeed, intriguing, but it lacks support from period documents.

Further, there is no evidence that indicates that St. Lusson continued west on Lake Superior to search for copper on the Ontonagon River. Neither St. Lusson nor anyone in his retinue, nor any Jesuits or traders in the region at the time, mentions anything at all about his traveling 525 miles along the coast west of the Sault to locate copper mines. According to Talon, "The place to which the said Sieur de Saint Lusson has penetrated is supposed to be no more than three hundred leagues from the extremities of the countries bordering on the Vermilion or South Sea. . . . According to the calculation made from the reports of the Indians and from Maps, there seems to remain not more than fifteen hundred leagues of navigation to Tartary, China, and Japan."[12] St. Lusson's report is based on information he received from the tribes at the Sault and perhaps projections or prognostications based on the 1669 Jesuit map. St. Lusson was dispatched "north" to "discover the South Sea and the Copper Mine," but he accomplished neither and there is no credible evidence that he even attempted to do so.

St. Lusson was back in Quebec by the late summer of 1671. In October he was instructed by Talon to continue to open the communication link between Pentagout (Castine, Maine) and Port Royal (Annapolis Royal, Nova Scotia) and to report back to him. Talon planned to relay the information he received from St. Lusson to the king. St. Lusson returned to Quebec in November, as Talon reported, "so broken down by the fatigue of his journey, and so enfeebled by hunger he suffered, that I doubt his ability to go to France."[13] But he recovered, and he was back in France by January 1672.

Donnelly, another Jesuit historian, wrote, "When Father Marquette arrived with his band of frightened Hurons [the Wendat at the Sault in 1671], he and Dablon must have spent *long hours* with Louis Jolliet discussing the geography of the vast, unexplored areas to the west and south of the Sault."[14] Donnelly's claim is refuted by Dablon himself, who wrote:

> And as, in transmigrations of this sort, people's minds are in no very settled condition, so Father Marquette, who had charge of that Mission of saint Esprit, had more to suffer than to achieve for those people's Conversion; for what with Baptizing some children, comforting the sick, and continuing the instruction of those professing Christianity, he was unable to give much attention to converting the others. He was obliged to leave that post with the rest, and to follow his flock, undergoing the same hardships and incurring the same dangers.[15]

In fact, so busy with the tribesmen was Marquette that the missionary never completed his annual report, a document that was required by Jesuit policy to be submitted by missionaries to their superior.[16]

What accurate information can we glean from the historical record about Jolliet and Marquette at the Sault? First, there is no evidence that Marquette ever stopped at Jolliet's trading post to discuss with Louis their future voyage to the Mississippi. If he had, Marquette would have left the frightened Wendat and Odawa who were fleeing for their lives to discuss a future voyage with someone he never met. We ask, how would Marquette have even known to speak to Jolliet, a newcomer to the region, about exploring the Mississippi?[17]

Second, Marquette did not attend St. Lusson's pageant. As we discussed earlier, Nicolas Perrot was one of three men who spoke to the tribes at that event, Allouez and St. Lusson (via an interpreter) being the other two. Perrot later wrote that "the report of this [St. Lusson's] taking possession was then drawn up, on which I placed my signature as interpreter, with that of Sieur de St. Lusson, the deputy; the reverend missionary fathers Dablon, Allouez, Dreuillette, and Marquet [Marquette] signed it further down; and below these, the Frenchmen who were then trading in those quarters."[18] However, St. Lusson's official report states that Father Louis André, who was working at the Sault and at Manitoulin Island at the time, not Marquette, had attended the pageant.[19]

Perrot was wrong; Marquette did not attend the event, as he was preoccupied with the Odawa and Wendat.[20] It is possible, too, that Marquette passed through the Sault *before* Louis arrived, if Jolliet had been part of St. Lusson's convoy. Marquette wrote that the La Pointe tribes typically left their villages "after the Easter Holidays." Whether this was the case in 1671 is uncertain. That year Easter Sunday was celebrated on March 29.[21] Marquette did, however, visit the Sault sometime *after* Jolliet and Dablon had left for Québec, *after* he and the Wendat and Odawa were settled in their new villages and were safe from the Nadouessi. During that time, Marquette left his Michilimackinac mission and traveled to the Sault to recite his final Jesuit vows on July 2, 1671, spending eight days there.[22] Why didn't Marquette recite his final vows when he passed through the Sault on his way to St. Ignace? Likely it was because he was too busy to do so. Marquette could not have met with Jolliet at this time to discuss plans to explore the Mississippi Valley.[23]

Jesuit historian Jean Delanglez brings up an interesting point about the witness list for St. Lusson's *procès-verbal*. According to Delanglez, "Strictly speaking, the names in the list are not signatures. For instance, Jolliet would not sign his name 'le sieur Jolliet,' but 'L. Jolliet' or 'Jolliet'; 'le sieur' was added by the copyist, just as he added the 'sieur' before the name of Nicolas Perrot."[24]

Could Jolliet and Marquette have met earlier, perhaps in Quebec, to discuss exploring the Mississippi? No! Marquette arrived in Quebec in June 1666, while Louis was studying at the Jesuit *collège*. Marquette remained in town for only about three weeks before heading to Trois Rivières to begin his studies. In July 1667, while Marquette was 124 miles away via canoe at Trois Rivières, Jolliet quit the seminary and sailed to France.[25] Marquette left eastern Canada on May 20, 1668, for the Sault, before Louis returned to Canada. Furthermore, the very idea of exploring the Mississippi Valley and visiting the Illinois Country could not have occurred until Allouez returned to Quebec in August 1667 with news of the Mississippi and the Illinois tribe and with pieces of copper ore. There would have been no reason for this voyage unless these three discoveries had been made. Further, neither Jolliet, who had been living at the *collège* studying for the priesthood, nor Marquette, who was relatively new to the colony, had ventured west of Trois Rivières or Cap de la Madeleine by this time. Neither of them had any real-life wilderness experience, and it is therefore highly unlikely that they would have undertaken such a perilous endeavor. Last, neither Marquette nor Jolliet ever wrote or mentioned anything at all about a future expedition to the

Mississippi with each other. The first reference to this alleged meeting is in 1674, when Dablon mentioned the two men "frequently agreed upon it together" in his introduction to his and Jolliet's meeting at Quebec. Dablon was mistaken. Jolliet and Marquette could not have met to discuss the voyage.

Leaving the Sault shortly after the pageant, Jolliet returned east. He next appears in the historical record in Quebec in September, although it is uncertain what he did there at the time.[26] After the pageant, Allouez returned to Wisconsin. He was promoted to superior of the Wisconsin mission in November by Henri Nouvel, now superior of the western missions, replacing Dablon, who had been elevated to superior of the Canadian missions, who, in turn, succeeded Le Mercier, who became prefect of the Jesuit *collège* at Quebec. Marquette resumed his work at St. Ignace, while Father André, who had worked under Druillettes at the Sault, was sent to assist Allouez in Wisconsin. André worked among the Menominee and the Potawatomi living in the Green Bay area. The veteran voyageur and woodsman Jacques Largillier would begin his work with Allouez as a lay helper.[27]

Talon's drive to locate mines, minerals, and water routes continued when he returned to Canada. As we have seen, during his first term as intendant, he personally searched for ore along the St. Lawrence and dispatched expeditions west, including those of Cavelier, Adrien Jolliet and Jean Péré, and St. Lusson. He also dispatched Jesuit Charles Albanel and Paul Denys de Saint-Simon north to Hudson Bay to establish trade with the local tribes, but more important to "reconnoiter whether there be any means of wintering ships in that quarter, in order to establish a factory that might, when necessary, supply provisions to the vessels that will possibly hereafter discover, by that channel, the communication between the two seas—the North and the South."[28] Talon's curiosity was further piqued when a man identified as Captain Poulet suggested an expedition be sent to not only locate the Northwest Passage, but also circumnavigate the continent by way of the North Sea or south through the Straits of Magellan.[29]

In a letter to Talon the following year, Colbert informed the intendant, "As, next to the increase of the Colony of Canada, there is nothing more important for that country and his Majesty's service than the discovery of the passage to the South Sea, his Majesty wishes you to offer a large reward to those who shall make that discovery."[30] This "discovery," as Colbert called it, was important because communication between Quebec, the administrative center of the colony, and France was suspended sometimes for five months during the winter.

Quebec was shut off from the Atlantic, and sea ice on the Gulf of St. Lawrence made travel hazardous. In fact, 1645–1715 were the coldest years in a climatic anomaly known to climatologists as the Little Ice Age.[31] Locating a suitable site for a port on the South Sea, on ice-free waters, would afford year-round communication between North America, France, and its other colonies. Claiming and securing access to the South Sea might also effectively check England and Spain from penetrating parts of today's southern United States.[32]

◇◇◇◇◇◇◇◇◇◇◇◇◇◇◇

The first official Jesuit house, not a cabin or temporary shelter to protect French traders and missionaries, was built at the Fox rapids in late fall 1671, which shortly thereafter burned down. Allouez lost in the fire his writing case and journal, which he later wrote "deprived me of The means of writing accurately of the most remarkable things that have occurred in connection with Christianity in The bay of saint Xavier."[33] The incident helps to account for missing information about the priest's activities during this time. Allouez scavenged what he could from the ashes and rubble and built a makeshift cabin that lasted until it, too, burned on December 22, 1672. Immediately after the second fire, the local Potawatomi began building him a "cabane," a reed-mat wigwam, a structure that could be disassembled and moved. By 1673 the mission was one of three in Ottawa country with permanent dwellings to house the Jesuits, a place where Allouez, André, and later Marquette reportedly "repair[ed] from time to time, to take a breath for a while."[34]

During the second half of 1671 and all of 1672, Marquette toiled at his St. Ignace mission. About this period, he wrote, "This year, the Tionnontateronnons [Tobacco tribe of Wendat] were here to the number of three hundred and eighty souls, and they were joined by over sixty souls of the Outaouasinagaux."[35] Although the missionary's plans to visit the Illinois were put indefinitely on hold, Marquette still hoped to visit them when time and circumstance allowed. He wrote to Dablon, "Meanwhile, I am preparing to Leave It in The hands of another missionary, to go by Your Reverence's order and Seek toward The south sea new nations that are unknown to us, to teach Them to know our great God, of whom they have hitherto been Ignorant."[36] What is important here is that Marquette still hoped to travel to the Illinois, just as he intended to do two years earlier, in the company of Illinois guides, not with Jolliet, voyageurs, traders, or any other secular French yeomen.[37]

A Wendat lodge at the Marquette mission site in St. Ignace, Michigan.
Photo by the author.

In August 1671 and again in December 1672, Cavelier was in Montreal, perhaps hoping to avoid Talon, to whom he had not reported after his foray west
the previous year. Reportedly, Cavelier was "in search of money" at this time.[38]
According to Jesuit Jean Delanglez, Cavelier spent the winter of 1672–73 in
Haudenosaunee country.[39]

Sometime during the first part of 1672, Talon determined to send out
yet another expedition to find the great river and, hopefully, the South Sea.
Although he had championed the search for strategic waterways, mines, and
natural resources, he had not accomplished any of these aims to anyone's satisfaction. Cavelier's expedition was supposed to locate a route to the sea via
a river the Haudenosaunee called "Ohio." From Allouez Talon learned about
another great river, the Mississippi. Were these two streams the same river, or
were they different ones? Perhaps, too, the failure to locate the water routes and
the copper gnawed at him, and he determined to try again.

It is unclear why he was chosen for the assignment, but responsibility for
settling the question about the rivers and reporting back to authorities fell to

Louis Jolliet. Why did Talon choose Louis for this mission? He was a newcomer to the Upper Country, not a seasoned woodsman or a voyageur.[40]

About the choice of Louis Jolliet for the assignment, Canadian Jesuit historian Lucien Campeau wrote that Jolliet had a clear association with the Jesuits. "They [the Jolliet brothers] were Canadians imbued with the spirit of the country and the missionaries were assured that their activity would not lead to the spiritual detriment of the missions." However, he continued, "Louis Jolliet did not have at this age the abilities that would make of him a true leader of the expedition. The royal officials in the time of Colbert did not like to see priests directing enterprises that had an official title. They gave their commissions to young laymen, but without qualifications or experience, in comparison to the clerics on whose qualities the success of the expeditions was placed."[41] Examples of worldly, educated, and well-rounded clerics chosen to participate in important expeditions led by relatively unqualified laymen at this time include Dollier, a former cavalry captain, and Galinée, a mathematician and cartographer, who were instructed to accompany the inexperienced Cavelier.[42] Jesuit missionary Charles Albanel was also directed to travel to Hudson Bay in the company of the lesser-experienced Paul Denys.[43]

Even though there were good reasons not to choose Louis Jolliet for this important assignment, it is likely that he was chosen because he was willing to finance the expedition himself.[44] Louis would have likely viewed the venture as a potential business opportunity, something much more important than an exciting jaunt into uncharted territory. We will see that Louis later sent men in his employ to trade in the Illinois Country during the winter of 1674–75. We will also see that he sought royal permission to establish a colony in the Illinois Country in 1676. However, another explanation might be that Canadian officials confused Louis with his brother Adrien.

Adrien was an experienced woodsman and voyageur. When he was sixteen or seventeen, he was captured by Haudenosaunee and kept prisoner for three months.[45] He spent two full years in the Upper Country between the summers of 1661 and 1663, and he traveled west to trade in 1666. In 1669 Adrien traveled west with Jean Péré to locate copper mines. Adrien was the first European to confirm that the Great Lakes are an interconnected waterway that flow from the Upper Country to the St. Lawrence and ultimately to the Atlantic.[46]

Adrien lived in Cap de la Madeleine, or "Au Cap," located about 124 miles by canoe from Quebec, Canada's capital and home to the governor and intendant.

From 1663 on, "Au Cap" was Adrien's permanent residence. Adrien did little of anything east of his home. He made a name for himself as a voyageur while Louis was studying to be priest or played the organ at the church in Quebec. As previously noted, prominent historians over the past century have wrongly attributed the accomplishments and exploits of Adrien to Louis. Much of Adrien's life remained in obscurity until Raymond Douville's "Life and Death of Adrien Jolliet—a Short, Honest and Very Full Life," in *Les Cahiers des Dix* (1979), brought attention to his activities and discoveries.

During the Haudenosaunee blockade between the late 1640s and 1665, little trade or communication occurred between Quebec, Montreal, and the Upper Country. By the mid-1660s, experienced canoe men and traders were few and far between. Men such as Largillier and Adrien would have been in demand when the rivers west opened for trade and travel, a prime reason for Talon's choice of Adrien to locate a route to transport copper from the western mines. Recall that Talon left Canada in November 1668 after he chose Adrien and Péré for the mission. Adrien headed west sometime after April 1669, after he gave Louis power of attorney. Talon was away, either shipwrecked off the coast of Portugal or in France when Adrien died in December 1669. Talon arrived back in Canada in August 1670. Since Adrien's death occurred 124 miles from Quebec, and Péré, not Adrien, was responsible for submitting a report on the status of the copper mines, Talon likely had no idea that Adrien was dead. It seems plausible that the intendant wanted the same "Jolliet" whom he sent west with Péré to participate in the voyage to locate the South Sea. Perhaps Talon may have thought that the "Jolliet" who traded at the Sault in 1671 was Adrien, who would have been a great choice for this expedition, especially if he could finance it himself.

By way of comparison, Marquette spent much more time in the Upper Country than Louis, having lived there for five years in smoky bark huts and sometimes subsisting on whatever scraps of food he could find while Louis was in France or at Quebec. Marquette was eminently more qualified for the mission than Louis. Even though Louis had attended the best school in Canada at the time, the Jesuit *collège* in Quebec, Marquette had attended some of the finest schools in Europe, Jesuit institutions, having achieved bachelor's and master's degrees. He was educated in the sciences, and he was a likely qualified cartographer and mathematician before he arrived in Canada. He studied Native languages and customs, having, by his own admission, learned six of them.[47]

Louis de Buade, Comte de Frontenac et de Palluau (simply known as Frontenac), the governor who succeeded Courcelles, had not yet arrived in Canada when Talon decided to send Marquette and Jolliet to the Mississippi. The mission was Talon's idea; Frontenac had little to do with it, even though Dablon mistakenly wrote that he did.[48] Frontenac wrote to Colbert on November 2, 1672, that Talon "has likewise judged it expedient for the service to send Sieur Joliet to the country of the Maskouteins, to discover the South Sea, and the Great River they call Mississippi, which is supposed to discharge itself into the Sea of California."[49] Frontenac acquiesced to the decisions about the voyage that were already made before he arrived in the colony (in September 1672). In historian Jean Delanglez's words, "Talon had chosen Jolliet for the expedition before the arrival of the governor at Quebec on September 7 or 8, 1672; but it belonged to the governor to ratify this choice."[50]

As to Talon's selection of Louis, Donnelly fashioned another tale wherein the intendant allegedly "summoned" Jolliet to his palace. Donnelly described the scene: "Resplendent in his great wig, a frothy, stiffly starched jabot at his throat, M. l'Intendant received the twenty-seven-year-old Louis Jolliet. Always the suave diplomat, Jean talon [Talon?] expounded grandly on the glorious future of New France, the vast, wealthy empire it could be when its still unknown areas were explored." He asked Jolliet if he would be willing to undertake the exploration of "the length of that mighty river to its very mouth." Jolliet's response, allegedly "enunciated a bit too hastily, was that he would happily accept the commission, which, he was certain, would be completed successfully to the great glory of France and God."[51] This is another colorful story indeed, but there is no evidence that this meeting, as portrayed by Donnelly, ever occurred.

Jean Talon, who had served two terms as Canada's intendant, 1665–68 and 1670–72, left for France for the last time in November 1672. He had been at odds with Courcelles from the beginning of their tenures, the governor maintaining that the intendant had at times overstepped his authority and had assumed the governor's responsibilities. Talon also grew weary of the ongoing disputes and power struggles between himself and merchants, and the Jesuits, and the Compagnie des Indes Occidentales.[52] After putting the colony on a path to prosperity by correcting the mistakes of former incompetent and ineffective administrators, he was ready to leave. Courcelles also left Canada for France in November. Talon's departure left a power vacuum; it would be three years until Jacques Duchesneau, the next intendant, arrived to keep check on the governor.

Before Frontenac departed for Canada, the king gave him specific instructions. He was directed to "apply himself" to the establishment of justice for all the king's subjects by way of the Sovereign Council and to make sure the poor were not oppressed by the wealthy and powerful. He was to protect the colony, to encourage the clearing of timber and cultivation of the soil, to promote the breeding of livestock, and to support Canada's fisheries, shipbuilding, and trade. Should an epidemic spread among the inhabitants, he was to immediately find its cause and, if possible, terminate it. To promote population growth, Frontenac was to encourage young Canadians to marry and to direct missionaries to "take young Indians for the purpose of instructing them in the faith and civilizing them." Finally, he was to keep a check on Jesuit power and influence, but also to protect the Sulpicians and Recollects from Jesuit abuse, to maintain a proper "counterbalance" between the Catholic religious orders.[53]

With Talon's departure, Canada was without an official to look after the colony's fiscal health, settlement policies, and economic matters. It also left a vacant seat on the Sovereign Council. Equally important, there was no longer a watchful eye on the governor to ensure that he did not abuse his power and authority (Frontenac was deep in debt when he arrived in the colony). It was into this vacuum, in the autumn of 1672, that Frontenac, arrived. Besides ruffling the feathers of Canadian officials and ecclesiastics, the new governor was a proponent of western exploration and trade, but in a way that he hoped could line his own pockets. But rather than look out for the king's subjects, Frontenac instead took advantage of the political void. He ran the colony without the oversight that Courcelles and later governors were obliged to tolerate. He was free to exploit any situation to his personal benefit,

In 1673 Frontenac dispatched Cavelier to Onontagué, the capital of the Onondaga Haudenosaunee, to invite their leaders to a council so that the French could obtain a small piece of land located on the east end of Lake Ontario, at the mouth of the Cataraqui River. There the governor, without notifying the Crown of his intentions to do so, hoped to build a fort and trading post to divert western furs to the French and away from British traders in New York.[54] He also planned to establish a French settlement around the fort. Arriving at the meeting site amid a show of pomp and circumstance, Frontenac and his entourage were seated before the Haudenosaunee leaders. Gifts were exchanged and speeches were given. While the talks were under way, the governor's engineers under le Sieur Rendin began stepping out lines and clearing brush along what would become the walls of Fort Frontenac.[55] Perhaps being preoccupied with more important matters, including wars against the Andaste and Mohegan, the Haudenosaunee acquiesced to the governor's proposals. The new fort and adjacent property were soon leased to Jacques Le Ber and Charles Bazire, but in 1674 were transferred to Cavelier, who would become seigneur and receive a title of nobility, officially becoming Sieur de La Salle.[56]

◇◇◇◇◇◇◇◇◇◇◇◇◇

To fund the western voyage, a stipulation to which Louis had agreed, he created a partnership that included François de Chavigny (the Sieur de la Chevrotière), Zacharie Jolliet (Louis's younger brother), Jean Plattier, Pierre Moreau, Jacques Largillier, and Jean Tiberge.[57] The pact was formed to spread potential financial risks that might destroy a single investor. Three of the signatories, besides Louis, were present at St. Lusson's pageant and were likely employees of Jolliet.[58]

While preparations for the Mississippi expedition were under way in Quebec, Allouez and André remained busy instructing and ministering to the Wisconsin tribes. In 1672 Allouez established the mission of St. Jacques at the Mascouten village where he spent four months among fifty cabins of Mascouten, ninety Miami, twenty Illinois, thirty Kickapoo, and some Wea, a Miami subtribe. During one of his commutes to St. Xavier, his canoe wrecked at the rapids near modern-day Appleton. Fortunately for the priest, he recovered his waterlogged belongings the next day. The group procured another canoe and continued down the Fox and eventually landed at the mission. He next traveled to the Potawatomi, where he had his converts plant a large cross on a plateau above Green Bay.[59] Leaving the Potawatomi, the priest briefly returned to his house at St. Xavier and then headed back to the Wolf River for his third visit to the Mesquakie, arriving in early November. There he cared for the sick, taught the interested, and baptized forty-eight people. Sometime during Allouez's visit, a group of Mesquakie returned to the village from a council with some Haudenosaunee. Allouez reported that the "evil spirit" working through the Haudenosaunee had turned these Mesquakie away from him and his Catholicism. Their obstinance soon spread to other people in the village. Making matters worse, the Nadouessi had recently killed thirty-six Mesquakie warriors who Allouez wrote "prayed to God before going to war."[60] Since prayers did not protect them from their enemies, the warriors shunned the priest and refused to provide him adequate lodging for the upcoming winter. Allouez was forced to take shelter in a dilapidated bark hut that, fortunately, his helpers repaired and made somewhat livable. They also erected a bark chapel next to their cabin. Eventually, some despairing Mesquakie women brought Allouez their sick children to be baptized, hoping that the sacrament might restore their health. In due course, many Mesquakie came to call on the missionary.

Allouez left the Mesquakie on April 30 and paddled to the Mascouten village, where he was, again, well received. So many villagers arrived at his chapel for prayer that most were not able to enter it. Some ripped away the bark panels or poked holes through them to hear the priest speak. Allouez left the village on May 22 and returned to the Mesquakie, his fourth visit to the village.

While Allouez labored at the Fox and Wolf River villages, André was busy among the Menominee and the Potawatomi. He tells an interesting story about an incident that occurred while he was with some Menominee fishermen. Sturgeon fishermen, the missionary wrote, typically hung an image of the sun tied to the end of a brightly painted pole to which were attached sheaves of cedar that acted like floats above their nets. The image was an appeal to the sun to have pity on them and to fill their nets with sturgeon. Although the Menominee expected the river to be full of spawning fish, none had been seen or were caught, a troubling circumstance since sturgeon was a primary food source for the village. André asked the fishermen if he could switch the representation of the sun with an image of the crucified Christ, to which, having little to lose, they consented. The next morning, according to the priest, their nets were full of sturgeon.[61]

In autumn Jolliet and five men headed to St. Ignace in canoes laden with goods and supplies, arriving at the mission on December 8. Marquette was probably quite surprised—and thrilled—to see the group, having no idea that they were en route to the mission. He was also elated to learn that he had been chosen to participate in the voyage. Marquette's plans to explore the Mississippi and visit the Illinois in their country would finally be realized.

Marquette understood that he and Jolliet were about to embark on a dangerous voyage. He wrote, "I found myself in the blessed necessity of exposing my life for the salvation of all these peoples, and especially of the Ilinois, who had very urgently entreated me, when I was at the point of st. Esprit, to carry the word of God to Their country." The two explorers took great pains to prepare for the journey, making sure, as much as possible, that they knew where they were going and that they had the best information available to guide them. The two men also pressed the tribesmen for any information they might have about the route to the Mississippi, including any notable landmarks, the location of villages, and the distances between important points, information that the priest reduced to a rough map. The chart was also reported to have outlined the course of the Mississippi.[62] Marquette also surely shared with Jolliet what he learned from the Illinois at La Pointe about the waterways leading to their villages. It is possible, too, since Marquette had likely not spoken any Miami-Illinois during the past two years, that he and Largillier practiced their language skills, testing their memories and quizzing each other about words and phrases. Considering the scope of their mission and the dangers involved, there was little room for error, and the explorers wanted to know all they could about what they were getting themselves into.

The crew would embark on one of the most important early voyages in Canadian and American history. They prepared, studied, and honed their skills before venturing into territories unknown to the French, a voyage that would indelibly link their names to waters, lakes, and cities in today's Great Lakes states and the Mississippi Valley.

CHAPTER 4

St. Ignace to the Des Moines River

After the two bark canoes had been loaded with supplies, trade goods, guns and ammunition, reams of paper, navigational equipment, food, and priestly vestments and items needed to celebrate Mass, Jolliet, the missionary, and five canoe men pushed off from shore on May 17 and paddled into the aqua-blue-colored waters of Lake Huron.[1] They were embarking on a voyage of discovery that would take them through lands and up and down waterways that were unknown to the French. Marquette noted that the crew was excited, "animated" as he phrased it, singing songs of the voyageurs as they paddled out of the bay and toward the straits, which, he added, "rendered the labor of paddling from morning to night agreeable to us."[2]

Along their route, the explorers would visit each Native settlement they encountered and speak with the village headmen. They hoped to make a positive first impression on the tribes, intending to establish amicable relationships with them from the start. Unlike the British and later American models, the French were generally inclusive, not exclusive, and they worked to cooperate with the tribes, not defeat, expel, and exclude them.[3] This is why unlicensed and unregulated *coureurs des bois* were so harmful to French interests, as both Marquette and Jolliet were fully aware. These "runners of the woods" acted on their own behalf, for their own interests, and on their own impulses, not those of the Crown or church. Jolliet and Marquette also wanted to learn from the tribesmen as much as they could about dangers that lay ahead, human, natural, or otherwise. As linguist, cartographer, and Jesuit scout, Marquette was interested in the people his group would meet. Were they receptive to instruction in Catholicism, or were they predisposed against it? Where were their villages located? How many people lived in them? Could he communicate with them? Jolliet would likely take in and analyze what he and Marquette learned about the people to see if there was an opportunity for trade or even settlement, something that he might eventually benefit from personally.

In a few miles, the canoes entered Lake Michigan, where they followed the sandy shorelines of Michigan's Upper Peninsula. The group reached the Garden Peninsula where the islands of the Niagara Escarpment meld into the mainland and form the eastern edge of Big Bay de Noc. They soon passed Little Bay de Noc, and in another fifty-five miles they reached the Menominee River, the stream that separates present Michigan's Upper Peninsula from Wisconsin. Steering their canoes into the river, they paddled to a village of *folle avoine*, as Marquette called them, a tribe known to us today as the Menominee, where they disembarked.

The French were no strangers to the Menominee. Marquette's fellow Jesuits knew them and had instructed them prior to the voyage. Marquette already knew that several "good Christians" lived at this village, the result of the dedicated work of Father André, who was likely living among the Potawatomi on the eastern bank of the Door County Peninsula at the time.

The explorers had little time to spend with the Menominee; their minds were focused on the long voyage that lay ahead and the challenges they would face. Pulling their canoes ashore, they would have been greeted by several village leaders followed by a group of onlookers. The headmen would have led the explorers to a lodge where the calumet was smoked. It would have been there that Marquette told them that he was going to distant nations to teach them the "mysteries" of his faith. The Menominee were taken aback by this, and they told him of the perils that they would face, including hostile warriors, navigational hazards, river monsters, and a giant demon who would block their path. And even if they survived the warriors, hazards, and monsters, the summer heat would surely kill them. Marquette thanked the Menominee for their concern but stressed to them that the "salvation of souls was at stake" and that his party was prepared to defend itself against men and beasts.

Marquette scribbled a few lines in his report about how the Menominee harvest, winnow, and prepare wild rice or wild oats, *Zizania aquatica*. It is possible, though, that this information may have been added to Marquette's narrative by Dablon, who edited Marquette's report, since he, Dablon, and Allouez were in the Fox Valley at the time wild rice was traditionally harvested by the Menominee (the grain is harvested in September, and Marquette's visit was in May). After a prayer and a few words of instruction, Jolliet and Marquette left the council and, with the others, boarded their canoes and set out down the coast of Green Bay.

The explorers arrived at the Fox River. Two and a half years earlier, Dablon and Allouez paddled the stream and directed their men to throw into the river the idol that was worshipped by the locals.

From the Native American perspective, the Fox Valley had many advantages. Wild rice that grew in the river attracted flocks of ducks, geese, and other fowl. Fish were plentiful, as were an assortment of nuts and berries. Along the river, wide prairies were bounded by timber, ideal border habitat for game mammals such as whitetail deer. The stream was a thoroughfare for regional tribes who not only communicated but also traded with each other. A missionary wrote that ten nations, or fifteen thousand potential Catholic converts, called the area home. It is no wonder then why the Jesuits considered the Fox Valley an important mission field.[4]

Arriving at the first set of rapids, the crew disembarked and began dragging their canoes through the shallows, over rocks that reportedly were sharp enough to rip the hulls of their canoes and cut the feet of the men pulling them.[5] Located along this *sault* was the St. Francis Xavier mission.

Except for a *coureur des bois* or perhaps a local Indian or two, the mission was probably vacant when Jolliet and Marquette passed the site. Father André was away with the Potawatomi, and Allouez was busy among the Mesquakie on the Wolf River, where he remained until sometime in June.[6] A permanent structure stood at the site when Jolliet and Marquette passed it, for why else, as we will see, would have Marquette have remained there for thirteen months after the voyage before returning to the Illinois Country?

Above the rapids, the crew paddled the gentle current through shallow lakes where stands of wild rice grew sometimes to the middle of the stream. Hiding in these grasses were shorebirds, waterfowl, herons, and cranes. Reeds, lily pads, cattails, and a host of other marine plants grew in the shallows. Along the shorelines, they saw elm, ash, maple, aspen, and, inland, oaks. Farther upstream the group encountered other rapids, including the Grand Kakalin rapids, where Allouez and his group had suffered a canoe wreck the previous September; the Petit Colimi rapids; and the Grand Colimi rapids and falls, where Allouez's canoe men used wooden poles to push their craft over the river's rocky bottom to reach the Petite Lac Butte des Morts (Hill of the Dead Little Lake), located just above present Neenah.[7] Passing Doty Island, they paddled into Lake Winnebago, where the Upper Fox meets the Lower.

Lake Winnebago is Wisconsin's largest inland lake. A large yet shallow body, Lake Winnebago's more than 130,000 acres and approximately eighty-eight miles of shoreline extends into Calumet, Fond du Lac, and Winnebago Counties. Today the lake has a maximum depth of only twenty-one feet.

The canoes would have hugged the lake's western shoreline for the next fourteen miles until they reached today's Oshkosh, where the Upper Fox discharges into the lake. A traveler who navigated the Fox in 1767 called the Upper Fox the "Crocodile River" because local tribesmen reportedly killed a large animal there, the description of which, in his view, could have only been a crocodile or alligator, an obvious impossibility.[8]

In about four miles, the canoes entered Grand Lac Butte des Morts. Located at the modern-day community of Highland Shore, along the south side of the lake, is an area that researchers, including Jeffery Behm of the University of Wisconsin–Oshkosh, have written was once a large village, an encampment sometimes referred to as the Grand Village of the Mesquakie and the Bell site, 47-Wn-9. If this thesis is correct, this village was the target of French and Indian military campaigns in 1716, 1728, and 1730. The latter struggle forced the Mesquakie to abandon eastern Wisconsin.[9]

In 1673 the Fox entered Grand Lac Butte des Morts on its northwestern end where the explorers continued for two more miles before reaching the river's juncture with the Wolf. The Wolf begins its journey in lake country, flowing south for more than two hundred miles, where it widens to become Lakes Poygan and Winneconnee. At the river's confluence, the Fox flows north before taking a ninety-degree turn to the east where it enters Grand Lac Butte des Morts.

Marquette wrote that his party stopped somewhere along this stretch of river to search for a "medicinal plant," one that the local inhabitants claimed was an antidote for snakebites. The plant, he reported, "is very pungent, and tastes like powder when crushed with the teeth; it must be masticated and placed upon the bite inflicted by the snake."[10] Snakes were said to flee from whoever rubbed the powdered plant on their bodies. Marquette found and collected a few specimens just in case they needed them later during the voyage. Reembarking, the men soon reached the present town of Berlin, where on a hill above the south bank they saw the large village of Mascouten.

The town reportedly sat overlooking vast prairies dotted with groves of trees that, according to one observer, "nature seems to furnish solely for the gratification of the eye, or to meet the needs of man, who cannot dispense with wood." Similarly, Marquette also noted, "The soil [at the village] is very fertile, and yields much indian corn. The savages gather quantities of plums and grapes, wherewith much wine could be made, if desired."[11]

Sentries or barking dogs would have alerted the village of the approaching Frenchmen. At the river's edge, Jolliet and Marquette were met by a delegation of village headmen and warriors. After greetings were exchanged, the group walked the path up to the village, leaving the crew, or most of it, to guard the canoes and cargo. Passing a mineral spring, Marquette crouched down, cupped his hands, and sampled the water.

Marquette described the village as a collection of elm-bark and reed-mat huts of different sizes and shapes. In the center, they saw a large cross adorned with skins, red belts, and even bows and arrows, what appeared to have been a Christian symbol that would have been raised at the behest of Allouez. What Marquette did not know was that the cross had nothing to do with Christianity. It was a symbol of the Midewiwin Society, which, according to René R. Gadacz, writing for the *Canadian Encyclopedia*, "is a religious society made up of spiritual advisors and healers, known as the Mide. The Mide serve as spiritual leaders for the general populace. They perform religious ceremonies, study and practise sacred healing methods, and strive to maintain a respectful relationship between humanity and Mother Earth. The Midewiwin is an essential part of the worldview of the Ojibwa and of some other Algonquian and Eastern Woodland Indigenous peoples." Ethnologist Frances Densmore wrote that her informant, an Ojibwe elder named Gagewin, told her that the "Midewiwin has always had the idea of a cross connected with it." Moreover, the cross was said to be "a sacred post, and the symbol of the fourth degree of the Midewiwin."[12]

Nicolas Perrot spent a week at the village sometime between 1665 and 1670 during which time he attended councils with chiefs and elders and where he encouraged mutual friendship and trade. He also reported that the village was

palisaded, a common defensive feature during times of war. This was corroborated by Dablon, who pointed out a year and a half earlier that the Mascouten,
Kickapoo, and Miami lived there in "common defense," to protect themselves
from Haudenosaunee war parties. Displaced bands of Indians had been pouring
into the Fox River area, so many that by 1675 people from twelve nations, speaking three different languages, would be living in this village alone.[13] After the
formalities of smoking and exchanging words of goodwill were finished, both
Jolliet and Marquette told the chiefs the purpose of their visit. Jolliet spoke first,
spelling out to them that that he had been sent by Onontio, the governor of New
France, to discover new countries. Jolliet also told them that his God, the "sovereign Master" of his, Jolliet's, and Marquette's lives as the explorer phrased it,
wanted all nations to know him, and by doing his will, by bringing their master's
word to them, Jolliet feared not death. After giving the leaders a present, he asked
that they provide his party a pair of guides to escort them upstream, a request to
which the chiefs readily agreed. The chiefs also reciprocated and presented the
Frenchmen with a mat that was reportedly large enough to serve as a bed during
the entire voyage.[14] This was the last time Jolliet would speak with tribal leaders
during their journey. He was familiar with two Native languages, Algonquin-
Ottawa-Ojibwe, the language spoken by tribes at the Sault, and Montagnais,
but was now at the limit of his linguistic capability.[15] Both Marquette and Jolliet spoke to Indians while engaged in their respective professions, Marquette
to teach and convert them to Catholicism and Jolliet while trading. However,
Marquette spoke Huron and four dialects of Algonquin-Ottawa-Ojibwe, and
he was also becoming familiar with Miami-Illinois, an important prerequisite
for the 1673 voyage, an expedition that would take the two explorers down the
Mississippi and into the country of the Illinois, today the states of Wisconsin,
Missouri, Illinois, and Iowa. Since Jesuits and other missionaries worked to
convert the tribes of North America to Catholicism, it was imperative that they
not only speak Native languages, but also understand their morphology, syntax,
and pragmatics, language issues that the Jesuits would work out by the late 1680s.
The Jesuits were linguists in the purest sense, not just polyglots.[16]

Conspicuously missing from Marquette's report of the voyage is any mention of Jacques Largillier, voyageur, woodsman, and one of six investors in Jolliet's company. Largillier was not only familiar with Native languages such as
Algonquin-Ottawa-Ojibwe, but he, like Marquette, was also learning Miami-Illinois. Trading contracts reveal that Largillier was in the Upper Country between

1669 and 1671, even attending St. Lusson's pageant at the Sault.[17] And we saw that Largillier worked as a lay helper to the Jesuits in the western Great Lakes beginning in 1671, including Allouez at his mission at the Sault. Largillier was no doubt familiar with the languages and dialects of the regional tribes, and by extension the Miami-Illinois tongue, too, since both Allouez and Marquette had extensive interaction with Miami-Illinois-speaking people. What linguistic role if any Largillier played during the voyage is unknown. Was he present during councils, or was he relegated to canoe-man status? It seems likely that he may have, in some way, large or small, assisted Marquette with language issues.

Since Marquette, Jolliet, and Largillier were well versed in Ojibwe, they would have used a combination of Miami-Illinois and Ojibwe when speaking with tribal leaders at the village. They would not have used Mascouten, but, while they are not mutually intelligible, Ojibwe and Miami-Illinois are reasonably close grammatically speaking, and there would have been people at the Mascouten village who could speak Ojibwe at least to some degree. Naturally, Marquette's and Largillier's growing knowledge of Miami-Illinois would have also helped.[18]

After spending the night at the village, the explorers and their escorts boarded their canoes and headed upstream before a crowd of people who gathered at the river's edge to watch the send-off.

Above the Mascouten village, the river narrows and bends, then widens and narrows again, where bulrushes extended far into the river, limiting visibility from canoe level, and where shallows thick with cattails and phragmites could conceal an awaiting ambush along the shore. Passing through today's Marquette and then Columbia Counties, the Frenchmen and their Miami guides pulled to shore and disembarked at the Fox-Wisconsin portage.

The portage is the strip of land at the Continental Divide that separates waters that flow to the Great Lakes and empty into the Atlantic and those that flow to the Mississippi and ultimately the Gulf of Mexico. The portage was level, flat, without hills or bluffs between the two waterways. Carrying their cargo and canoes to the Wisconsin would have been a laborious task made somewhat easier with the help of their Miami guides. During their crossing, some of the men may have held their guns at the ready in case an ambush lay waiting in the brush ahead.

Marquette recorded that the portage was 2,700 steps long. Jonathan Carver, who traversed it in October 1767, wrote that the portage was 1.75 miles long. Midway through it, Carver wrote that it was "a morass overgrown with a kind of long grass, the rest of it a plain, with some few oak and pine trees growing thereon." In the timber, Carver saw "a great number of rattle-snakes."[19] Coincidentally, this observation dovetails with Marquette's comments about searching for the plant that the tribesmen believed was an antidote for snakebites.

The Fox River end of the portage in Marquette's day appears to have been located a short distance upstream from today's historical marker located a few yards north of State Route 33, across the road from the "Surgeon's Quarters" at old Fort Winnebago. Maps dating to the 1830s through 1850s locate the east, actually the north, end of the portage at an approximate forty-five-degree bend in the river south of Route 33. Today a pseudoportage follows the Wauona Trail, a street that connects Route 33 at the Fox to East Wisconsin Street where a stone marker commemorates the portage site. The Wisconsin River end of the portage was several hundred yards southeast of the stone marker.

An American expedition led by Lewis Cass that included Henry Schoolcraft crossed the portage in August 1820. Schoolcraft described the portage as a level prairie, 1.5 miles across, with a "good wagon road" connecting the two rivers. He noted that a Frenchman lived at the portage who kept horses and cattle that were used to transport goods and merchandise for a fee—twenty-five cents per hundred weight.[20]

Before the advent of railroads and highways, the nation's rivers and lakes were important transportation routes, and their associated portages were vital links along these thoroughfares. To secure the portage between the Fox and Wisconsin, and to protect newly arrived settlers and miners who trespassed on Ho-Chunk lands, the U.S. military erected Fort Winnebago near the Fox River end of the portage.

Reaching the shore of the Wisconsin River, the realization set in among the men that from this point forward they would be alone; their fate, as Marquette wrote, was "in the hands of providence." Before starting on the new leg of their journey, the group took a few moments to beseech the "blessed Virgin Immaculate" for protection for themselves and for the success of the mission. When they finished, the crew, after "mutually encouraging" each other, boarded their canoes and set out on the Wisconsin.

Sailing downstream, the explorers zigzagged between islands, sandbars, and "shoals," as Marquette called them. The river flowed above a "bed of sand," according to Schoolcraft.[21] From their canoes, the men saw herds of bison and deer on the meadows. More important, especially to Jolliet, the group saw what appeared to be iron mines, or more likely lead mines, on the bluffs above the river.[22] They passed sites that a century later would become home to the Sauk and Mesquakie. Another noticeable feature they passed was "Tower Hill," where during the nineteenth century workers would pour molten lead through a strainer on top of the hill to make lead shot, a process known as the "Watts Method."[23] Traversing southwestern Wisconsin's Driftless Area, the explorers beheld the lush green hills and gray limestone cliffs—one bluff, some distance to their left, being the popular overlook known today as Point Lookout at Wyalusing State Park.

With great joy, and probably a bit of unease, the group reached the Mississippi on June 17. Although French explorers Radisson and Groseilliers may or may not have reached the northern part of the river in the 1650s, this was the first time that duly appointed agents of France would explore the central parts of the stream and report their findings to authorities.

On the Iowa side of the river, the explorers saw "very high mountains," as Marquette described them, elevations known today as the "Paleozoic Plateau,"

A photo of the confluence of the Wisconsin and Mississippi Rivers where Jolliet and Marquette's party arrived on June 17, 1673. Photo by the author.

some of which is part of Pike's Peak State Park. Steering their canoes south and sailing with the current, they viewed the shores of Grant County, Wisconsin, on their left and Clayton County, Iowa, on their right.

They also passed Catfish Creek, located just south of modern-day Dubuque, Iowa, on the west bank of the Mississippi, where the Cass-Schoolcraft expedition visited the village of the Kettle Chief, a Mesquakie camp of nineteen lodges, or a population of about 250. Mesquakie women reportedly mined lead in the cliffs and bluffs above the village and then transported the ore to an island opposite the Mesquakie camp where the traders would purchase and then smelt the mineral.[24] This area was known in Schoolcraft's time as the Dubuque Lead Mine District.

South of the district, the river gradually widened.[25] Wooded hills bordered the river on both sides until they reached the floodplain at Thompson, Illinois, where the ancient Mississippi left the present channel and flowed east-southeast through Whiteside County, connecting with the Illinois River at the Big Bend near Hennepin. Marquette opined that islands along this stretch were covered in "finer trees" than those farther upstream, likely a reference to nut-bearing hardwoods such as walnut, oak, and hickory. Deer and bison were plentiful, as were molting waterfowl. They also saw what seems from his description to have been a cougar. Large fish reportedly filled the waters, one of them even hitting one of their canoes with such force that they thought they had struck a submerged log.[26]

Traveling in unfamiliar territory and having been warned that tribes lived along the river who would certainly defend their villages from intruders, the men were always on guard, alert, and ready to defend themselves. They took other precautions, too, including cooking their food before nightfall over small fires just large enough to grill their dinners, and soon after they finished eating they would douse the embers with water. They also slept in their canoes, which were anchored a short distance from shore. A sentry always kept watch.[27]

By the time they reached Clinton, Iowa, there were fewer backwaters and sloughs, the waterfowl and shorebirds they had seen were no longer plentiful, while turkeys and bison were abundant. At the northern end of today's Quad Cities, the canoes encountered a long stretch of rapids, a well-known geological feature illustrated on early maps, including Marquette's 1673 holograph map.[28] They would have also passed Rock Island, the future site of Fort Armstrong, one of a series of American forts along the Mississippi that were built to keep a check on French and British traders, to protect American settlers from Indian attacks, and to keep peace between the tribes to prevent interruptions of the fur trade. In seven miles, the group passed the mouth of the Rock River, a stream that began its nearly three-hundred-mile journey to the Mississippi just south of Lake Winnebago, not far from where the explorers had been a few weeks earlier. Not far up the Rock, a large Sauk village known as Saukenuk, would be established in the mid-1730s. Saukenuk would be home to the famous war chief Black Hawk.

Between Le Claire and Muscatine, Iowa, the Mississippi flows southwesterly and then, from the mouth of the Rock, nearly due west. At Muscatine the river curves almost ninety degrees to the south, but the current remains gentle. The French passed the Iowa River, the Yellow Banks, and the Des Moines Rapids before reaching the Des Moines River, the state line between today's Iowa and Missouri.

Marquette wrote, "Finally on June 25 we noticed human tracks at the edge of water and a little, rather beaten path that went into a beautiful prairie. We stopped to examine it, and judging that it was a way that led to some Indian village, we decided to go reconnoiter it; we then left our two canoes under the protection of our people."[29] Beaching their canoes, Jolliet and Marquette decided to investigate; they would follow the path to discover where it led. Finding it prudent to keep their men at the river's edge to guard their canoes rather than proceed with an armed escort, Jolliet, carrying a backpack of gifts of goodwill, and Marquette cautiously headed up the trail. After walking about two leagues (just over five miles), Marquette wrote, they saw a village situated on a hill above the bank of an oxbow lake. From their vantage point, they would have seen, a half league beyond, two more villages. Moving silently forward, the two men drew so close to the settlement that they could hear people talking. Finding themselves in this precarious situation, the two men yelled out loud with all their energy, as Marquette wrote, to announce their presence. Hearing their shouts, the villagers left their huts and rushed to see who was causing the commotion. They were likely surprised to see two Frenchmen, one of whom was wearing a long black gown.[30]

From the Illinois Villages
to the Illinois River

Realizing that the two Frenchmen were not a threat, four elders came forth, at first walking slowly and deliberately toward the explorers, two of them holding brightly adorned calumets, smoking pipes with beautifully colored feathers attached to them. Approaching the explorers, the two men raised their calumets to the sun as if offering them to the sun to smoke. Marquette, who was intimately familiar with customs and the etiquette of many tribes, knew that this ceremony was performed before visitors who were held in high regard. When the elders had come within easy speaking distance, Marquette asked them in Miami-Illinois who they were. The elders replied that they were Illinois; more specifically, the French would learn that many of them were Peoria, a large Illinois subtribe.[1] After offering the explorers a puff from their calumets, the group walked to the village where a crowd of inquisitive bystanders had gathered.

The villages that Jolliet and Marquette had stumbled upon were located at today's Illiniwek Village State Historical Site in Clark County, Missouri. Archaeological excavations conducted there during the 1990s uncovered two of the three villages recorded by Marquette. The entire site, known as 23-CK-116, is divided into two smaller units, the northern one known as the Haas Site, likely the first village that Jolliet and Marquette encountered, and the second or more southern one called the Hagerman Site. The third village, that of the Illinois subtribe known today as the Moingwena, has not been located. The 23-CK-116 site dates from around 1640, possibly earlier, to about 1677 and again between 1680 and 1683.[2] Archaeologists working at the site have uncovered an abundance of Danner Cordmarked pottery, sometimes known as the "pottery of the Illinois," and a significant assemblage of seventeenth-century trade goods.[3]

Historians argue that the Illinois moved west of the Mississippi to avoid attacks by Haudenosaunee war parties.[4] This premise is supported by archaeological evidence that indicates these Illinois villages had been established around the time of the so-called Beaver Wars, when Haudenosaunee war parties raided Huronia and the Great Lakes region, forcing tribes such as the Mesquakie, Sauk, Wendat, and others to flee west. The villages were not located on a large river but were instead tucked away just less than two miles inland at a secure water source, a large, clear, and deep oxbow lake that was not visible from the river. Relocating west of the Mississippi would have put the Illinois at or beyond the limit of Haudenosaunee striking range. However, it is possible too, albeit less likely, that the Illinois moved west of the Mississippi by or possibly before 1640 in order to be closer to large bison herds that other tribes who lived farther up

The Hagerman site at the Illiniwek Village State Historic Site in Clark County, Missouri, where Jolliet and Marquette visited two Illinois villages. Photo by the author.

the Des Moines, such as the Otoe, incorporated into their seasonal subsistence cycle.[5] This hypothesis is corroborated by historian Wayne Temple, who wrote that the 1673 villages were summer hunting camps, not semipermanent agricultural villages.[6] Marquette did mention "corn," maize, a crop typical of summer agricultural villages in the part of his report detailing his and Jolliet's visit, but only insofar as it related generally to Illinois crop production, not his personal observations about the sites.

These people may have been from the same village that Marquette planned to visit two years earlier, before intertribal warfare forced him to cancel his journey.[7] Marquette was now with the tribe with whom he hoped to instruct and convert, people whose language he had studied so diligently to learn.

The explorers were led to a hut where they were greeted by an elderly man, a village chief, who heard the commotion outside but perhaps as a matter of protocol remained at his lodge. Seeing the Frenchmen, the chief held his hands high to the sun and said to them, "How beautiful the sun is, O frenchman, when thou comest to visit us! All our village awaits thee, and thou shalt enter all our Cabins in peace."[8] The French entered the lodge where, as honored guests, they were the first to be given the calumet to smoke before it was passed to the others.

Not long afterward, the French were invited on behalf of the great captain, or head chief of the Illinois, to join him at a council at the second village, a request they readily accepted. The villagers were mesmerized by the French; hundreds followed them en masse, while others lined the trail to the chief's village, while still others who had walked well ahead of the French retraced their steps to see the explorers again. Arriving at the lodge, Jolliet and Marquette were met by the chief, who stood between two elders. The chief greeted the visitors, congratulating them on their arrival. As Illinois custom prescribed, the calumet was given to the two Frenchmen, which they smoked as they entered the lodge.

Inside, Marquette presented the assembled chiefs and elders four gifts, the first three accompanying statements that explained the purpose of their visit, while the fourth sought information about other nations they would encounter along their way and any information chiefs might have concerning the sea. When Marquette finished speaking, the head chief, resting his hands on the head of a young Indian boy, spoke to the explorers, thanking them for their visit and for the trouble they took to travel to his village, a visit that, according to the chief, made the earth more beautiful, the rivers calm and clear of rocks, the tobacco taste better, and the maize appear finer.[9] He next presented them a slave boy, and then a calumet, an item the chief valued more than the boy.

The chief begged the explorers on behalf of his nation to go no farther because many dangers awaited them. Undeterred, Marquette told the chief that he did not fear death and that he would be happy to give his life in the service of his God. After the council, the explorers feasted on *sagamité*, fish, and bison, the fattest pieces being placed in their mouths by the tribesmen. Freshly cooked and fatty bison meat suggests that the animal had been recently killed and butchered, something that was more likely to have occurred at a summer hunting camp mentioned by Temple than at a semipermanent agricultural village.[10]

The chief was more than thrilled that the explorers had visited his village. But this raises the question of why. Was it because the chief wanted to tap into the power of a Catholic deity who could give his people luck in war, luck during the hunt, and luck healing the sick, or was it perhaps because they wanted local access to trade goods, items that some Illinois had traveled all the way to Lake Superior to purchase?

As we have seen in a previous chapter, the French first encountered the Illinois at La Pointe, a cluster of winter villages located near present Ashland, Wisconsin, hundreds of miles away from the Des Moines River. What did they have to offer in trade for items of European manufacture? Slaves. Marquette wrote, "They [the Illinois] are warlike, and make themselves dreaded by the Distant tribes to the south and west, whither they go to procure Slaves; these they barter, selling them at a high price to other Nations, in exchange for other Wares."[11] One of the primary nations from which the Illinois procured slaves was the Pawnee, one band of which in 1673 lived some distance above the Illinois villages on the Des Moines. About Pawnee slaves and the Illinois, historian Carl Ekberg wrote available data indicates that "sixty-eight percent of Indian slaves in Canada for whom tribal designations are available were identified as 'Panis [Pawnees]' which is an astonishingly high number even when taking into account that 'Panis' was often employed generically to mean 'Indian slave.'" Also according to Ekberg, the "tribes of the Illinois nation had the best access to slaves who had been captured west of the Mississippi River, whereas the Ottawa tribes had the best access to manufactured goods coming from France via the St. Lawrence Valley."[12] Guns, knives, and tomahawks purchased by trading slaves made the Illinois a formidable enemy. Marquette continued, "They [Illinois] also use guns, which they buy from our savage allies who Trade with our french. They use them especially to inspire, through their noise and smoke, terror in their Enemies; the latter do not use guns, and have never seen any, since they live too Far toward the West." Access to trade items made the Illinois middlemen in the Amerindian trade business, making tribes with little access to them dependent on the Illinois.

European trade goods and weapons were important to the Illinois for power, prestige, and protection. Missionaries were the key that opened the door to purchase these goods.[13] This may have been one reason the chief tried to dissuade Jolliet and Marquette from continuing their journey: he did not want them to encounter other tribes who, too, might attempt to trade with the French.

It should be noted, too, that by the 1670s, European manufactured trade goods were not curiosities or rare and bedazzling items to the Illinois and people of the western Great Lakes; they were commonplace. According to archaeologist Robert Mazrim, "The Zimmerman site [located on the upper Illinois River near present Utica, Illinois] has also produced one of the largest protohistoric trade goods samples in the Lower Great Lakes dating as early as the 1630s and acquired by the Illinois through down-the-line trade," not by face-to-face barter with traders.[14] Previously, we saw that the Ho-Chunk, who lived around the southern end of Lake Michigan, possessed European trade goods prior to 1630.[15] It is possible, perhaps, that since Jolliet and Marquette had traveled all the way to their village, the Illinois hoped that the French might establish a trading post near them, thus eliminating the long voyage through Nadouessi-claimed territory to reach French trading posts located around the Great Lakes.

Furthermore, of all the Illinois groups, the Peoria, the name that Marquette designated to these villages on his 1673 map and who were likely the largest Illinois subtribe at the time, were the least amenable to Christianity until the early decades of the eighteenth century. Like other Illinois groups, the Peoria had their own spirituality, their own way of understanding nature, and their own manitous, beliefs, and practices that they were not at all ready to abandon. Peoria shamans were powerful and influential members of their community, and they opposed, at this time, the Jesuits, the Jesuit's manitou, and the Catholic religion. The name "PE8ARE8A," as transcribed by the earliest French Jesuits, signifies "someone who dreams in relation to, with the help of, entities in the spirit world." The Peoria were the traditionalists, the "Dreamers," who held to their spiritual bonding to and understandings of their world as steadfastly as the Jesuits held to theirs.[16] Many Peoria resented Jesuit disrespect toward their beliefs and their interference in spiritual matters.[17] In fact, Jesuit missionary Jacques Gravier would in 1705 receive a mortal wound from an arrow shot by a Peoria warrior at his Lake Peoria mission.

But even though the Peoria appear not to have been predisposed to Christianity, it is possible that they and the other Illinois groups may have sought to access the mysterious power of the Jesuits' God, a mighty manitou who Marquette, Allouez, and others claimed was the creator of the universe and master of their lives. Even though the Illinois had no concept of a single monotheistic deity, they still, in their view, understood that the Black Robe had contact with this strange yet powerful being, and they hoped that by befriending the missionary, they might have access to him too.

When the council and feast ended, Jolliet and Marquette were given a guided tour of the "whole" village. Whether "whole" village means only the second village or both is unclear. If the number of cabins at the site was three hundred, as Marquette reported (meaning a population of about six thousand), this would suggest that they visited both villages. However, a population of six thousand indicates that other Illinois subtribes must have been living at the site among the Peoria. Joseph Zitomersky's population study of the Illinois estimates that the total Illinois population in 1677 to have been about ninety-six hundred, a number that does not include the Michigamea, who later joined the Inohka alliance.[18] Six thousand people living at the two Illinois villages seems to be consistent with Allouez's statement that the Illinois had been reduced to two villages but does not take into account other Illinois groups living elsewhere, including the Kaskaskia.[19]

As the two men toured the village, their hosts presented them with gifts such as belts and curios made from bear and bison hair dyed red, yellow, and gray, articles that may have had value among the Illinois, but none to the French. They saw that the Indians still used ladles made from bison skulls but also owned guns and other trade wares. Marquette recorded cultural information about the tribe, including what he had learned about war parties, calumets, dances, music, clothing, and medicines. These activities, however, are beyond the scope of this narrative and will be discussed only as they relate to the 1673 voyage. There is, however, one issue that needs to be addressed, one that pertains to the name Illinois.

Marquette wrote that when "one speaks the word 'Ilinois,' it is as if one said in their language, 'the men,'—As if the other Savages were looked upon by them merely as animals. It must also be admitted that they have an air of humanity which we have not observed in the other nations that we have seen upon our route."[20] Jesuit missionaries after the time of Marquette such as Jacques Gravier and Jean-Antoine Robert Le Boullenger noted that the Illinois, who spoke Miami-Illinois, an eastern Great Lakes Algonquin language, called their alliance of subtribes "In8ca." Based on what is known about this word, the currently accepted phonemicized form is *inohka*; however, the vowel lengths for *i* and *o* are unknown.[21] What *inohka* means is also unknown. The word "Illinois," pronounced "*ilinwé*" by the early French, is a French shortening of Miami *ilenweewa*, "he/she speaks in a regular way"[22] Linguist Michael McCafferty of Indiana University, Bloomington, notes that in forming "*ilinwé*" (that is, "Illinois"), the French heard the stressed syllable -*wee*- of the Miami-Illinois term and made that the last syllable of their reformulation, since the French language across the board stresses the last syllable of any word. Moreover, the word "Illiniwek" is an Ojibweyan plural reformulation of the Miami-Illinois name. McCafferty further states that the best explanation for Marquette's misinterpretation of "Illinois" as "men" is that the missionary was a fluent speaker of Algonquin-Ottawa-Ojibwe before he started learning Miami-Illinois, and in Old Algonkian, the term for "man" was *irini*, and "he is a man" was *iriniiwi*.[23]

Jolliet and Marquette spent the night at the cabin of the great chief. What they did the following morning is unknown; perhaps they visited Illinois lodges and made the observations noted above. By about noon, they would have begun the hike back to their canoes. Following closely behind were hundreds of admirers. After promising to return to their village the following year, Marquette bid the Illinois adieu; the canoe men shoved their canoes from shore and struck a course down the Mississippi.

The explorers stopped intermittently and examined and sometimes even tasted a few of the fruits, roots, and nuts they found, perhaps while taking a few minutes to rest on shore. One of these was a plant with roots similar to that of a turnip that reportedly tasted like a carrot. They also found mulberries, another fruit that looked like an olive but tasted like an orange, and they came across other fruits and nuts that were unfamiliar to them.

The group passed the mouths of the Fabius, Wyaconda, and Salt Rivers of present Missouri. Before reaching the confluence with the Illinois River, the canoes passed what later cartographers called "Handsome Rocky Cliffs," located on the Illinois side of the river.[24] They also passed the mouth of the Quiver

River, where in 1804 several Americans who illegally settled on Native hunting territory were killed by Sauk warriors.[25] At a ninety-degree bend in the Mississippi, the French passed the mouth of the Illinois, a stream they would ascend on their return journey. On a limestone cliff just south of Alton, Illinois, the crew saw two griffon-like images that had been painted on the bluff face, mythical creatures known today as the Piasa. Marquette described them:

> While Skirting some rocks, which by Their height and Length inspired awe, We saw upon one of them two painted monsters which at first made Us afraid, and upon Which the boldest savages dare not Long rest their eyes. They are as large As a calf; they have Horns on their heads Like those of deer, a horrible look, red eyes, a beard Like a tiger's, a face somewhat like a man's, a body Covered with scales, and so Long A tail that it winds all around the Body, passing above the head and going back between the legs, ending in a Fish's tail. Green, red, and black are the three Colors composing the Picture. Moreover, these 2 monsters are so well painted that we cannot believe that any savage is their author; for good painters in france would find it difficult to paint so well,—and, besides, they are so high up on the rock that it is difficult to reach that place Conveniently to paint them. Here is approximately The shape of these monsters, As we have faithfully Copied It.[26]

What were these "monsters," and what did they represent? Fortunately, Marquette sketched their likenesses and included them in his report. The familiar name "Piasa" comes from the Miami-Illinois word *páyiihsa*, meaning a "small supernatural entity."[27] The best evidence indicates that the Piasa represented water monsters, mythological creatures found in Amerindian cultures, including Siouan and Algonquian. It was not uncommon for Native groups to paint or cut images of water monsters above whirlpools and other hazardous stretches of rivers.[28] The Piasa may have been meant to be a warning to travelers of dangers that lay ahead. By late 1698, little remained of them; they were "now nearly effaced," according to one traveler.[29]

While the explorers sailed down the calm and clear river, as Marquette described it, perhaps exchanging opinions about the river monsters, they heard at a distance the sound of rushing waters, a "rapid." They proceeded with caution. Approaching present-day St. Louis, they saw logs, whole trees, even "floating islands" in a muddy torrent pouring into the Mississippi from the Missouri River, the river *peekihtanwi*, as Marquette referred to it, meaning

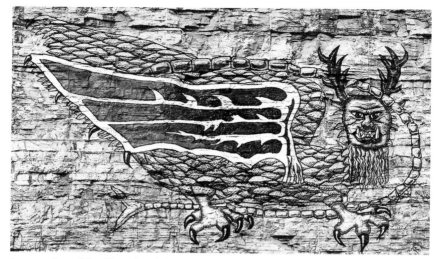

A re-creation of the Piasa that Jolliet and Marquette encountered during their journey. The replica is located near Grafton, Illinois. Photo courtesy of Wikimedia Commons.

"it-flows-muddy."[30] From this point forward, the character of the Mississippi would be much different from the waters above the Missouri.

Three missionaries of the Société des Missions Étrangères (Society of the Foreign Missions, also known as the Seminary Priests), en route to the Arkansas River in 1698, including Fathers François Jolliet de Montigny, vicar-general of the group; missionaries Antoine Davion and Jean-François Buisson de St. Cosme; a priest, Dominic Thaumer de la Source; several lay brothers; a few voyageurs; and the group's guide, Henri Tonti, reached the Mississippi by way of the Illinois on December 6. St. Cosme wrote in his memoir that the Mississippi was "very clear" until they reached the Missouri, where the waters were so muddy that they dirty the Great River.[31]

Marquette's observations about the clarity of the Mississippi are supported in accounts dating as late as 1846. William Hervey Lamme Wallace, second lieutenant in the First Regiment of Illinois Volunteers, was bound for New Orleans aboard a steamboat to join General Zachary Taylor's Army of Occupation during the war with Mexico. About the confluence of the Missouri and Mississippi, he wrote, "I have been studying this strange river all day [the Mississippi]. As we left Alton I saw we were sailing on a clear and beautiful stream. My attention was called to business in the cabin and when I looked again, the river was as muddy as a frog pond. My first impression was that we were running in shoal water, but in looking around, it was all the same, the river seemed to have undergone some necromantic change—that some demon was stirring the 'Father of Waters.'"[32]

To avoid colliding with trees and debris gushing into the river, the French party would have hugged the Mississippi's eastern shore while the canoe men watched for snags and other navigational hazards.

Zebulon Pike, who passed the Missouri in the opening years of the nineteenth century, reported that the banks of the Missouri were timbered with buttonwood, ash, and cottonwood and that hackberry, called *bois inconnu*, "unknown wood" by the French, grew in sandy soil.[33]

The French party passed Cahokia Creek, where three miles east of the river once stood the Native American metropolis of Cahokia. Cahokia was a Mississippian period settlement, the largest of several urban areas that spread out along the Mississippi, Ohio, and Tennessee River valleys. It appears that its first occupants may have settled at the site sometime around 600 C.E. Slowly, the population of Cahokia grew and by the eleventh century may have reached between ten to twenty thousand inhabitants, not counting the scattered villages and various settlements that encircled the city.[34] Cahokia's layout included plazas, wooden henges, orderly streets, and arranged neighborhoods. Earthen mounds dotted the site, the largest of which is Mound 38, also known today as Monk's Mound, the largest man-made earthen mound north of Mexico.[35] The metropolis was located near major river systems that made possible trade and communication with other groups throughout the central parts of the United States. By the mid-twelfth century, Cahokia's population began to decline, most likely due to destruction of the natural resources, climate change, and flooding. The site was probably abandoned by the mid-fourteenth century. During the late 1600s, the Cahokia subtribe of the Inohka alliance would establish a village along the creek where French missionaries would toil among the tribesmen, traders would peddle their wares, and habitants would farm the rich soil.

A few miles downstream, the party passed the site where the Tamaroa, another Illinois subtribe, would establish a village. Ten leagues or more beyond, the explorers passed today's Randolph County, Illinois, where French settlements including Kaskaskia, Prairie du Rocher, and St. Anne would be founded and where Fort de Chartres, the first of four forts by that name, would be constructed in 1720. The second Kaskaskia would become the first capital of the state of Illinois in 1818. On the opposite shore of the Mississippi, the French town of Ste. Genevieve would be established. The rich bottomlands along this part of the river would be the breadbasket for French Louisiana and later acquire the nickname the American Bottoms.

Somewhere below these future settlements, the men saw high above the eastern shore what appeared to be an iron mine. From their canoes, they reportedly saw several veins of ore. The discovery of iron deposits would have been of great interest to colonial authorities and their agent, Louis Jolliet. The canoe men paddled to shore to investigate. Upon closer inspection, they saw a vein of ore a foot thick mixed with pebbles, impurities that could be removed by smelting. They found what the missionary called a "sticky," multicolored earth of purple, violet, and red. They also found a heavy red sand.[36]

The canoes sailed southward in the swift current, gliding between the many islands, reaching, as Marquette noted, "a Place that is dreaded by the Savages, because they believe that a manitou is there,—that is to say, a demon,—that devours travelers." The explorers had been forewarned about this place by the Illinois, a site described as "a small cove, surrounded by rocks 20 feet high, into which The whole Current of the river rushes; and, being pushed back against the waters following It, and checked by an Island near by, the Current is Compelled to pass through a narrow Channel."[37] According to St. Cosme, the demon cove was "an island or rather a rock about one hundred feet high, which makes the river turn very short and narrows the channel, causing a whirlpool in which it is said canoes are lost during the high waters. On one occasion fourteen Miamis perished there." The spot was dreaded by the Indians who reportedly offered sacrifices to the rock whenever they pass it. To frustrate the alleged power of the demon, St. Cosme and the other missionaries climbed the rock and planted a cross on its summit, while the rest of the crew members sang *Vexilla Regis* and fired their muskets.[38] The site seems to have been located just above present Grand Eddy, in Perry County, Missouri.

West of the Mississippi was Missouri's lead-mine district where towns such as Old Mines, Irondale, Ironton, Mine La Motte, and Potosi, the latter formerly known as Mine au Breton, were established by the French during the early eighteenth century.

The party arrived at the mouth of the Ouaboukigou, the name Marquette applied to today's Ohio River. The pre-1673 Miami-Illinois name for the Ohio is *akaanseasiipi*, "Quapaw River."[39] The Ohio is a 981-mile stream that begins in Pennsylvania, at the confluence of the Allegheny and Monongahela Rivers. Reaching the Ohio and determining from whence it flowed was an important objective for Jolliet, who had been tasked with finding out whether the river Iroquoian speakers called "Ohio" was the same river some Algonquian speakers identified as Mississippi. Now, knowing that the Ohio entered the Mississippi from the east not only settled the issue of whether the two rivers were the same, but also brought to the fore questions about the course of and source of the Ohio, answers to which La Salle had set out to find but failed to resolve during his 1669 and 1670 expeditions.

The explorers began to see canes and reeds along the shore, some stands so thick that it was difficult for bison to pass through them.[40] Farther downriver they saw the marshes, bayous, and backwaters of eastern Missouri and western Tennessee. As the group descended into warmer climes, mosquitoes, which had not yet been a problem for the crew, became one. To protect themselves from swarms of buzzing mosquitoes, local tribesmen set smoldering fires beneath scaffolds on which they slept and covered themselves with bark. The explorers, who were confined to their canoes, instead made a sort of cabin, as Marquette called it, from their sails, which somewhat abated the mosquito onslaught and also sheltered them from the scorching sun.

Near modern-day Hickman, Kentucky, the Mississippi begins to bend and twist, taking a serpentine-like course that continues nearly all the way to the Gulf. Floods and even an earthquake have so altered the course of the stream in time that portions of states east of the river are now located west of it. Islands dotted the river, as they had since the explorers first entered it in Wisconsin.

The group's first potential clash with tribesmen occurred some distance below the Ohio when they saw armed men on shore waiting for them, a situation the explorers took as a threat. Hoping to avoid a confrontation Marquette held high the calumet he had been given by the Peoria while the others waited, guns in hand, just in case the missionary's peaceful overtures went unheeded or unnoticed. Marquette called out to them in Huron, but they mistook his words as a signal for war. As they drew closer to shore, the French realized that they had misread the tribesmen's intentions—the men meant no harm; they wanted to meet the explorers and to show them a bit of hospitality. Although it is by no means certain, it seems likely that the village belonged to the "MONS8PELEA," a tribe Marquette noted along this stretch of river on his holograph map.

The village headmen were both friendly and accommodating to the explorers, offering them bison meat, bear grease, and fruits, including plums. The Frenchmen saw guns, hatchets, knives, glass flasks, and cloth, all items that the chiefs claimed to have purchased from people who lived to their east. One chief quipped to Marquette that some of the people with whom they had traded looked like him. More important, the chiefs told the explorers that the sea was only ten days' journey from their village, a point that, although factually incorrect, was encouraging news to the French. After their visit, the crew reembarked and continued their trek downstream with a new sense of enthusiasm.

Pushing forward the missionary recorded the species of trees that he saw growing along shore, primarily cottonwood, elm, and basswood, and he saw birds, including parrots and quail. Bison were so close that they could hear them bellowing in the prairies just beyond the river.

Near modern-day Memphis, Tennessee, the canoes passed the site where a temporary fortification known as Fort Prudhomme would be built nine years later. The fort's name comes from an incident that occurred in 1682 when the gunsmith of La Salle's Gulf expedition, Pierre Prudhomme, lost his way in the forest while hunting and was missing for ten days before reuniting with the others. The fort was also where La Salle spent several weeks recuperating from a debilitating illness during his return trip from the Gulf.

Approaching the mouth of the St. Francis River in present Arkansas, the Frenchmen saw a village at a distance. Drawing closer they heard war cries and saw warriors on the shore rallying the men to action. Warriors boarded dugouts and paddled out to intercept the French. Some men dove into the river, hoping to swim to the canoes, but turned back after hurling war clubs. Beseeching their patroness, the Virgin Mary, for divine protection and with guns at the ready, the men prepared for the worst. Throughout the melee, Marquette held high his calumet, but to no effect. Eventually, some village elders who had been watching the incident from shore saw the calumet and called off the attack. Drifting into the shallows, several warriors threw their weapons into the French canoes as a sign to the crew that they were safe. Two elders motioned to the Frenchmen to paddle to shore. The explorers soon learned that the village belonged to the Michigamea.

The pre-Jolliet-Marquette expedition history of the Michigamea remains somewhat clouded in obscurity. Wisconsin historian Louise Phelps Kellogg

described the group being of Algonquian origin who had at one time separated from the Illinois but later rejoined the alliance. She also wrote the Michigamea had been driven north during the late 1600s and "coalesced" with the
Kaskaskia. Jesuit teacher, writer, and traveler Pierre-François Xavier de Charlevoix, who traveled the Illinois and Mississippi Rivers in 1721, wrote that the
Michigamea were a "foreign nation" who had been "adopted" by the Kaskaskia.
Having much more archaeological, documentary, and linguistic information
today about the tribe, linguist Michael McCafferty wrote that the Michigamea,
meehčaakamia, meaning "large stream person" in Miami-Illinois, had been a
Dhegiha Siouan–speaking group who, according to the oral tradition of the
Quapaw, Kaw, Omaha, Ponca, and Osage, were along with the latter people,
at one time, a single tribe. While there is no extant ceramic evidence to support this, onomastics substantiates the connection between the Quapaw, Kaw,
Omaha, and others because, as mentioned above, the Miami-Illinois name for
the Ohio is *akaanseasiipi*, "Quapaw River." Moreover, the cognate Shawnee
name for the Ohio translates to "Kaw River."[41] Whether the Michigamea had
been driven north as posited by Kellogg is uncertain. What is known is that by
1698, the Michigamea were reported living a short distance below the Cahokia
and that the Cahokia, Tamaroa, and Michigamea were all speaking the Miami-
Illinois language.[42] By 1703 the Michigamea had joined the Kaskaskia and were
living along the Kaskaskia River.[43]

Marquette attempted to speak with the Michigamea elders, but his efforts
were to no avail. His group had traveled beyond the limits of his linguistic capabilities, forcing the two parties to communicate via sign language and gestures.
Perhaps because some Michigamea had had prior contact with the Illinois, an
elderly man who knew a few Miami-Illinois words came forward to serve as an
interpreter between the tribe and the French. Language issues aside, the Michigamea headmen became more attentive and understanding after Marquette
gave them several gifts, after which the missionary communicated to leaders
that he and his party were en route to the sea. This the Michigamea chiefs "very
well" understood but communicated back that they would learn more at another
settlement a little farther downriver, at a village called Akansea, which is the
source of today's Arkansas. While the priest had their attention, Marquette tried
to sneak in a word of two about his Catholic faith, but it is unlikely that they
understood what he said. The explorers spent the night with the Michigamea.

The next morning, the crew boarded their canoes and headed down the river
led by ten Michigamea warrior escorts and the interpreter. A mile or so before

reaching the village, the party was intercepted by two dugouts of Arkansas; in one of them, a chief held high a calumet. Pulling their dugouts alongside the canoes, the two parties drifted down the river, serenaded by the chief. As a sign of friendship, the captain offered the Frenchmen food and tobacco. After their meeting, he signaled to the French to follow him to his village, but to do so slowly.

Later accounts place the Arkansas village a short distance upstream from the mouth of the Arkansas River.[44] In nine years, La Salle would grant his second-in-command, Henri Tonti, a seigniory near the site, where in 1686 Tonti granted land to several men, including Louis Delaunay and Jean Couture, who built a "house surrounded by stakes."[45] The following year, news would reach the Frenchmen living there that La Salle had been murdered. In late 1698, de Montigny's group arrived at the same site, where they began their mission to the Lower Mississippi River.

Arriving at the Arkansas village, Jolliet and Marquette were led to a space below a scaffold, as Marquette called it, that belonged to an important war chief. The room was described as clean and carpeted with reed mats on which Jolliet and Marquette were seated. Around them sat village chiefs and elders, while behind the headmen were warriors and, at the periphery, everyone else. As luck would have it, a young man, as Marquette described him, who attended the council spoke Miami-Illinois and Dhegiha Siouan, the latter the language of the Arkansas.

Marquette began the proceedings by presenting gifts to the chiefs. Then, as he had done at the other villages, he spoke a few words on behalf of his religion. The words apparently resonated with the Arkansas, who considered keeping the priest at their village to learn more. After greetings had been given, kind words had been spoken, and the calumet had been smoked, Marquette questioned the chiefs, through his interpreter, about what lay ahead down the river. They told him that the sea was only ten days' journey from their village (it was roughly 625 miles), but that they seldom traveled there because it was too dangerous to do so. They told him that their well-armed enemies barred the way to the Gulf and attacked anyone who tried to reach the Europeans (the Spanish) who traded with tribes living near it. It had been so long since they had been there that they no longer knew which nations lived along the river. When asked how they acquired what few trade items they did have, they replied that they obtained them from a tribe to their east and the Illinois who lived to their west.[46] Like other tribes had before them, the Arkansas warned the explorers of dangers that awaited them if they continued to the Gulf. What the Arkansas leaders told them must have alarmed Jolliet and Marquette. Powerful and well-armed tribes reportedly lived between the Arkansas and the sea, a situation evidenced by the paucity of European manufactured goods at the village and the Arkansas' inability to access them. Further, the Michigamea, whom the explorers encountered before reaching the Arkansas, at first, and unlike the Native groups the French met in Wisconsin, Michigan, and Missouri, seemed easily provoked and ready to defend themselves from what they believed were intruders, enemies. Europeans lived there too, Spanish, who would arrest any Frenchmen who trespassed in their sphere of influence. Unlike the Menominee and Illinois, who tried to convince the French not to continue their voyage, probably to prevent tribes living beyond their territory from accessing French trade goods, the explorers saw the dearth of simple everyday foods such as meat at the village, a sign that they were indeed telling the truth. The fact that the Arkansas had nothing to gain if the French continued downstream was something to seriously consider.

A feast followed the council—whole corn, *sagamité*, and watermelon were brought out on wooden and earthen platters. Even though their hosts had fewer amenities than other tribes, they were generous with what they had. So poor were they that bison skins, a common commodity at other villages, were a sign of wealth.

That evening the explorers learned that several Arkansas planned to rob and kill them, perhaps because the younger warriors were desperate to get the guns and knives that the French carried. The village chief, however, learned of it, too, and foiled the plot. Likely angered and embarrassed that his people had the audacity to harm their guests, the chief called Jolliet and Marquette to his scaffold and danced the calumet for them. When he finished, he gave the explorers the calumet to cover his people's transgression.

Although what they learned at the council may not have been what they wanted to hear, they learned a lot from the Arkansas, and the information seemed credible. The Arkansas were surrounded by enemies, warring tribes lived downstream, and the Spanish occupied the region, too. Jolliet and Marquette had explored the central parts of the Mississippi, a swath of North America that few Europeans had seen, let alone explored. They had collected a wealth of information, including latitude readings and approximate distances between important geographical points. They visited Native villages and met with their chiefs and elders, and they had documented the location of settlements and recorded for posterity many Amerindian customs and beliefs. They learned who was at war with whom and who had access to trade goods and who did not. They had learned the routes of major rivers and had collected plants and likely rocks and minerals as well as other items of possible interest to colonial authorities. More important, they learned that the Ohio was not the Mississippi and that the Mississippi flowed into the Gulf of Mexico, not to the western sea or Virginia. All things considered, they had accomplished just about everything that they had been tasked to do. Should they continue to the Gulf, or should they return to Canada? The two leaders chose the latter, to return north.

On July 17, the French left the Arkansas village and retraced their route up the Mississippi. The paddle back north would have been difficult during normal pool, but with rivers such as the flooded Missouri dumping trees and debris into the Mississippi, travel was slow and hazardous. Eventually, they would reach the Illinois River, the shortcut to Lake Michigan. About their trek back up the Mississippi, Marquette wrote, "We therefore reascend the Missisipi [from the Arkansas village] which gives us much trouble in breasting its Currents. It is true that we leave it, at about the 38th degree, to enter another river, which greatly shortens our road, and takes us with but little effort to the lake of the Ilinois."[47]

CHAPTER 6

From the Mississippi to Kaskaskia

A t the southernmost point of Calhoun County, Illinois, the Mississippi curves ninety degrees, flowing northeasterly for several miles and then bending again to the southeast. Today the confluence of the Mississippi and Illinois is a wide expanse, about a mile in breadth. Travelers who passed the juncture during the late 1600s and early 1700s recorded their impressions. According to St. Cosme in 1698, "The Miçissipi is a fine, large river flowing from the north. It divides into several channels at the spot where the River of the Illinois falls into it, forming very beautiful islands."[1] In 1710 nineteen-year-old Joseph Kellogg, the first *known* Englishman to have traveled down the Illinois, wrote, "The River Missasippi where the River Ilinois Joyns it is more than half an English mile broad, and very deep water."[2] In 1673 there were, and still are, several large, wooded islands at the confluence, including today's islands 525 and 526 and Mason Island that, viewing the river from a canoe, can obscure the entrance to the Illinois River's main channel. Approaching the mouth of the river, Jolliet's and Marquette's canoes likely hugged the left shore of the Mississippi (northern shore or to their right), passing the bright white cliffs that tower above today's Illinois Route 100.

The best evidence indicates that the expedition began their ascent of the Illinois River on August 25. According to Jesuit historian Raphael Hamilton, "It is almost certain that the last leg of the voyage was begun from the mouth of the Illinois River on August 25, which is the feast of St. Louis, king of France."[3] Catholic missionaries often named mission sites, rivers, and lakes after the saint on whose feast day they arrived at the site. Allouez established the mission of St. Marc's to the Mesquakie on the feast day of that saint, April 25. He also dedicated the St. Francis Xavier mission in Wisconsin to the saint who the priest believed protected his party's voyage on the day he began his mission to the Fox Valley tribes, December 3. Recollect priest Louis Hennepin named the large body of water located between Lakes Huron and Erie Lac Ste Claire in honor of that saint's feast day, August 12, the day he and La Salle's crew entered the lake onboard the explorer's bark, the *Griffon*.[4] To determine whether Jolliet and Marquette could have entered the Illinois on August 25, it is instructive to reexamine that portion of their voyage.

Marquette wrote that their party left the Arkansas on July 17: "We therefore reascend the Missisipi which gives us much trouble in breasting its Currents."[5] Jolliet reported, "Its depth [the Mississippi River] is as much as ten brasses of water; and it flows very gently, until it receives the discharge of another great river, which comes from the west and north-west, at about the 38th degree of latitude [the Missouri River]. Then, swollen with that volume of water, it becomes very rapid; and its current has so much force that, in ascending it, only four or five leagues [approximately 10 to 13 miles] a day can be accomplished, by paddling from morning to night."[6] The canoes struggled against the powerful current, likely dodging trees and other hazards. It must have taken sheer determination to paddle day after day, for 440 grueling miles, to reach the mouth of the Illinois. The mental and physical strain in the hot, humid Mississippi Valley summer would have been exhausting, and it is likely that the Frenchmen stopped frequently to rest, hydrate, and regain their strength. If the party reached the Illinois on August 25, it would have taken them forty-one days to paddle approximately 440 miles, an average of 11 miles per day, up the swollen Mississippi. Considering conditions, the distance they covered in that amount of time is reasonable.

For the first 6 miles up the Illinois, their course was southwest and then north. The explorers would have seen to their left a mélange of wetlands and shallow mud-bottomed lakes and sloughs that were pooled in a forest of silver maple, cottonwood, sycamore, and black willow. This was prime habitat for migratory waterfowl (ducks, geese, swans), migratory game birds (rail, snipe, woodcock), fur-bearing mammals (beaver, mink, muskrat, bobcat, raccoon), and game mammals (whitetail deer, black bear, rabbit). On the prairies beyond the wetlands, the explorers may have seen bison, elk, and whitetail deer. On the opposite shore, they saw tall bluffs that eventually turned to hills that soon veered inland.

The diversion of the Chicago River in 1900, the series of locks and dams, the draining of wetlands, river sedimentation made worse by mechanical farming methods, upland field tiling, and pollution have permanently altered the composition of the Illinois and Mississippi. Moreover, the system of levees that were built to contain the rivers within artificial boundaries inadvertently channeled floodwater and amplified the river's speed, force, and depth, which increased exponentially as the rivers flowed south, amplifying the likelihood of a levee break farther downstream. These levees also contributed to the demise of floodplain ecosystems, which upset the natural cycle that had fed, watered, and sheltered fauna and flora since the end of the last Ice Age. For millennia before the levees, dams, and river reversals, floodwaters seeped onto floodplains where they were absorbed into the soil before evaporating, drained into creeks, or filled backwater lakes and sloughs, providing water for nesting migratory birds, spawning fish, and a multitude of aquatic plant life species. As summer neared, river levels dropped, allowing other types of plant life such as smartweed and wild millet to thrive in the water-soaked soil, their seeds becoming food for migrating birds and waterfowl in the fall. Furthermore, the Mississippi and the Illinois today contain massive amounts of sediment, much more than they did in 1673. Sediment is topsoil that has been washed by rains and melting snow from upland agricultural fields and deposited into creeks, which ultimately flow into the rivers. Flash floods we experience today can be the result of excessive field drainage and tiling that artificially funnel water down the watershed and into the rivers. According to the Illinois State Water Survey, "13.8 million tons (MT) of sediment are delivered to the river [Illinois] valley annually from tributary streams. Of this, 5.6 MT are carried to the Mississippi River while 8.2 MT are deposited in the valley, including the floodplain and backwater and side channel lakes. Additional sediment is derived from stream banks and bluffs."[7]

The Illinois current was slow and gentle, not turbulent and debris laden like the Mississippi below the Missouri, a welcome relief to the canoe men. Marquette wrote that the Illinois not only shortened their road, but also took them "with but little effort to the lake of the Ilinois."[8] Later travelers made similar observations. In September 1687, survivors from La Salle's failed Gulf expedition en route to Fort St. Louis at present-day Starved Rock paddled up the Illinois guided by four Arkansas Indians. Henri Joutel, the group's chronicler, wrote, "We found a great alteration in that river [the Illinois], as well with respect to its course, which is very gentle, as to the country about it, which is much more agreeable and beautiful than that about the great river [the Mississippi], by reason of the many fine woods and variety of fruits its banks are adorned with." About his journey up the Illinois in 1821, Henry Schoolcraft wrote, there is "perhaps no stream in America whose current offers so little resistance in the ascent."[9]

The Illinois flows nearly due south just beyond the west end of Gilbert Lake, which would have been a large slough in 1673 and is today a public recreation area managed by the U.S. Fish and Wildlife Service in Jersey County, Illinois. Across the river from Gilbert Lake are today's Swan and Bundy Lakes, which would have been large, shallow backwaters. About one mile above Gilbert Lake the river bends to the north.

Schoolcraft noted that along the river, both banks are bordered by a "dense forest of cottonwood, sycamore, and other species common to the best western bottom-lands."[10] Up on the hills the Frenchmen saw upland forests of white oak, black oak, red oak, shagbark hickory, black walnut, red cedar, and American basswood.

Three miles above Gilbert Lake were narrow backwater lakes, including today's Deep, Long, Flat, Brushy, Eagle, and Fowler, former channels of the Illinois River. The crew would have passed Twelve Mile Island, aptly named for being located approximately twelve miles from the river's mouth, and immediately above it Helmbold Island (also spelled Hembold). Five miles above Helmbold Island, the canoes rounded Mortland Island and then passed the mouth of old Macoupin Creek, the boundary line between today's Jersey and Greene Counties.[11] In 1773 Macoupin Creek was about twenty yards wide, the shore was "low on both sides; the timber, bois connu [hackberry], or paccan [pecan], maple [silver maple] ash, button-wood." The shoreline was "well timbered and covered with tall weeds."[12]

Two miles north of today's Hardin, the explorers would have paddled between Tip and Diamond Islands or between Diamond Island and the shore. North of Hardin, timbered bluffs shadow the river, while on the opposite shore a wide floodplain extends to the bluffs some distance beyond. Schoolcraft wrote, "Of the fertility of the soil [along this stretch of river], no person of the least observation can for a moment doubt; but at the same time, the insalubrity of the climate, particularly during the summer season, must be considered as presenting a formidable, impediment to its speedy settlement."[13]

They passed a series of islands, including Willow, Crater's, Hurricane, Diamond, Van Geson, Bridge, Pearl, Wing, Spar, Fisher, and Twin Islands, some of them so large that ponds and sloughs were located inside of them.

About the cliffs and bluffs along the Lower Illinois, Schoolcraft noted, "Not unfrequently, springs of clear water issue from these cliffs, which, as that of the river was absolutely bad, we were constantly on the alert to discover." His party encountered what he described as a "scum or froth of the most intense green color, and emitting a nauseous exhalation, that was almost insupportable." One of the men collected a sample of the odorous water, but its fermentation reportedly "baffled repeated attempts to keep it corked."[14]

The crew saw the lands along the river were littered with dead trees and rotting logs, some covered with mushrooms and assorted fungi. Piles of sticks and branches that were washed by floods lay scattered about, and between them decaying leaves covered the forest floor like a carpet. The smell of decomposing organic material filled the air. The backwaters were muddy, and the mud stank, attracting swarms of mosquitoes and flies that hovered above the rotting vegetation. Fields of stinging nettles and clearweed grew in clearings. Beaver cuttings, some tree trunks left half-cut, too large to fell or perhaps left to take on another day, dotted the marshy floor. Cattails, phragmites, and assorted rushes grew in the swampy earth. In the standing timber, a variety of birds, including woodpeckers and red-winged blackbirds, fluttered from tree to tree, searching for food or a place to hide. Some trees bore the marks of hungry pileated woodpeckers, who ripped the bark and chiseled the wood, searching for insects. Cavities in tree trunks were home to nesting wood ducks, buffleheads, and common mergansers. The shallow waters were home to schools of large fish, including the redhorse, catfish, dogfish, and gar, which were taken by spear, bow and arrow, or seine. Snapping turtles and softshell turtles sunned themselves on dead logs during summer months. Macoupins (*Nuphar advena*) grew and were harvested in these backwaters.[15] In the paleo-channels, fur-bearing animals such as beaver, mink, and muskrat took refuge in dens made from piles of sticks and cattails. Flocks of molting ducks and Canada geese dabbled and dived as they waited for their new flight feathers to grow. Duckweed, prime food for shoveler, mallard, teal, and other puddle ducks, grew in the shallows. Herons and egrets silently stalked their aquatic prey, and bullfrogs croaked, warning others that trespassing into their lairs could be fatal.

They reached Big Blue Island, located at today's river mile 58, a site described by Englishman Patrick Kennedy in 1773: "At one o'clock we passed an island called Pierre. A fleche or arrow stone is gotten by the Indians from a high hill on the western side of the river near the above island; with this stone the natives make their gunflints, and point their arrows [their arrow points]."[16] According to Duane Esarey, retired, formerly of the Dickson Mounds Museum in Lewistown, Illinois, "This location certainly describes Big Blue Island and the bluff running from Big Blue Creek up to Flint Creek" (a distance of approximately two and a half miles, or four kilometers). Esarey continued, "One notable aspect of this locale is that, as one descends the Illinois River, these are the first outcrops of chert suitable for flintknapping to be found for over 100 miles."[17]

Beyond Big Blue Island, the explorers would have seen to their right the large backwater lake known during the late nineteenth century as Burr Lake, the width of which was twice as wide as the Illinois River. Two miles farther was Mauvaise Terre Creek (Bad Land Creek). About the "bad land," Schoolcraft wrote, "A ridge of alluvial earth here forms a prominent shore, for some distance, and admits of a convenient landing. The quality of the soil, as the name denotes, is poor, but this term is to be understood only in a comparative sense. In a country where the lands are so generally fertile, the slightest appearances of aridity are seized upon to mark a positive distinction." The site was a "favorite spot for encamping, from the earliest period," wrote Schoolcraft.[18] Across the river flowed McKee Creek. This area, like that of Pierre à la Fleche and Mauvaise Terre, would later become winter hunting territory for the Kickapoo and Mascouten.[19]

Just above modern-day Naples, Kennedy reported that the "banks of the river are high, the water clear," and the river bottom consisted of "white marl and sand." Marl is a sediment or sedimentary rock that is a mixture of clay and calcite ($CaCO_3$).[20]

Approaching present-day Meredosia, the explorers would have seen oxbow lakes, ancient river channels, and sloughs, as well as a wide expanse of prairie to the west, fertile ground where Illinois farmers would one day grow corn, soybeans, wheat, and rye. Heading upstream near Meredosia, the canoes coursed to the northeast. Passing Meredosia the canoes would have glided by the entrance to Meredosia Lake, a large backwater that is separated from the river by an isthmus, which in 1673 would have been approximately five miles long and at places three times wider than the river itself. With a small island in front of the lake's entrance, it may have appeared that the opening was a channel, not a large backwater lake. Today Meredosia Lake is a 690-acre waterfowl hunting area that is managed by the Illinois Department of Natural Resources. The U.S. Fish and Wildlife Service manages the adjacent Meredosia Wildlife Refuge.

As the French traveled farther up the Illinois, they encountered several large wetland areas like the one at Meredosia, marshlands containing lakes, large and small sloughs, channels that led to dead ends, islands large enough to hold weedy ponds and lakes, everglades, bayous, wooded peninsulas, and isthmuses that appear as islands, coaxing canoe men unfamiliar with the river into shallow, muddy bays. A turn into the wrong channel could lead to a swampy maze from which it could take a day or more to find the way out. This is why the Peoria chief gave the explorers the slave boy, someone who could guide the party through the labyrinths and up the 273-mile river. According to seventeenth-century historian Claude-Charles le Roy de La Potherie, also known as Bacqueville de La Potherie, who claimed to have spoken personally to Jolliet, "The Illinois [the slave boy] who had accompanied him [Jolliet] brought him back by another route, shorter by two hundred leagues, and had him enter the Saint Joseph River [Illinois River], where Monsieur de la Sale [*sic*] had begun a settlement."[21] This was not the first time the explorers depended on guides to direct them through the unknown; we recall that they asked for guides to lead them up the Fox to the portage with the Wisconsin. The boy was more than just a gift from a chief; he was a valued member of the crew.

Kennedy's party passed "La Mine" River, today's La Moine, the mouth of which he described as "fifty yards wide and very rapid."[22] From the La Moine to today's Beardstown, the French would have seen that the floodplains widened considerably; the hills and bluffs that had paralleled the river veered sharply to the west and east. Large backwater lakes and sloughs, including Fair, Swan, Big, and North, and a multitude of small ponds that dotted the floodplain lay secreted beyond the band of silver maples that grew on the isthmuses.

At Beardstown the river bends and flows nearly due south. At the curve and to the right is the entrance to "Muscooten Bay," a large backwater lake. The Woermann Maps (1905) reveal that the opening to the lake was nearly as wide as the Illinois River. The lake also appears to have been deeper than most other backwaters associated with the stream. At the time of mapping by the U.S.

Army Corps of Engineers, the lake had depths, at normal pool, of up to thirteen feet. A few hundred yards into the lake was the southern tip of an isthmus that separated Wood Slough from Muscooten Bay. Wood Slough is a narrow channel that extends to the northwest before curving around a peninsula that formed the western bank between Baujan Slough, a shallow backwater, and Muscooten Bay. Just beyond the far north end of Muscooten Bay were Hager's Slough, Coleman's Lake, and Treadway Lake, three interconnected backwaters. On the west side of the Illinois sat Stewart Lake, a body of water separated from the main river channel by an isthmus covered with heavy underbrush and timber. An inlet on the north side of Stewart Lake curved behind the isthmus and led to a channel between the river and one that flowed between Hickory Island and the west shore of the Illinois.

Continuing north Jolliet and Marquette would have passed Elm Island and a smattering of lakes and sloughs, including Dutchman Lake to the east and Sangamon Lake to the west. Amid this seemingly endless series of interconnecting sloughs, creeks, and lakes was a broad prairie that was interspersed with patches of brush and stands of timber, ideal habitat for deer and bison, a wide assortment of migratory and game birds, and fur and game mammals.

Eventually, the French canoes would have glided past the mouth of the Sangamon River. In 1673 the Sangamon met the Illinois about nine miles north of the present-day river, which was channelized in 1949. As an important geographical feature in the middle of a vast wilderness, the mouth of the Sangamon was mentioned in the correspondence and reports of seventeenth-, eighteenth-, and nineteenth-century travelers, including Charlevoix, a French army officer named Legardeur Delisle, and Patrick Kennedy, and it appeared in an unpublished French trader's itinerary that dates from the late 1750s to the early 1760s.[23]

The party next passed two shallow backwater lakes, Chain Lake to their right and Big Lake to their left. Near today's river mile 107, the explorers saw the end of a long, narrow peninsula, a point of land that extended far out into the river. Was this an island or an isthmus that separated the Illinois from the mouth of yet another river? They would soon learn that the point was the end of a six-mile-long island that the French later would call Île Grand (Grand Island). Today the eastern channel is known as the Bath Chute, named for the town of Bath, which is located about three-quarters of the way up the channel. Shallow remnants of paleo-channels crisscrossed Grand Island. Some of the wider ones included Jack, Horseshoe, Eagle, Swan, Bell, Goose, Grass, and Lynch Lakes.

Brush, lowland timber, and wetland prairies would have covered the island in 1673.

Passing Grand Island, the canoe men would have seen Shepard Island, behind which would have been a narrow chute that led to Matanzas Bay. In 1902 the Army Corps of Engineers recorded that Matanzas Bay was one of the deeper backwaters along the river, having depths of between three and four feet. East of the bay were small hills, some of them thirty to forty feet high, which were interspersed with clearings. West of the river was a broad plain full of sloughs and lakes. A short distance upstream, at today's river mile 120, the explorers would have reached the site of the present town of Havana, across from which empties the Spoon River, a 150-mile stream that drains approximately 1,850 square miles of west-central Illinois land between today's Galesburg and Lewistown.[24] Patrick Kennedy reached the Spoon River, a stream he called the river Demi-Quian, which he noted was fifty yards wide and enters the Illinois from the west. To the west beyond the Spoon, the lands, Kennedy reported, were flat, with no visible high ground, home to bison, deer, elk, and other wildlife. His party camped on the southeastern side of the Illinois near today's Havana, where he noted the "fine meadows, extending farther than the eye can reach, and affording a delightful prospect."[25]

The canoes reached what appeared to have been four channels, the two on their right being the main river channel separated by an island, one leading to a dead end at Sieb's Lake, and the one on their left, the entrance to Flag Lake. The boy likely directed the canoes to take one of the two channels to their right. The French were now entering today's Emiquon National Wildlife Refuge.

In 1687 Joutel's party of Texas survivors, following the instructions of a voyageur he had met at the Arkansas post, mistakenly paddled into Flag Lake, where they were lost for more than a day.[26] Kennedy described the lake, a place he called "Lake Demi-Quan," as "circular," six miles across, that empties into the Illinois by way of a small channel. Joutel's group found its way out of Flag Lake and soon thereafter reached Quiver Lake, where the Frenchman recorded seeing two symmetrical earthen mounds later known as Deux Mammelles, or "two breasts." Joutel's observations are one of the first historical references to the site. Joutel also saw several camp sites where local tribesmen stayed while fishing Quiver Lake.

Schoolcraft's party included canoe men who were familiar with the channels that coursed through Emiquon. He wrote, "We embarked on the following morning, as soon as the dawning day permitted our canoe men to descry the proper channel. This is a precaution that occasional visitors will do well to attend to, in ascending this stream as the number of false channels, or lagunes, is calculated to divert, and mislead him." But even though Schoolcraft's group included experienced guides, they still followed a false channel from which they had to return. He wrote, "Notwithstanding the wariness of our steersmen on this point, we had not proceeded many miles, when we entered one of those lagunes, and did not perceive our error until we began to approach its termination."[27] His group spent the next two hours retracing their route.

During the nineteenth century, Flag and adjacent Thompson Lake were known as "two of the most productive backwater lakes in the Illinois River Valley."[28] They were separated from the Illinois River in 1924 and reduced to ditches that drained agricultural fields. In the year 2000, the Nature Conservancy purchased the property and seven years later began restoration of the lakes. The Illinois River Biological Station of the Prairie Research of the University of Illinois monitors both aquatic vegetation and fish communities at Emiquon.

Before levees and the lock-and-dam system, wetland ecosystems such as Emiquon, as mentioned earlier in this narrative, went through a natural annual cycle of flooding, growth, and evaporation that produced habitat and food for fish and wildlife. Since the river's natural flooding and draining cycle has been altered by levees and dams, conservationists now take the place of nature and use pumps to flood and drain Flag and Thompson Lakes.

The canoes passed the opening that led to Quiver and Dog Fish Lakes. To their right was a long isthmus that paralleled the river, on the other side of which was today's Liverpool Lake. Wetlands to their right were purchased by the U.S. government in 1936, which became today's Chautauqua National Wildlife Refuge. A short distance upstream and to their left was the present-day town of Liverpool, while to their right was the opening to Goose Lake. A mile above Goose Lake, a narrow peninsula to their right separated Clear and Mud Lakes from the river, the former paralleling the Illinois for about three and a half miles.

At the Mason-Tazewell County line, the canoes passed the channel that led to Pikehole Slough and Spring Lake. To their left was Senate Island, an island so large that mile-long Senate Lake fits comfortably within its boundaries. From the present-day Peoria-Fulton County line along the west side of the Illinois, timber and brush interspersed with small potholes dotted the floodplain.

Near today's Banner, the French party passed Copperas Creek, a small river that flowed into the Illinois from the west, which was known in the later eighteenth century as the "Seseme-Quain" river, a stream reportedly forty yards wide at its mouth and navigable for sixty miles.[29]

At Kingston Mines, just below Kingston Lake, the French would have seen that the Illinois curved to the east as it approached the mouth of the Mackinaw River. In 1722 Delisle called the Mackinaw the "Carp River," a stream he described as "50 yards wide," and navigable for about ninety miles. He also reported that "between 30 and 40 small islands are cluttered at its mouth," which at a distance "appear like a small village." Delisle saw a healthy forest at the Mackinaw, mainly cedar, pine, maple, and walnut.[30] Turkey Island, known to the French as "L'Evantaille," was located about a quarter mile above the mouth of the Mackinaw.

A short distance above today's city of Pekin, the expedition passed the future site of Fort de Crèvecoeur, a wooden fortification that men under the supervision of the explorer La Salle constructed during the early months of 1680. A short distance beyond the possible fort site, or at river mile 162, Jolliet and Marquette and their crew entered Lake Peoria.

Lake Peoria is a long and wide stretch of the Illinois River. The lake is actually two lakes, the upper lake, the larger of the two, and the lower lake. The two lakes are separated at the narrows between river miles 166 and 167.

The first *known* contact between the Illinois and Europeans at the lake was in early January 1680 when La Salle's expedition into the Illinois Country encountered an Illinois winter village on the lake's western shore consisting of 80 "cabins," or a population of about sixteen hundred people. Between 1691 and the early 1750s, some Peoria groups lived on the lake.[31] In the fall of 1691, the French built a second Fort St. Louis in the Illinois Country on the western shore adjacent to the Illinois camps.[32] A Jesuit mission was also established at the lake, which was abandoned in 1705, but reestablished in 1712. By 1763 two small French settlements had been formed, one near the old French fort and another along the lake. A new French settlement known as "La Ville de Maillet" was founded on the lake in 1778. During the early 1790s, Potawatomi tribesmen settled north of La Ville de Maillet. The U.S. Army built Fort Clark at Peoria in 1813, which burned down the following year.[33] In 1819 the first permanent American settlers arrived. The town of Peoria was organized in 1835 and incorporated as a city in 1845.[34]

The Miami-Illinois speakers who lived at the lake called it and the surrounding area *pimiteewi*, a word the French transcribed as *Pimitéoui*.[35] Later in the French regime, the post was known by monikers such as "Au Pay" and "Opa," meaning "at the Peoria"; "Dupee," meaning "of the Peoria"; and "Le Pe," "the Peoria."[36] American cartographers who mapped the Illinois River in 1790 called Lake Peoria "Lake de Aussee," "Lake Daussee," and "Illenois Lake."[37]

The explorers paddled the lake's calm waters. On the heights around it, they saw hills covered in mature upland timber. Charlevoix wrote, "The lake and river swarm with fish, and the banks of both with game.[38] Schoolcraft, a keen observer of Native American life and nature and student of the natural sciences, wrote, "The waters of this lake [Lake Peoria] are beautifully clear, and as they are well stocked with fish, of the kinds before mentioned [catfish, buffalo, gar], they afford the natives a fine theater for exercising their skill in throwing the spear; an exercise, in which, standing on the gunwales of their canoes they exhibit great dexterity, and show off their slender forms to much advantage."[39]

Passing through the narrows, the channel that separates the lower from the upper lake, they reached present-day Mossville and Spring Bay. Schoolcraft's party harvested wild onions somewhere along this rush-lined shore.[40] In front of today's Rome sat Partridge Island. Above the island, the lake began to narrow; the main channel would become as narrow as it had been below Lake Peoria.

Approaching Lacon, the French would have seen a series of bays, backwaters, and sloughs that, in a disconnected and haphazard layout, continued for the next forty-five to fifty miles. At Henry they passed the mouth of Sandy Creek, which enters the Illinois from the east, an area that was reported by later travelers as "generally low and full of swamps, some a mile wide, bordered with fine meadows, and in some places the high land comes to the river in points, or narrow necks."[41] Above the town of Henry, Jolliet and Marquette continued to see shallow, muddy sloughs and backwaters; the largest of these included today's Mud, Sawmill, Hennepin, Hopper, and Senachwine Lakes. In one of these backwaters, Schoolcraft's canoes became mired in mud after paddling some distance into a false channel, a situation from which it took the men an hour and a half to extricate themselves.[42]

Just above Hennepin, they would have passed Hennepin Island and, just to its west, the entrance to Hickory Ridge Lake. In another half mile, they would have passed Bureau Creek, near the future site of American Fur Company post during the first half of the nineteenth century. In another half mile, they would have seen the channel that led to Coleman Lake, which, depending on river levels, is three lakes, two of them being separated by a peninsula.

The next significant geographical and geological feature that the French would have encountered is the "Big Bend" of the Illinois River, located about two and a half miles above Hennepin. The Big Bend is where the westerly flowing Illinois River, a young stream, meets the southerly flowing Illinois, or the ancient Mississippi.

Briefly, about 15,500 years ago, toward the end of the last Ice Age, glacial meltwater that had been trapped behind the Marseilles Moraine, a C-shaped earthen dam formed by glaciers pushing their way south into Illinois, eventually poured over and cut through the moraine, sending a torrent of water over the landscape and carving an entirely new river channel, the upper Illinois. The deluge cut its way west where it reached the ancient Mississippi at the Big Bend, and the two streams became one. The volume of water that poured into the ancient Mississippi would have been "inconceivable," and it continued for several thousand years. But in time, with the retreat of the glaciers and the change in Lake Michigan drainage, the water eventually ebbed and became the Illinois River that Jolliet and Marquette paddled in 1673.[43]

Geologist Raymond Wiggers describes the river current below the Big Bend as "to the point of being downright lethargic." He continues, "Geologists call it an aggrading river, one that is building up its bed rather than cutting down through it because it receives more sediments than it can carry away. In the neighborhood of Havana, it has an extremely flat gradient of only 3 inches drop per horizontal mile." The river is so sluggish that, where Sandy Creek near Henry empties into the Illinois, the river, instead of carrying away sand and silt deposited by the creek, flows around it, creating backwaters and wetlands that the explorers saw during their journey up the middle Illinois.[44]

Immediately to their left after rounding the Bend, the Frenchmen would have seen the entrance to Lake Depue, while a mile farther upstream and to their right, they would have seen, through a line of silver maple trees, Turner Lake and a number of smaller sloughs. Approaching today's city of Peru, they would have seen the wide entrance to a backwater known today as Husse Lake, and a short distance farther they would have passed the western terminus of the future Illinois and Michigan Canal, an artificial channel that connected the Illinois River at La Salle with Chicago. (More about the canal will be forthcoming in a later chapter.) Also to their left was the mouth of the Little Vermilion River, where Illinois's second land grant commenced, a parcel of property La Salle awarded to Pierre Prudhomme, his expedition's gunsmith in August 1683, property that included parts of today's city of LaSalle.[45]

Rounding an *S* curve in the Illinois, the French would have arrived at the Aramoni, today's Vermilion River. Entering the Illinois from the south, the stream was an important geographical marker to traders, travelers, and explorers. La Salle recorded the stream's name as "Aramoni," the Miami-Illinois word for red ocher. The Aramoni is Illinois's only northward flowing river for its seventy-five-mile length, beginning in far southeastern Livingston County. Most of the river's lower course is shallow, rocky, and bordered by tall, steep limestone cliffs. As it approaches its juncture with the Illinois, the river deepens and its current slows. According to La Salle, coal was abundant at the Aramoni, and local tribesmen reported having often found bits of copper along its banks.[46] The Aramoni was used by Shawnee who traveled between the Illinois and their Ohio Valley villages.[47] For the next 20 miles, the Illinois becomes a far different stream than the one Jolliet and Marquette had paddled for the last 227 miles.

At the mouth of the Vermilion grew a lowland timber, primarily silver maple, cottonwood, and sycamore. Behind it a long limestone outcrop separated the lowlands from the uplands above. The uplands were bordered by black oak, white oak, red oak, shagbark hickory, white pine, red cedar, and red elm. Across from the mouth of the Aramoni, a thin strip of silver maple interspersed with willow lined the river, partially blocking the view of a wide meadow that stretched for several miles eastward that was crisscrossed by a series of paleo-channels.

About one mile above the Aramoni, the explorers would have seen the exposed end of a long sandstone promontory known as Little Rock. Little Rock is the terminus of at least one paleo-channel that at one time ran parallel to today's Illinois River and about a hundred yards to the south. Little Rock likely formed at the same time as the Appalachian Mountains when the collision of the North American and Eurasian continents deformed and folded the crust. Little Rock marks the crest of the La Salle Anticline, the westernmost fold of the Appalachian tectonics. Deformation breaks in the solid St. Peter Sandstone were greatest along the crest of this fold. Subsequent erosion of these cracks produced crevices that can still be seen.[48]

Little Rock marked the point where the first land grant in today's Illinois commenced. In April 1683, La Salle awarded the grant to Jacques Bourdon d'Autray, a trusted member of his inner circle. The property extended approximately 4.57 miles up the south shore of the Illinois and was about 1.5 miles deep.[49]

About a hundred yards west of Little Rock was a small island that was formed by alluvial deposits emanating from the creek that flows along the west edge of the promontory. At the east end of the island was a ferry crossing during the nineteenth century. Later accounts mention rapids and the difficult passage that began from a mile or so above the Aramoni, several of which come from travelers who navigated the river during summer months, during the same time of the year as the Jolliet-Marquette expedition. On September 30, 1721, Charlevoix's party descended this stretch of river. He wrote, "The same evening we passed the last part of the river [heading downstream], where you are obliged to carry your canoe; from the place forwards, it is every where, both in breadth and deepness equal to most great rivers in Europe."[50] In June 1722, rapids prevented Delisle's bateaux from ascending above the Aramoni.[51] Patrick Kennedy's group could go no farther upstream than about a mile above the Vermilion during their August trek up the Illinois in 1773.[52] Lieutenant Armstrong's U.S. Army cartographers wrote in 1790 that, heading downstream, "the river is not very deep to the entry of the Vermillien [sic] River, where the river [the Illinois River] is near 150 yards broad."[53] Schoolcraft's group encountered the rapids about a half mile above the Vermilion in August 1821 where his canoe "would no longer float without rubbing against rocks."[54] To their right, the river was bordered by silver maple; hidden behind them were tall, sheer sandstone cliffs.

The explorers next reached the first of the next series of islands, today's Plum Island. The river's depth would, for the next several miles, fluctuate between only a few inches and two and a half feet. This portion of the rocky, shallow, and rapid-strewn Illinois River has the steepest declivity, and hence the swiftest current, of any stretch of the stream.

The explorers passed between Plum and Leppold Islands, where they saw on their right two tall sandstone bluffs, their summits covered in red cedar, white cedar, white pine, and white oak, a scene reminiscent of more northern environs. The first of these was a bluff the French would later call Le Rocher, the Rock, present-day Starved Rock. Le Rocher is a 125-foot-high isolated St. Peter Sandstone bluff. Its summit is about two-thirds of an acre in size. Le Rocher has a long Amerindian history, one dating back between ten and twelve thousand years. Native Americans used the top of the bluff as a campsite, as a place to inter their dead, and as a lookout.[55] Archaeologist Richard Hagen, who excavated parts of the summit in 1949 and 1950, wrote, "The Rock is unique: its cap of soil contains cultural remains which cover a greater period of time than any other single site in the state [state of Illinois]."[56]

Le Rocher gained notoriety when men working under the authority of La Salle built Fort St. Louis on the summit during the first months of 1683. The fort became the center for trade in the Illinois Country and served to facilitate

Franco-Amerindian diplomacy. The fort was abandoned in 1691 when the Illinois groups who lived near Le Rocher relocated to Lake Peoria.

The second bluff is known today as Lover's Leap–Eagle Cliff bluff. By the late eighteenth century, the bluffs would become landmarks known as "Little Rocks" and "Small Rocks," by the late nineteenth as Maiden Rock and Camp Rock, and by the twentieth as Lover's Leap and Eagle Cliff.

Above Little Rocks, they approached the largest of the many islands along this stretch of river, today's submerged Delbridge Island, known during the nineteenth century as Grass and Goose Island. The canoes would have struck a course between Delbridge Island and the river's north shore, where they would have seen at a distance a village located at the lower end of a portage, a site the French would call "Kaskaskia."[57]

CHAPTER 7

Kaskaskia to Lake Michigan and Beyond

Apporaching Kaskaskia, Marquette would have stood and held high the calumet. Barking dogs would have alerted the village, people may have shouted and run about, some calling out "Black Robe, Black Robe!" in Miami-Illinois. Armed warriors, onlookers, chiefs, and other officials walked to the shore to greet the strangers. The Kaskaskia probably expected the French, that is, if they had survived the rigors of the Mississippi, the snakes, the whirlpools, and the river monsters. Information sharing between the Illinois groups was essential for survival. Keeping current on trade opportunities and threats from enemies, announcing the time and location of feasts (a time when young Illinois men and women searched for potential mates), developing strategies for bison hunts, and preparing for war were commonly communicated between villages. Kinship bonds, intratribal relationships among family members living at different villages, were the glue that kept the Inohka alliance together. It seems likely that as soon as the explorers left the Des Moines, a runner was dispatched to tell the headmen at Kaskaskia that the French should be on their way, the slave boy guiding them.

The village, part of the present-day Grand Village of the Illinois State Historic Site (11-LS-13), was called *kaaskaaskinki* by the Illinois and *Kaskaskia* by the French. It was named for the Kaskaskia Indians, the Illinois subtribe who lived at the site in 1673.[1] The village was located along the north bank of the Illinois

River, about a mile upstream from today's Starved Rock.[2] Part of the village is now under water, having been submerged after construction of the lock-and-dam system, or has been washed away by the river.

The site was first identified by Dr. Sara Jones Tucker of the University of Chicago in the 1940s. Numerous archaeological excavations and surveys have been conducted at the site, including ones in 1947, between 1970 and 1972, 1985, 1987, 1991, and a five-year investigation between 1992 and 1996. Archaeological work at Kaskaskia reveals that it had been intermittently inhabited by people who grew domestic crops since Early Woodland times (600–300 B.C.E.).[3] Successive occupations at the site, including those of the late Woodland traditions, Upper Mississippian, Proto-Historic, and Historic were also discovered. The Illinois whom Jolliet and Marquette met at Kaskaskia were relative newcomers to the present Illinois Valley. The best and most recent archaeological evidence reveals that the proto-Illinois left their homelands south of Lake Erie and settled in the Illinois Valley at Kaskaskia sometime during the early 1600s, perhaps in the 1630s.[4]

Kaskaskia was strategically located to exploit the area's natural resources and for defense. In front of the village was the rocky Illinois River, a stream shallow enough to cross on foot during summer months, which also acted as a defensive barrier that protected the Kaskaskia people from attack, as enemies would have been forced to approach the village on foot, without cover, which would have exposed them to arrows or musket fire. Also in front of the village was a portage where travelers would have carried their canoes or wooden dugouts around the shallow water and associated rapids.

That the village was located at a rapid at all, instead of along calm or sluggish water, was a testament to the Kaskaskia and earlier occupants of the site and their understanding of how sicknesses and diseases such as malaria were contracted and spread. Disease from sluggish water sources, according to Brad Bartel, university provost, anthropologist, and archaeologist, at Middle Tennessee State University, was a "negative consequence" of sedentism, the transformation from hunter-gatherers to agriculturalists.[5] The river water at Kaskaskia was aerated, naturally filtered, and oxygenated, and it supplied a clean, fresh source of water to the inhabitants.

Behind the village, sheer sandstone cliffs and rugged outcrops separated the seemingly endless tallgrass prairies and uplands that stretched north into Wisconsin. Muddy paleo-channels lay between the village and the bluffs where game, fish, and other aquatic life were harvested. Bison, the primary large game animal consumed by the Illinois, which not only fed the village but also provided leather, wool, horns, and bones such as scapula that Illinois women used to till the soil, roamed in large herds near Kaskaskia. The wooded-prairie borders around the village were ideal habitat for two of the three other most utilized big game animals by the Illinois: whitetail deer and elk.[6]

Huts, reed-matted "cabins," as Marquette called them, lined the river. Wooden dugouts, or *pirogues* to the French and *mihsoora* to the Illinois, both large and small, would have been lying along the shore, some upside down, while others would have been fastened to trees or exposed roots. The village had no walls or outer defenses. Dogs with a mixed profusion of bloodlines, used for hunting, as sentries, and sometimes as food, would have roamed the village. Smoke from the many fires, in- and outside of cabins, used for light and heat and to cook, would have likely hung heavily in the summer air.

Five miles downstream was the Aramoni, a route that led to modern-day Indiana and beyond, while the Pestekouy, or the Fox River, flowed from Wisconsin and emptied into the Illinois about six miles upstream. Farther east were the forks of the Teakiki or Kankakee and the Des Plaines, the route to the Lac des Ilinois. Along the south shore of the Illinois River were the canyons, cliffs, and clear, cool streams of what is today's Starved Rock State Park, as well as a salt spring that was located directly across the river from the village.[7] Kaskaskia itself sat upon a terrace, residual sand that was washed to the site by the torrent that carved out the Upper Illinois Valley. The sandy loam soil was ideal for farming with tools fashioned from bone, shell, stone, and antler.

Jolliet and Marquette and village representatives would have smoked the calumet and exchanged pleasantries. The explorers would have been escorted to a lodge where they were seated on the floor on mats. Before discussing business, a chief may have lit another calumet and passed it to the others; everyone would have smoked it, even Marquette, who wrote, "This [smoking the calumet] must not be refused, unless one wishes to be considered an Enemy, or at least uncivil; it suffices that one make a pretense of smoking. While all the elders smoked after us, in order to do us honor."[8] Formalities completed, the Kaskaskia leaders were ready to hear what the French had to say. Marquette would have started the council by explaining to the chiefs the purpose of their visit. The missionary would have presented them with a few gifts, tokens of goodwill. Food including *sagamité*, bison meat, and dog would have been served, some of it likely being fed to the French by the hands of their hosts, and a chief may have danced the calumet for their guests.[9] It is probably at this time that an Illinois chief agreed, or offered, to escort the French to Lake Michigan, now that the slave boy had guided them to Kaskaskia.[10]

When the assembly ended, the Kaskaskia delegates would have, as they had done at the villages on the Des Moines, given the Frenchmen a tour of their town, which afforded Marquette the opportunity to count the site's seventy-four cabins, a number that represented about 1,480 people.[11] On the outskirts, they would have seen fields of maize, beans, squash, pumpkins, melons, and tobacco and, beyond, the remains of the deceased lying in their scaffolds.[12]

How long the explorers stayed at Kaskaskia is unknown. Gauging this visit by the length of time they spent at other villages, probably not long. They were eager to return north with their collection of curiosities and souvenirs, the geographical and anthropological data they had collected, and their lives. Before leaving, the chiefs obligated Marquette to return to instruct them in his Catholic faith, a request that the missionary would fulfill two years later. At the east end of the portage, the group boarded their birch-bark canoes and headed up the Illinois in the company of their Kaskaskia escorts.

It is interesting that, even though the explorers likely portaged around rapids on the Fox River and perhaps the Mississippi, this is Marquette's only reference to a portage along a river not located between waterways such as the Fox and Wisconsin or Des Plaines and Chicago Rivers in his report. It is possible that he did not mention the portages that we know they had to traverse because portaging around rapids was simply part of river travel. However, La Salle, Tonti, and others pointed out just how problematic the rapids on the Des Plaines and the Illinois, especially the ones in front of Kaskaskia, were. In a 1680 letter to Canada governor Frontenac, La Salle complained that the Illinois River, upstream from Kaskaskia, is "innavigable [sic] for forty leagues, the distance to the Great Village of the Illinois [Kaskaskia]. Canoes cannot traverse it during the summer and even then there are long rapids this side of that village."[13] Henri Tonti, who had been living among the Kaskaskia in September 1680, attempted to leave the village and travel to Michilimackinac. After a short and difficult journey upstream, he returned because the river was too shallow, even for his canoe.[14]

A mile above Kaskaskia, the French and their guides passed a large sandstone cliff on their left, today's Buffalo Rock. Buffalo Rock would be the site of a Miami village during the 1680s, where a group of French Canadian soldiers and their Odawa allies spent the winter of 1760–61, and today it is the site of Buffalo Rock State Park.

After rounding a bend, they would have encountered a series of narrow, elongated islands beginning just below the present-day town of Ottawa and a short distance beyond, the mouth of the river the French referred to as Pestekouy, the Fox River, a stream that charts a course southward from southern Wisconsin and ends at the Illinois. At the juncture of the two rivers was *la Charboniere*, or coal pits, as travelers called them.[15] La Salle claimed to have found a nugget of copper and another bronze-like metal he could not identify there. Charlevoix observed, "Nothing is to be seen in this course [of river] but immense meadows, interspersed with small copses of wood, which seem to have been planted by hand; the grass is so very high that a man is lost amongst it, but paths are every where to be found as well trodden as they could have been in the best peopled countries." Another traveler noted, "We consider the soil excellent, the lands finely diversified, handsomely elevated, and well-watered; and bating the general deficiency of forest timber."[16]

The group reached the Marseilles Moraine, the remnants of the earthen dam that was breeched by glacial meltwaters that carved out the Upper Illinois Valley. The moraine extends between today's towns of Ottawa and Seneca.

Approaching present Marseilles, the explorers would have noticed that the water had again become shallow. In front of them was another set of rapids, a *sault* with a portage an eighth of a league in length.[17] During the late 1700s, these rapids were known as "Demi Charge" and "Rapid of Mamor."[18] Travelers, traders, and explorers mentioned them in their reports and memoirs. In 1688 Henri Joutel complained that negotiating these rapids was the most difficult part of his journey between Le Rocher and Quebec.[19]

Above Marseilles the river remained rocky and the current strong. Just downstream from Seneca, the canoes passed two Kickapoo Creeks, one that entered the river from the north and one from the south. The streams are located about a mile apart. Catholic and local traditions hold that Gabriel de la Ribourde, a Recollect priest attached to La Salle's first expedition into Illinois, entered the timber near one of the creeks to pray and was killed by Kickapoo warriors.[20]

Beyond the moraine and above Seneca, wide plains bordered both sides of the river. Conspicuously missing were the pine-studded sandstone bluffs the explorers saw near Kaskaskia. The river was also narrower than it had been below the Big Bend.

Just below Morris they passed Waupecan Island, a site once known as Sugar Island. About three and a half miles above Sugar Island, the Mazon River enters the Illinois from the south. The twenty-eight-mile Mazon cuts its way through northern Illinois coal country, land today dotted with strip pit lakes and slag piles, visible remnants of past mining operations.

The explorers and their Kaskaskia guides passed Hutchins and Perry Islands before reaching Aux Sable Creek near today's river mile 268. Neatly tucked away in a niche along the river's south shore across from the mouth of the creek was Aux Sable Island. In 1722 a traveler noted seeing flocks of parakeets, as many as fifty to sixty birds, had gathered in the area.[21]

They soon passed what cartographers in 1790 called Twin Islands, today's Big and Little Dresden Islands, and two miles farther, following a southerly bend in the river, they reached the confluence of the Kankakee and Des Plaines Rivers, where the two streams merge to become the Illinois, a place that would be known as the Forks.[22] About this area, Charlevoix would write, "It is not possible to behold a finer and a better country than this which it waters, at least as far as the place from whence I write."[23] The explorers would follow the Des Plaines River north.

For about a mile above the confluence, the Des Plaines flowed from the southeast, whereas to their left wooded bluffs shadowed the river. According to linguist Michael McCafferty, *la plaine* likely refers to red maples (*Acer rubrum*) that grow along the river. Although "la plaine could in the 17th and 18th centuries mean maple, as in the silver maple (*Acer saccharinum*), a tree that grows along nearly all Midwestern rivers," the distribution of red maples is limited to southern Illinois and only in northeastern Illinois along the Des Plaines River corridor, with some growing in adjacent Lake and McHenry Counties and nearby Winnebago County. An isolated population of red maple was reported in McDonough County in western Illinois.[24] Considering that wild red maples are not common in northern Illinois, it seems much more likely that the Des Plaines is a reference to that particular tree species.

At the next bend, they coursed to the northeast, and in another half mile they reached a broad floodplain; the tall bluffs they had seen veered inland and away from the stream. In two miles, they passed the Du Page River, where the wooded hills again met the Des Plaines. Above the Du Page was Treats Island and, a mile further, a bend in a wide stretch of river known by early-twentieth-century cartographers as Lake Joliet. The lake was three hundred yards across at its widest point. Wild rice grew along its shores. To their left, at the north end of the lake, the French and Kaskaskia saw another important landmark, the mound that would be called Mount Jolliet.

Mount Jolliet (or Joliet, Juliet) was located just west of today's Larkin Avenue and a short distance north of the Illinois and Michigan Canal. The mound stood about 200 yards from the riverbank, plainly visible to passersby. American cartographers wrote that "Mount Juliet stands on a delightful Grassy plain and is a beautiful work of nature. The side that fronts the river is about fifty perches [825 feet] in length and is near thirty [495 feet] in breadth. Its ascent is a straight slope with the elevation of 45 degrees. Its perpendicular height above the Surface of the plain is 60 or 70 feet; the top is a perfect level."[25] According to St. Cosme, the Indians say "that at the time of the great deluge one of their ancestors escaped, and that this small mountain is his canoe which he upset there."[26] Miami-Illinois speakers called the hill *mihsooratenwi*, meaning "dugout canoe hill."[27] The mound was composed of clay, which ultimately led to its demise because the clay was excavated and used to manufacture sewer tiles for the growing city of Joliet during the mid-nineteenth century.

Shoals, rocks, boulders, and rapids marked the river's course for the two miles above Lake Joliet. To the right, the explorers would have seen Sugar and Hickory Creeks, two meandering tributaries, their channels separated by three islands before emptying into the Des Plaines. In about eight miles, the canoes encountered the next significant landmark, an island known as Isle à la Cache, or "Island of the Cache," at today's Romeoville.

The river between Mount Jolliet and Isle à la Cache was normally shallow and rapid strewn. St. Cosme wrote that "everything has to be portaged [between Isle à la Cache and Mount Jolliet], as there is no water in the river except in the spring." It took his party three days to travel the four leagues, roughly eleven miles, between Isle à la Cache and Mount Jolliet.[28] Gurdon Hubbard, a leading figure in the development of the city of Chicago, who worked for the American Fur Company in 1818, wrote that below Isle à la Cache, his crew was forced by low water to empty their boats and carry most of their cargo on their backs, while dragging their boats over the rocks and shoals. It took his group three weeks to go from Isle à la Cache on the Des Plaines to the mouth of the Fox River at Ottawa and another two days to get from the Fox to Starved Rock.[29]

Although local legends attempt to explain the origin of the island's name, the most likely explanation comes from an incident that occurred in early 1681 when two of La Salle's men, Jacques Bourdon d'Autray and a man only known to history as "the surgeon," spent nearly three months on the island, guarding a cache of goods and supplies.[30] St. Cosme reported that the island was called Isle à la Cache as early as 1698.[31]

During late summer, stands of wild rice grew around the island, where in some places "the whole breadth of the river is full of it."[32] Pierre Deliette, Henri Tonti's younger cousin, who spent decades among the Illinois trading between Chicago and Peoria during the late seventeenth and early eighteenth centuries, remarked that between Isle à la Cache and Mount Jolliet, "you ordinarily begin to see buffalo [while heading downstream]. As for turkeys, there are quantities of them."[33]

Schoolcraft drew a "line of distinction," as he called it, between the lands and waters at Lake Peoria and those at Chicago. Above Lake Peoria, he wrote, the lands were "pleasing and beautiful," with forests and prairies that were "finely watered and so delightfully elevated." Below it the region was one of "warmth and fertility." However, much of it was "low and swampy" and "decidedly barren." He added that there were two months of the year when people who live in the Lower Illinois are "exposed to fevers and augues [sic], which render life irksome."[34]

The canoe men paddled another 20 miles upstream, where they reached the west end of the portage between the Des Plaines and the south branch of the Chicago River.

The Chicago Portage, also known as the "Portage of the Oaks," was a 7.5-mile passage through a depression known as Mud Lake. The portage marked a Continental Divide that separated waters that flow to the Great Lakes and ultimately the Atlantic and those that empty into the Gulf of Mexico. When waters were high, the portage was relatively easy; a canoe could be paddled over most of it. However, when waters were low, the portage could be very difficult to traverse. Deliette wrote that when the waters were low, a traveler would walk about a quarter league across it (roughly ¾ of a mile), while when the waters were high, a traveler would only walk about an arpent (approximately 58.5 meters).[35]

In his autobiography, Gurdon Hubbard relates how difficult crossing the portage was for him and his crew: "Mud Lake drained partly into the Aux Plaines [Des Plaines] and partly through a narrow, crooked channel into the South Branch [of the Chicago River], and only in very wet seasons was there sufficient water to float an empty boat [bateau]. The mud was very deep, and along the

The monument commemorating Jolliet and Marquette's portage located at the Chicago Portage National Historic Site in Lyons, Illinois. Photo by the author.

edge of the lake grew tall grass and wild rice, often reaching above a man's head, and so strong and dense it was almost impossible to walk through them."[36]

Hubbard continued, "only at rare intervals" did they find water in the lake. To get through the tall reeds and tangled roots, forked tree branches were fastened to the ends of wooden poles and used to push their bateau forward, while some of the men waded in the mud, physically pushing the boat by hand and "constantly jerking it along." While some crewmates pushed, pulled, and poled the boat forward, others carried cargo on their backs to lighten the boat and to give the vessel more freeboard. Those who pushed the boat often "sank to their waist [in the mud], and at times were forced to cling to the side of the boat to prevent going over their heads." Reaching the Des Plaines, they removed the leeches that "stuck so tight to their skin that they broke in pieces if force was used to remove them." Not only did leeches menace the men, but swarms of mosquitoes made it impossible to sleep. The men who waded through the mud, according to Hubbard, "suffered great agony, their limbs becoming swollen and inflamed, and their sufferings were not ended for two or three days." It took his crew three days to cross the portage.[37]

Jolliet later suggested that a canal a half-league long be excavated through Mud Lake that would allow canoes, boats, and barks, large commercial vessels, to pass through the morass. More about Jolliet's canal will be forthcoming in a later chapter.

The French and Kaskaskia arrived at the south branch of the Chicago River, a "small stream," according to one traveler, that was "only two leagues long bordered by prairies of equal dimension in width." Another traveler wrote that the Chicago was "a little river that afterward loses itself in the prairies."[38] In a few miles, the stream merged with the river's main branch, the channel that took the group through the area that would one day be the city of Chicago.

The shoreline of the future city was a sandy and windblown plain where groves of stunted pines, scrub oak, and sand-dune willow grew amid patches of marram grass, sand reed grass, and sand cherry.[39] Sand and minute bits of gravel from the shoreline farther north were carried by the lake's counterclockwise current and deposited at the river's mouth, forming a peninsula that blocked the river's sluggish current, causing it to veer south where another peninsula guided it into the lake.[40]

Reaching the lake, Jolliet, Marquette, and company said good-bye to their Kaskaskia escorts and steered their canoes north along the coastlines of present-day Illinois and Wisconsin. Travel was sometimes dangerous because the windblown shallows offered no protection from winds and rough seas. Joutel's party was stuck at Chicago for eight days in the autumn of 1687 while waiting for winds to abate and the lake to calm. He complained that the surge of water was so great at the Chicago River that his party was forced to carry their canoes up the shoreline in hopes of finding a place from where they could access the lake and embark. Eventually, they boarded their canoes and paddled eight or ten leagues up the coast, but wind and waves made conditions so hazardous that they returned to the river and paddled back to Le Rocher. St. Cosme warned, "One must be very careful along the lakes and especially Lake Mixcigan [*sic*], whose shores are very low, to take to the land as soon as possible when the waves rise on the lake, for the rollers become so high in so short a time that one runs the risk of breaking his canoe and losing all of its contains. Many travelers have already wrecked there."[41]

From what we can gather from Marquette's *relation* and Jolliet's testimony at Quebec in August 1674, it appears that their three-hundred-mile voyage from Chicago to Green Bay was uneventful. Reaching the Door County Peninsula,

The route of the 1673 voyage. Photo taken at the Starved Rock State Park Visitor Center by the author.

they portaged at the marsh and channel that led to Sturgeon Bay and entered Green Bay.[42] Marquette reported that his party reached the Baie des Puants at the end of September.

What happened from this point forward is unclear. We know that Marquette spent the winter at the St. Xavier mission. We know that Jolliet, the Indian boy, and some crew members, perhaps all of them, paddled to Jolliet's trading post at the Sault, where they wintered. We also know that Jolliet carried with him a copy of Marquette's report, a document that included a "very exact chart," a map of the rivers and countries that he and Jolliet explored.[43] Jolliet was to give the *relation*, the annual report that Jesuit missionaries were required to submit to their superior, to Dablon when he, Jolliet, arrived in Quebec.

Marquette wintered at the St. Xavier mission rather than continue to St. Ignace because he planned to return to the Illinois the following year, even though he still needed Dablon's approval to do so. St. Xavier's was the closest mission to Kaskaskia, and by retracing the route up the Fox and down the Wisconsin and Mississippi, he could reach Illinois who lived on the Des Moines.[44]

However, Marquette wrote that he was sick during the summer of 1674. His now famous journal states, "Having been compelled to remain at st. François throughout the summer on account of an ailment, of which I was cured in the month of September [1674], I awaited there the return of our people from down below, in order to learn what I was to do with regard to my wintering." Dablon, writing in hindsight, seems to suggest that Marquette was ailing when he arrived at the mission. He wrote, "The great hardships of his first voyage had Brought upon him a bloody flux, and had so weakened him that he was giving up the hope of undertaking a second."[45] The explorers ate infrequently, drank river water, and were exposed to wind, rain, heat and humidity, and clouds of mosquitoes. They passed through regions where diseases such as yellow fever and malaria were common, where only people with the healthiest constitutions and strongest immune systems could survive. That Marquette's debility was caused by conditions he and the crew endured during their journey, and that he was ill when he arrived at St. Xavier's, seems reasonable. Although Marquette lived at mission sites on the clear and cool waters of the Great Lakes for five years before leaving on the voyage, he may not have had the innate predisposition to survive the daily physical hardships and biological assaults inflicted on his body. By the time he reached St. Xavier's, he was likely physically and mentally worn out.

It is interesting, too, that even though Marquette described the waterways, landscapes, and mines and animals they observed; the practices and customs of Native people; and even how the Menominee harvest wild oats and about a plant that cures snakebites in his report, he mentioned very little at all about his and Jolliet's journey up the Illinois River. He dedicated only ten sentences to about a thousand miles of travel from the Arkansas River to Green Bay. And it appears, too, that Dablon may have added at least the last two sentences to Marquette's report before forwarding it to France.

During their journey through today's Illinois, the explorers learned that the Illinois and Des Plaines Rivers linked Lake Michigan to the Mississippi, and hence the Gulf of Mexico. The river was where the Kaskaskia, a large Illinois subtribe, lived, people to whom the missionary dedicated his last days visiting and instructing. From Kaskaskia they saw that the river was a springboard not only to the Mississippi Valley, but to other regional streams and villages. And they saw that the lands that bordered the Illinois were ideal for settlement, agriculture, and hunting. Marquette's report includes only a minimum amount of information about that stretch of the voyage. The silence in Marquette's *relation* is confounding. What else did he not mention about the voyage between the mouth of the Illinois River and the St. Xavier mission? Did the French party encounter other Native groups or villages that later explorers and missionaries mention living along the Illinois River, by Lake Michigan, or at the Door County peninsula? What else did the French see or experience at Kaskaskia? Was the group sidelined along the coast of the lake due to rough seas? Who was at the St. Xavier mission when Marquette arrived at the site? When did Jolliet and Marquette part company? Why did Marquette devote only a few sentences to this important part of the voyage?

When Marquette would have given Jolliet a copy of his report is uncertain. Did he, since he was likely both ailing and exhausted, give a copy to Jolliet just before they reached the St. Xavier mission, hoping that Dablon, who edited the report, might add a few remaining sentences? Did he give it to Jolliet at the mission, where Marquette might have jotted down a few final lines? Or did he make a copy of his journal from the original one that was forwarded to Dablon in 1675, while Jolliet and the others waited? Regardless, Jolliet and some of the others left the mission with a copy of Marquette's report.

According to historian Raymond Douville, Marquette spent the winter of 1673–74 and the summer of 1674 at the St. Xavier mission. That summer the missionary reportedly suffered from a debilitating illness. With him, wrote Douville, "were two crew members of the voyage, one of whom one was Largillier."[46] However, Jesuit historian Jean Delanglez argues that Largillier continued with Jolliet to the Sault, where he wintered, and then returned to Green Bay in the spring of 1674.[47]

Jolliet hoped to reach the Sault before foul weather and rough seas made travel both difficult and dangerous. His party paddled up the coast of Green Bay, passing the Oconto, Suamico, Peshtigo, and Menominee Rivers. Reaching the St. Ignace mission, the crew may have stopped briefly to rest or purchase food or a few supplies.[48] Leaving St. Ignace, the crew headed due east. Upon reaching the De Tour Channel, they steered their canoes north, passing today's Lime Island, after which they ascended Munuscong Lake. They continued to Nicolet Lake, a widening in the St. Mary's River, and in a few miles arrived at Jolliet's trading post.

Most of what we know about the 1673 voyage comes from Marquette's report, even though it had been edited by Dablon, who likely deleted a few things and added a few others before sending it to France. What is curious is that although Marquette did mention Kaskaskia was located on a portage, neither Marquette nor Jolliet mentioned rapids or stretches of shallow water on the Illinois or Des Plaines River. Does this mean that both rivers were flooded when the group ascended them, or did they simply not think that it was important to mention the *saults*, the rocky river bottom, or other hazards?

Earlier in this narrative, we saw that La Salle, Tonti, Joutel, Charlevoix, Delisle, Kennedy, Armstrong's cartographers, and Schoolcraft noted that stretches of the Illinois River were oftentimes impassable because of shallow water and rapids, and these examples occurred during summer months, including August and September, about the same time the Jolliet-Marquette expedition paddled the Illinois River. We also saw that Marquette reported that Kaskaskia was located at a portage, which indicates that at the time of the voyage, the site was located along a stretch of river where the water was too shallow to traverse.

The U.S. Army Corps of Engineers monitors river levels across America, including the Illinois. Charts and graphs from prediversion times (prior to 1900), including those recorded at Havana, clearly demonstrate that river levels fluctuate from very shallow at times to flood stage. These same charts and graphs record, from between October 1878 and December 1899, a consistent pattern of floods/high water during the spring, and low water, sometimes very low water, during summer months.[49]

What this means is that it is difficult to determine with absolute certainty if the Illinois River was bone dry, at flood stage, or somewhere in between in August–September 1673. This is important because Marquette's report, except his mention of the Kaskaskia portage, and, as we will see, Jolliet's testimony to Dablon in 1674, makes it appear that barks, large commercial vessels, could sail the Illinois and Des Plaines between the Chicago Portage and the Mississippi.

Furthermore, Marquette wrote that the Illinois–Des Plaines "greatly shortens our road, and takes us with but 'little effort' to the lake of the Ilinois." If floods had inundated the Illinois and Des Plaines and river levels were high, it would have taken much effort to paddle these streams, as it had when the group paddled up the Mississippi from the Arkansas village. Moreover, Marquette's report says nothing about flooded meadows, submerged islands, floating trees and debris, or a strong current, things typically associated with floods and high water. And, as we will see in a later chapter, Marquette reported high waters and ice floes on the Chicago River during his return voyage to Kaskaskia.[50] Other than the inundation at the Missouri River, he mentioned nothing about strong currents, flooded meadows and timbers, submerged islands, or anything else related to floods. But this raises the question of why Marquette never mentioned the navigational hazards on the Illinois and Des Plaines that nearly all later travelers wrote about in their memoirs, reports, and journals. Why didn't he mention the long stretches of rapids and shallow waters of the Illinois and Des Plaines Rivers or even describe the demanding portage at Mud Lake?

A possible explanation is that rapids and portages were just part of travel during that time. There were several experienced voyageurs in Jolliet's and Marquette's party, men who, in all likelihood, carried the cargo, dragged the canoes, and shot the rapids while Jolliet supervised the men and Marquette studied the landscape, took latitude readings, or just followed along. Allouez never mentioned anything about the Illinois rapids or floods in his report of his journey to Kaskaskia in 1677, even though he wrote about the difficult winter journey down the coast of Lake Michigan. La Salle and Tonti paddled up and down the Illinois and Des Plaines many times, the former mentioning rapids only in hindsight as a geological feature that marked the location of his fort or in a complaint against Jolliet whom he perceived to be a competitor to his, La Salle's, Illinois trade concession. If this is the case, it seems likely that the streams were at normal summer pool and that river depth and water volume were similar to those encountered by later travelers; Jolliet and Marquette just never thought rapids and portages were important enough to mention.

Another issue that remains unclear is Marquette's reference to a Peoria village where he baptized a dying child. His *relation* states, "For, when I was returning, we passed through the Ilinois of Peouarea, and during three days I preached the faith in all their Cabins; after which, while we were embarking, a dying child was brought to me at The water's edge, and I baptized it shortly before it died,

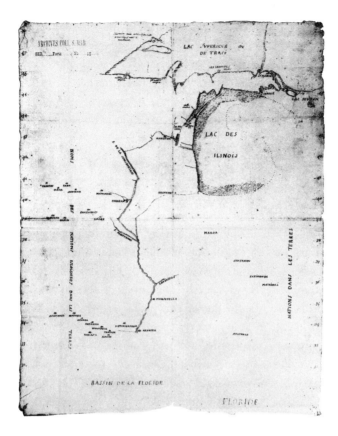

Marquette's 1673 autograph map. Image courtesy of Archives des Jesuites au Canada.

through an admirable act of providence for the salvation of that Innocent soul."[51] Where was this village located?

As far as we can tell, Marquette's report and map document the location of every Native village he and Jolliet encountered and some they did not. His map illustrates the villages of the PANA, MAHA, and KANSA, and rough designations for geographical territories claimed by entire tribes, such as the MOROA. CHA8ANON (Shawnee), and APISTONGA, information based on what he had learned from the tribesmen he and Jolliet visited.

The only Peoria villages mentioned by Marquette are the ones near the Des Moines where he and Jolliet stayed only one night, not three. If some Peoria had been living on Lake Peoria, as some historians have speculated, Marquette would have certainly included that information in his report or, if the village was large enough, illustrated it on his map. Historian Emily Blasingham, in her depopulation study of the Illinois Indians, conjectured that the Peoria village was located near the mouth of the Missouri, which, again, was not mentioned by Marquette, who passed the site twice.[52] Did the explorers encounter a group of Peoria somewhere along the Illinois River? If they did, did the group have many "cabins," as Marquette's report states? Was this a semipermanent settlement or a summer hunting camp? Why would the explorers have stayed three days with a small group of Peoria on the Illinois when they stayed only one night at the large villages near the Des Moines? Is it possible that the child the priest baptized was a Peoria, but that the incident occurred at Kaskaskia? If so, then why didn't Marquette say that? Furthermore, the sentence containing the Peoria village reference appears as if it had been added to the end of the report sometime later, perhaps by Dablon, who may have inserted it for effect before forwarding it to France.

Adding to the muddle are a series of charts known as the Manitoumie maps. The maps are based on Marquette's 1673 holograph map included in his *relation* of the voyage. The first two of the series were, according to Canadian historian Lucien Campeau, probably drawn in Quebec by a Jesuit, or perhaps at the behest of the Jesuits.[53] A variant of the second Manitoumie map was drawn by Melchisédech Thévenot in France and was published in 1681. The focus of the map is the Mississippi Valley, but also includes important points of interest such as the possible location of mines, Native settlements, and the Chicago and Door County portages. The map also illustrates what its author, or, more likely, what Jesuit officials, believed was an overland route taken by the explorers between the Peoria villages on the Des Moines and the Illinois River, the *chemin du retour*. According to the author(s) of the Manitoumie map, the French group, after leaving the Arkansas, would have returned to the Peoria villages on the Des Moines and stayed there for three nights. During this second visit, Marquette would have baptized the child before leaving for Kaskaskia. Leaving the Des Moines, the French party would have crossed the Mississippi and set out overland, across the prairie, where they eventually reached the Illinois River somewhere near Kaskaskia. There are many problems with this interpretation. To begin, the overland route has no support from Marquette's report or map. Marquette wrote that his party began their ascent of the Illinois at about the 38th degree, "which greatly shortens our road, and takes us with but little effort to the lake of the Ilinois."[54] The latitude of Grafton, Illinois, at the mouth of the Illinois River is 38.9700484. Neither Jolliet nor Marquette mentioned anything at all about a more than one-hundred-mile trek on foot across tallgrass prairies interspersed with creeks, sloughs, and forests while carrying two canoes,

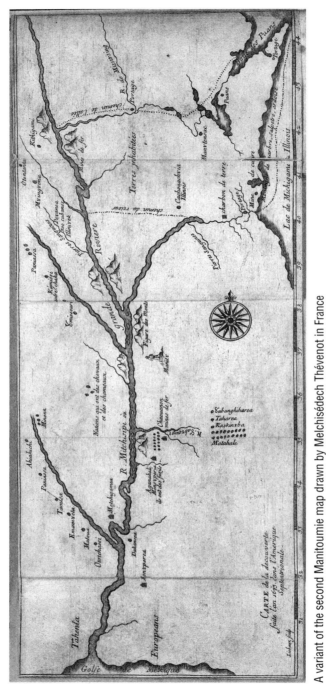

A variant of the second Manitoumie map drawn by Melchisédech Thévenot in France and published in 1681. Image courtesy of the Library of Congress.

supplies, boxes and bags of items they had collected, guns and ammunition, and more, a herculean task, to say the least.[55] Furthermore, Marquette could not have drawn such an accurate map of the course of the Illinois if he did not personally see it and study it. Considering the evidence, the French group did not take, or could not have taken, the *chemin du retour* across western Illinois. If they had, Marquette would have certainly written about it in his report, especially since he was likely ailing at the time, and Jolliet would surely have mentioned it to Canadian authorities when he returned to Quebec. The location of this alleged Peoria village, if it existed at all, remains a mystery.

The Jolliet-Marquette expedition traveled more than twenty-one hundred miles into the middle of a continent, most of it through lands unknown to the French. They were the first people of European descent to explore the central Mississippi Valley and the first to paddle the Illinois–Des Plaines–Chicago Rivers and into Lake Michigan. The surviving account of the voyage chronicles many of the crew's adventures: it describes the fauna and flora of lands through which they passed, it lays to rest speculation about the course of the Mississippi River, it illustrates the location of Amerindian villages, and it details important anthropological information pertaining to the life, customs, and attitudes of the Illinois and other Native groups. The voyage was an important milestone in the exploration, establishment of trade, religious conversion, and later colonization of the Mississippi Valley.

CHAPTER 8

Canada, Jolliet, and Marquette

Not long after he assumed possession of the lands around Fort Frontenac, La Salle hired François Dauphin de la Forest as a clerk to look after his legal interests and manage his day-to-day operations. La Forest was also the garrison's adjutant while La Salle was away.[1] Also joining on with La Salle was Jacques Burdon d'Autray, a trusted aid, confidant, and Canadian nobleman, son of the first procurer general of Quebec. La Salle later hired Michel Accault, who would become La Salle's bison-hide trader and an important figure in early Illinois history.

La Salle worked to develop the lands of his seigniory, as both a settlement and a trading post. He oversaw construction of walls that were built around the fort, introduced cattle to the lands, and had vessels built for trading on Lake Ontario.[2]

During this same time, Dablon was busy in Quebec serving on the Sovereign Council, editing the annual reports of his missionaries, and performing other administrative duties. Allouez worked at the Mascouten village and among the Mesquakie, while André remained busy with the Green Bay–area tribes. Father Nicolas, who worked with Allouez at La Pointe during the winter of 1667–68, labored at a new mission site near Sept-Îles, on the Lower St. Lawrence. Jesuit Antoine Silvy, who arrived in Canada in September 1673, the next year, would begin his mission to the tribes at Michilimackinac along with fellow Jesuit

Philippe Pierson.[3] Gabriel Druillettes would work among the Ottawa tribes at Sault Ste. Marie, where superior of the western mission Henri Nouvel would oversee the responsibilities of missionaries under his authority.

No one knows exactly what Jolliet did during the winter of 1673 and 1674. After landing at his trading post at the Sault, Jolliet's crew unloaded their canoes and brought the items collected to cabins and huts where they were stored. Jolliet would have met with his younger brother Zacharie to get an update on the events that occurred at and around the post while he was away and to evaluate rumors that may have been circulating among the Indians. He would have also met with the local Jesuits Druillettes, Bailloquet, and Nouvel.[4] During the long, cold winter, Jolliet probably began putting to paper his observations, impressions, and thoughts of the voyage, some of the information likely coming from long conversations in the canoe with Marquette. He may have also learned about the new settlement and fort at Cataraqui, Fort Frontenac, a site that could affect his trading operations.

After ice-out, Jolliet, two hired hands, and the boy given to him by the Peoria chief left the Sault for Quebec. Also in the canoe were curios collected during the voyage, personal items, paperwork that included Marquette's report and map, and likely important business documents and records pertaining to Jolliet's business dealings. The party took the shortest and most traveled route between Sault Ste. Marie and Quebec, the Ottawa–French River route.

While Jolliet and his party were paddling to Quebec, ten Nadouessi warriors who had traveled to the Sault to negotiate the release of eighty Nadouessi prisoners were attacked and killed by Kiskakon and "sauteurs," Odawa and Ojibwe tribesmen who lived near the village and Jesuit mission. Sometime during the melee, the house of the missionaries was burned to the ground. Reportedly lost in the fire was a copy of Jolliet's account of the 1673 voyage. Jolliet later claimed that he left a copy of it with the Jesuits there for safekeeping.[5]

If Jolliet had written a journal of the voyage, what kind of information would he have included in it? His journal would have likely contained basic information about the route he and Marquette traveled, including descriptions of the lands and waterways and any reports about English or Spanish influence along the Mississippi. He would have certainly written that the Ohio and Mississippi were two different streams, that the Mississippi emptied into the Sea of the South, and that he had located mines along the Wisconsin and Mississippi Rivers. He may have included a few stories about some minor discoveries pertaining to plants and animals that he and Marquette had encountered. Perhaps not as obvious in his report would have been information about the number of trade goods he saw at villages (if any), the types of wares the Indians possessed, and from whom the tribes obtained them. His journal would have been written from the perspective of a secular government agent and of a businessman eyeing potential trade opportunities. Marquette's report, on the other hand, was written from the perspective of a Jesuit scout and missionary who noted the location of Native villages, the geographical range of Native languages, and anthropological information about Native customs, practices, and spiritual convictions that would benefit future Jesuit missionaries who would work among western tribes.

By June Jolliet and his crew reached the St. Lawrence River. At a rapid within sight of Montreal, Jolliet's canoe capsized, and everything aboard—the men, the boy, and the box—was thrown into the water. As best as can be determined, everything and everyone were lost except Jolliet, who reportedly struggled in the water for four hours before being rescued by fishermen. Jolliet no longer had physical evidence to prove to authorities that he and Marquette had explored the Mississippi. For now the only information about the voyage would come from Jolliet.

While he was sidelined at Montreal, Jolliet was served papers that summoned him to court. The plaintiff was his ex-sister-in-law, Jeanne Dodier-Normandin, widow of his brother Adrien. One of her allegations against Louis concerned "three to four hundred pounds" that he owed her late husband. The money that Jolliet owed was for property his mother, Marie d'Abancourt, had sold to Monsignor Laval in 1668. In the transaction, Laval agreed to pay 2,400 pounds, of which Marie received 1,200. The remaining money was to be divided equally among her four children, Adrien, Louis, Marie, and Zacharie (300 pounds each). On April 13, 1669, Louis Jolliet signed a receipt for 780 pounds he received from Laval, 300 of which rightfully belonged to Adrien. Louis never gave his brother the money, nor did he pay Adrien's widow.[6] Louis also owed Jeanne "six months of rent," "40 skin robes" and "30 other robes," a canoe, payment for a forge he had been "using for three years," and a "white blanket."[7] In addition, Jeanne and her new husband, Mathurin Normandin, asked for accounts due by "various *voyageurs*" be produced (likely those under Jolliet's employ), that he pay for other robes that were still in the Ottawa country, and that he pay for canoes Jeanne had lent to him as well as for various articles of "*lingerie*" (clothing).[8] They also asked that he return "the forge, five sacks of wheat, sixteen roles of wire, some iron wire, and some hatchets." The money and rent Jolliet owed and finances relating to the company are specifically mentioned in Adrien's will, a document written in the presence of Father Bailloquet, Master Surgeon Félix Thuné, Sol Desmarais, Claude Caron, Michel Paroissien, and Cusson (the notary). Jolliet owed Jeanne a lot of money and merchandise. And it appears he did not intend to pay her or return the property until he had been officially summoned to court. On July 7, a decision in the case was rendered that substantiated most of the charges against Louis. On July 13, he was notified of the verdict by the notary Bénigne Basset. Jolliet subsequently "acquiesced and acquiesces without disagreement." An agreement was reached to which the Normandins were reportedly "satisfied."[9]

Despite the accident and his court appearance, Jolliet completed his journey to Quebec, arriving there in July. He may have taken up residence at the seminary, where he had once lived. If he did, it may have been there that he met Jean-Baptiste Louis Franquelin, whom Jolliet would ask to draw two maps that illustrated the route of his voyage and lands through which they had passed.[10]

Franquelin arrived in Canada in 1672, according to historian Lucien Campeau, as a guard for Governor Frontenac. The following year, Franquelin entered the seminary at Quebec. As of this point in his life, it appears that he had no formal training in cartography or mathematics but was a skilled calligrapher.[11] Some historians believe that Franquelin brought with him from France instruments, brushes, and other items commonly used by calligraphers and artists. Franquelin was probably the only person in Canada who had the tools and skills necessary to produce colorful art. It is likely, too, that Governor Frontenac convinced Franquelin to create charts that were based on information provided by explorers that the governor would forward to the French Court.[12]

On August 1, Jolliet met with Dablon to give the Jesuit superior a verbal account of his and Marquette's expedition. This raises the question of why Jolliet met with Dablon before corresponding with Canada's governor or another high-ranking secular authority. According to Jesuit historian Raphael Hamilton, Jesuit missionaries were required to submit to their superiors annual written reports that detailed their work at their respective missions. A collection of these reports, sometimes called a "short catalog," was then forwarded by each Jesuit provincial to headquarters in Rome. The provincial was also required to submit a summary of what was contained in the reports.[13] Considering this administrative mandate in light of the historic importance of the 1673 expedition, Jolliet, a good Catholic and friend of the Jesuits, met with Dablon to give him a verbal account of their journey—Marquette's report that Jolliet had been carrying and was lost in the St. Lawrence River. This explains why the discussion of the missing map and *relation* was so central to Jolliet's August meeting with Dablon.[14]

About the meeting, Dablon wrote, "We cannot this year give all, the information that might be expected regarding so important a discovery, since sieur Jolliet, who was bringing to us the account of it, with a very exact chart of these new countries, lost his papers in the wreck which befell him. . . . However, you will find herein what we have been able to put together after hearing him converse, while waiting for the relation, of which father Marquette is keeping a copy."[15] Until Marquette's copy arrived in Quebec (May 1675), Dablon would hear what Jolliet could tell him about the voyage.

Concerning the Illinois Country, according to Jolliet, "At first, when we were told of these treeless lands [by the Indians], I imagined that it was a country ravaged by fire, where the soil was so poor that it could produce nothing. But we have certainly observed the contrary; and no better soil can be found, either for corn, for vines, or for any other fruit whatever." Jolliet told Dablon, "A settler would not there spend ten years in cutting down and burning the trees; on the very day of his arrival, he could put his plow into the ground." In addition, Jolliet reported, "Game is abundant there; oxen [buffalo], cows, stags, does, and Turkeys are found there in greater numbers than elsewhere."[16]

Besides describing the fertile lands and the variety and abundance of game in the Illinois Country, Jolliet reported that a "bark," a large commercial sailing vessel, could sail from Lake Erie to Florida, "by *easy* navigation," something that Dablon wrote was a "very great and important advantage, which perhaps will hardly be believed." The only obstacle along this route lay at the marshy stretch of land located between the Chicago and Des Plaines Rivers where, according to Jolliet, it would be necessary to dig a canal a half-league in length to connect the two streams. Dablon recorded the route that the bark would take: "The bark would be built on Lake Erie, which is near Lake Ontario, it would easily pass from Lake Erie to Lake Huron, whence it would enter Lake Illinois. At the end of that lake the canal or excavation of which I have spoken would be made, to gain a passage into the river Saint Louis, which falls into the Mississippi. The bark, when there, would easily sail to the Gulf of Mexico."[17] Furthermore, Jolliet described the Illinois River as "wide and deep, abounding in catfish and sturgeon," indicating that the stream was deep enough for large vessels. With the exception of the portage between the Des Plaines and the Chicago Rivers, Jolliet reported no navigational impediments between Niagara Falls and the Gulf of Mexico.

There are several problems with Dablon's account of his meeting with Jolliet, most of which have gone unquestioned by historians. For instance, the Jesuit claimed that Jolliet had "joined Father Marquette [at the St. Ignace mission at Michilimackinac], who awaited him for that voyage." This passage means that Marquette knew that Jolliet was headed to his mission from whence they would set out for the Mississippi and that Marquette awaited his arrival. How would Marquette have known that Jolliet was en route to St. Ignace? Dablon answers this question: Jolliet and Marquette "had long premeditated that undertaking [the 1673 voyage], for they had frequently agreed upon it together."[18] Dablon is saying that the two men had discussed their voyage sometime before Jolliet arrived at Marquette's mission. However, in chapter 3 we saw that there is no credible evidence that Jolliet and Marquette ever met, let alone discussed a future voyage. Their first meeting appears to have been at the St. Ignace mission in December 1672. Dablon was wrong; Jolliet and Marquette did not discuss their expedition prior to Jolliet's arrival at St. Ignace. Jesuit historians have taken Dablon at his word, and rather than question if his claims are legitimate, they have, instead, as we have seen, fashioned incredible and implausible scenarios to justify Dablon's words.

About the voyage, Dablon wrote, "For this purpose, they could not have selected a person endowed with better qualities than is sieur Jolliet, who has *traveled much in that region*, and has acquitted himself in this task with all the ability that could be desired." He also wrote, "They were not mistaken in the choice that they made of Sieur Jolyet [*sic*], For he is a young man, born in this country, who possesses all the qualifications that could be desired for such an undertaking. He has experience and *Knows the Languages spoken in the Country of the Outaouacs*, where he has passed several years."[19]

Again, we saw in chapter 3 that Jolliet was a relative newcomer to the Upper Country when he was selected to explore the Mississippi. By that time, his only experience in the western wilderness was when he operated a trading post at the Sault in the spring of 1671, where he may have stayed for only two months. He had never traveled beyond Trois Rivières or Cap de la Madeleine prior to October 1670, and there is no evidence that he returned to the Upper Country between the time he left the Sault in June 1671 and when he arrived at St. Ignace in December 1672. Jolliet had neither "traveled much in that region," as Dablon claimed, nor had he "passed several years" there. It appears much more likely that Dablon, like Talon, had confused Louis with his older brother, Adrien, an experienced woodsman and voyageur.

Dablon also claimed that Jolliet knew the languages spoken in the Ottawa country. This claim is only partly true. Jolliet knew French, likely learned Latin and possibly Greek in the Jesuit *collège*, and likely knew Algonquin-Ottawa-Ojibwe.[20] There is no evidence that he knew Wendat or any Iroquoisan dialects, languages also spoken in the upper Great Lakes. Marquette knew the above languages and spoke Wendat and others, including Algonquin-Ottawa-Ojibwe. He also knew Miami-Illinois, to some extent, an important prerequisite for the 1673 voyage. Marquette's ability to speak some Miami-Illinois explains why he, and not Jolliet, spoke directly to the Peoria chiefs at two villages near the Des Moines River and at Kaskaskia and why Louis's last recorded speech was to the Mascouten at their village on the Fox River. Beyond the Mascouten village, Louis spoke only to his companions.[21]

Dablon's account also includes small errors, including the date when the expedition left St. Ignace, "about the beginning of June," as he wrote, when the group left on May 17. Dablon was prone to exaggeration as well. We saw that he wrote that Jolliet was chosen because he was an experienced woodsman when he was not, had lived in the Upper Country for several years when he had not, and could speak multiple language when he could not, and that he and Marquette had collaborated before setting out on their voyage when they did not.

Jolliet teamed up with Jean-Baptiste Franquelin in Quebec to draw a pair of maps, the 1674 *La Colbertie* and the 1675 *La Frontenacie*. Since information illustrated on both charts came from Jolliet's memory, both were less than accurate, their only value being to show the route from the east to the west by way of the Great Lakes. *La Colbertie*, showing the "newly discovered" western lands and the Mississippi River, was dedicated to French minister Jean-Baptiste Colbert. According to Jesuit historian Lucien Campeau, "They had for this part a very complete model, the Lac Tracy map. It was recopied entirely, with all its inscriptions, especially those for the Jesuit missions. Full of confidence and naiveté, the two young men did not suspect that the map was too Jesuit for Frontenac's tastes."[22] In other words, the part of *La Colbertie* that illustrates Lake Superior, Michigan's Upper Peninsula, the northern part of the Lower Peninsula, Lake Huron, and the Green Bay area were copied from Allouez and Marquette's earlier map of Lake Superior.

La Frontenacie named the western lands after Canada's governor Frontenac, and the Mississippi, which Jolliet christened Fleuve Buade, was so designated in honor of Frontenac's family name. Campeau described the Great Lakes as they are depicted on the map as "geometric forms." "Lake Superior is a trapezoid, Lake Huron is almost square, Lake Erie a triangle and Lake Ontario oval." Lake Huron is too large, while Lake Erie too small.[23] Furthermore, *La Frontenacie* depicts large expanses of the North American continent, regions that neither Jolliet, Franquelin, nor any other European had ever seen. Moreover, *La Frontenacie* includes the names of tribes living in the new territories, information conspicuously missing on *La Colbertie*. The likely explanation for addition of the names is because the papers compiled by Marquette, who died earlier the same year, which included the copy of the lost journal and map, had arrived in Quebec where Jolliet had had access to them.[24] *La Frontenacie* was likely completed, but still in Jolliet and Franquelin's possession, when the papers arrived. Jolliet then copied the names from Marquette's report and map and added them to *La Frontenacie*.[25] The names of tribes written on the map and in his report not only were important to Marquette personally but were also intended to show future missionaries who would serve in these far-off missions where whole villages of potential converts lived. Jolliet, on the other hand, operated a trading post at Sault Ste. Marie, more than a thousand miles away from many of these Mississippi River tribes. The names and locations of the tribes in that region would have been meaningless to him unless he had grand plans to establish a trading empire in the Mississippi Valley, designs of which there is no evidence. Colonization and agriculture are inseparable, and they are far removed from Jolliet's trading business in the upper Great Lakes. Last, the course of the Illinois River that wrongly depicts the stream flowing southwest, not south, illustrated on *La Colbertie* and *La Frontenacie* was the basis for other important maps that were drawn for the next century, including ones drawn by Franquelin (1684, 1688), Thevenot (1681), Corelli (1688), Hennepin (1698), Guillaume de L'Isle (1703, 1718), Popple (1733), Bellin (1745), Dinwiddie (1754), Mitchell (1755), Hutchins (1778), and Bradley (1796).[26] It was not until the early nineteenth century that maps of the Lower Illinois began to more accurately reflect the river's course, like the one drawn by Marquette.[27] Marquette's simple yet accurate rendering of the course the Illinois River and the countries explored went unobserved for more than a century. Marquette was far more qualified than Jolliet to draw a map of the countries explored in 1673.

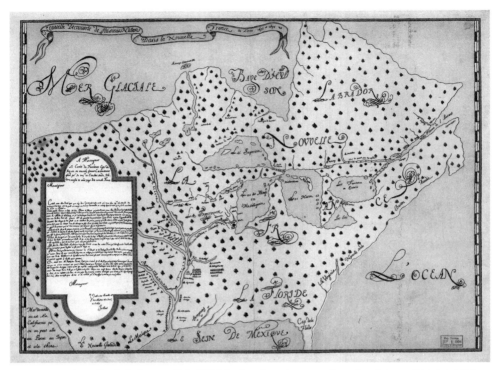

Jean-Baptiste Franquelin's 1675 *La Frontenacie*, a map based on information provided by Louis Jolliet. Image courtesy of the Library of Congress.

Both *La Colbertie* and *La Frontenacie* were, according to Campeau, petitions to French officials for "payment and a gratuity" for services rendered to the colonial and French governments. The maps contain dedicatory letters to Governor Frontenac. It is strange indeed, and at the same time revealing, that Jolliet, who some historians claim was a capable mapmaker, had to rely on Franquelin, a trader and skilled artist, not even a cartographer himself, to draw the two maps.[28] Jolliet was not a cartographer in 1674 or 1675, and Franquelin, the calligrapher who drew *La Colbertie*, and *La Frontenacie*, relied heavily on Marquette's "exact chart," a copy of the one he sent with Jolliet to Quebec and on the 1669 Jesuit map of Allouez and Marquette.

Jolliet attended the Jesuit *collège* in Quebec, where it is possible that he may have studied subjects that could have given him the necessary skills to draw a map. In a 1923 edition of the *Illinois Catholic Historical Review*, John Ely Briggs claimed that Jolliet drew a "remarkable map" of Anticosti Island and the Gulf of St. Lawrence while he was only thirteen years old. The map was said to have been housed in the Department of Marine in Paris.[29]

There are several problems with this claim. To begin, at age thirteen, Jolliet would have been enrolled in the Jesuit school at Quebec. According to the Jesuit Campeau, Jolliet had no special training in mathematics or cartography; he was a student of philosophy, hoping one day to be a priest.[30] We ask, when did young Louis travel more than seven hundred miles by canoe to the Gulf of St. Lawrence and circumnavigate the Gulf to draw a "remarkable map" of Anticosti Island? With whom would he have traveled? What cartographical training would a thirteen-year-old such as Louis have had that prepared him to draw a so-called remarkable map? What was the purpose of the map? Last, as of the time of this writing, this author has been unable to locate a copy of the mysterious Jolliet map.[31]

By way of contrast, Marquette's 1673 holograph map, for its time, was a much more accurate rendition of the territories and waters explored by the Frenchmen. It was the first *known* map to illustrate the Illinois River and the central parts of the Mississippi. What is especially interesting is the map's accuracy in depicting the southward course of the Illinois River between Meredosia and the stream's mouth. During the voyage, Marquette must have regularly noted latitude readings, reviewed compass points, and counted canoe paddle strokes to get an as accurate picture as possible of the streams he and Jolliet traveled.

Jolliet may have met with Frontenac to give him a verbal account of the expedition since Talon, who chose Jolliet to participate in the voyage, had returned to France. Frontenac was an ardent supporter of western exploration to expand France's claims into the yet so-called undiscovered territories. Considering these points, Frontenac would have likely wanted a verbal account of the voyage from Jolliet personally, not just a dedicatory statement on a map.

Regardless of whether Frontenac met personally with Jolliet or learned the details of the voyage some other way, the governor enthusiastically relayed Jolliet's report to French minister Colbert. However, the governor wrote that the only impasse between La Salle's Fort Frontenac and the Gulf was not at the Chicago portage, but at Niagara Falls. According to Frontenac, "[Jolliet] has returned three months ago, and discovered some very fine Countries, and a navigation so easy through the beautiful rivers he has found, that a person can go from Lake Ontario and Fort Frontenac in a bark to the Gulf of Mexico, there being only one carrying place, half a league in length, where Lake Ontario communicates with Lake Erie. A settlement could be made at this point and another bark built on Lake Erie." Continuing, Frontenac reported that Jolliet had traveled "within ten days' journey of the Gulf of Mexico, and believes that water communications could be found leading to the Vermeille and California seas, by means of the river [likely the Missouri River] that flows from the West into the Grand River that he discovered, which runs from North to South, and is as large as the Saint Lawrence opposite Quebec."[32]

In October, Jolliet wrote to his friend and benefactor Bishop Laval, who was, at the time, in France. The letter, according to historian Jean Delanglez, was a recap of the same information the explorer relayed to Dablon. Strangely, Jolliet wrote that there were no portages or rapids on the Mississippi, a river he described as being "as wide as the St. Lawrence at Sillery."[33] This statement is peculiar since he and Marquette, like later travelers, had to encounter rapids on the great river while approaching today's Quad Cities and near the Des Moines Rapids, a feature illustrated on Marquette's 1673 holograph map.

◇◇◇◇◇◇◇◇◇◇◇◇◇◇◇

Details about Marquette's stay at the St. Xavier mission after he returned from the voyage are unclear: Was he was sick when he arrived, or did he become ill sometime afterward? Further, who else lived at the mission with Marquette from September 1673 to October 1674? Did Largillier remain with Marquette, or did he continue to the Sault and join Marquette later?

It seems likely that Largillier, one of seven partners in Jolliet's company, would have continued to the Sault, where he wintered and may have received compensation for his contribution to the enterprise.[34] We saw that in September 1674, Marquette waited for his superior, Henri Nouvel, at the Sault to send someone with instructions about his wintering. It appears that Largillier and Pierre Porteret arrived sometime in autumn, perhaps October, and brought with them Nouvel's instructions directing Marquette to winter with the Illinois at Kaskaskia.

It is probably at this same time that Marquette learned about Jolliet's canoe accident on the St. Lawrence. Three people died in the wreck, two hired men and the Indian boy. The news surely sorrowed the priest. Marquette knew the boy. He had traveled with Marquette and Jolliet down and then up the Mississippi and guided the explorers through the labyrinth of sloughs, backwaters, and away from the false channels on the Illinois to reach Kaskaskia, a site he likely told them about on the way up the river. The boy was also with the explorers when they paddled Lake Michigan to get to St. Xavier's. Marquette and Largillier spoke to the boy in Miami-Illinois, which helped them to better learn and understand the language. It is possible that Marquette may have also known the two other men who died in the wreck. Marquette understood, too, that, besides their collection of ores, plants, and items given to him and Jolliet by the Indians, his report had been lost. Fortunately, Marquette kept a copy of it and entrusted it to a courier who carried the document to Dablon at Quebec.[35]

That Marquette kept a copy of his annual report raises the question of whether the one he sent to Quebec was an exact duplicate of the one he gave to Jolliet. Marquette was sidelined at St. Xavier's for more than a year. During that time, did he add information to his copy of the report, or was the copy he sent to Dablon in 1674 only a rough version of the one Jolliet carried? Or were both copies the same?[36] To these questions, we can never know answers.

At about noon on October 25, the priest and his two companions, Porteret and Largillier, boarded a canoe and began the long journey back to Kaskaskia.

CHAPTER 9

Marquette Returns to Kaskaskia

On October 3, about the time Marquette was preparing to return to the Illinois, Jolliet was summoned to court again, this time as a defendant in a case brought forth by Eléonore de Grandmaison (Demoiselle de la Tesserie), wife of the late Jacques Cailhaut de la Tesserie, and the mother of François Chavigny, one of Jolliet's partners.[1]

The suit stemmed from de la Tesserie's claim that Jolliet owed her a share of the profits in the company because she had invested 300 livres in the 1673 expedition.[2] After hearing the complaint, the council ordered Jolliet to produce all paperwork relevant to his trade business between 1672 and 1674. Jolliet provided the council numerous agreements, contracts, and notes, two of which are very telling. The first was a note "of the said defendant [Jolliet] of the fourth day of the said month and year [October 4, 1672] by which he acknowledges that the said plaintiff [de la Tesserie] has contributed three hundred *livres*, the share of one man, to the common fund, from which she [de la Tesserie] was to have half the profits of one share, the whole profit being divided into as many parts as there are partners." But he also produced another note, "signed by him [Jolliet] but undated, wherein he declares that he made no contract with the said Chartier and the Demoiselle de la Tesserie [the plaintiff]." The council sided with de la Tesserie, upholding "the sharing, made in ten parts with the defendant, of the pelts acquired in the trade by trading in the Ottawa country."[3] This was the second time in three months that a court had forced Jolliet to pay what was rightfully owed to others. About Jolliet Canadian historian Raymond Douville writes, "Louis Jolliet tried to dupe his brother Adrien and to exploit his career, his illness and his death to his personal advantage against his heirs."[4] In addition, Louis Jolliet also tried to cut Eléonore de Grandmaison (de la Tesserie) out of proceeds from the expedition. It seems strange, too, that even though Jolliet claimed to have lost his "minutes and journals" in the canoe wreck, he was able to produce contracts, agreements, and other documents pertaining to his trade activities between 1672 and 1674, paperwork that could have only originated and come from his trading post at the Sault, when required to do so in court. It seems possible that some of his papers would have been kept at his residence at Quebec. However, since either he or his brother Zacharie, while Louis was away on the expedition, operated his trading post at the Sault, records pertaining to the operations that occurred between the autumn of 1672 and spring of 1674 would have been kept at the Sault. The records would have included the paperwork for the "40 skin robes" and "30 other robes," a canoe, payment for a forge he had been *using for three years*," a "white blanket," as well as other robes that, Adrien's widow claimed, were still in the Ottawa country.[5]

◇◇◇◇◇◇◇◇◇◇◇◇◇◇◇◇◇

Paddling down the Fox, strong winds blowing off the bay forced Marquette's party to camp at the mouth of the river, where they met a group of Potawatomi at their village. There the priest learned that five canoes of Potawatomi and four of Illinois carrying trade goods had previously left the site and were heading to Kaskaskia. Marquette and his two companions remained at the Potawatomi village until the next afternoon. Leaving their camp, the French party caught up to the Potawatomi and Illinois at the Sturgeon Bay portage. There Porteret left the others to hunt, while Marquette, Largillier, and possibly a few Illinois began the difficult league-long portage across the peninsula. The French set up camp on the Lake Michigan side of the headland where later that day storms coming off the lake forced the group to move inland to a less exposed site. Porteret eventually arrived at camp after dark, but empty-handed—the Illinois and Potawatomi who had been traveling ahead of the French unintentionally scared the game away. Concerned for their safety, some Illinois came to Marquette and requested that he and his companions travel closely with them and to not strike out alone. To this Marquette wisely consented.

The next morning, with the help of a few Illinois women, the Frenchmen completed the portage, but strong winds and rough waters kept the group ashore. When the weather began to cooperate, the group boarded their canoes and headed south along the coast. Possibly near present Algoma, the party pulled ashore and camped near a small river next to a "good road," a land route that led to the Potawatomi. That night Marquette celebrated Mass before the French and perhaps a few inquisitive onlookers.

An Illinois named Chachagouessioua who seems to have been a chief or at least an influential figure among the Illinois at Kaskaskia, and who was in the canoes carrying trade goods, arrived at camp with a deer, parts of which he shared with the French.[6]

The French and Indians continued their journey down the coast. The priest reported that his group killed two raccoons that were "almost nothing but fat."[7] It seems probable that the animals were killed for their hides, not for meat.

During some downtime, Marquette walked the sandy Lake Michigan shore. He noted that it was covered in grass similar to the type that fishermen pull from the lake in their nets at Mackinac. The best evidence suggests that what he saw was American beach grass (*Ammophila breviligulata*), a common plant that grows along the eastern coast of the United States and the Great Lakes. He eventually reached a river and followed its course inland. Largillier and Porteret paddled to pick up the priest but found that the wind was so strong and the waves near the lake so high that they were trapped, unable to reach the lake. The French struggled to get out of their predicament. As they did, one canoe of Illinois arrived to help extricate Marquette's party, while the other canoes continued down the coast.

Between gusts of wind, smashing waves, stopping to hunt, or for personal reasons, the canoes often became separated and then reunited a day or two later. At one point, perhaps after spotting a herd of deer, the Illinois landed on the shore to replenish their meat supply. Marquette's group also pulled to shore at a "good camping ground," as the missionary called it. There the French party was forced because of "great agitation of the lake" to remain for five days. Finally able to leave camp, the group made a good day's travel until they pulled to shore, where they were forced to remain for three more days.

The weather was changing, temperatures were dropping, and travel was becoming even more unpleasant. Marquette reported that snow fell at night but thawed during the day.

Reaching the Port Washington area, the missionary's group camped along a series of sandy, windblown bluffs that Marquette wrote were "poorly sheltered," where winds delayed the group for two and a half more days. There Porteret left to do some scouting. During his foray, he reportedly came across a stream that Marquette described as a canal with banks as tall as the height of a man on both sides, levees made from windblown sand that had accumulated along the watercourse.

As the group advanced, so did winter. Temperatures plummeted, and as much as a foot of snow covered the ground, which, Marquette wrote, "remained ever since." The party landed ashore again along another river, where they were delayed for three more days. Unable to travel, Porteret took the opportunity to hunt, killing a deer, three "bustards," and three wild turkeys, meat that the French would need in case snow and cold prevented them from hunting. Some Indians in the group set out for the prairies, where at a distance they saw eight or nine cabins. They returned to camp with the news. The next day, Largillier and two Illinois hunters walked to the camp, where they learned that the group was a party of wintering Mascouten. Largillier, who likely picked up bits of different Algonquin languages while working as a voyageur and as a Jesuit *donné* learned that the Mascouten had separated from their main group to hunt. About Mascouten such as these, Marquette wrote, "They travel throughout the winter over very bad roads, the land abounding in streams, small lakes, and swamps. Their cabins are wretched; and they eat or starve, according to the places where they happen to be."[8] It was during this delay that Marquette was stricken with a bout of diarrhea, a warning that his illness was about to return.

Leaving camp, Marquette's group reached the lake. After traveling about three leagues, they reunited with some of the Illinois who were heading to Kaskaskia and who had killed several bison. To the priest, this was a welcome indication that they were getting closer to the village.

Marquette's party struggled to make headway on the lake through the "floating masses of ice," as the missionary called them. They reached the Chicago River in early December, which Marquette reported was covered by six inches of ice. Along the shore lay more snow than at any place they had seen since beginning their journey. Seeing animal tracks and the prospects for a good hunt, the party set up temporary camp at the river's mouth.

Leaving camp, Largillier and Porteret reportedly killed three bison and four deer. They also killed three or four turkeys that had ventured close to their camp. The weather was so severe that even the turkeys, as the missionary wrote, "were almost dying of hunger."[9]

Slowly making their way up the Chicago on foot, carrying some of their goods on their backs while dragging their canoes over the ice, Marquette's party approached the portage. Each step was difficult, a situation made worse by the relapse of the missionary's illness. Marquette was even unable to celebrate Mass on December 8, the Feast of the Immaculate Conception, an especially important holy day for him.[10] They could go no farther. About two leagues from the lake, the French determined to establish winter quarters. Some Illinois, one of whom was Chachagouessioua, the trader who had traveled south with the Potawatomi, set up camp next to the French.

Marquette's group was also joined by several passing Illinois from Kaskaskia who carried with them furs to trade with the French in the Great Lakes country. Marquette and his companions gave them some bison and deer meat from the animals they had killed a day earlier. Eager, perhaps even desperate, to get some tobacco, the Illinois reportedly threw beaver skins at the Frenchmen's feet. But hoping to keep as much of it as possible, the missionary told them that he could spare only a few pipefuls. He would need it when he arrived at Kaskaskia to give to the chiefs and elders as a token of goodwill and to further endear himself to the Illinois. Marquette eventually parted with a cubit of tobacco, trading the precious commodity for three bison skin robes, one for him and one for each of his companions.

Chachagouessioua and his group of Illinois left the French camp and continued on to Kaskaskia to deliver to his people the trade goods they carried and to tell them that the Frenchmen were en route to the village. After Chachagouessioua's departure, Marquette found the strength to celebrate the Mass of the Conception, but not long afterward he reported that his disease had returned with a vengeance, turning into what he called "a bloody flux." But mysteriously, a few days later, his ailment seemed to abate.[11]

With camp established, Largillier traveled six leagues to a winter Illinois village, several cabins composed of small family and clan groups. There he saw that the tribesmen suffered from hunger because snow and cold prevented them from hunting. Two Illinois, however, were fit enough to carry the news of Marquette's arrival to La Toupine and the "surgeon," a pair of Frenchmen who were living eighteen leagues from Marquette's camp, at or near Kaskaskia.[12] The surgeon and an Illinois packed some food, including dried blueberries and corn, and began the difficult winter trek to Marquette's camp.

Who were La Toupine and the surgeon, and what were they doing in the Illinois Country? La Toupine was the surname for Pierre Moreau, a Canadian, born near Xaintes, France, an experienced woodsman. At the time he learned that

Marquette was at Chicago, he was working for Jolliet. In 1671 Moreau attended St. Lusson's pageant at the Sault, and the next year he signed the contact that made him a financial partner in the 1673 voyage. Although it appears likely, it is uncertain if he was one of the five crew members of the expedition.[13] Moreau surely knew Marquette and Largillier, and he probably knew Porteret.

We can only speculate about who the surgeon may have been. The website Earlychicago.com says that the unnamed surgeon was Jean Roussel or Rousselière.[14] Other surgeons who may have been in the Illinois Country at this time include Jolliet's brother-in-law Louis Maheut and the surgeon of La Salle's 1682 Gulf expedition, Jean Michel.[15] The surgeon, like Moreau, was probably a trader working as an agent for Jolliet, being one of the first *known* Frenchmen trading in the Illinois Country. It is interesting that the unnamed surgeon called on the ailing Marquette and brought him blueberries and corn, while Moreau, a known associate of Jolliet, did not. This seems to indicate that Moreau, via Jolliet, was trading illegally in the Illinois Country. The surgeon remained at Marquette's camp long enough to perform his devotions before returning to Kaskaskia with Largillier. Both men carried a message to the Illinois that the priest was, at the time, physically unable to come to their village and would still have a difficult time getting there in the spring if his condition persisted.

A few days later, Largillier returned to the portage camp with some corn, pumpkins, dried meat, and a delicacy—fresh buffalo tongue from an animal he and an Illinois had recently killed. Arriving at camp, too, were three Illinois who brought on behalf of their village elders two sacks of maize, dried meat, pumpkins, and twelve beaver hides. They tried to convince Marquette that the presents were payment for gunpowder so they could hunt and to purchase a few trade items. But Marquette told them that he had come to instruct the Illinois, not to provide them with arms and goods. His mission was to restore peace, and he knew that if he gave the Illinois powder, they would use it against their Miami enemies. Marquette also told them that, although he appreciated that they brought him food, he and his companions did not fear hunger. Last, he told them that, when circumstance allowed, he would urge traders to come to Kaskaskia. Marquette's message was clear: he came as a missionary to instruct the Illinois in the Catholic faith, not to supply them goods and weapons. Marquette did give them a few small gifts, household items, including a few knives, a hatchet, and several glass beads and mirrors. He said that he would try to visit their village if his condition allowed, if only for a few days. The appreciative

Illinois told the ailing priest to "take courage," and if he died, his remains should remain in their country. They also agreed to carry Marquette's letters from the Illinois Country to the fathers at St. Xavier's.[16]

While waiting for ice-out, Marquette, in his free time, jotted down a few observations pertaining to the natural world at Chicago. He wrote that tides come and go on Lake Michigan several times each day, affecting the lake's tributaries, and that he saw "ice going [floes of ice moving] against the wind." What the priest likely saw was a combination of wind, current, barometric pressure, and perhaps high water that appeared to him as tides. According to the National Oceanic and Atmospheric Administration, "True tides—changes in water level caused by the gravitational forces of the sun and moon—do occur in a semi-diurnal (twice daily) pattern on the Great Lakes. Studies indicate that the Great Lakes spring tide, the largest tides caused by the combined forces of the sun and moon, is less than five centimeters in height. These minor variations are masked by the greater fluctuations in lake levels produced by wind and barometric pressure changes."[17] Father André also observed a similar phenomenon on the Fox River.[18]

Marquette also noted that although deer were plentiful near the lakeshore, they were so emaciated that Largillier and Porteret abandoned some that they had killed.[19] He also wrote that his hunters killed several partridges, noting that the males had "ruffs" on their necks, while the females had none.

Toward the end of March, the spring thaw arrived. Ice that covered the rivers began to melt, creating ice dams that caused the Chicago River to rise so fast that the French had to quickly break camp, flee to higher ground, and fasten their goods to trees to avoid losing them. Eventually, the dam broke and the waters subsided. On March 29, Marquette and his companions left their camp and continued their journey to Kaskaskia.

Crossing the portage, the party reached the flooded Des Plaines River, where the water had risen more than twelve feet, greatly increasing the speed and power of the current, making travel even more hazardous. Fortunately for Marquette, his canoe was steered by two experienced voyageurs who had many times negotiated turbulent waters. The current slowed as they paddled through Lake Jolliet and did again when they entered the Illinois. Shooting the swift water at Marseilles, the crew passed the Fox River and in a few miles saw in the distance Kaskaskia. Hugging the north shoreline, the Frenchmen landed at the eastern end of the portage. It took them eleven days to reach the village from their camp on the Chicago.

Arriving at Kaskaskia on Holy Thursday, the Thursday before Easter Sunday, the French were greeted by a crowd of Indians. Marquette himself was reportedly received "as an angel from heaven."[20] So welcoming were the Illinois that he may have even forgotten about his illness for a few moments. Illinois headmen probably escorted him to the cabin of a chief or other dignitary, while Porteret and Largillier secured the canoe and carried their cargo to their assigned lodging.

After settling in, Marquette gathered the chiefs, elders, and prominent men to a great council on the prairie adjacent to Kaskaskia, a site that was reportedly large enough to accommodate the entire village so that everyone could watch the assembly. Reed mats covered the ground, as did assorted animal hides and bearskins. Marquette directed them to set out in lines Chinese taffeta, colored silks, on which were attached four large images of the Virgin Mary on the mats and skins.[21]

Dablon, who edited Marquette's unfinished report, described the priest's visit, writing that 500 chiefs and village elders sat in a circle around Marquette, while the young men stood behind the village leaders. All told, he reported that more than 1,500 men were present, not counting the women and children who may have been busy sowing that year's crops in the adjacent fields.[22]

The village had grown considerably since Marquette's 1673 visit, when the priest counted seventy-four cabins, or a population of about 1,480 people. Now, in the spring of 1675, there were between five and six hundred fires, or a population of 5,000 to 6,000 people. The standard method for determining Illinois and Miami populations is based on the following assumptions:

1 family equals 1 warrior and 4 non-warriors
1 fire equals 2 families
1 cabin contains 2 fires, or 20 people
500 fires equal 250 cabins
600 fires equal 300 cabins
250 cabins equal about 5,000 people
300 cabins equal about 6,000[23]

From where did these other Illinois come, and why did they relocate to Kaskaskia?

Typically, the Illinois gathered at semipermanent agricultural villages such as Kaskaskia in early spring. After the crops were established, they left their villages for the summer bison hunt, which usually lasted about four weeks. In late summer to early autumn, the maize was harvested, shelled, and buried for safekeeping. The Illinois next left their summer villages for smaller winter hunting camps. After the hunt, they returned to their summer villages, and the cycle began anew.

In August 1672, Allouez reported that 20 cabins of Illinois, or about 400 people, likely Kaskaskia, lived at the Fox River village at Berlin. Jolliet and Marquette encountered Peoria near the Des Moines River in June 1673, villages that some researchers believe may have been summer bison-hunting encampments. He also reported that the Moingwena, another Illinois subtribe, lived just beyond the Peoria. By 1674 the Kaskaskia, Allouez wrote, had been at the Fox River village for a "year or two," while the Peoria, likely from the Des Moines, "are gradually coming here to settle."[24] This is about where any confidence about the location of Illinois settlements prior to April 1675 ends.

Marquette's 1673 holograph map records a tribe he called the Maroa, a possible reference to the Tamaroa, an Illinois subtribe that he located geographically in east-central Illinois and west-central Indiana, or possibly the Kankakee River country. However, neither Jolliet nor Marquette had traveled to Maroa territory. The priest based his assumption on information he received from chiefs and Native informants who told him that a tribe named Maroa lived in that region. Marquette's map sheds no light whatsoever about the size of their village or its specific location. Marquette also mentioned that during the winter of 1674–75, some Illinois bands lived in winter camps near present Chicago and at the portage, but, as we have seen, these groups were most likely from Kaskaskia.

Another problem is that the Miami and Illinois were sometimes considered one group.[25] Writing about the Mascouten village on the Fox, Dablon wrote, "It is united [the village], within the same palisade enclosure, to another people called the Oumami [Miami], who form one of the Nations of the Ilinois,—being dismembered, so to speak, from the rest, to make its home in these regions."[26] Sometimes the Illinois were considered Miami by the French, while at other times the Miami were considered Illinois.

As of April 1675, our understanding of the location and size of Illinois settlements, their purpose—meaning whether they were summer agricultural, winter hunting, large summer hunting camps, or if they lived among other nations—is limited, making it difficult to determine from where the Illinois who arrived at Kaskaskia between September 1673 and April 1675 may have come. As we will see in an upcoming chapter, the population of Kaskaskia would continue to swell until 1680, when nearly all Illinois subtribes would be living at the site.

Why did the Illinois subtribes gather at Kaskaskia? Although it is possible that the Illinois hoped to induce French traders to establish themselves in the Illinois Valley, which would afford them local access to trade goods, it seems more likely that the Illinois subgroups collected at Kaskaskia for defense, safety in numbers, to protect themselves from rumored Haudenosaunee attacks.[27]

At the assembly, Marquette relayed to the Illinois ten messages, each one represented by a gift that included an explanation of the "principal mysteries" of Catholicism, the reason for his return to the village. He also tried to explain to the tribesmen the purpose of Jesus's death on the cross. After Marquette finished his sermon, he celebrated Mass. For the next several days, he met with the villagers in their cabins and probably attempted to get a little rest between visits. He mustered enough strength to perform Mass on Easter Sunday. Dablon wrote that "by these two [the Mass celebrated on Holy Thursday and Easter Sunday], the only sacrifices ever offered there to God [at Kaskaskia], he took possession of that land in the name of Jesus Christ, and gave to that mission the name of the Immaculate Conception of the blessed virgin."[28]

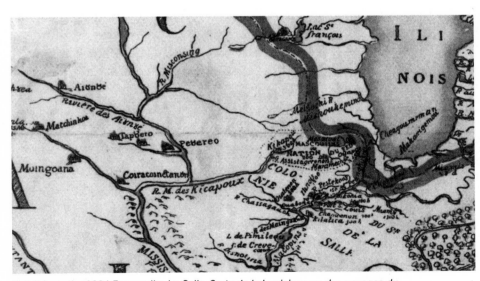

Detail from the 1684 Franquelin–La Salle *Carte de la Louisiane ou des voyages du Sr. De La Salle* showing the Peoria and other Illinois subtribes living west of the Mississippi River. Image courtesy of the Library of Congress.

Marquette remained only a short time at Kaskaskia. The missionary and his companions soon left the village to travel to his St. Ignace mission to receive whatever medical attention he might find there and to get some desperately needed rest. The party retraced its route to Lake Michigan and then headed south, passing the coastlines of Illinois, Indiana, and Michigan. But the missionary's health continued to worsen, and he was eventually unable to even move himself. Marquette never reached St. Ignace. He died, presumably near today's Ludington, Michigan, on May 19, 1675, where he was buried somewhere along the shore of the Marquette River by his two companions.

Porteret and Largillier continued their journey up the coast, likely arriving at St. Ignace sometime in late May. There they relayed the sad news of Marquette's passing to Fathers Pierson and Nouvel. Porteret and Largillier continued east, arriving at Cap de la Madeleine later that year.[29] The next year, Largillier's life would take a decided turn: he signed away all his material possessions and became a devoted assistant to the Jesuits, becoming a lay brother. He would perform the duties of "hunter, trader, and jack-of-all-trades" for the missionaries in the Upper Country and the Illinois, including Allouez and Jacques Gravier, and he would play a key role in the compiling, analyzing, and interpretation of much of the raw data of the Miami-Illinois language that the Jesuits had collected.[30] Largillier would never return to Quebec. What became of Porteret is less certain. Canadian historian Henri Béchard wrote that at the time he and Largillier arrived at Cap de la Madeleine, he was already a Jesuit *donné*. If he was, it is likely that he would have remained in that capacity, assisting other Jesuit missionaries until his death.

The stage was now set for the next phase of exploration and trade in the West, a situation made possible only because of the 1673 voyage. Jolliet had given a verbal account of the voyage; maps had been drawn showing the western rivers, lakes, lands, and location of villages; the Illinois mission had been established; and the Illinois were gathering at Kaskaskia. In Wisconsin the missions were expanding, too, as some nations were moving to the Fox Valley and Green Bay area to avoid the Haudenosaunee, and with the growth of these villages Jesuit activity, whether by way of missionary or *donné*, was also growing. In addition, the first *known* traders in the Illinois Country had arrived and were living among the Illinois. Kaskaskia was the magnet that would draw French trade, missionary activity, and settlement to the West.

CHAPTER 10

La Salle, Allouez, and Kaskaskia

While French interest in the West was growing, Jolliet remained busy with personal and business affairs in the East. On October 7, 1675, he married nineteen-year-old Claire-Françoise Bissot, whose late father, François Bissot, had been granted hunting and fishing rights between Île-aux-Oeufs (Egg Island) and Sept-Îsles by the Company of One Hundred Associates fifteen years earlier. He had also successfully petitioned Talon for cod and seal concessions in the area in 1671. Even though her father had passed, Claire's family still held commercial interests in the region. The next year Louis joined in partnership with Jacques de Lalande, Marie Laurence, and Denis Guyon, hiring the latter's bark to sail back and forth between Quebec and Sept-Îles to carry goods and furs. In November, Jolliet and Lalande purchased their own vessel, a two-masted ketch that sailed to Sept-Îles the following year.[1]

In October 1676, Louis's valued input was instrumental in setting the price of beaver in Canada. That same year, he petitioned French minister Colbert for permission to establish a colony in the Illinois Country with twenty men. The following April 1677, Jolliet learned that his request had been denied.[2] Colbert wanted to concentrate Canada's population in Lower Canada, rather than allow it to be strung out for a thousand miles in the West. The minister wrote, "We must increase the number of settlers [in Lower Canada] before thinking of other lands."[3] This veto, along with promising business prospects in the East, compelled Jolliet to sever his ambitions with the Upper Country. In fact, Jolliet was beginning to enjoy a bit of celebrity of sorts, not only in France and Canada, but, as we will see, even among the English. In 1678 Governor Frontenac consulted Jolliet and nineteen other Canadian "notables" about the issue of the trafficking of alcohol outside of the settlements, an assembly known today as the "Brandy Parliament."[4] Also in 1678, Franquelin drew another map based on information provided by Jolliet titled a *General Map of Northern [New] France Containing the Discovery of the Country of the Illinois*. According to historian Lucien Campeau, the map is a redrawing of *La Frontenacie*, but details on it are "more carefully added and more abundant."[5] Like *La Colbertie* and *La Frontenacie*, the chart was meant as a petition for a gratuity from Minister Colbert through then intendant Duchesneau. An interesting feature on the map is Jolliet-Franquelin's *Riviere de Messisipi*, not *Riviere de Buade*, a stream he formerly named on behalf of the governor. This name change seems to highlight a growing enmity between Frontenac and Jolliet, as Jesuit historian Jean Delanglez wrote, "The governor's antagonism is quite simple—the friends of the explorer [Jolliet] and his protectors were Frontenac's political opponents."[6]

While Franquelin was drawing his latest map and Jolliet was attending the Brandy Parliament, La Salle was in France, petitioning the court through Minister Colbert for permission to reach the Gulf of Mexico by way of the continent's inland waterways. We recall that locating a year-round port ranked second highest on Colbert's list of priorities for the intendant. La Salle's petition was successful; however, there were several important restrictions on his patent. These included a prohibition against trading with tribes whose furs were destined for Montreal, he was to trade in bison hides only, and he must complete his enterprise within five years.[7] In a nutshell, La Salle planned to trade for bison hides and transport them to an ice-free port on the Gulf, where they would be loaded onto ships bound for France. While he was still in France, La Salle recruited tradesmen, carpenters, shipbuilders, sawyers, and blacksmiths, skilled personnel he would need during his expedition to erect forts, build barks, construct shelters, and repair weapons and tools.

We know that before La Salle sailed to France for permission to locate the Gulf, he had access to, or was aware of, the substance of the August 1, 1674, meeting between Dablon and Jolliet. He had also studied Franquelin's *La Frontenacie*.

Of interest to La Salle, as it applied to his new enterprise, were the following statements by Dablon:

A "bark," a large commercial sailing vessel, could sail from Lake Erie to Florida, "by very *easy* navigation," something that was a "very great and important advantage, which perhaps will hardly be believed."

"It would only be necessary to make a canal, by cutting through but half a league of prairie, to pass from the foot of the lake of the Illinois to the river Saint Louis [Illinois River]."

"The place at which we entered [at the mouth of the Chicago River] the lake is a harbor, very convenient for receiving vessels and sheltering them from the wind."

"The [Illinois] river is wide and deep, abounding in catfish and sturgeon."

"A settler would not there [in the Illinois Country] spend ten years in cutting down and burning the trees; on the very day of his arrival, he could put his plow into the ground."

"Game is abundant there; oxen [buffalo], cows, stags, does, and Turkeys are found there in greater numbers than elsewhere."[8]

La Salle based the success of his new venture on the best and most up-to-date information available, Dablon's *relation* and Franquelin's maps. La Salle was led to believe that his ships could sail to the Chicago Harbor, where their cargo of trade goods, supplies, and other items would be unloaded and carried up the Chicago River and across the portage to awaiting barks on the Des Plaines. Sailing down the Des Plaines, the barks would reach the Illinois and, ultimately, the Mississippi and the Gulf. Conversely, bison hides obtained from the Illinois Country could be carried to the Chicago Harbor and transported in bulk east to Niagara. Then, after being transported across that portage, they would be hauled to La Salle's seigniory at Fort Frontenac. Other than the portage between the Chicago and the Des Plaines, neither Jolliet nor Dablon mentioned in reports, or illustrated on any maps, navigational hazards between Niagara and the Gulf. La Salle also knew that bison, the only animal hide of which he could legally trade, were abundant in the Illinois Country and the surrounding region. Not only had Jolliet reported that bison were plentiful there, but La Salle's trader, Michel Accault, had traded with tribes on the Des Moines, including the Iowa, Otoe, and Peoria.[9] Accault was at the forefront of the new bison-hide trading business. La Salle understood that hides purchased from the Des Moines area tribes could, with less difficulty, be transported downstream from their villages to the Mississippi and then carried downriver to the Gulf, rather than being transported up the Mississippi and Wisconsin Rivers, lugged overland to the Fox, through the Fox rapids to Green Bay, and then through the Great Lakes to the lengthy portage at Niagara and loaded onto another bark before they arrived at Fort Frontenac. And after forts had been built at strategic points between the St. Joseph River in Lower Michigan and the Mississippi, the French could farm the fertile lands without having to spend years clearing it. To La Salle, all the ingredients for a successful enterprise were in place. He would return to Canada in September and head for the Gulf.

◇◇◇◇◇◇◇◇◇◇◇◇◇◇

Pierson was busy among the tribes at St. Ignace. He wrote that by late April 1676, he had baptized there more adults than he had children, forty-seven of them, a remarkable accomplishment considering that the Jesuits generally focused their efforts on children. He was encouraged, too, that the tribal shamans were keeping their promises, in his words, to "abandon their juggleries [sleight of hand] and superstitions." Amid the good news, he feared that improving relations between the Haudenosaunee and the Wendat might be a ruse to convince the Wendat to leave the St. Ignace mission and, by doing so, would draw away many converts and potential converts and empower the Haudenosaunee. During the winter of 1676–77, Nouvel, who was also at St. Ignace, left the site to follow the Indians toward Lake Erie, where he reportedly suffered many hardships. From that camp, he visited other area tribes, as he wrote, "instructing and baptizing as opportunity offers."[10]

In July 1676, the aging Charles Albanel was appointed Jesuit superior of the St. Xavier mission where he worked with fellow Jesuits André, Silvy, and Allouez. The St. Xavier post was no longer an extension of the western missions administered from the Sault but had become headquarters for those in Wisconsin and the Illinois Country, including Kaskaskia. He would remain superior in the La Baie area until he was succeeded by Henri Nouvel in 1679.

The ever-busy André commuted between six different villages along both shores of Green Bay, some as far as thirty to forty miles apart, others closer. He wrote, "This compels me To Be always in the Field,—during The summer, in Canoes; during The winter, on ice,—to go instruct them, one after another. I have from 4 to 500 Christians on this bay." During this time, he reportedly baptized forty-five converts, and this number was amid the harassment of tribesmen, including one resentful Menominee who burned down his cabin.[11] Besides the Ho-Chunk, Menominee, and Potawatomi, André also visited a tribe for which he wrote "has no french name," the Otiasawatenon.[12]

Silvy wrote in April 1676 that he labored among the "many thousands" of Mascouten and Miami at the village on the Fox. However, he made it clear in this report that he was not there just to assist Allouez, but that he had come there to replace him, to "take charge of this mission."[13] This was because Allouez was preparing to travel to Kaskaskia to continue Marquette's work among the Illinois.

Allouez and Largillier spent early fall working in the La Baie area, traveling between the St. Xavier, St. Jacques, and St. Marc missions. In October, Allouez, Largillier, and another Frenchman loaded their canoe and set out on Green Bay, their destination Kaskaskia. They hoped to reach the village before winter. However, Allouez's party had not gone far before the temperatures plummeted. Ice began to form on Green Bay, first washing to shore with the waves, then piling in the shallows and mixing with slush. Travel became next to impossible. His party set up camp along shore and remained there until February, until the ice was strong enough to support the men and their canoe.

To better negotiate the ice, Allouez's men fastened a sail to their vessel, which, with the help from northerly winds, reportedly "made it go as [if it was] on water." When the winds stopped, the men tied ropes to the canoe and pulled it over the ice, "as horses draw carriages," wrote the missionary.[14]

Next, Allouez's party encountered a winter camp of Potawatomi. There the Indians told him that a young man he had baptized at La Pointe had been killed by a bear. Allouez learned that the victim had been hunting when he encountered a black bear at close range. The victim fired a quiver of arrows at the animal, and although he struck it repeatedly, he failed to deliver a fatal blow. The bear charged the victim, catching him and ultimately ripping his body to pieces. The villagers soon declared war on bears, hoping to kill as many as possible and while the animals still carried some of their prehibernation fat. The missionary reported that during their crusade, the Potawatomi killed more than five hundred black bears.[15]

Allouez's group portaged at Sturgeon Bay and slowly made their way south along the shore of Lake Michigan, "Lake St. Joseph," as the priest called it. The rivers they passed, Allouez recorded, remained frozen until April 3. Along one of these streams, his party planted a large wooden cross, a reminder to tribesmen who passed it of the catechism Allouez had taught them and to pray to God.[16]

They passed "pitch rock," as Allouez referred to it, presumably located at Whitefish Bay, a few miles north of Milwaukee.[17] There, the men took a portion of it and used it later to patch their canoe and to seal the priest's letters.

Beyond the dunes that lined the shore, the men saw vast prairies dotted by groves of trees arrayed in so orderly a fashion that they looked to have been planted by design. Herds of deer fed in the grass along the prairie borders. For sixty miles, the landscape remained unchanged. Ice piled high by the current was covered by snow drifts that resembled sand dunes. The temperatures were freezing, the men were cold and wet, and travel was extremely difficult. Eventually, the party reached the Chicago River.

Somewhere on the Chicago, the group encountered eighty cabins of Illinois, wintering tribesmen from Kaskaskia who, upon seeing the Frenchmen, walked to greet the visitors. In front of them was the village chief who, upon reaching Allouez, placed a calumet in the missionary's mouth and lit the tobacco with a firebrand. Allouez knew how important it was to smoke when greeted by his hosts, whether he liked it or not. He was next escorted to the chief's cabin, where he, Allouez, was seated in a place of honor.

Inside, the chief beseeched Allouez, pleading with him to allow him, the chief, to escort his party to Kaskaskia. He believed that as a holy man, one who spoke to spirits through prayer, Allouez had the power to protect his "nephews," as he called them, his warriors, during war, and to provide prosperity to his people. Fate would be unkind to him and his people, the chief believed, even fatal, if he failed to take advantage of the mysterious power that was in Allouez.

Not long after their meeting had ended, the French and their Illinois escorts departed for Kaskaskia. It was April, temperatures were rising, the rivers were now ice free, and the paleo-channels and ponds were covered in migrating waterfowl. Illinois women were busy sowing the seeds for the year's crops. The chief and his people were anxious to return home to Kaskaskia, especially since they were bringing with them their French guests. Paddling down the Des Plaines and then the Illinois, Allouez and his guides arrived at the village on April 27.

Pulling their canoes ashore, the French were met by a delegation of chiefs and leading men who escorted Allouez to a cabin that his hosts alleged housed Marquette two years earlier. Assembled inside were the village chiefs and elders, while outside gathered hundreds of curious onlookers. Without mincing words, the missionary told the Illinois that he had come to their village to "preach to them the true God, living and Immortal, and his only son Jesus Christ."[18] The Illinois headmen listened attentively to the priest's harangue,

The village site known today as the Grand Village of the Illinois State Historical Site where Jolliet and Marquette visited the Kaskaskia during their ascent of the Illinois River in 1673 and where Allouez taught and ministered to the Illinois subtribes in 1677. The village was permanently abandoned by the Illinois in 1691. Photo by the author.

and when he had finished, they thanked him for the trouble he had taken for their salvation.

That Allouez could so quickly garner the respect of the Illinois is interesting. He must have carried himself with great authority; his demeanor commanded respect. We saw that no sooner had he arrived at La Pointe, his first western mission assignment, than he had a confrontation with a powerful shaman; as soon as he met with tribal leaders at villages he visited, he spoke openly and boldly to the headmen that he had come to teach them about Jesus; he felt no compunction about destroying idols that the tribes honored on the Fox River; and he supervised the construction of large crosses at villages and along waterways, statements of Catholic hegemony. Perhaps because the Indians such as the Illinois lived in a warrior culture where bravery and prowess in hunting and war were important qualities, Allouez's bold bearing and fearless manner resonated with the tribesmen. It is possible, too, that, in time, the priest had grown to understand the Native psyche and felt confident coming across as proud and assertive. Allouez was not a meek and unassuming celebrant who quietly performed his duties among the Natives. He was a bold and sometimes rash purveyor of what he believed was the only antidote for their unbelief. His approach was in stark contrast to Marquette's accommodating and nonconfrontational style, preferring instead to work within the parameters of accepted tribal norms than confront them and their ancient customs.

By the time Allouez arrived in the Illinois Country, the Illinois seemed to have regarded him as someone who possessed magical power, a force they hoped to access through prayer. The Mesquakie, whom Allouez had visited several times at their Wolf River village, were led to believe that prayer to the priest's Christian manitou would bring them luck in war, a lesson they learned was not necessarily the case.[19] The Illinois he met near the Chicago Portage also believed he was in touch with supernatural powers. He probably understood, too, that since they believed that he had direct access to manitous who could protect their people in war and provide prosperity during the hunt, he could use those beliefs to the church's advantage.

Allouez toured the village, walking between shacks, lodges, wooden drying racks, piles of sticks and firewood, and through smoke emanating from cabin doors and gaps in their walls. He talked to the villagers, learning all he could about Illinois habits, customs, and beliefs. During their conversations, the Indians told him that they not only grew maize, but also domestic crops, including squash and beans, and they supplemented their diet with fourteen kinds of wild roots and forty-two different types of fruits and nuts. They also fished, reportedly catching twenty-five different species of fish and eels, and hunted twenty-two species of game, fur-bearing and other mammals, as well as forty species of birds.[20]

Archaeological investigations at the Kaskaskia site, known by archaeologists as 11-LS-13, or the Zimmerman Site, confirm much of what the Illinois told the priest about the animals they hunted, fish and marine life they caught, and crops they grew. Remains uncovered at the site during surveys and excavations include the three most utilized large game mammals by the Illinois, bison, elk, and whitetail deer.[21] Black bear remains as well as coyote, wolf, and dog were also unearthed. In 1677 northern Illinois would have been home to at least fourteen species of fur-bearing mammals, the most common for trade and personal use being beaver, muskrat, bobcat, otter, coyote, gray wolf, raccoon, and mink. Although the Illinois likely hunted cougar, no remains were found during excavations between 1970–72 or 1992–96.

Because some remains decompose more quickly than mammal bones and teeth, only a limited number of fish species, mostly rough fish, were recovered from the site, the most common being gar, freshwater drum, and channel catfish. Other fish remains include flathead catfish, bowfin, river redhorse, and black buffalo. The remains of six turtle species were also found. Although American eel were extant in the Illinois River in 1677, no eel remains were located.

Game bird remains include grouse, turkey, quail, and rock dove.[22] Bald eagle and red-tailed hawk remains were also found, birds that would have been taken for ceremonial or religious purposes, not for food.

The Illinois also told Allouez that slate was located near their village, as were rocks containing pitch, which, when cut open, the Indians say, they would find silver. Allouez did reportedly find "little pieces" of red copper along the banks of the Illinois River, something that would have certainly been of interest to colonial authorities.

Allouez described the landscape around the village. He wrote, "On one Side of it is a long stretch of prairie, and on the other a multitude of swamps, which are [render the atmosphere] unhealthy and often Covered with fog,—giving Rise to much sickness, and to loud and frequent Peals of thunder; they delight, however, in this location, as they can easily espy from it their enemies [from the sandstone bluffs along the river]."[23] Kaskaskia sat on a sandy terrace on a wide flood plain that was crisscrossed by paleo-channels appearing as long, narrow swamps. When snow melts and the air temperatures rise above ground temperatures, clouds of fog form and hang heavily above the ancient channels and above the canyons across the river from Kaskaskia, becoming what Allouez mistakenly believed were clouds that gave rise to sickness.

The missionary described the Illinois men as "high-spirited, valorous, and daring, who wage war with 7 or 8 different nations." They preferred the bow and arrow to guns, the former being more reliable and virtually silent, an important feature during ambushes. Illinois warriors also carried war clubs and shields made from bison skins that protected them from arrows.

During his saunter through the village, the priest counted 351 cabins, a number that represented about seven thousand people from eight Illinois subtribes.[24] From where did these other Illinois come? Unlike trying to determine from where the Illinois subtribes came by 1675, when Marquette visited the village, Allouez gives us some information about the new arrivals. He wrote that they came from the "neighborhood" of the Mississippi River.[25] This seems to indicate that some or possibly all the Illinois came from the two villages near the Des Moines and the Moingwena village located some distance upstream from the Peoria. Marquette reported that in 1673, there were 300 huts, a number that represented about six thousand people at one or perhaps both villages he and Jolliet visited.

Michel Accault, La Salle's bison-hide trader, traded with the trans-Mississippi tribes on the Des Moines in 1677. It appears that he traded with them in 1678.

Accault, according to La Salle, reportedly had a slight acquaintance with the Miami-Illinois language, evidence that he had had contact with the Illinois tribe.[26] With which Illinois group would Accault have traded? The Peoria near the Des Moines or another Illinois band?

In July 1678, La Salle dispatched fifteen men carrying 7,000 to 8,000 livres of merchandise to the Illinois living "in the neighborhood of the Mississippi," the same words used by Allouez.[27] Whether Accault was part of the fifteen-man group that was sent to the Illinois or not, he arrived at an island on Green Bay, possibly Washington Island, with 12,000 livres of bison hides that he obtained by trade that were loaded onto La Salle's bark, the *Griffon*. It appears that the only *known* Illinois groups at the time living in the "neighborhood of the Mississippi" were the ones residing near the Des Moines. Would Accault have traveled as far as Kaskaskia and traded with the Illinois there? Probably not because, as we have just seen, Accault met La Salle on the island on Green Bay, La Baie being where the Fox River empties into Lake Michigan and the Fox being the best known and most direct route between Green Bay and the Des Moines River.

Another possibility is illustrated on a map drawn by Franquelin in 1684, a chart based on information he received from La Salle, the *Carte de la Louisiane ou des voyages du Sr. De La Salle*. The map purports to show La Salle's travels between 1678 and 1683. It places the Peoria and Tapouaro, Illinois subtribes, on what appears to be the Des Moines River, and the Coiracoentanon and Moingwena, both Illinois subtribes, on the Wyaconda River in today's northeastern Missouri. The map also depicts the Tamaroa and Cahokia living near the Mississippi in southern Illinois between the Missouri and Ohio Rivers. The question is, did any of these Illinois subtribes depicted as living in the "neighborhood" of the Mississippi on Franquelin's map relocate to Kaskaskia by 1677? Making the map problematic is that La Salle had never been to the Des Moines or the Wyaconda. He must have based his information about the Peoria, Tapouaro, Coiracoentanon, and Moingwena on what he had heard from other Illinois, read on earlier maps (*La Frontenacie*), or perhaps from information he had learned from Accault. Although many Illinois relocated to Kaskaskia by 1677, it appears that the groups living on the Des Moines were the ones most likely to have settled at the village.

Why did the Illinois gather at Kaskaskia? The best explanation, among several, seems to be that at the time of Allouez's visit, rumors of a Haudenosaunee invasion were rampant among the Illinois groups. Their headmen certainly discussed what their best course of action should be: Should they move beyond the Mississippi to be further away from Haudenosaunee war parties, or should they consolidate at Kaskaskia? They chose to consolidate at Kaskaskia. It seems possible, too, that the tensions between the Illinois and Haudenosaunee may have been a dispute over geography, meaning position and power. The Illinois claimed that section of the Mississippi, they claimed the Illinois River Valley, and they were bringing people into their fold, by force, by enslavement, and by trade. Their clashes with the Haudenosaunee may have been the result of the Illinois defending their claimed territory from Haudenosaunee aggression. The Illinois probably hoped that along with French missionaries and traders would come French arms and French support. Throughout this period and into the future, the Haudenosaunee would remain enemies of the Illinois, and the conflict between the two people would continue to grow and intensify.

It was not long before Allouez devoted himself to the purpose of his visit, to teach and preach to the Illinois. He wrote that he visited a chief of a subtribe, indicating that the Illinois were likely living among their own subgroups and in their own areas of the village, not scattered about the site and mixed with the other subtribes. Allouez showed some of the curious Illinois a crucifix, an item that the Indians may have viewed as a charm or one showing a new torture technique to use on captured prisoners.

Jesuits and other Catholic orders commonly used crucifixes, crosses, and other religious-related iconography to attract inquisitive Indians and to help instruct them in Catholicism. We saw that Marquette set up four large pictures of the Virgin Mary in front of the assembled Illinois at Kaskaskia, icons that were meant not only to pique the curiosity of the tribesmen and draw them close, but as visual aids so they could see a heavenly image of whom the priest represented. The use of icons and symbolism, as well as the recitation of creeds and the saying of prayers, have been used by Catholic and Eastern churches to teach people who could not read or write since the first century.[28]

Icons, as they are called in the Eastern Christian tradition, were an essential part of worship and instruction, especially during the first years of Christianity when the sweeping majority of people, mainly non-Jews, were illiterate. Even though some people could add numbers or scratch their name, roughly 90 percent or more of people who lived in the ancient Greco-Roman world could not read or write. That is why people who were literate—scribes, priests, and early church leaders, for example—wielded much power and attracted large followings.[29] At that time, most people learned the Gospel message verbally, from people who told and retold the stories that would eventually be included in the Christian New Testament. Religious iconography was symbolic, consisting of images that represented the teachings of the church, and these images gave believers a visual sense of that mystical world of saints, martyrs, and others who inhabited it. Further, Christianity eventually spread like wildfire through the non-Jewish world, through Greek and Roman lands inhabited by people who were not bound by Tanakh, Mosaic Law restrictions that prohibited the use of images and iconography.[30] To the believer, these images were mystical representations of heavenly beings, and they added a sense of awe to their religious experience.

Besides sermons and preaching, Christian leaders also developed creeds, an easy method of inculcating church doctrine into believers in almost modern-day "bullet-point" fashion. Creeds were not only confessions of faith that promoted particular doctrinal beliefs, but, like the Nicene Creed, also statements against nonorthodox views, including the teachings of Arius of Alexandria and the Gnostics. As it applies to the Indigenous peoples of North America, creeds not only promoted the church's doctrine, but they were also meant to be a tool to counteract the influence of long-held tribal beliefs and practices of village shamans who rejected Catholicism. Prayers, on the other hand, were expressions of thanks or petitions for divine intervention from God. Jesuit priests taught creeds and prayers to their converts. Allouez writing in 1673, for example, wrote that he would not baptize adult Mesquakie converts at his St. Marc's mission unless they memorized the Our Father, Hail Mary, and the Apostles Creed (Nicaean Creed) in their own tongue.[31]

Converting French into Miami-Illinois, or any Amerindian language for that matter, was a difficult task. As with many languages today, there are few exact translations for words and phrases. Further confounding the matter were Christian religious terms and associated abstract religious concepts that were utterly foreign to Native languages and thought. Imparting theological notions such as original sin and transubstantiation would have been beyond the missionary's linguistic capabilities. Even translating simple prayers could be exceedingly difficult. For example, the first few lines of the Lord's Prayer, also known as the Our Father, were transcribed by Jesuit Sébastien Râles as follows:

The prayer verse: Our Father who art in heaven,
The Illinois phrase: *88ssemiranghi kigig8nghi epiani,*
Translation by Râles: "We (exclusive) have you as a father / in the sky / you are at that place

Hallowed be thy name,
kitiramat8tche ki8ins8rimi.
It is prestigious / your name

Thy kingdom come,
he nag8siani 8anataki apianghi kati,
As / you appear / peacefully / we will sit . . ."[32]

Other prayers such as the Hail Mary were translated with similar difficulty. Considering the complexity of translating prayers, creeds, and concepts into Miami-Illinois, where there were no words to convey deep theological concepts, ideas that were utterly foreign to non-Christian people, religious iconography, creeds, and prayers were important tools to help potential converts understand Catholic doctrine.

Native Americans believed in the power of charms, as omens of good luck and for other purposes. Ethnologist Frances Densmore, who studied Native American life, music, and culture while working for the Smithsonian Bureau of American Ethnology, wrote that the Ojibwe, for example, used charms for love, to attract worldly goods, to ensure safety and success, to influence or attract animals, to work evil, and for protection.[33] Likewise, Wendat men utilized charms to bring them luck in hunting, fishing, gambling, fighting, and love. According to Canadian anthropologist and ethnohistorian Bruce Trigger, "A charm was an object that had associated with it an *oki*, or spirit capable of helping the person who possessed it." He also wrote that "some charms could confer many types of benefits on their owners; others were useful for only one purpose. Those of proven worth were highly valued and were inherited from one generation to the next."[34] Catholic iconography, as well as crosses and crucifixes, were also considered charms by Native groups. As we have seen, while with a group of Menominee fishermen on Green Bay, André saw that they carried a pole with an image of a sun painted on it that was used as "an exhortation" to bring spawning sturgeon into their nets. André convinced the fishermen to replace the sun image with that of "Jesus crucified," the crucifix. The following morning, the sturgeon reportedly arrived "in abundance." The Menominee were reportedly awed by the spirit in the image and the power of prayer, so much so that the incident convinced the tribe to become more agreeable to the missionary's message, and it encouraged them to discover more about prayer.[35] The Mesquakie, who had been involved in ongoing wars with the Nadouessi, Ojibwe, and Haudenosaunee, incorporated Catholic symbolism into their cosmology, including the cross and crucifix. To demonstrate the power of the Catholic

God, Allouez erected large crosses in villages where he labored, including one at the Sault and one at the Mesquakie village on the Wolf River where, according to historian R. David Edmunds, "in the months that followed many of the Foxes [Mesquakie] incorporated the symbol on their lodges and possessions." Believing that the power in the cross would protect them in battle, Mesquakie warriors painted the symbol on their weapons and clothing to test the magic before setting out, in one case, to attack the Nadouessi. Although one Mesquakie group was successful against a small band of Nadouessi, a different Mesquakie war party bearing the same symbol lost more than thirty warriors, which turned many Mesquakie against Allouez and led them to believe that his "prayer had caused them to die."[36] There is no doubt that, besides impressing the Illinois with glorified images of Mary, brightly colored vestments, chants, incense, smoke, and esoteric Catholic rituals, items such as crucifixes and crosses were regarded as charms that brought luck and protection to those who believed in their power.

Claiming Kaskaskia and its people for the church, Allouez supervised the raising of another cross, one thirty-five feet tall, that was hoisted in the middle of their village, the official stamp of church dominion over it. As the people raised the cross, the missionary and the others chanted the "vexilla," a vexilla being a standard, banner, or icon used by Roman troops, and later, the church, to identify and distinguish themselves from other groups. The missionary believed that these Illinois were sincere, and that they understood his instruction. Moreover, not only did the cross represent the church's seal of protection, approval, and possession of Kaskaskia, it was also a statement, a warning, to secular influences to stay out of Jesuit territory and away from their Indians. Even though many of Allouez's converts included women and children, Illinois converts to Catholicism who joined the celebration wanted the cross so firmly planted that it would "never be in danger of falling."[37]

Allouez and the others left Kaskaskia, promising to return. The missionary was satisfied with the status of his mission. To him, his teachings resonated with the tribesmen, but even those who rejected his instruction still respected him as a person. He hoped to return to Kaskaskia sometime during the next year and remain there for two, but, according to Dablon, ongoing warfare between the Illinois and the Haudenosaunee put Kaskaskia at risk of attack.

Hudson Bay, La Salle in the Illinois, and the Recollects

A round the time Allouez was leaving Kaskaskia, a large party of Kiskakon returning to Michilimackinac from their winter hunt stumbled upon Marquette's grave. The Kiskakon knew Allouez, Nicolas, and Marquette, the latter having taught, converted, and baptized many of them both at La Pointe and at St. Ignace. The Kiskakon respected Marquette, so much so that they determined to remove his remains and reinter them at the St. Ignace mission where they would remain forever close to the tribe.

The Kiskakon defleshed, cleaned, and laid the bones in the open air to dry, a practice they performed on people for whom they "professed great respect." It appears that while the Kiskakon prepared the bones, runners were sent to St. Ignace to relay the news that Marquette would soon be returning to his mission. Not long afterward, some Ottawa and even a few Haudenosaunee arrived at the grave site to participate in the funeral procession. After the bones were prepared, the Kiskakon placed the missionary in a birch bark container and loaded them into a canoe. As the convoy approached Michilimackinac, some local Frenchmen and a crowd of Indians waded into the water to greet it. In the group were Fathers Pierson and Nouvel who, rather than accept the assertion that the bones the Indians carried were those of Marquette, queried the Kiskakon about them. Satisfied that the bones belonged to the late missionary, the two priests led the group in *de profundis*, a sort of dirge or requiem to express their heartfelt sorrow for the missionary's premature passing. The remains were next carried to the church, where they were covered by a "pall," a cloth, and where they laid in state. After the proper Catholic rites had been performed, the box containing the late missionary's bones was lowered into a small subterranean vault located in the middle of the church where, as Dablon wrote, they rest "as the guardian angel Of our outaouas [Ottawa] missions." Local tribesmen often visited the grave to pray, some of them attributing physical healings to prayers recited at the site.[1]

Jesuit Jean Enjalran, who arrived in Canada during the summer of 1676, traveled to his first duty assignment, at St. Ignace. From there he informed Dablon that of the four tribes whose Christians were dependent on the mission, about thirteen hundred of them were Kiskakon, while about five hundred were Wendat.[2] At the Sault, the aging Jesuit Gabriel Druillettes labored among the Odawa, as Henri Nouvel remarked, "with almost unparalleled energy."[3]

The presumed location of Marquette's grave located at his Odawa and Wendat mission at St. Ignace, Michigan. Photo by the author.

Back east in March 1679, Canada intendant Jacques Duchesneau granted Jolliet and Jacques de Lalande, stepfather of Louis's wife, Claire-Françoise, a concession east of Sept-Îsles and north of Anticosti Island, part of the Mignan Archipelago, where the two men were permitted to establish cod and seal fisheries. A year later, Anticosti Island was appended to the grant, but awarded to Jolliet alone.[4] Also, in 1679, Jolliet and seven men were dispatched by Charles Aubert de La Chesnaye (Jolliet's uncle) and Josias Boisseau, a manager of the Ferme du Domaine du Roy (the King's Domain), territory detached from the colony whose concessionaires possessed exclusive trade rights in the region, to make the arduous trek to Hudson Bay to assess the influence of English trade there, and to survey the possibility of establishing trade alliances with the regional tribes.[5] Arriving at the bay, Jolliet's group encountered several Englishmen who received them hospitably, so much so that they gave Jolliet's party biscuits and flour for their return trip to Quebec. One of the Englishmen, Governor Charles Bayly, who had heard of Jolliet's voyage to the Mississippi, made the explorer an offer to work for the English. Jolliet kindly refused. After completing his reconnaissance, Jolliet and company began the long trek back to Quebec.

From this survey, Jolliet realized that the Hudson Bay area was a literal bonanza in furs and seals. He also understood that with the region under British control, trade along the Lower St. Lawrence and Gulf, where his concession was located, could suffer. Furthermore, Boisseau believed that Jolliet and Lalande's concession on the Mignan would siphon furs away from the King's Domain.[6] He demanded that the intendant cancel Jolliet's Anticosti grant and restrict Louis and Lalande's trading privileges. Boisseau also falsely accused the two men of trading illegally with the British, and he demanded that their boats and goods be confiscated. Boisseau's complaints against Louis and Lalande, and his efforts to curb their trading activities, came to naught. He was dismissed from his position in 1681.[7] With Anticosti firmly in his possession, Jolliet built a summer home on the island.

◇◇◇◇◇◇◇◇◇◇◇◇◇◇

Dablon began his summary of the Ottawa missions for 1679 by describing the hardships his missionaries endured, the trials they faced, and the contempt they received from tribesmen. About Jesuit Pierre Bailloquet, the Jesuit superior wrote, "Father pierre Bailloquet has charge of these two missions; he has worked hard in them and suffered much for six years, since he must Seek out these peoples, who are scattered in various places along these two lakes, and caver [cover] more than 200 leagues of country, which he accomplishes in a Canoe during the summer, and in winter over the ice, with Incredible hardships." Further,

> He has been, as well as other missionaries, many times in danger of being murdered by some of the more licentious among these barbarians, who would not suffer his reproofs. One of them three times raised a hatchet over his head; others have Driven him from their Cabins and closed their doors on him when he called to Instruct them, or to look for their sick. Others have made him obnoxious by their Calumnies Because he combatted their superstitions and diabolical Juggleries. In addition, these Expeditions entailed upon him hunger and thirst, together with a hundred other Inconveniences,—which, nevertheless, were much mitigated by the fruit which they produced.[8]

In Wisconsin Allouez and Silvy remained busy among the Mascouten and Mesquakie. Dablon wrote that the villages were filled with refugees with populations that numbered twenty thousand, an incredible number, if accurate.[9]

While Jolliet was traveling between Hudson Bay and Quebec, and Boisseau was arguing with Canadian officials, La Salle was en route to the Gulf of Mexico. His expedition reached the forks of the Kankakee and Des Plaines in late December 1679 and arrived at Kaskaskia on January 1. Unlike Marquette and Allouez, who traveled to the Illinois via the Chicago and Des Plaines route, La Salle's party, instead, ascended Michigan's St. Joseph River and portaged to the Kankakee, a stream that La Salle held was the real Illinois, the Des Plaines being only a tributary.

Their journey on the Kankakee took the explorers down a meandering watercourse that wound through marshes and wetlands of what later became known as the Grand Kankakee Marsh, what was once one of the largest wetlands in today's United States.[10] So winding was the stream that La Salle quipped that his group "sometimes found after paddling a whole day that they had not advanced two leagues in a straight line."[11] Reeds, cattails, and scattered potholes broke the tallgrass plains that stretched as far as the voyageurs could see. So marshy was the ground that there were few places to camp, only an occasional frozen mound of earth where the men could rest and build fires. The area was devoid of game because the Miami, according to La Salle, had burned the plains during their fall bison hunts, leaving nothing but scorched earth littered with bison skulls and bones. La Salle wrote that when the Miami located a bison herd, hunters set the prairies aflame around it. Leaving only a few openings through which they tried to escape, the bison charged through the gaps and were killed by the hunters. La Salle was obviously interested in these hunts since the success of his enterprise was directly tied to the number of bison hides Native hunters traded to him. Besides bison La Salle also reported that deer, beaver, and otter, as well as a variety of game bird species, were plentiful during spring and summer months along the Kankakee. La Salle wrote that fish were abundant, the soil was fertile, hemp was plentiful, and the timber was suitable for shipbuilding. Moreover, the climate was "temperate and wholesome" and the country well watered. He reported there were mines of coal, slate, and iron and that bits of "pure red copper" could be found.

Entering today's state of Illinois, they passed the present town of Momence. At present Aroma Park, they passed the Iroquois River, a 103-mile stream with headwaters in northwestern Indiana. Beginning at Aroma Park, the Kankakee flows northwest, winding its way through the modern-day city of Kankakee. From there the river wavers between shallow and rocky, with stretches of deeper water interspersed with elongated islands. About a mile after passing present-day Langham Island, at today's Kankakee River State Park, the canoes passed Rock Creek, a clear, cool, stream, about 25 miles in length with branches that drain the prairies of southern Will and northern Kankakee Counties. In about 12 miles, the canoes reached the present town of Wilmington and, in 12 more, the forks of the Kankakee and Des Plaines Rivers. La Salle's party was the first *known* group of European descent to have traveled the St. Joseph–Kankakee River route.

Heading west from the Forks, La Salle's thirty-three-man crew followed the same course taken by Marquette and Allouez a few years earlier. These lands, La Salle later wrote, were "the most beautiful country in the world. The Indians call it Massane, on account of the large quantity of hemp there. Nothing could be better intersected by streams and diversified with meadows, islands, clumps of trees, hills, valleys and plains where the land is excellent and, best of all, the river."[12]

To La Salle's surprise, and probably to his chagrin, the crew encountered a set of rapids at Marseilles, a riverine feature that neither Jolliet nor Marquette mentioned in their reports or on their maps. We recall that Jolliet relayed to

Robert Cavelier, also known as La Salle. La Salle arrived at Kaskaskia on January 1, 1680. Photo courtesy of Wikimedia.

Dablon that, other than the difficult portage at Chicago, there were no rapids or other hazards on the Illinois; the river was deep enough to float barks.[13] Marquette, however, did mention a portage at Kaskaskia.[14] La Salle's group likely portaged around the *sault* to avoid tearing their canoe hulls on the rocks. Passing the rapids, the crew struggled in the late-December cold. Ice coated the rocks protruding from the river, water froze on their paddle handles (making them harder to grasp and heavier), and the late-December winds chilled the men to the bone. La Salle likely prodded his cold, hungry, and discouraged men along with promises of food and shelter at Kaskaskia, even though he knew the village would be deserted when they arrived. Hugging the north bank of the river, the convoy finally reached the portage at Kaskaskia. Pulling their canoes ashore, La Salle's men saw an empty town; all that remained were the previous year's cabins, lodges, and shelters. The men were hungry, and they soon began rummaging around and through the structures searching for anything to eat. Snow likely covered the ground, concealing any clue to where the Illinois might have buried their maize. Perhaps seeing footprints, or dirt scattered on the snowy ground, the work of Indians who had found the maize before the French arrived, the men took from the cache the equivalent of about forty bushels of the grain. To the Illinois, the theft was a serious offense; taking it could mean the difference between survival and hardship when they returned to the village in the spring.

While the men searched for food, the three Recollect priests assigned to La Salle's group, Zénobe Membré, Louis Hennepin, and Gabriel de la Ribourde, began counting cabins to estimate the number of people who lived at Kaskaskia. Missionaries counted huts and cabins, not heads, to determine populations. Missionaries wanted to know how many potential converts lived at a village, colonial authorities wanted to know how many warriors they could muster to fight, and traders wanted to know the extent of trade, that is, customers and suppliers, within a geographical area. La Salle wrote that the Recollects counted 460 "lodges" at Kaskaskia, structures that he described as "built like long arbors, and thatched with double mats of flat reeds, so well sewn as to be impervious to wind, snow, and rain."[15] This number was even more than the 351 that Allouez had counted during his 1677 visit. Every cabin, La Salle wrote, "has four or five fires, and every fire has one or two families, living all together on good terms." This number represented, if accurate, and if the structures were dwellings and not public lodges, more than nine thousand people.

La Salle chose Recollect priests to accompany his group, not Jesuits; the latter he later blamed for attempting to sabotage his expedition. About the Recollects, according to Hennepin, La Salle had, before leaving for the West, given the order property at Fort Frontenac and planned to include them in his will. The priest claimed that "he [La Salle] afterwards mark'd out a Church-yard; and having created a publick Notary, he order'd him to draw an Instrument whereby the said M. *La Salle* gave to our Order the property of Eighteen Acres of Ground along the side of the Lake *Ontario* near the Fort, and above a Hundred Acres more in the next Forest to be clear'd and grubb'd up. We accepted this Gift in the Name of our Order, and figu'd the Deed, which was the first that ever was transacted in that Country. The Notary's Name was *la Meterie*."[16]

The Recollects had a discontinuous history in Canada. In 1614 the order was requested to send missionaries there by the colony's merchants, as well as other influential Frenchmen. Leaving France, the first Recollects, a group that included Fathers Denis Jamet (who became the first superior of the Canadian missions), Joseph Le Caron, Jean Dolbeau, and one brother, Pacifique Duplessis, arrived with Samuel de Champlain in 1615. The men set to work immediately after their arrival. Dolbeau and Duplessis constructed housing for their fellow priests and built a chapel at Quebec, where Dolbeau celebrated the first Catholic Mass in that town.[17] Jamet and Le Caron traveled as far up the St. Lawrence as Montreal, arriving there in June. Later that same year, Le Caron traveled to Huronia, where he encountered the Wendat. In 1623 Recollects Nicolas Viel and Gabriel Sagard arrived in the colony and, within three weeks, set off for Wendat Country.[18] Realizing the enormity of the Canadian mission, the Recollects requested help from the Jesuits, who had labored in Acadia as early as 1611. The Jesuits obliged and dispatched missionaries who arrived in Canada in 1625. The two orders worked together until 1629, when both were forced to leave after the fall of Quebec to the British. After Quebec had been returned to the French, the Jesuits became the most powerful and influential religious order in the colony. In 1670 the Recollects returned to Canada, auspiciously, in the words of Canadian historian William Eccles, "in a deliberate attempt to reduce the influence of the Jesuits."[19] One of the first to arrive was de la Ribourde, in 1670. Both Membré and Hennepin landed in 1675, aboard the same ship as La Salle, during the explorer's return to the colony after receiving his title of nobility in France.[20]

Membré worked as a priest at Beaupré and then Trois Rivières, remaining there in that capacity until 1678, when he was selected to accompany La Salle on his Gulf expedition.[21] Membré was a chaplain who ministered to the French in La Salle's group, not a trained missionary who knew the language and culture of the Miami and Illinois. Although Hennepin claimed in early 1680 that Membré had lived with the Illinois and could speak their language, there is no credible evidence that he did.[22]

De la Ribourde spent his first three years in Canada at Quebec, reportedly restoring the Recollect seigniory there and renovating and repairing the monastery and church of Notre-Dame-des-Anges. In the autumn of 1673, he traveled to the newly constructed Fort Frontenac, where he remained until 1676. He returned to Quebec as superior of the monastery and then moved to the mission at Trois Rivières. From Trois Rivières, de la Ribourde returned to Fort Frontenac, where he joined Recollects Membré and Hennepin and assumed the informal title of "spiritual leader of the expeditionary party."[23]

After he arrived at Quebec, Hennepin wrote that he spent time wandering, sometimes traveling "Twenty or Thirty leagues off the town [of Quebec]," on snowshoes with his dog, or in a canoe to learn Native customs, to receive their confessions, and to administer communion.[24] Hennepin traveled to Fort Frontenac with fellow Recollect Luc Buisset, where he, Hennepin, helped construct a mission house at the fort. He returned to Quebec, where he wrote that he had prepared and sanctified himself for the upcoming journey with La Salle. However, it is uncertain when he was assigned to La Salle's expedition, perhaps while at Fort Frontenac or perhaps earlier. Either way, Hennepin returned to Fort Frontenac, where he joined de la Ribourde and Membré, who, too, were assigned to La Salle's team. Boarding a vessel, the three Recollects sailed with other members of the expedition to Irondequoit Creek, where they remained until early July. Heading next to a site above Niagara Falls, where La Salle's men constructed a bark known as the *Griffon*, a supply ship meant to carry trade goods and supplies west and heavy bison hides east, the three Recollects eventually boarded the ship and sailed to Michilimackinac.

Why did La Salle travel the Illinois River to get to the Mississippi and not the Fox-Wisconsin or perhaps the Lake Erie to the Allegheny River to the Ohio route? About the Ohio River route, La Salle in a letter to Governor Frontenac in 1680 claimed that "there is yet another route, the Ohio, which is shorter and better, and is navigable for sailing vessels [than the Illinois]." And if a bark sailed the Ohio River, it would avoid the "difficulty of the harbor at the end of the lake of the Illinois." The problem with La Salle's statement is that there is no credible evidence that he had ever seen the Ohio, let alone navigated it. Although in 1750 the French claimed that La Salle had discovered the Ohio River in 1669, this statement is without support from period documents—it was a French claim against British interests prior to the last of the French and Indian Wars to show that the Ohio Valley was part of their territory, not that of the British. La Salle's above statement was part of a letter that he wrote to Frontenac against Jolliet and the latter's embellished description of the course of the route through the Great Lakes and down the Illinois River that was, as we have seen, quite different from what La Salle saw when he arrived at Kaskaskia.[25]

But despite its rapids, shoals, and other hazards, the upper Illinois River was still, in La Salle's view, the best route to the Mississippi from Lake Michigan because it flowed through territory claimed by the populous Illinois tribe with whom he hoped to establish a trade alliance. And since La Salle's patent restricted his trade to that of bison hides, La Salle found at Kaskaskia four reasons to believe that his enterprise would succeed: the village was large, it was situated in lands where bison were plentiful, it was occupied by bison-hunting people, and the village was located along a route that linked the Great Lakes to the Mississippi. To La Salle, all the ingredients for a successful business venture were in place, and Kaskaskia was its epicenter. However, La Salle had entered the domain of the Jesuits, territory Allouez had staked out and marked with a thirty-five-foot-tall cross, and La Salle was not welcome.

La Salle and his men left Kaskaskia and paddled down the semifrozen river. Four days later, they entered the north end of Lake Peoria. From there they saw at a distance a winter camp of Illinois. The next day, La Salle's group arrived at the village, where he met with the chiefs and elders in council. Among several matters they discussed, he persuaded the headmen to accept his offer of repayment for the pilfered maize. Sometime that night, a Miami chief named Moonswa, who had been sent by Allouez, according to La Salle, to turn the Illinois against the explorer, arrived at the village.[26] Moonswa reportedly told the Illinois that La Salle breathed Haudenosaunee breath, that he planned to pin the Illinois between their enemies to their east and west, and that even the Jesuits "abhorred" him, considering him to be an ally of the Haudenosaunee. La Salle was also said to have carried a potion that could poison everyone in the village. After presenting the Illinois obligatory gifts of kettles, hatchets, and knives, Moonswa and his associates disappeared into the snowy night and returned to the village on the Fox.[27]

Not only had Allouez sent Moonswa to turn the Illinois against the explorer, but La Salle alleged that the Jesuit had tried to convince some Mascouten and Miami to join with the Haudenosaunee to "carry on war against the Illinois," to undermine La Salle's efforts to establish a trade alliance with them.[28] Allouez wanted La Salle out of the Illinois Country and away from his Indians and would, if necessary, use whatever means he could to do so.

Although it seems counterintuitive for Allouez to bring war upon the very people he was trying to convert, he probably figured that he could use the situation to his advantage. If the priest could set the Mascouten, Miami, and Haudenosaunee against the Illinois, Illinois hunters would be less likely to hunt to provide La Salle with the bison hides that he needed to pay for his expedition. If La Salle's claims about Moonswa and Allouez are credible, Allouez was attempting to turn the Illinois against him and turn the tribesmen against each other.

Coureurs des bois, many of whom the priest believed were part of La Salle's entourage, were the bane of Jesuit missionaries. Their disruptive behavior and less than civilized antics at Native settlements were well known. Marquette,

Allouez, Silvy, Le Mercier, André, Dablon, Druillettes, and other Jesuits had risked their lives to instruct the tribes, not only enduring harassment, physical abuse, and death threats, but also suffering from hunger, cold, and illness. Allouez wanted *coureurs des bois* and other secular influences away from his converts, and he was willing to do whatever was necessary to keep the rabble out of the Illinois Country. Although some historians are convinced that since many of the complaints about Allouez's bad acts come from La Salle's biased writings, Allouez himself later admitted that he meant to disrupt La Salle's western operations. Henri Joutel, chronicler of La Salle's failed Gulf expedition who wintered at Le Rocher during the winter of 1687–88, wrote:

> I related before that the Jesuit father [Allouez] had been alarmed by what we had told him, that M. de La Salle could well be coming to the fort, according to what he had told us before leaving us, and as this father [Allouez] feared that said *sieur* [La Salle] would meet him, either because he had gone among these men, as well as I believe I noted, something that was not to the benefit of said *sieur*, the [Jesuit] fathers had promoted certain things to counter the enterprise and had tried to separate several nations of the Indians, which had given themselves to M. de La Salle. They had even gone all the way to wanting to destroy Fort St. Louis, having built one at Chicago, where they had attracted some of the Indians, not being able in any way to take possession of said fort.[29]

Having learned of Moonswa's late night visit by an Illinois chief named Omoahoha, La Salle addressed Moonswa's claims in council with tribal leaders the following afternoon. La Salle told the principal chief, Nicanapé, before the assembled group, that he, the explorer, was surprised that the chief believed Moonswa's lies. Why, La Salle asked Nicanapé, did Moonswa come in secret at night and then slip away soon after telling his lies? La Salle reminded Nicanapé that he could have killed him and his people when he and his men first arrived at the village since most of the warriors were away hunting. Further, he informed the chief that he could kill everyone now if he chose to do so. La Salle also challenged Nicanapé to search the French canoes to see that they carried only tools and trade goods, not weapons.

La Salle's words resonated with the chiefs. Although they considered taking up the chase to catch Moonswa, a snowfall that night obliterated the Miami's trail. Nevertheless, La Salle thought it best to leave the village and relocate elsewhere.

Leaving the Illinois village, La Salle and his men landed some distance downstream, where they began constructing a fortification dubbed Fort de Crèvecoeur. The men also began building a forty-two-foot bark that La Salle hoped to use to carry trade goods, supplies, and heavy bison hides back and forth between the Illinois Country and the Gulf. Locating the Gulf via the Mississippi was La Salle's number-one priority.

In late February, La Salle dispatched Michel Accault, the priest Hennepin, and a man named Antoine Aguel to the Mississippi. Accault, who had traded on behalf of the explorer with the Iowa and Otoe on the Des Moines, was to reestablish himself with the tribes, while Hennepin was to introduce them to Catholicism. It is possible, too, that La Salle chose Hennepin because he wanted to rid himself and his group of the annoying priest.[30] But before Accault, Hennepin, and Aguel had reached the Des Moines, the three Frenchmen were captured by a Nadouessi war party. They were taken to a Nadouessi village believed to have been located at Mille Lacs Lake in Minnesota, where they were later released.

By this time, La Salle's carpenters had run out of rigging, tackle, iron, canvas, and other materials needed to complete the bark. Hearing nothing about his missing vessel on the Great Lakes from men assigned to watch for it, the explorer and several men left de Crèvecoeur and trekked to the St. Joseph River, where his men built a small unassuming post the previous November, to find out what he could about the ship's whereabouts.

Before leaving for Michigan, La Salle appointed his second-in-command, Henri Tonti, to command at the fort. Judith Franke, former director of the Dickson Mounds Museum, wrote that "Tonti is arguably one of the most important explorers of the Americas to have gone almost unnoticed by history."[31] Writing about Tonti's death at Mobile, Alabama, in 1704, historian Charles Balesi proclaimed, "Thus ended the exploits of one of the least known—yet most important—figures of the French conquest of North America."[32]

Tonti, an Italian by birth, served in both the French army and the French navy. He lost a hand by a grenade during the battle against the Spanish at Libisso. Taken prisoner by the Spanish, he was released six months later in exchange for the governor's son. He returned to France but soon volunteered to work in the galley of a French naval vessel. In 1678 he returned to France, where he was introduced to La Salle, who had recently obtained his royal patent to explore the Mississippi. The two men, along with thirty hired hands, sailed for Canada, arriving at Quebec in September.[33]

Tonti was exactly the type of man La Salle needed in his retinue. He was loyal and honest, and La Salle could depend on him to obey orders without question. As a seasoned military officer who had fought in wars against the Spanish and the Dutch, Tonti knew how to manage and inspire men under his command. At Fort de Crèvecoeur, Tonti was left in charge of a group of disgruntled and disillusioned Frenchmen whose time in the wilderness with La Salle had been discouraging, difficult, and dangerous. Most of them wanted out, away from La Salle and the calamities associated with the voyage. Some hoped to desert to the British and ultimately find a way back to France. Tonti probably feared that without his or La Salle's commanding presence among the men, the men would desert and the expedition would fall apart.

Slogging their way through ice and slush, La Salle encountered two men whom he had instructed to keep a watchful eye out for his missing bark. The men told him that the *Griffon* had never arrived at the St. Joseph and that, although they had traveled around Lake Michigan searching for it, they had neither seen it nor learned of its whereabouts. Disheartened by the news, La Salle next sent the men to Fort de Crèvecoeur to instruct Tonti to examine a site for a new fort near Kaskaskia, at a bluff the French would later call Le Rocher. Leaving the explorer, the men arrived at de Crèvecoeur and gave Tonti La Salle's instructions. Although he likely knew that leaving his men unsupervised was a bad idea, Tonti, true to form, complied with La Salle's orders. After examining the fort site, he returned to Fort de Crèvecoeur to find that, as expected, most of the men had deserted. Unfortunately for Tonti and the five loyal French with him, a small group that included the priests de la Ribourde and Membré, the deserters took just about everything of value with them. Tonti and the others, none of whom were experienced woodsmen who could survive in the wilderness without the help of voyageurs or Indians, were forced to leave the fort and ask the Illinois, who had since returned to Kaskaskia from their winter hunt, if they could stay at their village until La Salle returned. The Illinois skeptically acquiesced to Tonti's request, thinking that their guests just might be Haudenosaunee spies, an idea planted in their minds by Moonswa several months earlier. Tonti and the French spent the summer at Kaskaskia, likely learning some Miami-Illinois language, accompanying the Illinois during their summer bison hunt, and learning about Illinois life and customs. After the village maize had been harvested, shelled, and stored, Illinois clans and family groups began leaving the village for winter hunting camps.

In the meantime, the ongoing conflict between the Haudenosaunee and the Illinois had come to a head. What had been scattered raids, some of them bloody indeed, was about to become an invasion. Incensed by La Salle's attempt to arm and ally with the Illinois and perhaps believing that the French were attempting to confine their tribe's influence to boundaries determined by the French, the Haudenosaunee moved to attack Kaskaskia, the de facto capital of the Illinois.[34]

In September a Shawnee who had been living with the Illinois at Kaskaskia stumbled upon a five- to six-hundred-man Haudenosaunee war party a few miles from the village on the Aramoni River, and this at a time when most Illinois had already left for winter camps. The horrific news was verified by Illinois scouts. That night the Illinois sent their noncombatants to hide in the marshes downstream while the men prepared themselves for battle. The next morning, Tonti led a group of Illinois toward the Haudenosaunee camp to hopefully broker a peace or, if necessary, fight. Approaching the Haudenosaunee, musket fire erupted. The skirmish ended after Tonti, who had been stabbed, captured, and interrogated by the Haudenosaunee, tricked his inquisitors into believing that a large Franco-Illinois force was waiting in the wings and was prepared to attack. Unsure if their captive was telling the truth, Tonti was released. Tonti and the Illinois next returned to Kaskaskia, the Haudenosaunee following menacingly behind. Reaching the village, the Illinois lost heart and left to reunite with their families downstream—Kaskaskia now belonged to the Haudenosaunee.

Two days later, the Illinois returned to the village, hoping to strike a peace agreement with the Haudenosaunee. After learning that no such Franco-Illinois force existed, Tonti and the French were ordered by the victors to leave the Illinois Country the next morning. Boarding their canoes, the French group traveled about five leagues up the river before pulling ashore to repair leaks in their canoe and to dry their clothes and cargo. Disregarding Tonti's advice to remain with the others, de la Ribourde entered the timber to pray. He was never seen alive again. The priest was reportedly killed by a group of Kickapoo who had been in the area searching for Haudenosaunee stragglers.

With the French gone, the Haudenosaunee took their anger out on the Illinois, destroying Kaskaskia, burning most of the remaining crops, and chasing them down the river, all the way to the Mississippi. There the Illinois groups scattered, some heading south, others north, while the Peoria and some others more than likely returned to their old camps near the Des Moines. Passing

Fort de Crèvecoeur, the Haudenosaunee plundered what remained of the site, including La Salle's unfinished bark, an act meant to send a message to the explorer that they resented his meddling in tribal affairs.

For part of one year, 1680, the Recollects, not the Jesuits, were the face of Catholicism in the Illinois Country, albeit not as missionaries who had come to stay, but as priests and chaplains. From this point, September 1680 until May 1684, no Catholic missionaries or priests would serve in the region.

Looking at the significance of the 1673 mission as it applies to the Illinois Country, we see that the voyage led to a short-lived French presence in the Illinois Valley. Allouez continued Marquette's work among the Kaskaskia, La Salle made contact with the Illinois at Lake Peoria, and the French constructed the first French post in the Illinois Country, Fort de Crèvecoeur. And to stop the French, who were now infiltrating the region, promising to arm and aid the Illinois, the powerful Haudenosaunee attacked the Illinois and drove them from their own territory. But French penetration into the Illinois and Mississippi Valleys, and their secular and religious influences, would persist and would forever change the dynamics of the region's lands and people.

CHAPTER 12

La Salle, the Illinois Country, and the Gulf

In the West, Jesuit influence among the tribes was spreading. They had established missions in Michigan, Wisconsin, and Illinois and had sent missionaries, including Allouez, Silvy, André, Albanel, Nouvel, Enjalran, and their *donnés* and helpers, to work among the regional tribes. Although their presence in the Upper Illinois Valley was put on hold after 1677, they would return.

In early 1681, La Salle was at his St. Joseph River post preparing to return to the Illinois Country, hoping to locate some Illinois tribesmen who survived the Haudenosaunee onslaught the previous September and convince them to tell their leaders to end their wars with the Miami and to ally with him. Just before leaving for the Illinois Country, about 150 Shawnee warriors and their chief arrived at the post and asked La Salle for French protection against the Haudenosaunee. La Salle communicated to the chief that if he would accompany him, La Salle, to the Gulf, he would put his people under the protection of the French king. The chief gladly accepted La Salle's offer and promised the explorer that he would rendezvous with him at the Miami post that fall.

On March 1, 1681, La Salle left the St. Joseph post for the Illinois Country with 15 well-seasoned woodsmen. During their journey they encountered a winter village of Mesquakie and then a group of Illinois hunters. La Salle communicated to the Illinois that they should end their wars with the Miami and ally with him. If they didn't, La Salle explained, the Haudenosaunee would destroy their villages individually. Since La Salle needed the Illinois to ensure the success of his enterprise, he likely stressed to them that peace would not only provide security from the Haudenosaunee, but also open local access to trade with him. He asked them to relay his message to their leaders.

Returning to the St. Joseph River, La Salle met with the representatives of "seven or eight different tribes," according to La Salle, the Moraigane, Anhanagane, Mahigane (likely Mohegan), and the Minissens from today's Massachusetts, New York, and "the borders of Virginia."[1] La Salle told them through his interpreters Nanangoucy and Ouiouilamet of the advantages of settling in the Illinois and Miami Country—the lands were fertile, game and fish were plentiful, and they would be far away from their British enemies in the East. They would also enjoy the protection of the king of France. But first, La Salle made known to them that he must locate the mouth of the Mississippi in order to bring to them much-needed trade goods and livestock and other items they once enjoyed in their homelands. One condition of La Salle's arrangement, however, was they must work with La Salle to unite the Illinois and the Miami.[2] The tribes accepted La Salle's proposals.

The next day, La Salle met with Miami leaders. He stressed to them that they needed to end their conflict with their Illinois cousins and ally with him, the benefits being protection from the Haudenosaunee and access to trade goods. The following day, the Miami leaders met La Salle at his lodge and, after presenting the explorer with gifts of beaver hides, told the Frenchman, "Do not count our gifts, my brother; it is all that we have left. The Iroquois [Haudenosaunee] have stripped us of everything, but we offer thee our hearts, hoping that in the spring we may be able to give thee greater tokens of our love and gratitude."[3] For the time being, the Miami, like the northeastern tribesmen, had accepted La Salle's proposals.

In January La Salle and a group of Frenchman, and some tribesmen and their wives, left the St. Joseph area and began the long journey to the Gulf, a voyage that had been postponed for nearly two years. The group traveled along the west coast of Lake Michigan, then paddled up the Chicago River. Crossing the Chicago–Des Plaines portage, they entered the Des Plaines, following that stream to the Illinois, and then the Illinois to the Mississippi. The group arrived at the Gulf on April 6. Three days later, La Salle claimed for France all lands and waters that flowed between the Appalachians and the Rockies. To the literally millions of Native Americans who lived in this vast country, La Salle's claim was absurd.

But to colonial powers who vied for control of the continent, La Salle's claim was the means by which the newcomers asserted royal ownership and authority of Native lands, in effect opening them to trade, colonization, exploitation of natural resources, and investment. La Salle did, however, accomplish what Jolliet and Marquette had failed to do, arrive at the Gulf via the Mississippi.

Likely during the voyage back north, La Salle granted Tonti land at the Arkansas River, the southern terminus of Jolliet and Marquette's journey. Four years later, Tonti would allow several men to establish a trading post at the site. French influence was now beginning to spread to the Lower Mississippi.

A few months later, La Salle learned that his ardent supporter Governor Frontenac had been recalled to France. Spiteful, pretentious, and at times bombastic, Frontenac had managed to anger both secular and ecclesiastical authorities. He promoted haphazard western expansion through men such as La Salle, he failed to contest British encroachment into French trading territory, and he failed to protect French settlements and aid Canada's Indigenous allies when requested to do so. These shortcomings led to growing Haudenosaunee aggression, one manifestation of which was their attack on Kaskaskia. Frontenac's leadership, or lack thereof, hurt trade, threatened settlement, and destabilized tribal relations.

Appointed in Frontenac's stead was a man who before his arrival in Canada was a naval captain, governor, and civil administrator—Le Febvre de La Barre. Landing with him at Quebec was Canada's new intendant, Jacques de Meulles. La Barre had been instructed to concentrate Canada's population along the Lower St. Lawrence, protect the colony's licensed fur trade, and prevent Haudenosaunee attacks on Native allies and the French. His first act as governor was to call together prominent secular and religious leaders to determine the best course of action in dealing with, in the view of French colonial officials, the increasingly aggressive Haudenosaunee. What he learned was quite disturbing. Canadian officials agreed that the Haudenosaunee planned to strike Canada's Indian allies and later focus their efforts against French settlements.[4] Colbert, Talon, and even Jesuit officials sought mines, minerals, and a route to the sea, as well as information about the people who lived in the Upper Country and beyond, but these objectives were meant to be slow and deliberate. While the French were inching west, the situation in the east was critical. La Barre needed to consolidate Canada's population and strengthen the settlements before exploration, trade, and settlement could continue.

Learning of the change in Canada's administration, La Salle wrote La Barre, apprising him of the situation in the West, believing that the new governor was supportive of his efforts. But La Salle was mistaken. He informed the governor that he intended to build a fort in the Illinois Country and convince the Miami and Illinois to establish villages nearby. He also told La Barre that he planned to award land grants to settlers. But La Barre saw that what La Salle had been allowed to do was everything contrary to what he, the governor, had been sent to Canada to prevent. La Salle and his enterprise had to be stopped. Since La Salle was still in the West, and seven months remained on his royal patent, La Barre was restricted in what he could do with his nemesis.

During the winter of 1682–83, while La Salle's men were building a palisaded stockade on top of Le Rocher, a post named Fort St. Louis, La Salle returned to Miami country to put into action the proposals he presented to the north-eastern tribes and the Miami two years earlier. The situation was now urgent because the Miami, who had been paying tribute to the Haudenosaunee in beaver hides, believed their departure from their St. Joseph villages and their alliance with the Illinois and the French would invite Haudenosaunee attacks. With Frontenac gone and La Barre in charge, La Salle could no longer guarantee that the French could help protect them from the Haudenosaunee. Moreover,

A model of La Salle's Fort St. Louis at the Starved Rock State Park Visitor Center. Photo courtesy of Tom Williams.

La Salle's royal patent would expire in May, and his time in the West would be brief. The Miami had two choices: remain in their villages and live under the Haudenosaunee yoke or relocate to the Illinois Country. Most Miami groups and some northeastern tribesmen, including several Mohegan, agreed to move to the Illinois Country.[5]

That spring numerous Miami groups, including the Atchatchakangouek (Miami), Peanghichia (Piankashaw), Ouiatanon (Wea), Pepikokia, and the Kilatica, established new settlements in Illinois. The villages were scattered across northern Illinois from between the Iroquois River in Kankakee County in the east to Bureau Creek in Bureau County to the west. Miami groups also built new villages at the forks of the Des Plaines and Kankakee, near the mouth of Illinois's Fox River, on today's Buffalo Rock, and near present Hennepin. One Shawnee group established a village near the Vermilion River in La Salle County, while a group of trans-Mississippi tribesmen, the Otoe (depicted as Ouabona on Franquelin's 1684 map), settled near the Big Bend of the Illinois River.[6] About six thousand Illinois who had been run out of their territory by the Haudenosaunee in 1680 returned to Kaskaskia. Historians inaccurately call this amalgamation of tribes "La Salle's Indian Colony." La Salle's fort on Le Rocher would be headquarters for Franco-Amerindian trade and diplomacy in the region.

While La Salle's men were constructing his Illinois Country fort, La Barre dispatched two officers to take command of strategic French outposts in the West. Olivier Morel, Sieur de La Durantaye, was dispatched to Mackinac and Chevalier Louis-Henri de Baugy to Fort St. Louis at Le Rocher. Since La Salle's patent had expired, Baugy was ordered to take possession of the fort and seize any and all items he believed had been obtained in violation of La Salle's former patent. Pressured by Montreal merchants who resented La Salle's presence in the West, believing him to be an illegitimate competitor, and likely having yet to be reimbursed for the money they loaned the explorer, La Barre seized La Salle's seigniory at Fort Frontenac on the premise that he failed to maintain the fort's defenses. He also began a "smear campaign" against La Salle to the new French minister, Jean-Baptiste Colbert, Marquis de Seignelay.[7]

With the French in the Illinois Valley, the tribes encamped across northern Illinois, La Salle's arrival at the Gulf, and his sweeping claim to all lands and waters of the midcontinent, the door to the West was beginning to open. Unfortunately, because of the many setbacks that thwarted his enterprise, including

Haudenosaunee invasions, the loss of ships, and desertions, the door opened too late for him to complete his primary objectives. With his license expired, La Salle remained in the Illinois Country to do what he could to guide his new enterprise. To the governor's chagrin, La Salle awarded large parcels of land to two of his loyal men, Jacques Bourdon d'Autray and Pierre Prudhomme. These properties, La Salle hoped, would eventually be the very first settlements in the Illinois Country, but more important, at the time, they made it more difficult for the governor to extract La Salle and his men from the region.

Having few trade goods to barter with the tribes moving into the region, La Salle sent two men to Canada to get firearms and other goods. They left with a letter written by La Salle requesting that the governor allow the men to purchase the needed items and return to Fort St. Louis, using as an excuse defense against the Haudenosaunee and "Panimaha," who were soon expected to attack. He also requested tools for cultivating the soil, implying that he was there to stay since settlers, not *coureurs des bois*, used shovels and other tools.[8] But the governor detained La Salle's men. Without trade goods, a primary reason for why the tribes relocated to Illinois, La Salle was forced to sail to France to plead his case before the court to allow for an extension to his patent. The foundation for his enterprise was in place, but he was without the means to sustain it.

La Salle and several men left Le Rocher that summer, leaving Tonti in charge of the fort. Along the way, he met Baugy and his detachment. Baugy informed La Salle that he had been instructed to take command of the fort. He also delivered to La Salle orders to report to the governor at Quebec as soon as possible. La Salle continued his journey and somehow managed to avoid the governor. At Quebec he boarded the first ship leaving for France and for the last time left Canada. Aboard the vessel with him was Franquelin, the artist/mapmaker; François de La Forest, who managed La Salle's affairs at Fort Frontenac; Zénobe Membré, the priest who had accompanied La Salle during his expedition to the Gulf; as well as other influential Canadians who might hopefully vouch for La Salle's testimony.

La Salle had to lay out a very convincing case to the court if he were to receive permission to continue his enterprise. The king's policies had changed much since La Salle had received his royal patent in 1678. The monarch and his advisers wanted Canada's population consolidated along the Lower St. Lawrence, they wanted French settlements protected, they wanted more restrictive trade policies, and they wanted the Haudenosaunee subdued. What La Salle was asking for would divert to his venture resources, men, munitions, and supplies from Canada, where they were desperately needed. La Salle hoped to reach the Mississippi by sea, a route never before taken by French mariners. It was into this political mix that La Salle would ask for the king's permission to establish a settlement more than two thousand miles from Quebec and more than a thousand miles from the closest French outpost. This was a tall order, indeed. La Salle devised a twofold approach: he would use arguments and maps.

In his petition to the minister Seignelay, La Salle laid out his case. He began by embellishing the accomplishments of his first patent (including his construction of Fort St. Louis on the Illinois), his placing of settlers near the fort, and the fact that he had allegedly brought together eighteen thousand emigres who were building houses and tilling the soil, the beginnings of, as he wrote, a "powerful colony."[9] He wrote that his claims could be verified by former governor Frontenac, Minister Colbert (but now deceased), the cleric Membré, and the others who had arrived in France with him. Not only could these people validate what La Salle had accomplished, but they could also help refute accusations against him by Governor La Barre, Intendant Duchesneau, and other enemies who had smeared his name and downplayed his successes. La Salle tried to convince the court that the hard work had already been done and that he had achieved these success while sick, while "almost daily" fighting Indians, and in doing so had endured great financial loss and personal misfortune. He also tried his best to explain to the king that he would never ask for permission to do anything that might disgrace him, La Salle, before the monarch.

La Salle's claims were true, but only to varying degrees. He wanted to show that he was forming a colony, not just managing an outpost at the edge of the wilderness. He had awarded land to settlers, but as far as surviving documents indicate, the land in the Illinois Country was apportioned to only two individuals, d'Autray and Prudhomme, and only d'Autray's land had been awarded, while La Salle's patent was still valid. Other land grants may have been awarded after 1683, perhaps by Baugy, or later by Tonti or La Forest, but as far as it can be known today, La Salle awarded only two in the Illinois Country.[10]

La Salle's petition also stated that eighteen thousand Indians resettled near his fort and were tilling the soil. There are many problems with this claim. While in France in 1684, Franquelin drew a map titled *Carte de la Louisiane*, a map based on information provided by La Salle. Briefly, what La Salle wrote about the fort and the tribes moving to the region in his reports and correspondences are contradictory and irreconcilable with information illustrated on Franquelin's map. His numbers are inflated, the illustrations denoting populations are vague, and several Illinois subtribes he mentioned in his correspondences as relocating to Kaskaskia are illustrated on the map living in Iowa, Missouri, and southern Illinois.[11] Eighteen thousand Native allies in northern Illinois, if the map was accurate, means that the French could muster thirty-six hundred warriors to support La Salle on the Gulf if necessary. The map was a propaganda piece that was meant to influence the court to aid La Salle to obtain permission to sail to the Gulf.

La Salle offered other reasons for why his patent should be extended, including that he would be well positioned to conquer Spanish silver mines. Evidence for this claim included Franquelin's map. The chart shows the Mississippi, beginning just below its juncture with the Ohio, rolling west-southwest and then due west through today's states of Arkansas and Oklahoma, flowing between six and seven hundred miles away from its proper course. The river next bends to the southwest and then curves to the southeast, through the Texas Panhandle and the central part of the state, emptying into the Gulf somewhere near the modern-day city of Corpus Christi. The Mississippi, according to the Franquelin–La Salle map, flowed in the direction of the Spanish-claimed territory that would put La Salle, in his mind, in position to conquer the silver mines. Considering La Salle's ability to negotiate the western rivers, lakes, and forests, combined with his having studied physical sciences such as geography, astronomy, and hydrography at Jesuit schools in France, a misrepresentation of the course of the Mississippi of this enormity could not be attributed to a broken compass, as the explorer had tried to claim.[12] He intended to deceive the French Court to improve his chances of receiving an extension of his patent.[13]

La Salle also hoped to convince the court that the Mississippi was navigable for oceangoing ships and that a port on the river would be well suited for repairing and refitting naval vessels and for procuring supplies. Ship hulls could be built from the region's timber, material for making rope and rigging was abundant, and iron mines might be found to make tools and cannons. La Salle reported that the climate was pleasant and natural resources were plentiful and cheap. The land was so fertile, he wrote, that colonists would voluntarily settle and remain in the region. The territory, he claimed, was easily defended from invasion. Domestic animals, including horses, pigs, and oxen, were abundant in "every part of the country," an obvious misrepresentation since no Europeans were settled along the Lower Mississippi at the time. And the Nations who lived in the Lower Mississippi, he claimed, were more inclined to Christianity than other tribes. All that was needed for a successful colony was La Salle's leadership and the Crown's permission.[14]

What was needed to establish a colony, La Salle explained, was one ship, some soldiers, munitions, two hundred men, and the vessels to bring supplies, merchandise, and people to the Gulf. He planned to maintain the colony through the "produce of the country." Everything else they might need would be purchased from the Indians. La Salle planned to build a viable, self-sustaining colony in the Mississippi Valley that would, theoretically, double the size of French-claimed territory on the continent.

◇◇◇◇◇◇◇◇◇◇◇◇◇◇

On March 21, 1684, while the northern Illinois tribes were still away on the winter hunt, two hundred Haudenosaunee warriors arrived at Le Rocher. Having been warned of their approach, twenty-four Frenchmen and twenty-two local Miami, Shawnee, and Mohegan tribesmen and their families fled to the safety of the fort. The defenders were low on ammunition, supplies, and food. A canoe convoy carrying merchandise and supplies bound for the fort had been three weeks earlier attacked and pillaged by the Haudenosaunee on the Kankakee. Considering the circumstances, the fort's defenders were forced to use restraint, shooting only when they knew they could kill, as Baugy wrote. Patiently waiting inside the palisades, the French and Indians hoped that the Illinois from Kaskaskia would soon return from the winter hunt and break the siege.

Three days into the incident, Baugy wrote a dispatch to La Durantaye at Mackinac requesting reinforcements, ammunition, and food. Somehow a courier carrying the message managed to slip through the besieging warriors and make his way to Mackinac. On day six of the siege, an Illinois contingent led by a large group of returning Peoria arrived and drove the Haudenosaunee out of the area, chasing them east and exchanging gunfire with them while they fled. Although the French and their Native allies in the fort had been surrounded and outnumbered by a well-armed and determined Haudenosaunee war party, the French still maintained their presence in the region and the fort atop Le Rocher still stood.

At the French post at Michilimackinac, La Durantaye gathered all the troops and supplies he could muster and headed to Le Rocher. La Durantaye's canoes traveled down the western shore of Lake Michigan and apparently stopped at the St. Xavier mission, where Allouez and Largillier joined the group. Since it is unlikely that anyone in La Durantaye's party had been to Kaskaskia or Le Rocher, Allouez and Largillier would have likely guided the canoes to the fort. The missionary and his *donné* had been to the area and were familiar with the route, including its portages, such as the ones at Sturgeon Bay and at Chicago, the distances between important geographical points, and the location of rapids and shallows. Their knowledge of the hazards would have been especially important since the group would have utilized large birch-bark canoes, vessels used by traders, soldiers, and Nations of the upper Great Lakes country, not two-man canoes that were typically used on the shallow and rocky streams of northeastern Illinois.[15] It is likely, too, that Allouez had heard that his adversary La Salle was away, either in France or on the Gulf, and he figured that it was safe to return to the area. La Durantaye's party arrived at Le Rocher in May, long after the siege had ended.

Allouez surely went right to work at Kaskaskia, rekindling former relationships with village leaders and converts and establishing new ones with others. And since he was the only chaplain in the region, he would have ministered to, or at least celebrated Mass before, the French at the fort. It is probable, too, that he traveled to local Miami villages like the one at located at today's Buffalo Rock, Hennepin, and perhaps others.

The Miami who relocated to northern Illinois at this time, if La Salle's writings can be trusted, fled their villages along the St. Joseph River in northwestern Indiana and perhaps southeastern Michigan.[16] What became of the Miami on the Fox River as reported by Allouez, and how many of them stayed in Wisconsin during this time? Did some of them leave Wisconsin and resettle on the St. Joseph before moving to the Illinois Country? If so, why? Did Allouez exaggerate the number of Miami who lived at his Wisconsin mission? Or did some Miami living in Wisconsin move to Illinois? Definite answers to these questions have been elusive, and La Salle's maps and correspondences are no help in this quest.

Attempting to establish a self-sufficient colony in Louisiana, La Salle and 280 colonists, soldiers, and missionaries set sail to the Gulf in four vessels—the frigate *La Belle*; the supply ship *L'Aimable*; a ketch, the *St. François*; and a battleship escort, *Le Joly*, commanded by Captain Taneguy Le Gallois de Beaujeu.[17] Beaujeu was in charge of concerns while the vessels were at sea, whereas La Salle was responsible for matters pertaining to the colonists. The inevitable overlap between Beaujeu's and La Salle's responsibilities and authority led to outbursts and accusations. While still in the Greater Antilles, the *St. François* was seized by privateers somewhere off the coast of modern-day Haiti.[18] Missing the mouth of the Mississippi, the three remaining vessels landed off the Texas coast at Matagorda Bay. There the *L'Aimable* was lost at Cavallo Pass, the entrance to the bay. The future colonists saw confusion and discord among their leaders, and La Salle's arrogant attitude toward them made matters even worse. Two vessels had been lost, heated arguments between La Salle and Beaujeu destroyed any cohesion within the group, and the French realized that they were at the edge of the known European universe, far from succor or a way to extricate themselves from their situation. La Salle's leadership failed to give any confidence to the future colonists that would assure them that this venture could succeed, let alone flourish. Between a harsh and unfamiliar environment, hostile Indians, and the threat of Spanish attack, most French believed it was better to return home than risk their lives and their future with La Salle. Beaujeu along with 120 soldiers and colonists returned to France. La Salle eventually moved the remaining French inland from Matagorda Bay, where they built another Fort St. Louis near Garcitas Creek. In early 1686, *La Belle*, the last of La Salle's ships, the one carrying what remained of the supplies, trade goods, and war matériel, was grounded in the bay during a storm. La Salle's colony was now alone, isolated from the rest of the French-known world. The nearest place of refuge was his outpost at Le Rocher, nearly two thousand miles away following Indian trails and the courses of rivers. La Salle now had no other options than to try to reach his Illinois Valley fort.

La Salle left Fort St. Louis Texas on January 12, 1687, with 16 others.[19] On March 19, he was led into an ambush by several disgruntled men in his group and was killed. With him, for the meantime, died France's hope of establishing a self-sufficient colony and strategic port in the Lower Mississippi Valley.

Twelve years later, Pierre Le Moyne d'Iberville would sail to the Gulf and locate the Mississippi, what La Salle had failed to do. But part of La Salle's legacy, including his sweeping and illegitimate claim to Native lands between the Rockies and the Alleghenies, and the waters that flow into the Mississippi, would become part of the new United States in 1803, the Louisiana Purchase, a transaction that doubled the size of the new country. It would become the legal basis for the American seizure and takeover of tribal lands west of the Mississippi, a grandiose yet greedy attitude that would lead to nearly a century of war.

With La Salle away, Tonti and La Forest supervised the explorer's restored Illinois concession, Tonti as captain at the fort and La Forest as administrator of contracts and the manager of business affairs at Montreal. Having heard nothing about La Salle or his Gulf colony by early 1686, two and a half years since the explorer had left Le Rocher, Tonti and a group of about thirty Frenchmen and some Shawnee left the Illinois Valley fort and headed south to search for the explorer. Reaching the Gulf, Tonti and the others saw no colony, no fort, and no sign of La Salle, and this after searching the coast for many miles on either side of the mouth of the Mississippi. Without any idea of La Salle's whereabouts, the group returned north. At the Arkansas River, ten members of the group that included Louis Delaunay and Jean Couture asked permission to remain at the Arkansas on land La Salle had given to Tonti in 1682. Understanding that La Salle had planned to establish the French in the region, and since there was no French trading post beyond the Le Rocher, Tonti allowed the men to remain at the site. Inch by inch, even with La Salle's Gulf experiment ending in disaster, the French had opened the central Mississippi Valley to local trade relations with the region's tribes and its occupation by French adventurers.

In the Illinois Valley, Allouez was busy among the Illinois at Kaskaskia. In September several survivors from La Salle's Gulf debacle—including a group of Frenchmen that included Henri Joutel; two Sulpician priests, Jean Cavelier and Anastase Douay; La Salle's nephew Colin Cavelier; and a man named Tessier—arrived at the fort. Unable to continue on to Quebec because of rough seas on Lake Michigan, the group spent the winter of 1687–88 at Le Rocher. There three priests shared religious responsibilities at the fort, Allouez performing daily Mass in the fort's chapel and the two Sulpicians performing Mass during feast days.[20] This is the first time that priests from two different and competing Catholic religious orders served at the same location in the West. Hearing from the Texas survivors that La Salle was headed back to the fort, a lie to obtain credit on La Salle's behalf that allowed them to hire canoe men and guides and purchase supplies to get to Quebec, Allouez, hoping to avoid the explorer at all costs, left Le Rocher in mid-February 1688 for southwestern Michigan. Not long afterward, Joutel, the two Sulpicians, and the others left for Quebec, eventually arriving in France in October. There they relayed to French authorities their story of the failed colony.

Allouez would never again return to what is today's northern Illinois. He traveled to the St. Joseph River country where the aging priest worked among

The stone marking the grave site of Jesuit Claude-Jean Allouez in Berrien County, Michigan. Photo courtesy of the Fort St. Joseph Archaeological Project.

some Miami who returned to their former villages. The priest died at his mission in August 1689.

Allouez was the first Jesuit to venture to the Upper Country while the Haudenosaunee blockade of the route to the Great Lakes was ending. He had been abandoned in the wilderness by the Indians and left to die on a frozen river by his countrymen. He suffered many hardships and faced many dangers. He worked among a long list of western tribes and had established the missions in today's Wisconsin, Illinois, and Michigan. Being the only Jesuit on Native land for hundreds of miles, Allouez had never flinched when it came to calling out what he believed in his mind was pagan or immoral, yet he could just as easily assuage the tribesmen's ill feelings toward him and other Frenchmen. He was an important figure in the exploration of the West and the recording of its history. Even though he had charted the trail that led Marquette to the Upper Country, he later followed in the footsteps of the Jesuit who opened the way west for him and his order, Jacques Marquette.

Epilogue

It is uncertain exactly when Jacques Gravier, the next Jesuit to work among the Illinois at Kaskaskia, arrived at the village. Lionel Lindsay writing for *The Catholic Encyclopedia* maintains that he succeeded Allouez at the Illinois mission in 1687 (Allouez was still in the Illinois Country in 1687 and part of 1688), while Charles O'Neill writing in the *Dictionary of Canadian Biography* wrote that he took residence among the Illinois in 1689.[1] According to Jesuit historian Charlevoix, Gravier arrived in the Le Rocher area after he learned of La Salle's death, which occurred in 1687. Jesuits Jacques Lamberville and Pierre-Gabriel Marest place him in the Illinois Country in about 1690.

Gravier landed in Quebec in 1685. There he lived at the Jesuit *collège* and soon after, like nearly all newly arrived Jesuit missionaries, moved to Sillery.[2] Heading west he labored at the Sault before arriving at Kaskaskia. While among the Illinois, he worked out the grammar of the Miami-Illinois language and contributed to the compilation of words and expressions that would become part of the well-known Illinois-French dictionary commonly but incorrectly attributed to him.[3] Working with Gravier, likely leaving St. Joseph after Allouez's death, was Jacques Largillier. Largillier not only worked as Gravier's scribe, but also assisted the priest "collecting, analyzing, and interpreting much of the raw data on the language."[4] Gravier's and Largillier's work among the Illinois was not only clarifying, categorizing, and solidifying what the Jesuits knew about the Miami-Illinois language, but also paving the way forward in the order's understanding, comprehending, and perception of the Miami-Illinois speaking people. Gravier's arrival among the Illinois began a new phase of the western ministry of the order.

◇◇◇◇◇◇◇◇◇◇◇◇◇◇◇

The inevitable disagreements and long-held grudges and animosities that had been festering beneath the surface among colony tribes, especially between the Miami and Illinois, began to emerge. By 1689 the non-Illinois groups abandoned the villages they had established in 1683. Some Miami groups began infiltrating the Chicago area, where in 1696, Jesuit Pierre-François Pinet established the Mission de l'Ange Gardien. Slowly and deliberately, the Illinois began leaving Kaskaskia and relocating at Lake Peoria, and, by 1690, only about a thousand of the original six thousand remained. By autumn 1691, Kaskaskia was abandoned. With the Illinois living 110 miles away by canoe, the French abandoned their Le Rocher fort and moved to Lake Peoria. Following the Illinois to the lake were Gravier, Largillier, and a missionary new to the Illinois Country, Sébastien Râles. Other Jesuits, including Julien Bineteau and Gabriel Marest, would later be associated with the Lake Peoria mission.

The Peoria, Kaskaskia, Moingwena, and other subtribes settled along the lake in about 260 cabins, or a population of about fifty-two hundred.[5] The new French Peoria settlement consisted of several structures, including one for lodging, a warehouse, soldiers' quarters, and outside of the palisades a chapel. After La Salle's death, his concession was transferred to Tonti and La Forest, who had invested heavily in the Illinois concession while La Salle was away. Tonti later ceded half his share in the company to his brother Alphonse, while La Forest sold half of his to Michel Accault. Trade at Lake Peoria was short-lived, however, because French markets were so overstocked with beaver that many western trading posts were closed. But still, the Lake Peoria post was allowed to operate but under strict limitations since officials suspected that the British would take advantage of the void left by the French if trade was outlawed entirely. Consequently, and with the exception of the Lake Peoria post, rather than contest the British in the West, the French decided, instead, to focus colonization efforts on the Lower Mississippi and the Gulf, essentially resurrecting a modified version of La Salle's scheme for the region.[6]

As mentioned in an earlier chapter, in late 1698 three missionaries of the Société des Missions Étrangères guided by Tonti and a group of French canoe men paddled down the Illinois and Mississippi. Their destination was the French post on the Arkansas River. The group planned to extend Catholic instruction and conversion beyond the Jesuit missions to the tribes of the Central and Lower Mississippi Valley.

About the time Tonti was escorting the missionaries to the Arkansas, Henri Joutel was in France, finalizing the journal of his voyage with La Salle and his subsequent trek to Quebec. The new French minister, Louis Phélypeaux, Comte de Pontchartrain, who succeeded the late Seignelay, requested from Joutel a copy of his journal to help guide a second expedition to locate the Mississippi via the Gulf, one led by naval officer Pierre Le Moyne d'Iberville. Joutel complied with the minister's request, and Pontchartrain provided d'Iberville a copy of the journal.[7] Leaving France in 1698, d'Iberville's expedition arrived at the Gulf the following January and reached the Mississippi Delta in early March. To secure the river mouth, he constructed a temporary fort at present Ocean Springs, Mississippi, and then sailed to France. Returning the following year, he erected a second fortification, Fort La Boulaye, also called the "Mississippi Fort," located on the Mississippi River, some distance below modern-day New Orleans.[8]

Perhaps having heard rumors that the French were now on the Lower Mississippi, and that traders might soon be headed north with canoes loaded with goods and supplies, the Kaskaskia at Lake Peoria and their missionary, Pierre-Gabriel Marest, separated from the Peoria and Moingwena and established a new village at Rivière des Pères, in present St. Louis. Other Jesuits including Father Jean Boré, Father François Pinet, and Brother François Guibert would live and work among the Kaskaskia with Marest.[9] It is likely, too, that La Salle's bison trader, Michel Accault, who had since returned to the Illinois Country after his capture by the Nadouessi and who had married a Kaskaskia woman at Lake Peoria, also lived at Rivière des Pères during this time. Accompanying the group to their new camps was Gravier, who recently returned to the Illinois Country from a stint as superior at Michilimackinac. Gravier would continue to the Lower Mississippi to determine if the French had, indeed, established a base near the Gulf.[10]

Gravier was against the breakup of the Illinois groups at Lake Peoria. The departure of the Kaskaskia was more than a simple relocation that might put them in a better situation to obtain trade goods. It struck at the core at what the Jesuits believed was the cohesion of the Inohka alliance, it put distance between the various Illinois groups, and it left the Peoria mission without a missionary. The move also provoked the resentment of the Peoria and Moingwena.

Gravier, and the Jesuits before him, viewed the Illinois mission as an assembly of subgroups that melded into a single entity. But by this point in their history, the Illinois groups were no longer collecting at one large village site; they were now separating into different groups at different locations. Perhaps some of the novelty of the Frenchmen had worn off and the Illinois simply returned to the settlement pattern that they practiced prior to French contact. The Peoria told Gravier that they would remain at Lake Peoria until the "great Chief who is at the lower end of the river" told them where to relocate.[11]

Reaching the Mississippi, Marest, Gravier, and the Kaskaskia passed a village of Cahokia who likely resided at Kaskaskia before its abandonment more than a decade earlier, and four leagues later, they disembarked at Rivière des Pères. After remaining with the Kaskaskia for four days, Gravier, Marest, and their entourage continued downriver until they disembarked at a Tamaroa village, located about two leagues south of the new Kaskaskia site.[12] There they were greeted by Marc Bergier, acting vicar-general of the region; his assistant, Michel Buisson de St. Cosme, younger brother of missionary St. Cosme, both of the Société des Missions Étrangères; and Jesuits Pinet and Joseph de Limoges.

Although the name "Tamaroa" was applied to the site, the Tamaroa tribe proper only accounted for about one-third of the Tamaroa village population. The village site was named Tamaroa in honor of the tribe who was said to have been the village's original occupant.[13] Also living there were some Cahokia, Peoria, Michigamea, and about two thousand sojourning Missouri Indians.

A jurisdictional dispute arose during this time between the Jesuits and the seminary priests. The Jesuits maintained that, as stated in a 1690 proclamation, the Illinois missions and those of the Miami and Nadouessi fall under their authority. The decree asserts that fathers of the Society of Jesus

> have been working in the mission of the Illinois which they were the first to discover and to which Father Marquette of the same Society announced the Faith, beginning in the year 1672 [1673], subsequently dying in that glorious occupation, which had been committed to him by our predecessor; and [knowing] that after the death of Father Marquette we placed in charge of it Father Allouez, also a Jesuit, after laboring there many years, closed his life, worn out by the excessive hardships which he endured in the instruction for the conversion of the Illinois, Miami, and other nations; and as, finally, we have delivered the care of this mission of the Illinois and other surrounding [tribes] to Father Gravier of the same Society, who has been engaged [in the work] with great

blessing of God upon his labors; for these reasons we continue and ratify what we have done and, altogether anew, we commit the mission of the Illinois and the surrounding [tribes] as also those of the Miami, the Sioux, and other [tribes] of the Ottawa country and towards the setting [sun] to the Fathers of the Society of Jesus and we give to the Superiors of the said missions all the powers of our Vicar-Generals.[14]

The Jesuits claimed that they were the first Catholic order to visit Illinois lands and to establish missions in Illinois villages, and they would continue to do so. Moreover, the relocation of the Cahokia, Tamaroa, Kaskaskia, and others to the Mississippi from the Illinois Valley had no bearing on their religious authority over the tribe. Gravier maintained that by virtue of the 1690 proclamation, his order was entitled to religious jurisdiction over the site. However, the seminary priests argued that Bishop St. Vallier's (second bishop of Quebec) letter of patent authorized them to evangelize the tribes located "on this side and that of the Mississippi River and along the entire length of that river and the tributaries discharging therein . . . without its being permitted to other missionaries of different bodies [the Jesuits] to make establishments unless with the consent of [the Seminary Priests] in places where they shall be established or either in other places which they shall have chosen in agreement with us or our Vicar generals."[15]

As we have seen in a previous chapter, the seminary priests, including Montigny, Davion, and St. Cosme, had been sent to the central/Lower Mississippi to work among the tribes there. Their presence along the Great River was authorized by St. Vallier, who maintained that a Catholic order other than the powerful Jesuits should be introduced to the Mississippi below the Illinois.[16] St. Vallier's proclamation was supported by Canadian bishop François de Laval. The seminary priests understood that the Tamaroa mission was the gateway to tribes who lived along the Missouri, Ohio, and Mississippi Rivers, where along the latter stream, from Tamaroa to the Gulf, Bergier estimated lived twenty thousand Indians.[17] Besides, while the Jesuits still worked among the tribes living at Lake Peoria, the seminary priests had settled among the Cahokia and Tamaroa, making them the first Catholic order to do so.

Although the jurisdictional dispute and interorder rivalry between the Jesuits and the Société des Missions Étrangères persisted, Gravier reported that Bergier and Pinet maintained a friendly and professional relationship. He wrote that Pinet labored among the Indians, while Bergier acted as chaplain to the French.

Gravier and his group left Marest, who was ill at the time, at the Tamaroa and with his group continued to the Gulf.

In 1701 a committee of French bishops determined that the seminary priests would maintain ecclesiastical jurisdiction over the Illinois groups headquartered at Cahokia and at the Tamaroa. The Jesuits would have authority among the Illinois groups residing at Lake Peoria and Le Rocher and, after 1703, at the second Kaskaskia.[18] Later, as the tribes established new camps along the American Bottoms, the Société des Missions Étrangères would have authority to send their priests to the new villages.

◇◇◇◇◇◇◇◇◇◇◇◇◇◇◇◇

Gravier carried with him as a guide to his journey down the Mississippi a copy of Marquette's 1673 report and a copy of La Salle's Mississippi memoir. He noted while at a Kappa Arkansas village that a chief told him that his people had danced the calumet dance for Jolliet and Marquette, a claim that the priest verified in Marquette's journal. Gravier also described, as Marquette had, the power of the calumet. The missionary wrote, "No such honors are paid to the crowns and scepters of Kings as those that they pay to it [the calumet]. It seems to be the God of Peace and of war, the arbiter of life and of death. It suffices for one to carry and to show it, to walk in safety in the midst of Enemies, who in the hottest of the Fight lay down their weapons when it is displayed. That is why the Illinois gave one to the late Father Marquette, as a safeguard among the tribes of the Mississippi through whom he must pass on his voyage, when he went to discover that river and the nations that dwell along It."[19]

About La Salle's memoir, Gravier mentioned passing Fort Prudhomme, where the explorer's gunsmith, Pierre Prudhomme, had been lost in the forest for several days; passing Rivière a Mayot, a stream named for a Mohegan in La Salle's group; and seeing the whirlpool that La Salle mentioned in his account. He may have also read Joutel's journal as the priest mentioned that La Salle's assassins fled to the Cenis, that La Salle had missed the mouth of the Mississippi, and that rather than acknowledge his error, out of spite, he continued for another eighty leagues. He also mentioned that La Salle's brother, "the priest," along with four others hiked across Arkansas country to reach safety in present-day Illinois and, ultimately, France.[20]

Contrary to La Salle's report to Seignelay, that the lands along the Lower Mississippi were fertile, natural resources were plentiful, and the climate was pleasant, Gravier saw the opposite; the air was filled with clouds of biting insects, mud along the shore was several feet deep, and snakes were plentiful, which reportedly even ate "lettuce and other vegetables down to the roots."[21] Further, the heat was intense, the Indians were destitute, conditions were favorable for fevers, and the river was too shallow to float French vessels.

Eighteen leagues from the Gulf, Gravier reached Jean-Baptiste Le Moyne de Bienville's Fort Mississippi on December 17, 1700.[22] The missionary reported that the post had neither walls, bastions, entrenchments, nor redoubts and that the roofs of the five or six cabins there were covered with palms.[23] The dozen or so pieces of artillery located along the side of a hill were not meant to impress the local warriors, but were meant to defend against the English who, a year earlier, had sent an exploratory expedition under a Captain Bond to occupy the Lower Mississippi.[24] The priest also learned that Bond had carried with him a copy of La Salle's *relation* to guide him during his voyage up the Mississippi.[25] The Frenchmen at the fort were also nearly out of food because some of their fields had been inundated by tide waters.

Gravier also traveled to d'Iberville's "Fort Bilocchi" (Biloxi), where he, d'Iberville, first constructed a fort that was located near the coast at present Ocean Springs, Mississippi. Two years later, both the Mississippi and the Biloxi (Fort Maurepas) forts would be abandoned, and a new site near Mobile would become headquarters for the French in the region.[26]

In only twenty-seven years, from the time of Jolliet and Marquette's voyage, the West was not only known to the French but *well known*. Soldiers, sailors, priests, and others who had infiltrated the region were learning the layout of the Lower Mississippi and beyond. In a letter to his brother, Tonti, who had volunteered to join d'Iberville on the Gulf, described in detail the rivers of the Lower Mississippi Valley, the location of villages along the rivers, the number of warriors who lived in the villages, and the estimated distances between the villages and the Gulf.[27] Other French, including Bienville, were, during the same time, exploring rivers such as the Red and the Ouachita.[28]

La Salle had convinced Seignelay that a colony near the Gulf would be self-sufficient, needing little support from France. But this was not the case. By 1710 only three to four hundred people had settled in Louisiana. France, having exhausted its wealth in the War of the Spanish Succession, was unable and unwilling to provide the resources needed to maintain the struggling colony. The Crown decided that Louisiana should be managed by concession, like Canada had been in its early days, and that Antoine Crozat would be its concessionaire. Crozat agreed to manage the enterprise based on exaggerated claims of Louisiana's potential wealth by the new civil governor, Antoine Laumet de Lamothe Cadillac. In 1712 he formed a company to develop Louisiana, Crozat contributing 600,000 to 700,000 livres of his own money to the franchise.[29] Crozat was granted complete control over Louisiana's trade, both foreign and domestic, including the African slave trade. He was authorized to appoint government officials, exploit mines, and control agriculture. For these privileges, he was required to send two ships of supplies and settlers each year and was obliged to "govern the colony in accordance with French laws and Customs."[30] Crozat and his enterprise was granted a fifteen-year lease. As promising as the Louisiana concession may have seemed to him, an enterprise based on embellished claims, Crozat soon realized that not even he could guide the colony into solvency. The lack of exploitable resources, few exports of goods, an unhealthy climate, sickness, his inability to relocate settlers, mismanagement by unqualified appointees, and his own failure to invest more in the colony eventually led to the company's collapse. Petitioning the court, Crozat was relieved of his responsibilities in 1717, the year Louisiana was removed from the jurisdiction of Canada and became its own colony. Waiting in the wings and believing that he could salvage what remained of Crozat's enterprise was Scottish financier John Law.

Law was well known in French social circles as the founder of a private bank, the Banque Générale, who had convinced the Crown to allow him to print paper money, a system based on the bank's gold and silver assets, to create a medium of exchange.[31] He offered to the public shares in his bank, money from which went to pay off the state's debt, which he also assumed. Law organized the Compagnie d'Occident, commonly known as the Mississippi Company, and he absorbed other trading firms into his orbit, essentially establishing a worldwide trade monopoly. He effectively maintained authority over all trade between France and Louisiana, Canada, Africa, and China. In Canada and Louisiana, Law's company, like Crozat's, had the power to control commerce and trade, exploit mines, appoint judges, and manage relations with the tribes, and it was given authority over all ports, forts, and garrisons.[32] The company also agreed to transport six thousand settlers and three thousand slaves before its twenty-five-year charter expired.[33]

Law created what appeared to be at the time a secure environment for investment.[34] In reality, speculation abounded in not only France but also Europe, and wealth became tied to paper money. But its value slowly began to diminish and eventually no longer reflected the bank's actual assets. Law printed promotional literature designed to convince potential stakeholders of the fortunes that could be made investing in his company. But the wealth his stakeholders believed would be extracted from Louisiana and New France never materialized; it was, in fact, never really there to begin with. By 1721 Law's so-called bubble had burst, and he and his company were forced into bankruptcy. Except for investors who had sold their interests before company stock plummeted, many were driven into financial ruin. Law himself was reportedly run out of Paris by a mob.[35]

◇◇◇◇◇◇◇◇◇◇◇◇◇◇

While the Illinois trade concession was coming to an end, another industry was attempting to break into the market, that of the tannery. In 1700 Charles Juchereau de St-Denys convinced the Crown, despite the king's desire to close the western posts, to allow him to establish a tannery near the confluence of the Ohio and Mississippi Rivers. The Wabash, Cumberland, Tennessee, and Missouri Rivers, the region's highways at the time, converged near the Ohio-Mississippi confluence, making the site a prime location for collecting hides. With the western trading posts closed, disgruntled French traders, feeling their livelihoods threatened, had no qualms about trading with the English. To prevent illicit trade and to keep the English in check, one reason for France's renewed interest in the Lower Mississippi, Juchereau was permitted to establish his tannery. The decision, however, was soon contested by the Compagnie du Canada, which believed Juchereau's tannery would invite illegal trade and eventually lead to the company's ruin. Although the tannery scheme seemed promising, it came to naught. Juchereau died in 1703, perhaps from an epidemic that spread through the region during that time.[36]

The Kaskaskia and their Jesuit associates at Rivière des Pères left their camps in 1703 and relocated to a site approximately two leagues upstream from the mouth of the "River Metchigamea," as it was called then, the Kaskaskia River, in present Randolph County, Illinois.[37] Also settling at the site amid the Kaskaskia and Jesuits were several French traders, their Illinois wives, and a large group of Michigamea. During its early years, Kaskaskia was a mission settlement, not a French settlement.[38] The large groups of Indians, disgruntled traders, and priests gathered at the site soon proved to be incompatible with each other. Traders, who had lost their livelihoods because Illinois trade had closed, incited the tribesmen to conduct raids against other tribes to capture slaves, which the traders would sell to the English. The Jesuits struggled to keep the traders' influence and interference to a minimum, but by 1708 the missionaries had finally had enough and requested help from Bienville, now civil governor of Louisiana. The governor sent a Sieur d'Eraque and six men to reestablish order at the village. The situation settled, but again, in 1711, Marest had to again request help to suppress the traders, who were now reportedly debauching Native women to prevent their religious conversion. This time the governor dispatched a sergeant and twelve men to establish and preserve order.[39]

One account of life at Kaskaskia during this time describes the settlement's church as a structure with a steeple and a bell. Inside were three chapels and a baptismal font. In the early morning, the settlement's converts arrived at the church for Catholic instruction and to recite prayers. When services concluded, the priest visited and comforted the village sick. Natives and habitants reportedly worked the fields together, tilling the soil, and planting and harvesting vegetables, even growing "excellent French melons."[40]

During the summer of 1714, an epidemic spread through the region. Two of its victims were Marest, the missionary, and Jacques Largillier, the voyageur, scribe, and Jesuit lay helper. In 1719 the Michigamea left the village and resettled downstream near the site of the future Fort de Chartres. The Kaskaskia also distanced themselves from the French.

The departure of the two Illinois groups from Kaskaskia is reflective of a new paradigm in the settling of the Illinois Country. Whereas a handful of French and large groups of Illinois lived in proximity to each other at Le Rocher, Lake Peoria, and at French Kaskaskia, the arrival of French military officials, settlers, and assorted tradesmen by way of the Mississippi switched the settlement pattern from coexistence to take over. With the establishment of Fort de Chartres in 1720, military officials imposed themselves and their order on the local Illinois. It is understandable that French officials, some of whom had never been to the frontiers of North America, and who had been sent to Louisiana to defend the young colony from hostile Indians as well as British and Spanish encroachment, would employ a less than cordial tone. The same sort of disinterested authority toward the tribesmen also occurred at new French posts located farther south.[41]

French Kaskaskia continued to grow, and by 1721 there were, according to village records, sixty-four habitants, forty-two "white laborers," twenty-eight married women, and seventeen children, considerably more Frenchmen than at Cahokia, where only seven habitants, one white laborer, one married woman, and three children lived.[42] That same year, Louisiana was divided into nine military districts, New Orleans, Biloxi, Mobile, "Alabamons," Natchez, "Yazouz," Natchitoches, Arkansas, and Illinois. In 1722 the first provincial council was established in the Illinois district. The council was tasked with "rendering justice in the first degree and with administering the affairs of the Company [the Mississippi Company]."[43]

Gravier returned from the South and reestablished his mission at Lake Peoria in 1702. Whether it was because the Peoria shamans, the "Dreamers," as we saw in a previous chapter, believed that their power was threatened by Gravier, or perhaps the priest's dogmatic attitude that disparaged long-held Peoria beliefs and customs was no longer tolerable, some Peoria began to develop an antipathy toward the Jesuits and their teachings. Gravier had been the target of at least two attempts on his life by the Peoria.[44] At one of the villages in 1705, a Peoria attacked the priest, shooting him with an arrow that entered his arm through his wrist, lodging in his elbow. The priest survived the attack but suffered greatly because the arrow point could not be removed. Gravier and Largillier escaped the village and traveled to Mobile from where Gravier sailed to France in search of a surgeon who could remove the point. Unsuccessful at this, Gravier sailed back to Mobile, where he died from his wound in 1708. With his departure, the Peoria mission was closed until 1712, when it was reestablished by Gabriel Marest.

◇◇◇◇◇◇◇◇◇◇◇◇◇◇

Kaskaskia on the Upper Illinois had been abandoned by the Illinois by the autumn of 1691. Other than possible temporary occupation by some small Native groups passing through the area, or perhaps by some wintering Illinois in the mid-eighteenth century, the village as a semipermanent agricultural site ceased to exist. The site next appears in the historical record in 1821, when the Cass-Schoolcraft party passed through the property on horseback during their journey to Fort Dearborn at Chicago from St. Louis, guided by a Potawatomi chief named Peerish. The site, according to Peerish, was where the Kaskaskia made their last stand before retreating to Le Rocher, where they were killed by their enemies, a traditional oral tale with no support from written sources or archaeology. Schoolcraft reported that the site had been "completely encompassed by a ditch and wall, the remains of which are still conspicuous, and the whole extent of the lines is easily traced."[45] Besides these anomalies, Schoolcraft noted that nothing else remained of any Native American occupation at the site.

Two months later, General Land Office surveyor William Rector surveyed the land of the Kaskaskia village, defining the west and north margins of the site. He described the river bottoms that surrounded old Kaskaskia as "an extensive prairie."[46] In 1852 the Sulfur Springs Hotel was built on the old village site along present Dee Bennett Road. The hotel's name comes from a sulfur spring located a short distance behind the structure, a feature not mentioned in any reports of traders or missionaries who visited the village during the seventeenth century. The structure was originally a tavern and hotel but by the 1860s was converted into a private residence. The hotel boasted twenty-eight rooms, each with its own fireplace. The first and second floors contained accommodations for sulfur treatments and were also used as parlors. In 1899–1900, the Army Corps of Engineers surveying the Illinois before the reversal of the Chicago River and the construction of the lock and dam system passed the Kaskaskia site, noting the shoreline, taking depth readings, and marking the composition of the river's bottom.[47] With construction of the Starved Rock Lock and Dam, completed in 1933, the depth of the Illinois River increased by approximately ten feet, which soon began eroding the old village shoreline and submerging several islands associated with the site.

Historian Francis Parkman came to La Salle County, Illinois, while writing his famous book, *La Salle and the Discovery of the Great West* (1867). During his visit, he met with a local landowner, Jim Clark, who owned property two miles west of the Kaskaskia site. Parkman, seeking to find the location of the Illinois village from the time of La Salle, inquired if Clark or his tenant had ever uncovered "Indian remains," to which Clark said "yes, on his [Clark's] land." However, the site where the items were found were not above Le Rocher, as period documents indicate, but more than a mile downstream from it. Parkman concluded that Kaskaskia was located two miles west of where period sources spell out where it was. Parkman and Clark did not know it at the time, but the relics found in Clark's field dated from the Woodland Period, two thousand years before Marquette's arrival in the region. Consequently, historians combining Parkman's mistake, local lore, and Peerish's statements to Schoolcraft wrote that Kaskaskia, by then erroneously known as La Vantum, or Illinois Town, concocted stories of tremendous battles that were fought at the site between the Illinois and their enemies before the Illinois fled to Le Rocher, now known as Starved Rock, where they were all killed. Some of these books and articles include John Dean Caton's *The Last of the Illinois: And a Sketch of the*

Pottawatomies (1870), Nehemiah Matson's *French and Indians of the Illinois River* (1874), Harry Spooner's *Indians of Northern Illinois* (1941), and others. During the 1940s, Dr. Sara Jones Tucker of the University of Chicago, referencing period writings, located the actual site of the Kaskaskia village.

In 1987 Thomas Emerson, chief archaeologist of the Illinois State Historic Preservation Agency, learned that the Landings Development Limited Partnership (LDLP) planned to construct on the village site a "181-lot, year-round private resort community" of "luxurious pole homes." The group also planned to turn the old Sulfur Springs Hotel into a private bed-and-breakfast. Although few local residents knew much about the actual history of the site, when the news broke that a developer planned to build a resort over the old village, interest grew. Spokespersons, including Emerson, communicated to media outlets to educate the public about the site's significance. In Emerson's words, "This is one of the two or three most important archaeological sites in the state of Illinois" and that the site was where "prehistory blends into history." Although the state of Illinois had several opportunities to purchase the property, there was no sense of urgency until the LDLP bought the property, in January 1988, for $485,000. Prior to LDLP's purchase of the site, former owner Mrs. Keating wanted $500,000 for it, but the state could pay only $200,000, being bound by laws that forbade it to pay over assessed value, except in rare cases. Interest in the development continued to grow. Regional and national groups grew concerned about the site's future, as were tribal groups, and even the Catholic Church, since the site was where Marquette established the first Catholic mission in today's Illinois. At this point, it looked as if the site was doomed for destruction. However, the state continued to negotiate with the LDLP, but to no avail; the company now wanted $4.2 million for the land. For the next two years, the state and LDLP continued to negotiate. In April 1991, an agreement was reached between the two parties, the state agreeing to pay $1,030,000. In October, the site became state property and was renamed the Grand Village of the Illinois State Historical Site. The following year, a $150,000 gift by James Gallop, a Chicago-area businessman, provided moneys to fund the Grand Village Research Project.[48] The next year, a five-year archaeological project and inventory commenced at the site. Although the state has done little to develop the property, the old village is now protected from development and vandalism.

What Marquette and later Jesuits in the Illinois Country hoped to achieve by Christianizing and Gallicizing the Illinois changed the tribe's culture, way of life, and identity, but not necessarily to its benefit. Both secular and religious forces/ influence, intentional or not, combined to strip the Illinois of their customs, culture, spiritual beliefs, and in time, under the British and American regimes, their land. European-borne disease, alcoholism, monogamy, domestic animal husbandry, war, and other forces worked to reduce the once proud tribe to one-fifth of its population in less than a century, and this even with the addition of the Michigamea to the Inohka alliance.[49]

The attempt to Christianize and assimilate Native Americans into white culture in the United States and Canada continued into the nineteenth and twentieth centuries. As it relates to Native American groups in the Upper Country, Indian boarding schools among the Odawa were established after the War of 1812, originally a cooperative effort between the local Odawa and Christian missionaries. The mission school at Little Traverse Bay in Michigan, built in 1829, was followed by the opening of Catholic schools at Cross Village, Middle Village, and Burt Lake. By 1887 the U.S. government began dictating standards to which the Odawa schools were required to follow. Some of the regulations imposed on Odawa children included forbidding them to speak their Native language and strict dress codes. In addition, they were prohibited from participating in tribal ceremonies. The children also spent long periods away from family and support. Failure to follow the federal mandates could result in severe punishment for the children. The church-state program to indoctrinate Odawa children led to the loss of their language, culture, and history. The mind-set behind their so-called assimilation into white culture at the time was best spoken by Richard Pratt, founder of the American boarding schools for Indigenous children, who said "that all the Indian there is in the race should be dead. Kill the Indian in him and save the man."[50] All told, in the United States, more than one hundred thousand Native American children were taken from their homes and forced to attend government schools, facilities "advancing eradication" of Native American culture.[51]

In Canada, too, Native children were forced to attend church-state-sponsored boarding schools. And the tragedy continues to this day. In the spring of 2021, a horrific discovery at the site of a former Tk'emlúps te Secwépemc First Nation boarding school in Kamloops, British Columbia, revealed the remains of 215 children, some as young as three years of age, in an unmarked mass grave. Then again, a month later, 751 bodies were discovered in unmarked graves near a former "residential school" for Indigenous children located about eighty-five miles east of Regina, Saskatchewan.[52] According to one report, of the 150,000

Indigenous children who attended Canadian Indian boarding schools, 6,000 of them never returned home.[53]

In the 1760s, the Illinois groups lived along the Mississippi River in southern Illinois near places such as Fort de Chartres, Kaskaskia, and at Cahokia. In 1766 about 1,000 Peoria relocated a few miles south of St. Louis. In spring 1775, one group of Kaskaskia settled south, first at the Arkansas River and then on the White River. By the end of 1777, these Kaskaskia had returned to Illinois and settled among the Peoria near St. Louis and at Cahokia. By 1778 only about 50 Illinois remained in southern Illinois, and eight years later only 8 to 10 Kaskaskia men called the area home.[54] The once populous Kaskaskia subtribe of the Inohka alliance, whose village on the Upper Illinois was the magnet that drew French missionaries and traders to the region, and men such as La Salle, who pinned his hopes of establishing a commercial trade route and empire through the interior of the continent, were reduced to no more than 100 people. The Illinois ceded what few parcels of land they claimed to the British (1773) and then to the Americans in 1804 (Treaty of Vincennes), 1818 (Treaty of Edwardsville), and 1832 (Treaty of Castor Hill), the last of which being the final compact that relinquished their remaining lands in Illinois and Missouri. That same year, the Illinois moved to the Osage River in Kansas, where in 1854 they merged with the Wea and Piankashaw, Miami subtribes, the group becoming the Consolidated Peoria. In 1868 the Peoria and the Miami moved to northeastern Oklahoma, where they became the Peoria Indian Tribe of Oklahoma. Today, the Peoria maintain tribal headquarters in Miami, Oklahoma.

By the mid-1700s, the Potawatomi began to fill the void left by the departing Illinois. Potawatomi villages in northern Illinois include ones at Chicago; the forks of the Kankakee and Des Plaines; on the Kankakee, Fox, and Illinois Rivers; at Indian and Somonauk Creeks; and at wooded groves throughout the prairies. By 1763 the Potawatomi had claimed all lands along the Illinois River between the Forks and Le Rocher as their hunting grounds.[55] Interspersed among the Potawatomi groups, once part of the *aniššina·pe·k*, were Odawa and Ojibwe families. During the early nineteenth century, the Odawa Shabbona, who was married to a Potawatomi woman, was chief of a band of Potawatomi in northern Illinois. At the end of the Black Hawk War of 1832, the second to the last U.S.-Indian war east of the Mississippi, the Sauk, Mesquakie, Ho-Chunk, Potawatomi, and Illinois were compelled to sign land cession treaties with the U.S. government for lands they claimed in today's Illinois and move west of the

Mississippi. In 1833 the *aniššina·pe·k* signed the final land cession, the Treaty of Chicago, relinquishing their remaining land in Illinois, also agreeing to move across the Great River.

◇◇◇◇◇◇◇◇◇◇◇◇◇◇

Despite the French administration's best efforts to keep their population along the Lower St. Lawrence, the Crown still allowed certain individuals like La Salle to explore, establish trade alliances with the tribes, and even colonize the restricted territories—a contradictory policy that led to confusion and, to some, ruin. The French population of North America was by 1720 thinly spread across approximately two thousand miles between Quebec and New Orleans. Besides their need to populate Lower Louisiana, exploit any and all natural resources discovered, and maintain order among themselves, the French also dealt with British encroachment onto French-claimed territory, attacks by the Chickasaw and Natchez, and keeping the Mississippi River open for traffic and safe from attack. The Mississippi was the lifeline, the vital link between the colony's breadbasket, the Illinois Country, and the Gulf. Furs, grain, and other commodities moved down the river, while supplies, slaves, and other goods were carried north. Settlement along the Lower Mississippi, whether by design or not, became the king's concern. To protect his interests and to accelerate trade into new territories, the French constructed forts and posts, including Fort Rosalie near present Natchez (1716) and Fort de Chartres in the Illinois district (1720). Branching out from the Mississippi, the French built Fort St. Pierre on the Yazoo River (1719), Fort St. Jean Baptiste des Natchitoches on the Red River in Louisiana (1716), and St. Louis de Caddodoches on the Red River in Arkansas (1719). In Alabama they built Fort Toulouse at the juncture of the Coosa and Tallapoosa Rivers (1717).

By 1719 Frenchmen had already explored parts of eastern Oklahoma, northern Alabama, and Arkansas. They established military and economic ties with the populous Choctaw tribe while at the same time working to appease the Chickasaw, consorts of the British, who used the Chickasaw to attack French bateaux on the Mississippi and who played to the disenchantment of the Choctaw concerning the French's inability to supply them trade goods. The British also encouraged the Choctaw and Chickasaw to form an alliance, a "reconciliation," that would threaten French occupation in the region. The Chickasaw also angered the French by sheltering and failing to hand over to them several hundred Natchez refugees, survivors of the French attempt to destroy the tribe after an "uprising" that occurred in 1729.[56] As allies to the French, the Choctaw were becoming increasingly unreliable.

To strike a blow against the Chickasaw, a Franco-Native force under Pierre d'Artaguette left Fort de Chartres in February 1736 and marched to Chickasaw territory. From the south, a forced led by Bienville was supposed to move north, the two forces trapping the Chickasaw in between. D'Artaguette had been instructed by Governor Bienville to proceed to a site near present Memphis and to wait there until receiving word that Bienville's force was in Chickasaw territory. Hearing nothing of Bienville's whereabouts, running short on supplies, and believing that the villages were vulnerable, d'Artaguette resolved to attack the Chickasaw at their town of Ogoula Tchetoka. But unbeknownst to d'Artaguette, the Chickasaw were expecting the French. Reaching the site, d'Artaguette's force was surrounded, overwhelmed, and crushed. D'Artaguette and several of his officers were captured and killed by the victorious tribesmen. Two months later, Bienville's tardy force was also defeated by the Chickasaw at their fortified village of Ackia. In 1740 Bienville launched another offensive against a fortified Chickasaw position, this time with forces drawn from Canada, Michilimackinac, Illinois, and New Orleans, the battle ending in a draw. Shortly thereafter, a peace agreement was initiated between the Chickasaw and French.[57] By 1743 the conflict, for all practical purposes, was over.[58]

◇◇◇◇◇◇◇◇◇◇◇◇◇◇◇

The Jesuits in the Illinois Country received financial support from wealthy donors and from the Mississippi Company. Their support included land grants, assorted stipends, and funds to construct a chapel and house at Kaskaskia. The order owned large tracts of land on which crops were grown and harvested, ground in their mills, and often used in their breweries. Labor on Jesuit-owned lands came from African and Indian slaves who not only labored on site, but also raised families, the children of which were required by law to be baptized in the Catholic Church. French *engagés*, essentially indentured servants, also worked on Jesuit land. The order not only owned property and relied on slave labor to work the fields, clear timberlands, and act as servants, but was also deeply involved in the African slave trade. In fact, by 1720 the Jesuits were the largest slaveholders in the Illinois Country. By 1752 40 percent of Kaskaskia's population was composed of enslaved Black people.[59]

The Côde Noir, the Black Code of 1724, was introduced as a law that regulated relations between Blacks and French colonists. Based on the 1685 *côde* that regulated the treatment of slaves in French territories in the Caribbean, Louisiana's Côde Noir required, among many things, that masters impart Catholic teachings to their slaves, that Sundays and religious holidays be observed, that all children born of slaves be slaves, that owners provide their slaves food and clothing, and that masters could exact corporal punishment on their slaves who damage or steal property. Conversely, slaves were forbidden to carry weapons or sticks, to own property, or to denounce or speak ill of their masters. Slaves were chattel with few if any rights enjoyed by the French, Catholic white population of Louisiana.[60] Viewed from today's perspective, the Côde Noir was cruel, racist, and a codified blight on humanity. Twentieth-century scholars including Louis Sala-Molins, author of the *Dark Side of the Light: Slavery and the French Enlightenment*, described the Côde Noir as "the most monstrous legal document of modern times," nothing more than a "weak barrier to the master's tyranny." The Enlightenment philosopher Voltaire, commenting on the 1685 *côde*, wrote that "the Black Code only serves to show that the legal scholars consulted by Louis XIV had no ideas regarding human rights."[61]

In 1838 the administration of Georgetown University, a Jesuit school, sold 272 enslaved Africans to pay off the university's debt. In 2021 the Jesuit Conference of Canada and the United States pledged $100 million to be used toward the education of descendants of those slaves.[62]

In Europe the activities of the powerful Jesuits were coming under close scrutiny; rumors about them abounded. Between the order's entanglement in political affairs, questions about their wealth, and conflict between the order and European monarchs, combined with rumors such as assassination lists that contained the names of European sovereigns, cached wealth in a British palace, and their alleged plans to undermine European civilization, the tide of popularity, or at least respect, they once enjoyed began to crumble.[63] The order was banished from Portugal in 1759 and from Spain and France in 1773. Their exclusion extended to the kingdom's colonial holdings. The decree banishing the Jesuits from Louisiana arrived in July 1763 and included some of the following provisions:

- Their constitution was considered hostile to royal authority.
- They were forbidden to take the name Jesuit and were prohibited from wearing Jesuit garb (except some wearing apparel).
- Their property was to be seized and sold at auction.

- Their ornaments and sacred vessels were to be forfeited to the Capuchins at New Orleans.
- They were to return to France.[64]

While the Jesuits had been banished from Louisiana, the few Sulpician clergy-men who remained in the district abandoned their own parishes.

On January 1, 1763, nearly all French territories east of the Mississippi fell under British dominion. From the Atlantic to the Mississippi, a new regime would now claim the Illinois Country as their own. Although, on paper, the former French territory became British, it was not until October 1765 that the French relinquished Fort de Chartres to the victors. The Mississippi Valley east of the Great River and the Illinois Country was now part of King George III's empire.

◇◇◇◇◇◇◇◇◇◇◇◇◇◇◇

It seems possible that Colbert's decision to concentrate Canada's population in Lower Canada rather than allow settlements in the Illinois Country may have been a primary factor that compelled Jolliet to sever his ambitions in the West and to consider more attainable goals in the East. Even though his personal ambitions in the Upper Country may have come to an end, Jolliet set about to chart a new course for his life in the East. Earlier we saw that his valued input was instrumental in setting the price of beaver in Canada and that Governor Frontenac consulted him and other Canadians about the issue of the traffick-ing of alcohol outside of the settlements. We saw that Intendant Duchesneau granted Jolliet and Jacques de Lalande a concession east of Sept-Îsles and north of Anticosti Island and that he led at least one expedition to Hudson Bay. In 1685 he completed a map of the St. Lawrence River and Gulf, an endeavor that likely helped him become royal hydrographer in 1697. In 1694 he sailed the shoreline of Labrador and sketched a map of the coast. In November 1695, he was chosen to guide the vessel *Charente* down the St. Lawrence because he was "perhaps the only man in this country, according to Frontenac, capable of performing this work properly."[65] Jolliet continued with the vessel to France, returning the following June. In 1697 Jolliet was awarded a fief on the Etchemin River. During winter months, he taught at the Jesuit *collège*. His death, however, remains a mystery. He was last reported at Anticosti Island during the summer of 1700, where he mysteriously disappeared. Jolliet was not only a musician, landowner, explorer, trader, teacher, and government official; he was also a respected citizen of Canada.[66]

Jolliet's Canal

We saw that Louis Jolliet, according to Dablon's account of his and Jolliet's August 1, 1674, meeting in Quebec, suggested that a canal be excavated to allow barks to travel through the marshy lowland between the south branch of the Chicago River and the Des Plaines, Mud Lake, at the Chicago Portage. According to Dablon, based on information he received from Jolliet, the canal would allow vessels to "easily" sail from the Great Lakes above Niagara to the Gulf of Mexico. Even though historians today cling to Jolliet's statement as proof that the Illinois and Michigan Canal that links Chicago with LaSalle, Illinois (completed in 1848), was Jolliet's idea, only six years elapsed before the claim came under direct scrutiny.

We saw that La Salle had read Dablon's *relation* and studied at least one of Jolliet's maps, complaining to Frontenac about some of Jolliet's claims after he had personally traveled Lakes Erie, Huron, and Michigan as well as the Des Plaines and Illinois Rivers. In the case of Jolliet's canal, La Salle wrote to the governor that the prairies at the portage were "flooded by a great volume of water flowing down from the neighboring hills whenever it rains," and because of this, he declared that not only would Jolliet's canal be very expensive to excavate, but it would also "immediately fill up with sand and gravel." And even if Jolliet's canal had been built, he argued that it would be impractical anyway, because "the Divine River [the combined Des Plaines and Illinois Rivers] is unnavigable for forty leagues, the distance to the Great Village of the Illinois [Kaskaskia]. Canoes cannot traverse it during the summer and even then there are long rapids this side of that village."[67] La Salle soon learned after traveling the lakes and rivers that Jolliet had given such a sterling review, that it was not only impractical to build and maintain the canal, but travel down the Des Plaines and Illinois in large vessels was not possible at all.[68]

The quest to link the Great Lakes to the Atlantic and the Gulf of Mexico moves to the first decades of the 1800s, in New York State. At that time much of America's manufacturing capability was located in the Northeast, along the rivers of New England, and many of its ports were located along the Atlantic and at New Orleans. People who lived in the western Great Lakes and the new state of Illinois wanted access to goods produced in the eastern states and Europe and to get their grain to eastern markets. To get the items to Lake Erie above Niagara Falls, the Erie Canal was excavated, completed in 1825. But even though barks could sail the Great Lakes, settlements, including Chicago, were still a long way from eastern markets and the Mississippi.

Towns such as St. Louis and New Orleans, settlements founded by the French, were doing quite well (with the exception of conditions caused by the Panic of 1819). Their populations were growing, and trade in everything from furs to cotton to wheat were bought, sold, and transported up and down the Mississippi. As it stood, the United States had two vital areas of commerce and trade, one in the East and one in the West.

The question became: How to connect the markets on the Mississippi with those in the East? We saw that the Illinois River was not navigable, even by canoes during summer months, and the land between the Des Plaines and Chicago was extremely difficult to traverse, even under the best conditions.

One idea was to build wing dams on the Illinois. Wing dams are long, rocky structures that protrude into the river, just under the surface, on an angle with the current, that funnel water to the center of stream in herringbone fashion. Although this may have seemed to have been a good idea at the time, it would not be a permanent solution to the problem.

We saw that in 1821, Henry Schoolcraft traveled from St. Louis to a site near Fort Dearborn, at today's Chicago, to assist Michigan territorial governor and superintendent of Indian affairs Lewis Cass in negotiating a land-cession treaty with the *aniššina·pe·k* of Lower Michigan. Arriving at the "ford of the Des Plaines," located on the Des Plaines River west of Chicago, Schoolcraft recognized that the river between this ford and the Vermilion, located about five miles downstream from Le Rocher, was rocky, rapid strewn, and shallow. He also described the Des Plaines below Lake Jolliet as "almost equally divided between ripples and still-waters."[69] Another hazard was what he called the Kickapoo rapids, which, according to Schoolcraft, fell about 6 feet in 1.25 miles. But these rapids were nothing, wrote Schoolcraft, compared to the ones on the Illinois near ancient Kaskaskia, which he estimated to be "twenty-four miles long" and only "a few inches" deep. This passage indicates that Schoolcraft, like La Salle, Hubbard, and others, saw that Jolliet's claim that large vessels could "easily" travel between Lake Michigan and the Mississippi River was not realistic, even if Jolliet's canal was built.[70]

By Schoolcraft's time, travelers estimated that a canal at the portage would have to be "eight or ten miles" in length, not 1.5 miles, as Jolliet had claimed. However, even if this hypothetical canal could be dug, Schoolcraft wrote, it would still "fall far short of the grand purpose." He believed that rather than excavate a channel through Mud Lake, it would be less expensive and more practical "to open an entire new channel, than to improve the natural bed of a shallow and rapid stream, or one that is subject to great and sudden fluctuations from vernal or autumnal freshets."[71] In other words, it was a better idea to dig a canal that bypassed the Illinois and Des Plaines River rapids altogether. Schoolcraft's canal was eventually built—the Illinois and Michigan Canal—an artificial channel that was completed in 1848. The canal linked the Illinois River below the Le Rocher rapids with Chicago.[72] It was 140 years after La Salle wrote his polemic to Frontenac that Henry Schoolcraft rightly assessed how a channel could be excavated to connect Lake Michigan with the Illinois River. He was the forerunner of engineers who established a commercial water link between the Mississippi and the Great Lakes, and credit for the idea to build that man-made channel, the Illinois and Michigan Canal, was more his idea than Jolliet's.

The Illinois and Michigan Canal at Lock 14 in La Salle, Illinois, near its confluence with the Illinois River. Photo by the author.

With the construction of the Illinois and Michigan Canal under way, towns such as Utica, Ottawa, Marseilles, Morris, and others were either established or were relocated from the river a short distance north to the new canal. Even though the Illinois and Michigan Canal connected the Illinois River to Chicago, and the conveyance of agricultural commodities, raw materials for manufacturing and building, and passengers between north-central Illinois and Chicago increased exponentially, navigational problems on the Illinois River below the town of LaSalle persisted, primarily because of the unpredictability of seasonal river levels. In an attempt to bring stability to the river, engineers constructed a series of locks and dams, including ones at La Grange, a project commenced in 1877 and completed in 1899; at Kampsville, which also commenced in 1877 but was completed in 1903; at Copperas Creek, completed in 1876; and at Henry, in 1870. The latter, along with dredging, created a seven-foot-deep channel to the Mississippi.[73]

Other dams on the Illinois River and its tributaries were also built and funded by local municipalities during this time. At Ottawa a low-head dam across the Illinois and one on the Fox, a short distance from its merger with the Illinois, were constructed by the Coldwell, Clark, and Company in 1871. The dam that stretched across the Illinois River was anchored on Bull's Island and, when completed, was 1,430 feet long and 16 feet high. It was constructed by filling wooden cribs with stone that were then covered with oak planks. The Fox River dam was 490 feet long and 15.5 feet high. No locks were constructed at the Illinois River dam at Ottawa, perhaps because the river below it would have still been too shallow for navigation. The Illinois River dam was short-lived. It was washed away by the river in 1876.[74]

Discussions and negotiations about widening and deepening the Illinois River channel between state and federal governments, including Congress, the War Department, the Army Corps of Engineers, and the Illinois governor's office, spurred on by lobbying groups such as the Citizens Association of Chicago and the Lakes-to-Gulf Deep Waterway Association, began in 1866 and continued for decades. Surveys of the Illinois River as well as cost and feasibility studies were conducted. At issue were concerns about the route and the depth of the new channel. For a 160-foot-wide channel, should the river depth be 7 feet, 8 feet, or 14 feet? Or perhaps as deep as 20 to 30 to accommodate oceangoing vessels? The amount of funds needed in respect to the width and depth of navigational channel and associated locks and dams varied widely. For example, at one point it was estimated that an 8-foot-deep navigational channel would cost $26,888,153, whereas a 14-foot channel would cost $48,282,763. Added to the mix were discussions about the type of vessels that would use the improved waterway. The Army Corps of Engineers studied three options, including "a 14′ [deep] channel from Lockport to St. Louis via the Des Plaines, Illinois and Mississippi Rivers, a 7′ [deep] channel from Joliet to LaSalle on the Illinois River, and an 8′ [deep] channel that used the same route as the second option." The Corps recommended the 14-foot option in 1905. In time it seemed to Illinois voters as though the federal government was paralyzed, unable to agree on a plan to modernize the river, and this at a time when Illinois manufacturing, such as steel production and the switch from the Bessemer process to the open hearth, was in full swing. By 1908 the state of Illinois decided to go at it alone, authorizing $20 million toward construction of a waterway between Lockport and LaSalle. To pay for the project, state officials believed that revenue generated from hydroelectric power that the state would sell would offset any debt incurred. However, before any construction could begin, the plans had to be approved by Congress, a tall order since the body refused to be drawn into conflicts between state and federal governments.[75] In 1915, despite not having federal authorization, the state of Illinois appropriated $5 million more toward construction of a waterway that incorporated existing canals on the river, construction of new ones, and the building locks and dams on the Illinois between Chicago and LaSalle. The chief engineer of the Army Corps of Engineers denied a permit for the proposed waterway, citing, among several issues, unknown or unforeseeable consequences of the project, the responsibility for which would fall squarely in the lap of the federal government. The back-and-forth between the state and the federal government continued until 1919 when the state finally received authorization to construct the waterway. The route was set, the dimensions were fixed, and a way to pay for the project was determined; the undertaking could now go forward.

Work began on the new dam and navigational canal at Marseilles in 1920 and was completed in 1925. By 1933 the Lockport, Brandon Road, Dresden Island, Marseilles, and Starved Rock Locks and Dams were in operation. The Peoria and La Grange Locks and Dams were fully operational by 1939. The Thomas J. O'Brien Lock and Control Works at the entrance to Lake Michigan were the last to be completed, in 1960. They became operational in 1965. It took 292 years from the time of the Jolliet-Marquette expedition to complete the commercial waterway that linked Lake Michigan to the Mississippi.

◇◇◇◇◇◇◇◇◇◇◇◇◇◇

The success of La Salle's western enterprise was directly tied to knowledge gleaned from the 1673 voyage. Even though Jolliet and Marquette failed to reach the Gulf, the knowledge they acquired of the region's waterways, lands, and people was the first step in European access to and dominion over the central and Lower Mississippi. La Salle claimed for France all lands and waters in the Mississippi drainage in 1682. France reaffirmed this claim for eighty years until 1762, at the close of the Seven Years' War, when the British would soon acquire France's holdings in North America. But before France signed the final accord with the British, they entered into an agreement with Spain, the Treaty of Fontainebleau, that secretly ceded the Isle of Orleans (New Orleans) and all claimed lands west of the Mississippi to the Spanish. The agreement effectively denied the British half of France's vast but undeveloped territories on the continent and gave Spain control of the Mississippi River. The following year, the French and British signed the Treaty of Paris, the document that officially ended the Seven Years' War and ceded to the British French lands claimed east of the great river. The Spanish maintained control of the territory until 1800, when the Treaty of San Ildefonso was signed, giving the Mississippi and the lands west of the Great River back to France. If the new United States wanted to access the Mississippi, it had to negotiate with Napoleonic France. With the influx of new American settlers and farmers into the interior of the continent came riverboats from the north with cargos of tobacco, corn, flour, hides and furs, salted and smoked meats, salt, lead, lumber, whiskey, bear grease, lard, tar, and pitch. New Orleans had, in stark contrast to its early days, become a thriving river port with nearly six hundred vessels mooring at the city's docks in 1801 alone.[76]

But even though New Orleans belonged to the French, Spanish authorities still maintained effective control of the city and its ports, the French having not yet replaced Spanish appointees. Further, in 1802, Spanish intendant Juan Ventura Morales, who likely suspected Americans were smuggling goods rather than paying required duties, closed the New Orleans ports to American boats. President Jefferson and other top officials understood just how important free travel, trade, and access to ports on the Lower Mississippi were to the American economy. Jefferson dispatched Robert R. Livingston to Paris to negotiate the purchase of Louisiana and later sent James Monroe. Not long after Monroe arrived in Paris in April 1803, French treasury minister François Barbé-Marbois and the American delegation came to an agreement: France would sell Louisiana to the United States in what is known as the Louisiana Purchase, the price tag $15 million.[77] The acquisition gave the United States unfettered access to the Mississippi and its tributaries, and, hence, to global markets. It also expedited American settlement to the region.

The French established their first presence in Canada at outposts where mariners and laborers at fish camps prepared codfish and other marine life for transport to Europe. The potential wealth to be made from fur soon supplanted fish and marine mammal markets and became the primary motivation for adventurers, speculators, and merchants to head to the Upper Country. Not long afterward, missionaries saw millions of potential Roman Catholic converts in the northern wilderness and then in the prairies and borderlands of today's Illinois and Mississippi Valleys. What Allouez learned at La Pointe, about copper, the Mississippi, and the Illinois people, led to the Jolliet-Marquette expedition of 1673, which in turn became the springboard that led to La Salle's drive to establish a continent-wide commercial empire that linked Canada with the Gulf of Mexico by way of the continent's interior waterways. Settlements that began as French outposts and missions such as St. Ignace, Detroit, Chicago, and Green Bay became popular American cities on the Great Lakes, while in the South and West, St. Louis, Biloxi, Mobile, New Orleans, Natchitoches, Natchez, Baton Rouge, and others were later founded. The 1673 expedition of Louis Jolliet and Jacques Marquette brought a modicum of certainty to the European understanding of the unknown parts of the interior of North America, and it opened the door through which the European and American occupation of the central and Lower Mississippi Valley would pass. The rest, as they say, is history.

APPENDIX

Timeline of Events

1534
- Jacques Cartier explores the Gulf of St. Lawrence. He reaches the St. Lawrence River the following year.

1541
- Spanish under Hernando de Soto cross the Mississippi River.

1598
- Troilus de La Roche de Mesgouez is appointed lieutenant-governor of Canadian territories.

1599
- Pierre de Chauvin de Tonnetuit obtains a monopoly of Canada's fur trade.

1602
- Aymar de Chaste is appointed Canada's viceroy.

1603
- Pierre Dugua de Monts receives a trade monopoly and is appointed lieutenant-governor "of the coasts, lands and confines of Acadia, Canada and other places in New France."
- Samuel de Champlain first arrives in Canada.

1608
- Champlain founds Quebec.

1609

- Champlain in the company of Algonquian and Wendat allies, slays two Haudenosaunee chiefs.

1611

- Realizing the enormity of the Canadian mission, the Recollects requested help from the Jesuits, including Pierre Biard and Ennemond Massé, who had recently labored in Acadia.

1615

- The first Recollects arrive in Canada with Champlain. The group includes Fathers Denis Jamet, Joseph Le Caron, Jean Dolbeau, and Pacifique Duplessis.

1622

- Jesuit missionary Claude-Jean Allouez is born in Haute-Loire, in south-central France.

1623

- Recollects Nicolas Viel and Gabriel Sagard arrive in Canada and within three weeks set off for Wendat Country.

1624

- The Mohawk attack the Mahican tribe, which forces the survivors to flee east to the Connecticut Valley.

1627

- Compagnie des Cent-Associés is formed.

1629

- Quebec falls to the Kirke Brothers.
- Jesuit and Recollect missionary work is suspended in Canada.

1632

- Treaty of Saint-Germain-en-Laye returns Canada to France.
- Missionary work resumes in Canada.

1634

- Jesuits Antoine Daniel and Ambroise Davost set out for Huronia.
- Between 1634 and 1639, the Huronia tribes lose an estimated half of their populations to European-borne diseases.

1635

- France enters the Thirty Years' War.

1637
- Jacques Marquette is born in Laon, France.

1640
- Canada becomes the principal source of furs for the European market.
- First *known* reference to the Mesquakie tribe appears in the historical record.

1642
- The village of Villa-Marie, later known as Montreal, is founded.
- Haudenosaunee begin raiding Wendat villages.

1643
- Robert Cavelier, later known as La Salle, is born in Rouen, France.

1645
- Louis Jolliet is born at or near Quebec.
- The Compagnie des Cent-Associés is driven to relinquish its fur trading monopoly to the Compagnie des Habitants.

1645–1711
- The coldest part of the "Little Ice Age," a period known as the Maunder Minimum, impacts the Northern Hemisphere.

1649
- Large-scale attacks by Haudenosaunee war parties on Wendat villages scatter the survivors. They seek refuge among the Neutral and Erie tribes. The Wendat also flee to Georgian Bay and Lake Nipigon. The following year, some Wendat move to Île d'Orléans, near Quebec.

1649–1650
- Haudenosaunee war parties attack the Nipissing and Petun tribes.

1650–1651
- Haudenosaunee war parties attack and decimate the Neutral tribe.
- As a result of the attacks, Wendat and Petun groups flee west to present Mackinac Island, then to an island on the Door County Peninsula. Sometime later, they move to mainland Wisconsin.

1654
- A temporary peace is established between the Haudenosaunee and the French.

1656
- A Haudenosaunee war party attacks the Wendat groups living on Île d'Orléans.
- Jesuit Léonard Garreau is killed by Haudenosaunee warriors near Montreal.

1657
- The surviving Erie are absorbed into the Haudenosaunee.

1659
- Marquette writes to J. P. Oliva, general of the Jesuit Order, requesting to be relieved of his studies and be sent to the foreign missions. His request is denied.
- Pierre-Esprit Radisson and Médard Chouart des Groseilliers reportedly travel to Lake Superior and into today's northern Minnesota.

1661
- With the death of Cardinal Mazarin, Louis XIV ascends to the throne of France.

1663
- Louis XIV declares Canada a royal colony.
- Alexander de Prouville de Tracy is appointed lieutenant-general of New France, and Augustin de Saffray de Mézy is appointed governor. Daniel de Rémy de Courcelles soon succeeds de Mézy.
- The Carignan-Salières Regiment is sent to Canada to strike the Haudenosaunee.
- Canada's Sovereign Council is established.
- The Compagnie des Cent-Associés goes out of business.

1664
- Jesuit missionary Louis Nicolas arrives in Canada to continue his training. He takes his Jesuit vows in 1667.

1665
- Jean Talon becomes Canada's intendant.
- Jesuit missionary Claude-Jean Allouez heads to the Great Lakes for the first time. He arrives at La Pointe on the southern shore of Lake Superior where he establishes the mission of St. Esprit.
- There, Allouez learns of the Mississippi River and that copper is found along the shores of Lake Superior. He also meets a delegation of Illinois.
- Marquette writes Oliva again, asking to be sent to the mission fields. His request is granted.

1666
- The first French incursion into Haudenosaunee country commences in January. The expedition nearly ends in disaster for the French.
- In September a second and better-organized French force heads into Haudenosaunee country. The foray convinces the Haudenosaunee to seek peace with the French.

- Marquette arrives in Canada in September. Twenty days later, he begins his instruction in Native languages and culture under Jesuit Gabriel Druillettes.
- Robert Cavelier petitions J. P. Oliva to be sent to China or Portugal. His request is denied. He soon leaves the order.
- Louis Jolliet's eldest brother, Adrien, prepares to journey west as a voyageur, into Ottawa country.
- Talon conducts Canada's census.

1667

- In May Allouez travels to Quebec to recruit missionaries and lay helpers to assist him at his La Pointe mission.
- While at Quebec, Allouez delivers copper nuggets he collected at La Pointe to his superior, François-Joseph Le Mercier. Le Mercier gives the copper nuggets to Talon.
- Jesuit Louis Nicolas is assigned to assist Allouez at La Pointe. Both missionaries travel to the Great Lakes country.
- Lieutenant-General Tracy leaves Canada and sails to France.
- Robert Cavelier arrives in Canada and receives a piece of land from the Sulpicians near Montreal.
- Louis Jolliet leaves the priesthood and sails to France. What he did there is unknown.

1668

- Allouez and Nicolas leave La Pointe and paddle to Sault Ste. Marie. Nicolas continues east, later working at Sept-Îles, Quebec, and in Iroquois country.
- Marquette arrives at Sault Ste. Marie to begin his work among the tribes there.
- Allouez and Marquette circumnavigate Lake Superior and gather information for the now famous Jesuit map.
- Louis Jolliet returns to Canada. He purchases a large supply of trade goods from his uncle Charles Aubert de La Chesnaye.
- In November Talon leaves Canada and returns to France.

1669

- An expedition that included Robert Cavelier and missionaries François Dollier de Casson and René de Brehant de Galinée heads west to locate and explore the Ohio River. The two priests separate from Cavelier and travel to the Sault. What Cavelier did is unknown.
- Jean Péré and Adrien Jolliet are sent to the Upper Country to locate copper mines and to find a way to transport the ore east. A Haudenosaunee prisoner shows Adrien the Great Lakes route. He encounters the Cavelier/Dollier and Galinée party near Tinawatawa.
- Adrien Jolliet dies at his residence at Cap de la Madeleine in December.

- Marquette succeeds Allouez at La Pointe, where he meets a delegation of Illinois. He is given a slave boy to teach him the Miami-Illinois language. During the winter, he conceives of a plan to travel to the Illinois Country.
- Allouez makes his last voyage to Quebec. He and his group deliver several Haudenosaunee prisoners that he had ransomed from the Odawa to governor Courcelles. Heading back west, he arrives in the Green Bay area. He visits a Potawatomi village near Lake Michigan.

1670

- Allouez and several Frenchmen paddle the Fox and Wolf Rivers and establish missions among the Mesquakie and Mascouten. He later visits villages of Kickapoo, Menominee, Ho-Chunk, and Potawatomi.
- Talon dispatches two more expeditions west, one led by Simon F. Daumont, Sieur de St. Lusson, to locate copper mines, and one southwest to find the route to Mexico and the Gulf, led by Cavelier. St. Lusson arrives at the Sault the following May. What became of Cavelier is unknown.
- In autumn, Jolliet heads west for the first time, to establish a trading post at the Sault. He most likely travels with St. Lusson's group.
- In the spring, Marquette leaves La Pointe and heads to the Sault. There he meets with Claude Dablon, Jesuit superior of the Western Missions, and reveals to him his plans to visit the Illinois in their country.
- Jesuit missionaries Gabriel Druillettes and Louis André are sent west to assist Allouez, Marquette, and Dablon. Druillettes is given charge of the mission at the Sault, while André will minister to the tribes at Green Bay.
- Back at La Pointe, Marquette notes that tensions between the Odawa and Wendat and the Nadouessi have reached a boiling point.
- Allouez and Dablon explore the Green Bay area and the Fox River. They successfully ease concerns of the tribesmen of ill-treatment by French traders. They note that the Illinois and Miami are living at the Mascouten village on the Fox.
- Dablon leaves Allouez and likely winters somewhere near today's St. Ignace, Michigan.
- Talon returns to Canada to serve a second term as the colony's intendant.
- The Recollects, including Father Gabriel de la Ribourde, return to Canada, "in a deliberate attempt to reduce the influence of the Jesuits."

1671

- St. Lusson holds a pageant before the representatives of fourteen regional Native groups, Frenchmen, and missionaries at the Sault. He claims all northern, western, and southern lands and waters for France.
- Soon after the pageant, Jolliet and St. Lusson's group return to Quebec.
- Hostilities between the Nadouessi and the La Pointe tribes cause the La Pointe tribes to flee to Mackinac and Manitoulin Island. Marquette follows

the tribesmen and settles at Mackinac, where he establishes the mission of St. Ignace.

- In July Marquette arrives at the Sault to recite his final Jesuit vows. He spends eight days there.

1672

- Louis de Buade, Comte de Frontenac et de Palluau (known as Frontenac), arrives in Canada, replacing Courcelles as governor.
- Talon determines to send out yet another expedition to find the great river that leads to the sea. Louis Jolliet is chosen to participate in the voyage.
- In autumn Jolliet and five Frenchmen head to St. Ignace, arriving at the mission on December 8. They spend the winter at the mission.
- Allouez and André are busy among the Wisconsin tribes. Allouez is at the St. Xavier mission on the lower Fox River, the Mascouten village on the upper Fox, and among the Mesquakie on the Wolf. Allouez spends four months among the Mascouten, where he reports that fifty cabins of Mascouten, ninety Miami, twenty Illinois, thirty Kickapoo, and some Wea were living.
- In November Talon leaves Canada for the last time and returns to France.
- André works among the Menominee and Potawatomi living near Green Bay.

1673

- In May Jolliet and Marquette set off from St. Ignace to travel on their famous voyage of discovery. They travel as far south as the Arkansas River before returning north.
- Marquette winters at the St. Xavier mission, while Jolliet spends the winter at his trading post at the Sault.
- Governor Frontenac dispatches Cavelier to Onontagué to invite Haudenosaunee leaders to a council to obtain a small piece of land. Fort Frontenac and a French settlement would be established at the site.

1674

- Fort Frontenac and adjacent property are leased to Jacques Le Ber and Charles Bazire.
- Cavelier sails to France. The fort and seigniory at Fort Frontenac are transferred to Cavelier, who receives the title of nobility, officially becoming Sieur de La Salle.
- After ice-out, Jolliet, two men, and the Indian boy given to him and Marquette leave the Sault for Quebec. Near Montreal their canoe wrecks in the rapids. Everything in the canoe is lost in the river. Only Jolliet survives.
- At Montreal Jolliet is served papers that summon him to court. The case is settled to the satisfaction of the plaintiff, Jeanne Dodier-Normandin.
- Jolliet reaches Quebec, where he meets with Jesuit superior of Canada, Claude Dablon. Jolliet gives Dablon a verbal account of his and Marquette's expedition.

- While in Quebec, Jolliet meets Jean-Baptiste Franquelin, who draws a map of the voyage based on information provided by Jolliet's memory. The map is known as *La Colbertie*.
- Jolliet is summoned to court in Quebec to answer charges that he failed to pay Eléonore de Grandmaison (Demoiselle de la Tesserie) her share of the profits in Jolliet's company. The council sides with de la Tesserie.
- Marquette spends the summer recuperating from illness at the St. Xavier mission. By October he is ready to travel. He, Jacques Largillier, and Pierre Porteret leave the mission and paddle to the Illinois Country.
- Marquette, Largillier, and Porteret establish a winter camp at today's Chicago. There they meet two of Jolliet's employees, the "surgeon" and Pierre Moreau.
- Jesuit Antoine Silvy begins his mission to the tribes at Michilimackinac along with fellow Jesuit Philippe Pierson.
- Jesuit Druillettes works among the Ottawa tribes at Sault Ste. Marie. Henri Nouvel is superior of the western mission.

1675

- La Salle returns to Canada. He hires François Dauphin de la Forest to manage his legal concerns and day-to-day operations at Fort Frontenac.
- Marquette and his companions arrive at Kaskaskia. Even though Marquette is battling an illness that will take his life, he celebrates Mass before a large audience and visits the villagers in their cabins.
- Claude Dablon, who edited Marquette's final report, noted that Kaskaskia has grown from about 1,480 people in 1673 to about 6,000.
- The ailing Marquette leaves Kaskaskia. He dies while en route to his Mackinac mission, presumably at Michigan's Marquette River.
- Franquelin and Jolliet collaborate to draw another map of the western lands and rivers known as *La Frontenacie*, named in honor of Governor Frontenac.
- In October Jolliet marries Claire-Françoise Bissot.
- Jacques Duchesneau becomes Canada's intendant.
- Recollects Zénobe Membré and Louis Hennepin arrive in Canada. They will accompany La Salle's expedition into the Illinois Country.

1676

- Jolliet joins in partnership with Jacques de Lalande, Marie Laurence, and Denis Guyon, hiring the latter's bark to sail between Quebec and Sept-Îles to carry goods and furs. In November Jolliet and Lalande purchase their own vessel.
- In October Jolliet's input is instrumental in setting the price of beaver in Canada.
- Jolliet petitions French minister Colbert for permission to establish a colony in the Illinois Country with twenty men.

- Father Pierson is busy among the tribes at St. Ignace. He writes that by late April, he had baptized forty-seven adults.
- Charles Albanel is appointed Jesuit superior of the St. Xavier mission.
- Allouez and Largillier leave the St. Xavier mission for Kaskaskia to resume Marquette's work there.

1677
- Jolliet learns that his request to settle in Illinois has been denied.
- La Salle sails to France to petition the court through Minister Colbert for permission to reach the Gulf of Mexico by way of the continent's inland waterways.
- Allouez and Largillier arrive at Kaskaskia in April. The missionary counts 351 cabins at the site, or a population of more than 7,000.
- Kiskakon hunters locate Marquette's remains and carry them to the St. Ignace mission, where they are reinterred.
- Jesuit Jean Enjalran arrives in the Upper Country to minister to the tribes at Mackinac.

1678
- Governor Frontenac consults Jolliet and nineteen other Canadian "notables" about the trafficking of alcohol outside of French settlements, an assembly known today as the "Brandy Parliament."
- Franquelin draws another map based on information provided by Jolliet titled a *General Map of Northern [New] France Containing the Discovery of the Country of the Illinois.*
- La Salle receives a five-year royal patent to explore the western lands of New France. He recruits skilled personnel needed to erect forts, build barks, construct shelter, and build and repair weapons and tools.
- La Salle returns to Canada, arriving in September.

1679
- La Salle's expedition reaches the Niagara Falls area, where his men build a ship known to history as the *Griffon.* The ship is later lost in Lake Michigan.
- La Salle arrives at Michigan's St. Joseph River in November. After constructing a small post near the river's mouth, he and his group ascend the stream and portage to the Kankakee. He continues down the Kankakee and then down the Illinois.
- Canada intendant Jacques Duchesneau grants Jolliet and Jacques de Lalande a concession east of Sept-Îsles and north of Anticosti Island, part of the Mignan Archipelago, where the two men establish cod and seal fisheries.
- Jolliet and seven men are dispatched to Hudson's Bay to assess the influence of English trade there and to survey the possibility of establishing trade alliances with regional tribes.

- Dablon writes that the Indian villages in the Green Bay–Fox River area are filling with refugees, some having populations that number 20,000.

1680

- La Salle's expedition arrives at Kaskaskia on January 1. He records 460 cabins at the site, or a population of about 9,000.
- Men working under La Salle construct Fort de Crèvecoeur near the Illinois River below Lake Peoria.
- In September a large Haudenosaunee war party attacks Kaskaskia. The Illinois abandon the village and flee the region.
- Father de la Ribourde, one of the Recollects attached to La Salle's group, is killed by Kickapoo warriors east of Kaskaskia.
- Jolliet is awarded a grant that includes Anticosti Island.

1681

- La Salle is at his post on the Miami River. There he speaks with Miami and Shawnee leaders.

1682

- La Salle leads a group of French and Native Americans to the Gulf of Mexico. He arrives there in April.
- Governor Frontenac is recalled to France. He is succeeded by Le Febvre de La Barre.
- Jacques de Meulles becomes Canada's intendant.

1683

- La Salle's men build Fort St. Louis atop Le Rocher, today's Starved Rock. He also grants land to some of his loyal men.
- Miami, Shawnee, and Otoe tribesmen settle in present northern Illinois in what history calls "La Salle's Indian Colony." The Illinois who had fled the region return to Kaskaskia.
- La Barre dispatches Olivier Morel, Sieur de La Durantaye to Mackinac. Chevalier Louis-Henri de Baugy is sent to take control of Fort St. Louis at Le Rocher.
- La Salle sails to France to petition the court for permission to sail to the Mississippi via the Gulf of Mexico to establish a colony. He makes exaggerated claims about the viability of the lower Mississippi for settlement.

1684

- La Salle's petition is successful. La Salle and 280 colonists, soldiers, and missionaries set sail for the Gulf in four vessels. His ships miss the mouth of the Mississippi and land at Matagorda Bay, Texas. A second Fort St. Louis is eventually built near the bay.

- In March 200 Haudenosaunee warriors besiege Fort St. Louis on the Illinois for six days but are driven away by local Illinois returning from their winter hunt.
- Allouez returns to the Illinois Valley.

1685

- Fort St. Louis at Le Rocher is returned to La Salle. Henri Tonti, La Salle's trusted associate, commands the fort.

1686

- Tonti and about thirty French and Shawnee leave Fort St. Louis to search for La Salle on the Gulf.
- Failing to locate La Salle, the group returns north. At the Arkansas River, Tonti allows two Frenchmen, Louis Delaunay and Jean Couture, to remain in Arkansas country. They establish the first post near the Mississippi south of the Illinois Country.

1687

- La Salle is murdered by his own men in today's Texas.
- Several survivors of La Salle's failed Gulf expedition arrive at Fort St. Louis in September. They winter at the post, keeping La Salle's death a secret. In spring they head for Quebec and ultimately sail to France.

1688–1689

- Allouez establishes a mission among the Miami in the St. Joseph River country.
- Jesuit Jacques Gravier arrives at Kaskaskia.

1689

- Allouez dies at his Miami mission in August.
- After Allouez's death, Jacques Largillier arrives at Kaskaskia to assist Gravier.
- Most non-Illinois groups have left the upper Illinois Valley.

1691

- The last of the Illinois at Kaskaskia abandon the village. Many resettle at Lake Peoria. The French abandon their Le Rocher fort and build another Fort St. Louis at Lake Peoria.

1697

- Jolliet is awarded a fief on the Etchemin River.

1698

- Three missionaries of the Société des Missions Étrangères guided by Henri Tonti and a group of Frenchmen paddle down the Illinois and Mississippi Rivers. Their destination is the French post on the Arkansas River.

- Naval officer Pierre Le Moyne d'Iberville sails from France to locate the Mississippi via the Gulf.

1699
- D'Iberville's expedition arrives at the Gulf and constructs a temporary fort at present Ocean Springs, Mississippi.

1700
- Jesuit Pierre-Gabriel Marest and the Kaskaskia separate from the Peoria and Moingwena at Lake Peoria and establish a new village at Rivière des Pères, in present St. Louis.
- Jesuit Jacques Gravier paddles down the Mississippi to surveil the lower reaches of the stream to report on the status of the French in the region.
- Charles Juchereau de St-Denys convinces the Crown to allow him to establish a tannery near the confluence of the Ohio and Mississippi Rivers.
- D'Iberville's men erect Fort La Boulaye, also called the "Mississippi Fort," located on the Mississippi River, some distance below modern-day New Orleans.
- Jolliet dies near Anticosti Island.

1702
- Jesuit Gravier returns from south Louisiana and resumes his mission work at Lake Peoria.

1703
- The Kaskaskia and the Jesuits at Rivière des Pères leave their camps and relocate to a site approximately two leagues upstream from the mouth of the Kaskaskia River.

1705
- Gravier is attacked by a Peoria at his Lake Peoria mission. He dies in 1708 from his wound.

1710
- Only three to four hundred people have settled in Louisiana.

1712
- Antoine Crozat forms a company to develop Louisiana. He is granted complete control over Louisiana's trade and is authorized to appoint government officials, exploit mines, and control agriculture.

1717
- Louisiana becomes a royal colony.
- Crozat is relieved of his responsibilities in Louisiana.

- In August, John Law forms the Compagnie d' Occident (Company of the West) and manages Louisiana. By 1721 the financial bubble he created burst. He is forced into bankruptcy.

1719

- The Michigamea leave Kaskaskia and resettle near the site of the future Fort de Chartres. The Kaskaskia also distance themselves from the French.
- By 1719 Frenchmen have explored parts of eastern Oklahoma, northern Alabama, and Arkansas.

1720

- The first Fort de Chartres is built.

1722

- The first provincial council is established in the Illinois district.

1724

- The Côde Noir, the Black Code, is introduced to regulate relations between enslaved Blacks and French colonists in Louisiana.

1736

- A Franco-Indian force under Pierre d'Artaguette leaves Fort de Chartres in February and marches to Chickasaw territory. D'Artaguette's force is surrounded, overwhelmed, and crushed.

1743

- The French-Chickasaw wars end.

1750

- French officials claim that La Salle had discovered the Ohio River in 1669. This statement is without substance.

1753

- The last of four forts named Fort de Chartres is constructed.

1763

- The Potawatomi, once part of the *aniššina·pe·k*, claim all lands along the Illinois River between the Forks and Le Rocher as their hunting grounds.
- The Jesuits are banished from Louisiana.
- Nearly all French territories east of the Mississippi fall under British dominion.

1765

- In October the French relinquish Fort de Chartres to British officer Major Thomas Stirling. He assumes supervision of the Illinois Country.

1773
- The Illinois cede parcels of land to the British.

1803
- Robert Livingston and James Monroe sent to Paris.
- The United States purchases from France what becomes known as the Louisiana Purchase for $15 million.

1804
- The Treaty of Vincennes is signed.

1815
- Indian boarding schools among the Odawa are established after the War of 1812.

1816
- The year becomes known as the "year without a summer."

1818
- Treaty of Edwardsville is signed between the Illinois and the U.S. government.

1820
- While exploring the south shore of Lake Superior, Henry Schoolcraft mentions a "remarkable mass" of pure copper he and his group encountered.

1821
- Michigan territorial governor and superintendent of Indian affairs Lewis Cass and Henry Schoolcraft pass the site of the old Kaskaskia village.

1825
- The Erie Canal is completed. It connects markets in the east with the Great Lakes.

1832
- The U.S. government signs treaties with the Winnebago, Sauk and Mesquakie, and Illinois, requiring them to leave Illinois. In 1833 the *aniššina·pe·k* signed their final land cession east of the Mississippi, the Treaty of Chicago.

1838
- The administration of Georgetown University, a Jesuit school, sells 272 enslaved Africans to pay off the university's debt.

1848
- The Illinois-Michigan Canal is completed. It connects the Illinois River at La Salle, Illinois with Chicago, bypassing the Illinois River rapids.

1854
- The Peoria merge with the Wea and Piankashaw, Miami subtribes. The group becomes the Consolidated Peoria.

1867
- Historian Francis Parkman visits the upper Illinois Valley while researching his book *La Salle and the Discovery of the Great West.*
- The U.S. Army Corps of Engineers makes the first detailed map of the Illinois River.

1868
- The Peoria and the Miami move to northeastern Oklahoma, where they become the Peoria Indian Tribe of Oklahoma.

1883
- The Army Corps of Engineers returns to Illinois to survey the Illinois River.

1887
- By 1887 the U.S. government begins dictating standards to which the Odawa schools are required to adhere.

1899–1900
- The Army Corps of Engineers surveys the Illinois River, noting shoreline features, taking depth readings, and marking the composition of the river's bottom. The maps later become known as the Woermann Maps.

1940s
- Archaeologist Dr. Sara Jones Tucker of the University of Chicago, referencing period writings, locates the actual site of the Kaskaskia village on the upper Illinois River.

1991
- The state of Illinois purchases the Kaskaskia village site and names it the Grand Village of the Illinois State Historical Site.

2021
- Horrific discoveries, including the remains of about a thousand Native American children from Indian boarding schools, are found in unmarked graves in British Columbia and Saskatchewan.
- The Jesuit Conference of Canada and the United States pledges $100 million to be used toward the education of descendants of slaves sold by their order in 1838.

Notes

Introduction

1. Daniel Weiss, "When the Inuit Met the Basques."

2. W. J. Eccles, *The French in North America, 1500–1783*, 1–2.

3. *The Canadian Encyclopedia*, s.v. "Fur Trade in Canada," by John E. Foster and William J. Eccles, last modified November 1, 2019, https://www.thecanadianencyclopedia.ca/en/article/fur-trade.

4. W. Stewart Wallace, ed., *The Encyclopedia of Canada*, vol. 2 (Toronto: University Associates of Canada, 1948), s.v. "Company of New France—Quebec History," accessed December 11, 2015, http://faculty.marianopolis.edu/c.belanger/QuebecHistory/encyclopedia/CompanyofNewFrance-QuebecHistory.htm; *The Canadian Encyclopedia*, s.v. "Company of One Hundred Associates," by John Boyko, February 10, 2020, https://www.thecanadian encyclopedia.ca/en/article/compagnie-des-cent-associes.

5. Eccles, *French in North America*, 36.

6. "The Huron called themselves Wendat, which means 'Islanders,' or 'Dwellers on a Peninsula.' This term may refer to the Huron country which was surrounded on three sides by large bodies of water, or to Huron cosmological beliefs." Bruce G. Trigger, *The Children of Aataentsic, a History of the Huron People to 1660*, 27. The name Iroquois is not from any language, it is of unknown origin, and it has no known meaning. The name was pronounced by the French (*irokwé*). The name Haudenosaunee comes in a variety of forms in the different Iroquoian languages with the basic idea "the people of the long house." Ives Goddard, in *Handbook of North American Indians*, ed. Bruce Trigger, 320.

7. W. J. Eccles, *The Canadian Frontier, 1534–1760*, 3; Eccles, *French in North America*, 96.

8. According to Trigger's *Handbook of North American Indians*, 478, Mohawk comes in many historical forms and is cognate with Unami *mhuwe·yɔk*, "cannibal monsters." Obvi-

ously, it's not what these people called themselves. The self-designation is *kanyęʔkehró·nǫʔ*, "people of *kanyęʔke.*"

9. Trigger, *Children of Aataentsic*, 464, 466.

10. *The Canadian Encyclopedia*, s.v. "Iroquois Wars," by Zach Parrott and Tabitha Marshall, last modified July 31, 2019, https://www.thecanadianencyclopedia.ca/en/article/iroquois -wars.

11. According to Reuben Gold Thwaites, ed., *Jesuit Relations and Allied Documents, 1610– 1791*, 41:81, the Wendat fought the Haudenosaunee with bows and arrows. Some arrows were tipped with poison.

12. Trigger, *Children of Aataentsic*, 820.

13. Michael McCafferty, "Peoria," 11.

14. "Memoir on the Savages of Canada as far as the Mississippi River, Describing Their Customs and Trade," in *Collections of the State Historical Society of Wisconsin*, ed. Reuben Gold Thwaites, 373.

15. However, sometimes during the early years of contact with the Huronia tribes, Frenchmen attempted to interfere with established trade by bypassing tribes such as the Wendat along the trade pipeline. See Duane Esarey and Kjersti E. Emerson, eds., *Palos Village, an Early Seventeenth-Century Ancestral Ho-Chunk Occupation in the Chicago Area*, 184, referencing Trigger, *Children of Aataentsic*, 473–76.

16. Thwaites, *Jesuit Relations*, 11:5.

17. Sagard observed and documented Wendat trade networks, which included identifying Wendat trade partners as well as enemies. He also noted how social factors such as privilege, tribal customs, and war impacted the Wendat trade. See Esarey and Emerson, *Palos Village*, 183–84.

18. The Jesuit missionary Jean Brébeuf in Thwaites, *Jesuit Relations*, 11:7.

19. Trigger, *Children of Aataentsic*, 500.

20. *Dictionary of Canadian Biography*, s.v. "Brébeuf, Jean de (Échon)," by René Latourelle, accessed November 14, 2019, http://www.biographi.ca/en/bio/brebeuf_jean_de_1E.html.

21. R. David Edmunds, *The Potawatomis: Keepers of the Fire*, 3. An Odawa chief named Keewaygooshkum who spoke at the 1821 council at Chicago stated that the Ojibwe, Odawa, and Potawatomi were originally one nation. He stated they were related "by the ties of blood, language, and interest." They reportedly separated at Mackinac. See Henry Rowe Schoolcraft, "Travels in the Central Portions of the Mississippi Valley: Comprising Observations on Its Mineral Geography, Internal Resources, and Aboriginal Population," 146. Other smaller Aniššinapeg groups included the Nipissing, Algonquin, and Mississauga.

22. "The most consistent native explanation connects this word [Ojibwe] with a root meaning 'puckered up,' the reference being to the form of Ojibwa moccasins." Trigger, *Handbook of North American Indians*, 769. Odawa is known as *o·tawa* in the Odawa language. There is no known etymology for the name Odawa (785). The name Potawatomi is from Ojibwe, *po·te·wa·tami.* The self-designation is *potewatmi.* The name Potawatomi has no known etymology (741).

23. Gary Clayton Anderson, *Kinsmen of Another Kind*, 20.

24. Michael A. McDonnell, *Masters of Empire: Great Lakes Indians and the Making of America*, 17.

25. "Sioux" is a shortened form of French "Nadouissiou," which appears to derive from Proto-Algonquian *natowe·wa, which itself appears to contain the verb *-atowe·, "speak a foreign language." "Nadouessiou" probably has a diminutive suffix, here written -ss-. Trigger, *Handbook of North American Indians*, 320; Michael McCafferty, linguist, Indiana University, Bloomington, personal correspondence, June 21, 2021.

26. G. Anderson, *Kinsmen of Another Kind*, 18. In 1712 Jesuit Pierre-Gabriel Marest encountered a Nadouessi war party on the Illinois River just below present Utica, Illinois. See Thwaites, *Jesuit Relations*, 66:289.

27. G. Anderson, *Kinsmen of Another Kind*, 26–27, 15.

28. William W. Warren, *History of the Ojibway People*, 256.

29. R. David Edmunds and Joseph L. Peyser, *The Fox Wars: The Mesquakie Challenge to New France*, 32. The Sauk, like many other people of the region, spoke an Algonquian language, or a possible variant without the tribal marker o- was used by neighboring Ottawa and Ojibwe to mean "those at the outlet." Their original self-designation was *osa:ki:waki* (pl.), later *asa:ki:waki*, meaning "people of the outlet," probably in reference to the Saginaw River. This name was transliterated by the French to "Saki," and eventually to English "Sauk" and "Sac." See Trigger, *Handbook of North American Indians*, 636, 654; and McCafferty, linguist, Indiana University, Bloomington, personal communication, June 23, 2021.

30. John Steckley, "The Early Map 'Nouvelle France,' a Linguistic Analysis," 19.

31. Edmunds and Peyser, *Fox Wars*, 9.

32. Map of Meskwaki and Sauk Migration, cartography by R. Vanderwerff and J. Artz, Earthview Environmental, Inc., Coralville, IA, based on historical research by Jonathan L. Buffalo, Meskwaki tribal historian, June 2013.

33. Jesuit Claude-Jean Allouez noted that some Mesquakie and Sauk were living at a winter village at La Pointe. Thwaites, *Jesuit Relations*, 51:44; Warren, *History of the Ojibway People*, 96, 183–84.

34. The "foot of the lake" means the geographic/cartographic end of the lake, not where the water leaves the lake and flows into Lake Huron.

35. Allouez in Thwaites, *Jesuit Relations*, 54:217–19.

36. Melville B. Anderson, trans., *Relation of the Discoveries and Voyages of Cavelier de La Salle from 1679 to 1681, the Official Narrative*, 263.

37. Louis-Henri de Baugy to Olivier Morel de La Durantaye, March 24, 1684, National Archives of Canada, Source RC 6515, call number MG1–Series C11A. Translation from a copy of the original by Michael McCafferty of Indiana University.

38. Michael McCafferty, *Native American Place-Names of Indiana*, 36–37.

39. Esarey and Emerson, *Palos Village*, 188–90.

40. See *Dictionary of Canadian Biography*, s.v. "Jean Nicollet de Belleborne," by Jean Hamelin, http://biographi.ca/en/bio/nicollet_de_belleborne_jean_1E.html; Charles J. Balesi, *The Time of the French in the Heart of North America, 1673–1818*, 8; and Claiborne Skinner in *The Upper Country: French Enterprise in the Colonial Great Lakes*, 8. Information found on websites including U.S. Forest Service, "History of the Nicolet National Forest, 1928–1976," https://foresthistory.org/wp-content/uploads/2017/02/History-of-Nicolet-National-Forest-1928-1976.pdf; and Wisconsin State Historical Society, s.v. "Nicolet, Jean, 1598–1642," wisconsinhistory.org/Records/Article/CS1665.

41. Michael McCafferty, "Where Did Jean Nicollet Meet the Winnebago in 1634: A Critique of Robert L. Hall's 'Rethinking Jean Nicollet's Route to the Ho-Chunks in 1634'"; Eccles, *Canadian Frontier*, 37; Esarey and Emerson, *Palos Village*, 188–92.

42. Duane Esarey in Esarey and Emerson, *Palos Village*, 192, citing Thwaites, *Jesuit Relations*, 44:247.

43. Illinois comes from Miami-Illinois *irenweewa*, "he speaks in a regular way." David J. Costa, "Illinois," 10. The name was probably used by the Miami to designate their linguistic cousins, the Illinois. Miami *myaamiaki* appears to mean the "downstream people." McCafferty, personal correspondence, June 21, 2021.

44. Brain Fagan, author of *The Little Ice Age* (New York: Basic Books, 2002), on *Little Ice Age, Big Chill* (DVD).

45. *Republican Farmer* (Bridgeport, CT), June 12, 1816. The unusually cool temperatures were made worse by the eruption of Mount Tambora in 1815. See "Mount Tambora," *Encyclopaedia Britannica,* accessed December 6, 2022, https://www.britannica.com/place/Mount-Tambora.

46. According to Congregational missionary the Reverend Thomas Robbins, see Connecticut History, s.v. "Eighteen-hundred-and-froze-to-death," by Wajda.

47. According to John P. Rafferty in *Encyclopedia Britannica*, s.v., "What Was the Little Ice Age," "In addition, temperatures of other regions (such as in eastern China and in the Andes Mountains of South America) were fairly stable, while still other regions (such as southern Europe, North America's Mississippi Valley, and parts of Africa and Asia) became drier, with droughts lasting several years at a time." https://www.britannica.com/story/what-was-the-little-ice-age, accessed November 17, 2019.

48. Robert Michael Morrissey, *Empire by Collaboration*, 17–18.

49. La Salle in Theodore Calvin Pease and Raymond C. Werner, eds., *French Foundations*, 2–4; Melville B. Anderson, trans., *Relation of Henri de Tonty Concerning the Explorations of La Salle from 1678 to 1683*, 35; Henry Rowe Schoolcraft, "Travels in the Central Portions of the Mississippi Valley: Comprising Observations on Its Mineral Geography, Internal Resources, and Aboriginal Population," 105.

50. Paul Le Jeune in Thwaites, *Jesuit Relations*, 46:205.

51. *The Canadian Encyclopedia*, s.v. "Company of One Hundred Associates," by Boyko.

52. *The Canadian Encyclopedia*, s.v. "Huron-Wendat," by C. E. Heidenreich, last modified October 10, 2018, https://thecanadianencyclopedia.ca/en/article/huron; *Dictionary of Canadian Biography*, s.v. "Garreau, Léonard," by J. Monet, accessed March 9, 2021, http://www.biographi.ca/en/bio/garreau_leonard_1E.html.

53. *Dictionary of Canadian Biography*, s.v. "Chouart des Groseilliers, Medard," by Grace Lee Nute, accessed March 9, 2021, http://www.biographi.ca/en/bio/chouart_des_groseilliers_medard_1E.html.

54. *The Canadian Encyclopedia*, s.v. "Intendant," by Jacques Mathieu, March 2015, https://www.thecanadianencyclopedia.ca/en/article/intendant.

55. *Encyclopedia Britannica*, s.v. "Sovereign Council: Canadian History," accessed February 18, 2021, https://www.britannica.com/topic/Sovereign-Council.

56. Jean Delanglez, *Life and Voyages of Louis Jolliet (1645–1700)*, 27.

57. Gilbert J. Garraghan, S.J., "La Salle's Jesuit Days," 95.

58. Joseph Zitomersky, *French Americans: Native Americans in Eighteenth Century French Colonial Louisiana*, 368–69.

Chapter 1. Confronting the Haudenosaunee, Searching for Ore, and Allouez in the Upper Country

1. *Dictionary of Canadian Biography*, s.v. "Prouville de Tracy, Alexandre de," by Léopold Lamontagne, accessed March 10, 2021, http://www.biographi.ca/en/bio/prouville_de _tracy_alexandre_de_1E.html.

2. *Dictionary of Canadian Biography*, s.v. "Talon (Talon Du Quesnoy), Jean," by André Vachon, accessed March 10, 2021, http://www.biographi.ca/en/bio/talon_jean_1E.html.

3. *Dictionary of Canadian Biography*, s.v. "Talon (Talon Du Quesnoy), Jean," by Vachon.

4. "Journal of the Jesuites," in Thwaites, *Jesuit Relations*, 50:181.

5. The name Mohawk comes in many historical forms. The self-designation is *kanyę̓kehró·nǫʔ*, "people of kanyę̓ʔke." Trigger, *Handbook of North American Indians*, 478; Michael McCafferty, linguist, Indiana University, Bloomington, personal correspondence, June 22, 2021.

6. Eccles, *French in North America*, 73.

7. Thwaites, *Jesuit Relations*, 51:167.

8. "Instructions to Talon," March 27, 1665, in *Documents Relating to the Colonial History of New York*, ed. Edmund Bailey O'Callaghan, 29, hereafter cited as O'Callaghan, *DCHNY*.

9. Talon to Colbert, in O'Callaghan, *DCHNY*, 30.

10. Claude-Jean Allouez, "Historical Essay," Wisconsin Historical Society, accessed March 10, 2021, https://www.wisconsinhistory.org/Records/Article/CS2822.

11. Allouez in Thwaites, *Jesuit Relations*, 50:277.

12. See Thwaites, *Jesuit Relations*, 50:277–81.

13. Raphael N. Hamilton, *Marquette's Explorations: The Narratives Reexamined*, 5–7.

14. Marquette to Jesuit General Oliva in Gilbert J. Garraghan, S.J., "Some Hitherto Unpublished Marquettiana," 16.

15. General Oliva to the Provincial, Roger, December 29, 1665, in Garraghan, "Some Hitherto Unpublished Marquettiana," 18.

16. *The Canadian Encyclopedia*, s.v. "Louis Nicolas," by François-marc Gagnon, accessed March 15, 2021, https://www.thecanadianencyclopedia.ca/en/article/louis-nicolas.

17. Garraghan, "La Salle's Jesuit Days," 94–96, 100, 98.

18. Delanglez, *Life and Voyages of Louis Jolliet*, 1.

19. *Dictionary of Canadian Biography*, s.v. "Jolliet, Louis," by André Vachon, accessed November 21, 2019, http://www.biographi.ca/en/bio/jolliet_louis_1E.html.

20. Allouez in Thwaites, *Jesuit Relations*, 50:283.

21. Gabriel Sagard wrote that the Wendat believed "there were spirits of a sort, or the spirits of the fish themselves whose bones were burnt, which would warn the other fish not to allow themselves to be caught, since their bones would also be burnt." See W. Vernon Kinietz, *Indians of the Western Great Lakes: 1615–1760*, 26.

22. René Descartes studied mathematics at the Jesuit Collège at Le Flèche. Garraghan, "La Salle's Jesuit Days," 95.

23. Allouez in Thwaites, *Jesuit Relations*, 50:299.

24. Allouez in Thwaites, *Jesuit Relations*, 50:301. Translation by Michael McCafferty.

25. Allouez in Thwaites, *Jesuit Relations*, 50:301–3.

26. Warren, *History of the Ojibway People*, 307.

27. Ives Goddard, "The West-to-East Cline in Algonquian Dialectology," 187–211; McCafferty, personal communication, March 12, 2021.

28. Allouez in Thwaites, *Jesuit Relations*, 54:219.

29. The description of the location of the Illinois village appears to have been on the Des Moines River, in present Clark County, Missouri.

30. This seems to indicate that some of the Illinois Allouez met at La Pointe were Peoria who, as we will see later in this narrative, were culturally the tribe's traditionalists. Further, by the 1660s, the Illinois had acquired firearms, which implies that the Illinois at La Pointe who claimed that they still used bow and arrows may have been Peoria.

31. Allouez in Thwaites, *Jesuit Relations*, 51:47.

32. Allouez in Thwaites, *Jesuit Relations*, 51:51.

33. Allouez in Thwaites, *Jesuit Relations*, 51:53.

34. Ives Goddard, "Mississippi," 12–13.

35. "Journal of the Jesuites," in Thwaites, *Jesuit Relations*, 50:189; Delanglez, *Life and Voyages of Louis Jolliet*, 2.

36. Joseph E. Donnelly, S.J., *Jacques Marquette*, 80.

37. Marquette to Father Pepin, rector of the college of Dijon of the Society of Jesus, in Garraghan, "Some Hitherto Unpublished Marquettiana," 21.

38. Donnelly, *Jacques Marquette*, 93, 100.

39. Donnelly, *Jacques Marquette*, 95.

40. Raymond Douville, S.R.C., "Life and Death of Adrien Jolliet—a Short, Honest and Very Full Life," in *Les Cahiers des Dix* (August 1979): 36–38.

41. Allouez in Thwaites, *Jesuit Relations*, 50:263–65, 54:159.

42. Mentor L. Williams, ed., *Schoolcraft's Narrative Journal of Travels*, 122.

43. Allouez in Thwaites, *Jesuit Relations*, 51:72–74.

44. Allouez in Thwaites, *Jesuit Relations*, 51:73.

45. Garraghan, "Some Hitherto Unpublished Marquettiana," 21.

Chapter 2. Copper Mines, Cavelier, and Wisconsin

1. Janell (Belisle *dit* Germain) Norman, "The Amazing Louis Jolliet," 6; Balesi, *Time of the French in the Heart of North America*, 13.

2. *The Canadian Encyclopedia*, s.v. "Louis Nicolas," by François-marc Gagnon, accessed March 15, 2021, https://www.thecanadianencyclopedia.ca/en/article/louis-nicolas.

3. Duane Esarey, Dickson Mounds Museum, "Paleography des Indes: An Overview of the Codex Canadiensis," PowerPoint presentation.

4. Louis Hennepin, *The French Regime in Wisconsin*, vol. 1, 1634–1727, 61n.

5. Thwaites, *Jesuit Relations*, 54:254.

6. *Dictionary of Canadian Biography*, s.v. "Dablon Claude," by Marie-Jean-d'Ars Charette, C.S.C., accessed March 17, 2021, http://www.biographi.ca/en/bio/dablon_claude_1E.html.

7. "Journal of the Jesuites," in Thwaites, *Jesuit Relations*, 51:149.

8. Thwaites, *Jesuit Relations*, 52:197; *Dictionary of Canadian Biography*, s.v. "Dablon Claude," by Charette.

9. *Dictionary of Canadian Biography*, s.v. "Jolliet, Louis," by André Vachon, accessed August 31, 2017, http://www.biographi.ca/en/bio/jolliet_louis_1E.html.

10. *Dictionary of Canadian Biography*, s.v. "Claude de Bouteroue d'Aubigny," by W. J. Eccles, accessed March 17, 2021, http://www.biographi.ca/en/bio/boutroue_d_aubigny_claude_de_1E.html.

11. René de Bréhant de Galinée in *Early Narratives of the Northwest, 1634–1699*, ed. Louise Phelps Kellogg, 191.

12. Delanglez, *Life and Voyages of Louis Jolliet*, 14, 15.

13. "Seneca" is of unknown origin and meaning. The self-designation of the Seneca is *onǫtawáʔka·ʔ.* Trigger, *Handbook of North American Indians*, 515–16.

14. Galinée in Kellogg, *Early Narratives*, 171. The name Shawnee, *ša·wanwa*, means "person from the south." Trigger, *Handbook of North American Indians*, 634.

15. Trigger, *Handbook of North American Indians*, 170.

16. Trigger, *Handbook of North American Indians*, 168.

17. Trigger, *Handbook of North American Indians*, 171.

18. Galinée in Kellogg, *Early Narratives*, 181.

19. Kellogg, *Early Narratives*, 190.

20. James Bruseth and Toni Turner, *From a Watery Grave: The Discovery and Excavation of La Salle's Shipwreck "La Belle,"* 18–19.

21. Patoulet to Colbert, November 1669, in Delanglez, *Life and Voyages of Louis Jolliet*, 10; O'Callaghan, *Documents Relating to the Colonial History of New York*, 9:787.

22. Delanglez, *Life and Voyages of Louis Jolliet*, 13.

23. Delanglez's examination of the matter demonstrates conclusively that the priests met Adrien, not Louis. See Delanglez, *Life and Voyages of Louis Jolliet*, 10–13.

24. Galinée in Kellogg, *Early Narratives*, 193. The 1641 *Nouvelle France* reveals that the French had some idea that present Lake Erie flowed into Lake Ontario. See also Steckley, "Early Map 'Nouvelle France,'" 26–27.

25. Douville, "Life and Death of Adrien Jolliet," 42.

26. Galinée in Kellogg, *Early Narratives*, 192.

27. Douville, "Life and Death of Adrien Jolliet," 45.

28. Kellogg, *Early Narratives*, 191–93.

29. Marquette in Thwaites, *Jesuit Relations*, 54:167, 169.

30. Roy W. Meyer, *History of the Santee Sioux: United States Indian Policy on Trial*, vii. Santee Sioux groups include the Mdewakanton, Wahpeton, Wahpekute, and Sisseton.

31. Marquette in Thwaites, *Jesuit Relations*, 54:183, 185, 189.

32. Marquette in Thwaites, *Jesuit Relations*, 51:47.

33. Marquette in Thwaites, *Jesuit Relations*, 54:189.

34. Marquette in Thwaites, *Jesuit Relations*, 54:211.

35. Marquette in Thwaites, *Jesuit Relations*, 54:221.

36. Jeffery A. Behm, "The Mesquakie in Eastern Wisconsin: Ethnohistory and Archaeology," 65–68.

37. Allouez in Thwaites, *Jesuit Relations*, 54:219.

38. Allouez in Thwaites, *Jesuit Relations*, 54:225–27.

39. According to Trigger's *Handbook of North American Indians*, 672, "Mascouten" may mean "person of the small prairie."

40. Allouez in Thwaites, *Jesuit Relations*, 55:201–3.

41. Allouez in Thwaites, *Jesuit Relations*, 54:233.

42. Allouez in Thwaites, *Jesuit Relations*, 54:229.

43. Allouez in Thwaites, *Jesuit Relations*, 54:263.

44. John J. Wood, *The Mascouten Village*, 1.

45. Lynn A. Rusch, "The Springview Site: A Possible Late Seventeenth-Century Mascouten Village," 165; W. A. Titus, "Historic Spots in Wisconsin: The Lost Village of the Mascouten."

46. *Oshkosh Daily Northwestern*, July 7, 14, and 18, 1964.

47. Rusch, "Springview Site," 157.

48. Rusch, "Springview Site," 158–64.

49. *Berlin Journal*, January 26, 1995.

50. According to linguist Michael McCafferty, who specializes in Native American languages, the term *Kitchigamich* as written is probably from Ojibwe-Ottawa. The ethnonym derives from Proto-Algonquian *keʔčikamyi, literally meaning "big-water," referring to one of the Great Lakes, presumably Lake Michigan. (The ʔ is the symbol for a glottal stop.) Personal communication, March 20, 2021. Menominee is from Ojibwe *mano·mini,* "wild rice people." The self-designation is *omɛ·ʔnomene·w,* which is not related to the Menominee word for "wild rice." Trigger, *Handbook of North American Indians*, 723.

51. Ho-Chunk, the self-designation is *ho·čągra,* "big fish" or "big voice" (Winnebago is from possibly Potawatomi *winpyeko,* "people of the dirty water"). Trigger, *Handbook of North American Indians*, 706.

52. "Talon to Colbert," November 10, 1670, in Delanglez, *Life and Voyages of Louis Jolliet*, 33.

53. Marquette in Thwaites, *Jesuit Relations*, 54:183.

54. Marquette in Thwaites, *Jesuit Relations*, 52:115.

55. Marquette in Thwaites, *Jesuit Relations*, 55:169.

56. Dablon in Thwaites, *Jesuit Relations*, 55:189, 207.

57. Dablon in Thwaites, *Jesuit Relations*, 55:205, 207.

58. Donnelly, *Jacques Marquette*, 168. He bases his assumption on Dablon's report found in Thwaites, *Jesuit Relations*, 50:157–61

59. Dablon in Thwaites, *Jesuit Relations*, 55:157.

60. Dablon in Thwaites, *Jesuit Relations*, 55:159.

61. Dablon in Thwaites, *Jesuit Relations*, 55:159.

62. Dablon in Thwaites, *Jesuit Relations*, 55:219, 58:41.

Chapter 3. St. Lusson, Marquette, Jolliet and the Sault, Adrien Jolliet, and Frontenac

1. Talon to Minister Colbert in Jean Delanglez, S.J., "Jolliet Early Years," 16.

2. For example, Henri Joutel, the chronicler of La Salle's disastrous Gulf expedition, and his group were unable to continue their voyage from today's Chicago to Michilimackinac

in the autumn of 1687 because eight days of "contrary winds and the bad weather" on Lake Michigan prevented them from continuing their journey. Pierre Margry, *Découvertes et établissements des Français dans l'ouest et dans le sud de l'Amérique septentrionale, 1678–1685,* 3:486 (translation by Michael McCafferty).

3. Nicolas Perrot, "Memoir on the Manners, Customs, and Religion of the Savages of North America," in *Indian Tribes of the Upper Mississippi Valley and Region of the Great Lakes,* ed. Emma Helen Blair, 1:221–22.

4. "Taking Possession, in the King's Name, of All the Countries Commonly Included under the Designation Outaouac," in Kellogg, *Early Narratives,* 214.

5. Kellogg, *Early Narratives,* 218.

6. Speech of "Simon Francois Daumont Esquire Sieur St. Lusson" at the Sault St. Marie pageant in O'Callaghan, *Documents Relating to the Colonial History of New York,* 9:803, hereafter cited as O'Callaghan, *DCHNY.*

7. Delanglez, *Life and Voyages of Louis Jolliet,* 6–7.

8. André Vachon, writing in *The Dictionary of Canadian Biography,* for example.

9. According to Thwaites, *Jesuit Relations,* 50:105, St. Lusson "repaired to sainte Marie du Sault early in May" 1671, apparently meaning that he left his Manitoulin Island camp for the Sault in early May.

10. Even Claude Dablon, who was alive at the time and met with Louis, wrote about him, "For this purpose [the 1673 voyage], they could not have selected a person endowed with better qualities than is sieur Jolliet, who has traveled much in that region, and has acquitted himself in this task with all the ability that could be desired." Thwaites, *Jesuit Relations,* 58:93.

11. Rafael N. Hamilton, S.J., *Father Marquette,* 42; Mark Walczynski, "Claude Dablon and Louis Jolliet, Constructing a Narrative from Presuppositions," 65.

12. Talon in O'Callaghan, *DCHNY,* 9:72.

13. Talon in O'Callaghan, *DCHNY,* 9:72; *Dictionary of Canadian Biography,* s.v. "Daumont de Saint Lusson, Simon-François," by Léopold Lamontagne, accessed June 2, 2021, http://www.biographi.ca/en/bio/daumont_de_saint_lusson_simon_francois_1E.ht.

14. Donnelly, *Jacques Marquette,* 197 (emphasis added).

15. Dablon in Thwaites, *Jesuit Relations,* 50:169.

16. Thwaites, *Jesuit Relations,* 56:115.

17. For a full discussion of Jolliet and Marquette's alleged meeting to discuss the Mississippi voyage, see Walczynski, "Claude Dablon and Louis Jolliet," 61–69.

18. In Blair, *Indian Tribes of the Upper Mississippi Valley,* 1:224, 225.

19. St. Lusson in O'Callaghan, *DCHNY,* 9:804.

20. Blair, *Indian Tribes of the Upper Mississippi Valley,* 1:225.

21. Marquette in Thwaites, *Jesuit Relations,* 54:183.

22. Blair, *Indian Tribes of the Upper Mississippi Valley,* 1:177–78; Garraghan, "Some Hitherto Unpublished Marquettiana," 24. Marquette was away from his mission for fourteen days. Thwaites, *Jesuit Relations,* 57:249.

23. Later that year, Marquette and the Wendat and Ottawa relocated their island village next to a bay along the shoreline of Michigan's Upper Peninsula's, at today's St. Ignace.

24. Delanglez, "Jolliet Early Years," 18.

25. It should be noted that at this time, a "ferry" ran between Montreal and Quebec. Douville, "Life and Death of Adrien Jolliet," 29.

26. Delanglez, "Life and Voyage of Louis Jolliet," 258.

27. Michael McCafferty, "Jacques Largillier: French Trader, Jesuit Brother, and Jesuit Scribe, 'par Excellence,'" 191.

28. "M. Talon to M. Colbert," in O'Callaghan, *DCHNY*, 9:72.

29. *Dictionary of Canadian Biography*, s.v. "Talon (Talon Du Quesnoy), Jean," by André Vachon, accessed March 10, 2021, http://www.biographi.ca/en/bio/talon_jean_1E.html.

30. "M. Colbert to M. Talon," in O'Callaghan, *DCHNY*, 9:89.

31. The years 1645–1715 are specifically known as the Maunder Minimum.

32. William J. Eccles, *Canadian Frontier*, 106.

33. Allouez in Thwaites, *Jesuit Relations*, 57:263.

34. Thwaites, *Jesuit Relations*, 59:67.

35. Thwaites, *Jesuit Relations*, 56:247.

36. Marquette in Thwaites, *Jesuit Relations*, 57:261.

37. Marquette may have employed a Jesuit *donné* as an assistant. Jacques Largillier was a well-known *donné* (a man who donated his life and services to the Jesuits) who later worked in the company of Marquette, Allouez, and Gravier.

38. *Dictionary of Canadian Biography*, s.v. "Cavelier de La Salle, René-Robert," by Céline Dupré, accessed March 24, 2021, http://www.biographi.ca/en/bio/cavelier_de_la_salle _rene_robert_1E.html.

39. Jean Delanglez, "Calendar of La Salle Travels," 286.

40. Louis Jolliet "defended a thesis in philosophy" at the Jesuit church, an event that was attended by "All the public officials," including Intendant Jean Talon. Delanglez, "Jolliet Early Years," 5.

41. Lucien Campeau, "Les cartes relatives à la découverte du Missisipi [*sic*] parle le Père Jacques Marquette et Louis Jolliet," 88.

42. Kellogg, *Early Narratives*, 163–64.

43. Campeau, "Les cartes relatives."

44. Louis Jolliet formed a company of investors that included François de Chavigny (Sieur de la Chevrotière), Zacharie Jolliet, Jean Plattier, Pierre Moreau, Jacques Largillier, and Jean Tiberge. Delanglez, *Life and Voyages of Louis Jolliet*, 103.

45. Douville, "Life and Death of Adrien Jolliet," 29.

46. Galinée in Kellogg, *Early Narratives*, 191–92.

47. *Dictionary of Canadian Biography*, s.v. "Marquette, Jacques," by J. Monet, accessed September 11, 2017, http://www.biographi.ca/en/bio/marquette_jacques_1E.html.

48. Thwaites, *Jesuit Relations*, 58:91.

49. Frontenac in O'Callaghan, *DCHNY*, 9:92. It should be noted that O'Callaghan's translation of this document says, "He (Chevalier de Grandfontaine, Governor of Acadia and of Pentagouet)," not Talon. However, and Donnelly agrees, O'Callaghan was mistaken, as it was Talon, as demonstrated by other documents, who chose Jolliet for the expedition. See Donnelly, *Jacques Marquette*, 199n.

50. Delanglez, *Life and Voyages of Louis Jolliet*, 105.

51. Donnelly, *Jacques Marquette*, 199.

52. *Dictionary of Canadian Biography*, s.v. "Talon (Talon Du Quesnoy), Jean," by Vachon.

53. Frontenac's instructions from Louis XIV in O'Callaghan, *DCHNY*, 9:85–88, 120.

54. Eccles, *Canadian Frontier*, 107.

55. "Journal of Count de Frontenac's Voyage to Lake Ontario," in O'Callaghan, *DCHNY*, 9:104.

56. *Dictionary of Canadian Biography*, s.v. "Le Ber, Jacques," by Yves F. Zoltvany, accessed January 15, 2021, http://www.biographi.ca/en/bio/le_ber_jacques_2E.html.

57. Delanglez, *Life and Voyages of Louis Jolliet*, 103.

58. Speech of "Simon Francois Daumont Esquire Sieur St. Lusson" at the Sault St. Marie pageant in O'Callaghan, *DCHNY*, 9:804.

59. Marquette in Thwaites, *Jesuit Relations*, 57:37.

60. Thwaites, *Jesuit Relations*, 58:47.

61. Thwaites, *Jesuit Relations*, 58:271–73.

62. Thwaites, *Jesuit Relations*, 59:89–91.

Chapter 4. St. Ignace to the Des Moines River

1. Donnelly, *Jacques Marquette*, 209.

2. Marquette in Thwaites, *Jesuit Relations*, 59:89.

3. Denys Delâge, "French and English Colonial Models in North America," 14.

4. Dablon in Thwaites, *Jesuit Relations*, 56:119–23.

5. Marquette in Thwaites, *Jesuit Relations*, 59:97. Marquette mentioned these rapids in his report while writing nothing at all about other *saults*. Dablon also mentioned them in his report of his and Allouez's journey of the Fox in September 1670. See Thwaites, *Jesuit Relations*, 55:189–91.

6. Allouez reported that he had been among the Mesquakie but left them on April 30 to go to the St. Jacques mission at the Mascouten village. On May 22, he left the Mascouten to return to the Mesquakie where he remained until sometime in June. See Allouez in Thwaites, *Jesuit Relations*, 58:41.

7. Wisconsin Historical Society, s.v. "Carte du pays des sauvages Renards depuis la baye du lac Michigan jusques a leur dernier village," 1911 copy of a map drawn by Gaspard-Joseph Chaussegros de Léry in 1730, accessed December 6, 2020, https://www.wisconsinhistory.org/Records/Image/IM98535.

8. Wisconsin Historical Society, s.v. "Travels through the Interior Parts of North America, in the Years 1766, 1767, and 1768," by Jonathan Carver, 32, accessed November 29, 2020, https://content.wisconsinhistory.org/digital/collection/aj/id/13108.

9. Behm, "Meskwaki in Eastern Wisconsin," 7.

10. Marquette in Thwaites, *Jesuit Relations*, 59:99. The plant is probably today's snakeroot (*Ageratina altissima*).

11. Thwaites, *Jesuit Relations*, 59:197, 103.

12. *Canadian Encyclopedia*, s.v. "Midewiwin," by René R. Gadacz, June 8, 2021, https://www.thecanadianencyclopedia.ca/en/article/midewiwin; Frances Densmore, *Chippewa Customs*, 87.

13. Observation by Allouez in Thwaites, *Jesuit Relations*, 59:219.

14. Marquette in Thwaites, *Jesuit Relations*, 59:103.

15. See Delanglez, *Life and Voyages of Louis Jolliet*, 262.

16. Mark Walczynski, "Louis Jolliet and Jacques Marquette: Consistencies, Contradictions, and Misconceptions," 136.

17. McCafferty, "Jacques Largillier," 189.

18. Michael McCafferty, linguist, Indiana University, Bloomington, personal communication, November 26, 2020.

19. Wisconsin Historical Society, s.v. "Travels through the Interior Parts of North America," by Carver, 43.

20. Williams, *Schoolcraft's Narrative*, 238.

21. Williams, *Schoolcraft's Narrative*, 235.

22. Jonathan Carver stated that lead mines had been reported in the area. See Wisconsin Historical Society, s.v. "Travels through the Interior Parts of North America," by Carver, 49.

23. Tower Hill State Park, Wisconsin Department of Natural Resources, accessed November 29, 2020, https//dnr.wisconsin.gov/topic/parks/towerhill/history.

24. Williams, *Schoolcraft's Narrative*, 224–27.

25. Zebulon Pike, *An Account of Expeditions to the Sources of the Mississippi, and through the Western Parts of Louisiana, to the Sources of the Arkansaw, Kans, La Platte, and Pierre Jaun Rivers*, 43, accessed November 30, 2020, http://www.americanjourneys.org/aj-143/.

26. Marquette in Thwaites, *Jesuit Relations*, 59:107.

27. Thwaites, *Jesuit Relations*, 59:111.

28. It appears that the horizontal lines at this location illustrated on Marquette's 1673 map are a reference to these rapids. See McCafferty, *Native American Place-Names of Indiana*, 190.

29. Marquette in Thwaites, *Jesuit Relations*, 59:113, translated by Michael McCafferty, Indiana University.

30. From Marquette's report, the Frenchmen saw the path somewhere along the Mississippi near the mouth of the Des Moines River. The two men hiked "two leagues" (roughly five miles) to the Illinois village. This begs the question: Were the "tracks of men" on the "somewhat beaten path" located along the Des Moines or the Mississippi River? If the tracks and path were located along the Mississippi, as Marquette's report indicates, Jolliet and Marquette would have hiked more than seven and a half miles to reach the first village. And their trek would have taken them through river bottoms that would have paralleled the Des Moines River. However, if the French canoes would have conducted a reconnaissance up the Des Moines and observed the path along that stream, they would have walked less than two miles to the village. This raises another question: Why would the Illinois hike more than seven and a half miles to access the Mississippi from their village when they could reach the Des Moines in less than two?

Chapter 5. From the Illinois Villages to the Illinois River

1. Although the text of the narrative does not use the word "PE8ARE8A," Marquette's map 1673 illustrates the villages as Peoria.

2. Larry Grantham, "The Illini Village of the Jolliet and Marquette Voyage of 1673," 1–20.

3. Robert Mazrim, *Protohistory at the Grand Village of the Kaskaskia: The Illinois Country on the Eve of Colony*, 3.

4. Raymond E. Hauser, "Ethnohistory of the Illinois Indian Tribe, 1673–1832," 11; Zitomersky, *French Americans*, 78.

5. Such was the case with the Santee Sioux, whose bison-hunting activities on the prairies had increased from a few weeks every year, to several months. See G. Anderson, *Kinsmen of Another Kind*, 25–26.

6. Wayne C. Temple, *Indian Villages of the Illinois Country*, 17.

7. Marquette in Thwaites, *Jesuit Relations*, 54:183–89.

8. Thwaites, *Jesuit Relations*, 59:115.

9. Thwaites, *Jesuit Relations*, 59:119.

10. Zitomersky, *French Americans*, 80.

11. Zitomersky, *French Americans*, 125.

12. Carl J. Ekberg, *Stealing Indian Women: Native Slavery in the Illinois Country*, 10, 11.

13. Hauser, "Ethnohistory of the Illinois Indian Tribe," 58.

14. See Mazrim, *Protohistory at the Grand Village of the Kaskaskia*, 1, 147–48.

15. Esarey and Emerson, *Palos Village*, 188–90.

16. Michael McCafferty, "Peoria," 11.

17. The Jesuit Jean Mermet wrote to the Jesuits in Canada, "I write you news concerning the affairs of the Ilinois, some of which is good and some bad. It is good from this village, except that they threaten to leave us at the first word. It is bad, as regards both spiritual and temporal matters, among the Ilinois of Détroit,—otherwise, the Peoarias,—where Father Gravier nearly lost his life on two occasions, and he is not yet out of danger." See Mermet in Thwaites, *Jesuit Relations*, 66:49.

18. Zitomersky, *French Americans*, 201.

19. Marquette in Thwaites, *Jesuit Relations*, 51:47.

20. Zitomersky, *French Americans*, 201.

21. Michael McCafferty, personal communication, December 2, 2020.

22. See Costa, "Illinois." Recently, Costa discovered that the Kaw referred to the Ottawa as "Indokah." McCafferty speculates that "Indokah"~ *inohka might have been a word used by Siouan speakers south the Great Lakes to refer to Great Lakes Algonquians in general. Miami-Illinois had extensive prehistoric contact with Siouan speakers, as the term for the number "eight" in Miami comes from a Siouan language. McCafferty, personal communication, December 2, 2020.

23. In Old Miami-Illinois, *r* in this term shifted to *l*. McCafferty, personal communication, December 2, 2020.

24. Zebulon Montgomery Pike, *Map of the Mississippi River from Its Source to the Mouth of the Missouri*, [1811?], https://www.loc.gov/item/78692257.

25. A delegation of Sauk chiefs and one Mesquakie chief met with U.S. officials to make restitution for the murders. They were tricked into signing away their tribal lands in the so-called Treaty of 1804, a land cession for which they had no authority and no intent to negotiate. The treaty would remain a point of contention for the Sauk and Mesquakie for many years, and it eventually led to hostilities known as the Black Hawk War of 1832.

26. Marquette in Thwaites, *Jesuit Relations*, 59:137–39.

27. McCafferty, personal communication, November 19, 2020.

28. Natalia Marie Belting, "The Piasa—It Isn't a Bird!," 303–5. Canadian historian Lucien Campeau wrote that the original copy of the report Marquette sent to Quebec with Jolliet that was lost in the St. Lawrence included the sketch of the Piasa, but later copies did not. See Lucien Campeau, "Regard critique sur la narration du P. Jacques Marquette," 15. A modern reproduction of the Piasa is located on a cliff face along the Illinois River just below Grafton, Illinois.

29. Jean-François Buisson de St. Cosme in Kellogg, *Early Narratives*, 355.

30. McCafferty, personal communication, June 24, 2021.

31. St. Cosme in Kellogg, *Early Narratives*, 355.

32. Isabel Wallace, *The Life and Letters of General W. H. L. Wallace*, 15.

33. On an island just out from the confluence of the Missouri and Mississippi, a band of Kickapoo later resided in a small summer village. Zebulon Pike, *An Account of Expeditions to the Sources of the Mississippi, and through the Western Parts of Louisiana, to the Sources of the Arkansaw, Kans, La Platte, and Pierre Jaun Rivers*, 41, accessed November 30, 2020, http:// www.americanjourneys.org/aj-143/.

34. Alan G. Shackleford, "The Frontier in Pre-Columbian Illinois," 182–83.

35. Cahokia Mounds Museum Society, s.v. "Mound 38," October 22, 2015, https:// cahokiamounds.org/mound/mound-38-monks-mound/; National Park Service, "Cahokia Mounds State Historic Site: World Heritage Site," last modified July 23, 2020, https://www .nps.gov/articles/000/cahokia-mounds-state-historic-site-world-heritage-site.htm.

36. Marquette in Thwaites, *Jesuit Relations*, 59:143–45.

37. Marquette in Thwaites, *Jesuit Relations*, 59:141–43.

38. St. Cosme in Kellogg, *Early Narratives*, 356–57.

39. Michael McCafferty, "While Cleaning Up a Tribal Name."

40. Jesuit, traveler, and historian Charlevoix reported seeing canes as far north as Cap Antoine, in southern Illinois. Pierre-Francis Xavier de Charlevoix, *Journal of a Voyage to North America*, 2:239.

41. Kellogg, *Early Narratives*, 352–53n3; Charlevoix, *Journal of a Voyage to North America*, 2:228; McCafferty, "While Cleaning Up a Tribal Name," 178, 179–80.

42. St. Cosme in Kellogg, *Early Narratives*, 356.

43. According to Joseph Zitomersky, the Michigamea had been living among the Tamaroa and Cahokia as early as 1700. Zitomersky, *French Americans*, 93.

44. St. Cosme in Kellogg, *Early Narratives*, 360.

45. Tonti in "Memoir of Tonty," in Kellogg, *Early Narratives*, 308.

46. It is unknown who these Illinois could have been since no Illinois groups were known to live west of the Arkansas.

47. Thwaites, *Jesuit Relations*, 59:159.

Chapter 6. From the Mississippi to Kaskaskia

1. St. Cosme in Kellogg, *Early Narratives*, 354.

2. Raymond Phineas Stearns, "Joseph Kellogg: Observations on Senex's Map of North America (1710)." Kellogg was a passenger in one of two French canoes that traveled between Montreal and the Arkansas Post.

3. Hamilton, *Marquette's Explorations*, 179.

4. Louis Hennepin, *A New Discovery of a Vast Country in America*, 108.

5. Marquette in Thwaites, *Jesuit Relations*, 59:159.

6. Jolliet reported this to Dablon during their meeting on August 1, 1674. See Thwaites, *Jesuit Relations*, 58:93.

7. By John C. Marlin, PhD, "Evaluation of Sediment Removal Options and Beneficial Use of Dredged Material for Illinois River Restoration: Preliminary Report," accessed December 17, 2020, www.istc.illinois.edu/special_projects/il_river/sediment_removal_marlin.pdf.

8. Lake of the Illinois is today's Lake Michigan. Marquette in Thwaites, *Jesuit Relations*, 59:159.

9. Isaac Joslin Cox, ed., "Joutel's Historic Journal of Monsieur de La Salle's Last Voyage to Discover the River Mississippi," 2:204, 209; Schoolcraft, "Travels in the Central Portions of the Mississippi Valley," 85.

10. Schoolcraft, "Travels in the Central Portions of the Mississippi Valley," 85.

11. Macoupin Creek has been channelized and today empties into the Illinois River about three miles north of its prior channel. Macoupins were aquatic tubers that the Indigenous people of the Illinois Valley utilized for food.

12. Gilbert Imlay, ed., "Mr. Patrick Kennedy's Journal Up the Illinois River," 507.

13. Schoolcraft, "Travels in the Central Portions of the Mississippi Valley," 85.

14. Schoolcraft, "Travels in the Central Portions of the Mississippi Valley," 87, 91.

15. Macoupin, *mahkopina* in Miami-Illinois, literally "bear-potato," is "spatterdock, pond lily." Michael McCafferty, personal communication, July 31, 2021.

16. Imlay, "Mr. Patrick Kennedy's Journal," 507.

17. Duane Esarey, "Seasonal Occupation Patterns in Illinois History: A Case Study in the Lower Illinois River Valley," 206n3.

18. Schoolcraft, "Travels in the Central Portions of the Mississippi Valley," 87–88. Mauvaise Terre Creek is located about five miles below modern-day Naples on the east side of the river.

19. Esarey, "Seasonal Occupation Patterns in Illinois History," 204.

20. Arkansas geological survey, accessed February 21, 2020, https://www.geology.arkansas.gov/minerals/industrial/marl.html.

21. La Poterie is referring to the Illinois River, not the St. Joseph River. La Salle had not established a settlement on the St. Joseph by this time, and Jolliet and Marquette had returned north via the Chicago Portage to Lake Michigan where they followed the west coast of the lake to Green Bay. La Poterie in Blair, *Indian Tribes of the Upper Mississippi Valley*, 1:348. La Poterie wrote that he received much information about the voyage from Louis Jolliet personally. Blair, *Indian Tribes of the Upper Mississippi Valley*, 2:134–35.

22. Imlay, "Mr. Patrick Kennedy's Journal," 507.

23. See Kellogg in Charlevoix, *Journal of a Voyage to North America*, 2:217; Stanley Faye, ed., "The Journal of Legardeur Delisle, 1722," 54; and Archives de la Société de Jésus Canada Français, Montreal, "Chemin de S. joseph aux illinois par Le tiatiki," Ms. Pierre Potier, *Gazettes*, 171; and Imlay, "Mr. Patrick Kennedy's Journal," 508.

24. *Encyclopedia Britannica*, s.v. "Spoon River," May 19, 2008, https://www.britannica.com/place/Spoon-River.

25. Imlay, "Mr. Patrick Kennedy's Journal," 508.

26. Joutel in Margry, *Découvertes et établissements des Français*, 3:473–74.

27. Schoolcraft, "Travels in the Central Portions of the Mississippi Valley," 90.

28. Prairie Research Institute of the University of Illinois, Illinois River Biological Station, "The Emiquon Preserve," accessed November 4, 2020, https://illinois-river-bio-station.inhs .illinois.edu.

29. Imlay, "Mr. Patrick Kennedy's Journal," 508.

30. Imlay, "Mr. Patrick Kennedy's Journal," 509.

31. Both Peoria groups lived at Le Rocher, Starved Rock, a 125-foot sandstone bluff located near present Utica in mid-1722, before the Mesquakie forced them to flee the Illinois Valley. The Peoria and some Cahokia returned to the Illinois Valley by 1730. See Mark Walczynski, *Massacre, 1769: The Search for the Origin of the Legend of Starved Rock*, 85–87.

32. The first Fort St. Louis was built on Le Rocher during the early months of 1683. Construction began in late December 1682 and was completed by March 1683. See Tonti in Kellogg, *Early Narratives*, 305.

33. Judith A. Franke, *French Peoria and the Illinois Country, 1673–1846*, 85–95, 35–36.

34. "Peoria History," *Peoria Journal Star*, accessed November 5, 2020, at https://www .pjstar.com/peoria-history.

35. For an in-depth reading on the name Pimitéoui, see Michael McCafferty, "The Illinois Place Name Pimitéoui," 177–87.

36. Franke, *French Peoria and the Illinois Country*, 3.

37. Coulton Storm, "Lieutenant John Armstrong's Map of the Illinois River, 1790," 51, 54.

38. Kellogg in Charlevoix, *Journal of a Voyage to North America*, 2:205.

39. Schoolcraft, "Travels in the Central Portions of the Mississippi Valley," 100.

40. Schoolcraft, "Travels in the Central Portions of the Mississippi Valley," 100.

41. Imlay, "Mr. Patrick Kennedy's Journal," 509.

42. Schoolcraft, "Travels in the Central Portions of the Mississippi Valley," 104.

43. Raymond Wiggers, *Geology Underfoot in Illinois*, 128, 129, 141.

44. Wiggers, *Geology Underfoot in Illinois*, 158–59, 142.

45. The city spells its name LaSalle, not La Salle.

46. La Salle in Margry, *Découvertes et établissements des Français*, 2:175–76.

47. Tonti in M. Anderson, *Relation of Henri de Tonty*, 35.

48. Joseph Jackupcak, retired geologist, personal communication, February 17, 2020.

49. *Cavelier de La Salle to Jacques Bourdon d'Autray*, deed in the French America Collection, Chicago History Museum Research Center; Pease and Werner, *French Foundations*, 19–27.

50. Kellogg, Charlevoix, *Journal of a Voyage to North America*, 2:204.

51. Faye, "Journal of Delisle," 55.

52. Imlay, "Mr. Patrick Kennedy's Journal," 510.

53. Storm, "Lieutenant John Armstrong's Map of the Illinois River," 51.

54. Schoolcraft, "Travels in the Central Portions of the Mississippi Valley," 105.

55. Allouez reported that the Illinois used these bluffs as lookouts. See Allouez in Thwaites, *Jesuit Relations*, 60:159.

56. Richard Hagen, "Starved Rock: An Illinois Time Capsule."

57. Marquette in Thwaites, *Jesuit Relations*, 59:159. Marquette also wrote that the portage was about a half-league in length.

Chapter 7. Kaskaskia to Lake Michigan and Beyond

1. Michael McCafferty, "Illinois Voices, Observations on the Miami-Illinois Language," in *Protohistory at the Grand Village*, by Mazrim, 122.

2. The site increased in size and by 1680 had a reported 460 cabins. Today the site is managed by the Illinois Department of Natural Resources.

3. Thomas E. Emerson, ed., *The Archaeology of the Grand Village of the Illinois, Report of the Grand Village Research Project, 1991–1996: Grand Village of the Illinois State Historic Site (11-LS-13), La Salle County, Illinois*, 207, 22.

4. See Mazrim, *Protohistory at the Grand Village of the Kaskaskia*, 1, 147–48.

5. Brad Bartel, "Power of Place: Catalhoyuk, the Development of the World's First Town," Middle Tennessee State University honors lecture, October 15, 2014.

6. John T. Penman in Emerson, *Archaeology of the Grand Village of the Illinois*, 207.

7. The Illinois reportedly processed salt from salt springs. The site across the river from Kaskaskia is called the "Salt Well" and is located in present-day Starved Rock State Park. See Hauser, "Ethnohistory of the Illinois Indian Tribe," 97–98.

8. Marquette in Thwaites, *Jesuit Relations*, 59:117.

9. The Illinois hand-fed the explorers at the Peoria village. See Thwaites, *Jesuit Relations*, 59:121.

10. It seems likely that, as Potherie claimed he had learned from Jolliet, the slave boy must have traveled the Illinois River between the Des Moines villages and Kaskaskia and was familiar with its course.

11. The Jesuits developed a simple yet efficient way to determine the population of Illinois villages and that of their close ethnic cousins, the Miami. Each Illinois cabin consisted of two fires, there were two families per fire, and each family consisted of one warrior and four nonwarriors for a total of about twenty people per cabin. See Zitomersky, *French Americans*, 219.

12. M. Anderson, *Relation of La Salle*, 211.

13. "La Salle on the Illinois Country," in *French Foundations*, ed. Pease and Werner, 3.

14. M. Anderson, *Relation of Henri de Tonty*, 35.

15. Including Deliette and Charlevoix. See Deliette in *French Foundations*, 306; and Kellogg in Charlevoix, *Journal of a Voyage to North America*, 2:200.

16. "Letters of Cavelier de La Salle and Correspondence Relative to His Undertakings (1678–1685)," 181, Miami Tribal History Document Series, Great Lakes—Ohio Valley Ethnohistory Collection, Erminie Wheeler-Voegelin Archives, Indiana University, Bloomington; Kellogg in Charlevoix, *Journal of a Voyage to North America*, 2:200; Schoolcraft, "Travels in the Central Portions of the Mississippi Valley," 112.

17. Pierre Deliette in *French Foundations*, 306.

18. Hugh Heward, *Hugh Heward's Journal from Detroit to the Illinois: 1790*, accessed February 23, 2013, http://archive.lib.msu.edu/MMM/JA/09/a/JA09a001p008.pdf.

19. Joutel in Margry, *Découvertes et établissements des Français*, 3:508.

20. M. Anderson, *Relation of Henri Tonty*, 45, 47.

21. Marquette in Thwaites, *Jesuit Relations*, 59:159; Pease and Werner, *French Foundations*, 306; Kellogg in Charlevoix, *Journal of a Voyage to North America*, 2:205.

22. Storm, "Lieutenant John Armstrong's Map of the Illinois River," 53.

23. Kellogg in Charlevoix, *Journal of a Voyage to North America*, 2:199.

24. Linguist Michael McCafferty, personal communication, April 28, 2021; Illinois Department of Natural Resources, *Forest Trees of Illinois*.

25. Storm, "Lieutenant John Armstrong's Map of the Illinois River," 50.

26. St. Cosme in Kellogg, *Early Narratives*, 349.

27. McCafferty, personal communication, December 26, 2020.

28. St. Cosme in Kellogg, *Early Narratives*, 349.

29. Gurdon Saltonstall Hubbard, *The Autobiography of Gurdon Saltonstall Hubbard*, 43–46.

30. M. Anderson, *Relation of La Salle*, 243, 265. La Salle returned to the island in March to retrieve the men and merchandise.

31. St. Cosme in Kellogg, *Early Narratives*, 349.

32. Storm, "Lieutenant John Armstrong's Map of the Illinois River," 50.

33. Pierre Deliette in "De Gannes, Memoir," in *French Foundations*, ed. Pease and Werner, 304.

34. Deliette in *French Foundations*, ed. Pease and Werner, 94–95.

35. Deliette in *French Foundations*, ed. Pease and Werner, 302–3.

36. Hubbard, *Autobiography*, 41.

37. Hubbard, *Autobiography*, 42–43.

38. Deliette in *French Foundations*, ed. Pease and Werner, 302; St. Cosme in Kellogg, *Early Narratives*, 347.

39. Illinois Natural History Survey, accessed November 13, 2020, https://www.inhs.illinois.edu/outreach/illinois-beach/dune-formatio/.

40. By the 1820s, soldiers stationed at nearby Fort Dearborn dug a channel that bypassed the old mouth of the Chicago River. *Encyclopedia of Chicago*, s.v. "Proposed Plan for Improving the Mouth of the Chicago River, 1830," http://www.encyclopedia.chicagohistory.org/pages/10761.html.

41. St. Cosme in Kellogg, *Early Narratives*, 346.

42. Marquette in Thwaites, *Jesuit Relations*, 59:165. The swampy portage site was excavated, channelized, and opened on July 4, 1879. The new canal is reported to be seventy-four hundred feet long. See Thwaites, *Jesuit Relations*, 59:313n43.

43. Dablon in Thwaites, *Jesuit Relations*, 58:91.

44. Thwaites, *Jesuit Relations*, 59:67.

45. Marquette in Thwaites, *Jesuit Relations*, 59:163, 183.

46. See Raymond Douville, "Jacques Largillier dit 'le castor,' coureur des bois et 'frère donné'"; and McCafferty, "Jacques Largillier," 190.

47. Delanglez, "Jolliet Early Years" 23.

48. Jesuit Philippe Pierson would have been in charge of the mission at the time. See *New Catholic Encyclopedia*, s.v. "Phillip Pierson," accessed November 16, 2020, https://www.newadvent.org/cathen/12080b.htm.

49. Historic river levels on the Illinois are available from the U.S. Army Corps of Engineers at https://rivergages.mvr.usace.army.mil/WaterControl/stationinfo2.cfm?sid =HAVI2&fid=HAVI2&dt=S.

50. Marquette in Thwaites, *Jesuit Relations*, 59:159, 179.

51. Marquette in Thwaites, *Jesuit Relations*, 59:161.

52. Emily Jane Blasingham, "The Illinois Indians, 1634–1800: A Study in Depopulation," 11–12.

53. Campeau, "Les cartes relatives," 42, 80–81, 84.

54. Marquette in Thwaites, *Jesuit Relations*, 59:161.

55. In addition, a straight line across the modern-day state of Illinois between the Mississippi and the Illinois on the map shows that that the French canoes did not paddle up a stream or small river to reach Kaskaskia.

Chapter 8. Canada, Jolliet, and Marquette

1. *Dictionary of Canadian Biography*, s.v. "Dauphin de La Forest, François," by Louise Dechêne, accessed January 18, 2021, http://www.biographi.ca/en/bio/dauphin_de_la _forest_francois_2E.html.

2. Reuben G. Thwaites, *France in America, 1497–1763*, 60.

3. *The Catholic Encyclopedic*, s.v. "Philippe Pierson," by Julia Zevely, accessed January 1, 2021, http://www.newadvent.org/cathen/12080b.htm.

4. Thwaites, *Jesuit Relations*, 59:215.

5. Delanglez, *Life and Voyages of Louis Jolliet*, 132; Thwaites, *Jesuit Relations*, 59:257–61.

6. Douville, "Life and Death of Adrien Jolliet," 38, 41.

7. The record states that Louis took the robes from the "said Community and made [them] his own without letting his sister [sister-in-law], know." The canoe was lent to him by his sister-in-law, which he apparently never returned. Douville, "Life and Death of Adrien Jolliet," 43–45. See also the will of Sieur Adrien Jolliet (45–46).

8. Not long after Adrien died, Jeanne married Antoine Baillargé. Antoine died about a year later. She then married Normandin. Delanglez, *Life and Voyages of Louis Jolliet*, 16.

9. Douville, "Life and Death of Adrien Jolliet," 44. See also the judgment written by the notary Basset in Delanglez, "Jolliet Early Years," 29. The case was heard by Louis Rouer de Villeray and Thierry de L'Estre. See also Walczynski, "Jolliet and Marquette," 139.

10. Campeau, "Les cartes relatives," 60.

11. Campeau, "Les cartes relatives," 60.

12. *Dictionary of Canadian Biography*, s.v. "Franquelin, Jean-Baptiste-Louis," by M. W. Burke-Gaffney, accessed June 27, 2021, http://www.biographi.ca/en/bio/franquelin_jean _baptiste_louis_2E.html.

13. Hamilton, *Marquette's Explorations*, 4. This mandate went into effect in 1681.

14. Walczynski, "Jolliet and Marquette," 134.

15. Dablon in Thwaites, *Jesuit Relations*, 58:91–93.

16. Dablon in Thwaites, *Jesuit Relations*, 58:105.

17. Dablon in Thwaites, *Jesuit Relations*, 58:103 (emphasis added).

18. Dablon in Thwaites, *Jesuit Relations*, 59:93.

19. Dablon in Thwaites, *Jesuit Relations*, 58:93, 59:87 (emphases added).

20. Jolliet also knew Montagnais as he acted as an interpreter for a Montagnais woman in 1694. Delanglez, *Life and Voyages of Louis Jolliet*, 262.

21. Marquette in Thwaites, *Jesuit Relations*, 59:105; Walczynski, "Jolliet and Marquette," 136.

22. Campeau, "Les cartes relatives," 60–61.

23. Campeau, "Les cartes relatives," 69.

24. Campeau looked into the matter of the arrival of Marquette's journal in Québec. He wrote, "The archives at St. Jérôme hold the paper that served as an envelope for Marquette's writings that were sent from Green Bay all the way to Quebec. We read there, in the handwriting of Father Allouez, the way it is addressed to Father Claude Dablon: 'To my reverend Father, father Claude Dablon, Superior of the Missions of the Company of Jesus in New France.' And in one corner, above this statement and in the same handwriting of Father Allouez, 'Letter and Journal of the late Father Marquette.' Nothing could be more explicit. This page nevertheless served as an envelope for a bigger packet, because Dablon wrote across it, in large handwriting, 'Everything pertaining to Father Marquette's voyage.'" On October 13, 1675, Marquette's death notice was written. Campeau, "Regard critique sur la narration," 35. Campeau's work was translated by Michael McCafferty, linguist, Indiana University, Bloomington, Indiana. As a member of the expedition, Jolliet would have surely had access to the narrative.

25. Campeau, "Les cartes relatives," 74.

26. Duane Esarey, "Mysteries, Misdirection, Mishaps, and Misdeeds: The First 150 Years of Illinois River Maps," PowerPoint presentation.

27. See David Buisseret and Carl Kupfer, "Validating the 1673 'Marquette Map,'" 267.

28. Campeau, "Les cartes relatives," 63, 71, 60. Franquelin also drew Jolliet's 1678 map. See also *Dictionary of Canadian Biography*, s.v. "Franquelin, Jean-Baptiste-Louis," by Burke-Gaffney; and Walczynski, "Jolliet and Marquette," 134.

29. Illinois Catholic Historical Society, "*Illinois Catholic Historical Review*, Volume VI Number 1–2 to Volume VI Number 3–4 (1923–1924)," *Illinois Catholic Historical Review (1918–1929)* (1923), bk. 11, http://ecommons.luc.edu/illinois_catholic_historical_review/11; Walczynski, "Jolliet and Marquette," 131.

30. Campeau, "Les cartes relatives," 60.

31. Walczynski, "Jolliet and Marquette," 131.

32. Count de Frontenac to M. Colbert in *Documents Relating to the Colonial History of New York*, ed. O'Callaghan, 9:121.

33. Delanglez, *Life and Voyages of Louis Jolliet*, 55–56.

34. Douville, "Jacques Largillier"; McCafferty, "Jacques Largillier," 190.

35. Dablon in Thwaites, *Jesuit Relations*, 59:163.

36. On his map describing the voyage of 1673, Marquette uses Ojibwe names for the Fox and the Potawatomi and a French-adapted Ottawa or Algonquin name for the Mascouten. (The name for the Fox is what the Ojibwe called them: *otaka·mi·k*, "people on the other shore.") Ives Goddard, in *Handbook of North American Indians*, ed. Trigger, 646.

Chapter 9. Marquette Returns to Kaskaskia

1. Delanglez, "Jolliet Early Years," 24.

2. Her son, François de Chavigny, was a signer of the partnership contract in October 1672. It appears that his mother provided the additional sum of 300 pounds and had not been paid what she was owed.

3. Delanglez, "Jolliet Early Years," 25.

4. Douville, "Life and Death of Adrien Jolliet," 43–44.

5. Walczynski, "Jolliet and Marquette," 138–39 (emphasis added).

6. Marquette in Thwaites, *Jesuit Relations*, 59:165. Marquette wrote "Chachag8essi8," and his last "8" represented *-wa*. The name is *šaahšaakweehsiwa*. Largillier defines it as "little mottled snake." It's thought to be the term for "garter snake." Jesuit Le Boullenger says it's the *couleuvre*, which is "garter snake." Linguist Albert Samuel Gatschet, however, got the term ca. 1890 and said then it meant copperhead. The term at the time of Marquette probably meant garter snake and two hundred years later had undergone semantic drift and had come to be the word for "copperhead." Linguist Michael McCafferty, personal communication, June 27, 2021.

This encounter, again, demonstrates that the Illinois traveled great distances to obtain European trade goods. As mentioned previously, they were active participants in the Franco-Native American trade by 1674.

7. Marquette in Thwaites, *Jesuit Relations*, 59:165. According to linguist Michael McCafferty, Marquette's "chat," literally "cat," was the old New World French term for raccoon. They were killed for their meat.

8. Marquette in Thwaites, *Jesuit Relations*, 59:169.

9. Marquette in Thwaites, *Jesuit Relations*, 59:171.

10. Marquette dedicated the 1673 voyage to the Virgin Mary and named the Illinois mission Immaculate Conception of the Blessed Virgin in her honor. See Dablon in Thwaites, *Jesuit Relations*, 59:189.

11. Marquette in Thwaites, *Jesuit Relations*, 59:177.

12. Marquette in Thwaites, *Jesuit Relations*, 59:173, 175. The location of the village, according to Marquette, was "near that place," meaning Kaskaskia.

13. Kellogg, *Early Narratives*, 214. The other partners included François de Chavigny de La Chevrotière, Zacharie Jolliet, Jean Plattier, and Jean Tiberge. See *Dictionary of Canadian Biography*, vol. 1, *1000–1700* (Toronto: University of Toronto Press, 1966), s.v. "Jolliet, Louis."

14. *Early Chicago*, accessed August 9, 2015, http://www.earlychicago.com/encyclopedia.php?letter=r&sel=surgeon#e3411.

15. *Dictionary of Canadian Biography*, vol. 1, s.v. "Louis Maheut," by Antonio Drolet; "Account of the Taking Possession of Louisiana by M. de La Salle in 1682," in *The Journeys of Rene Robert Cavelier Sieur de La Salle*, ed. Isaac Joslin Cox, 1:170.

16. Marquette in Thwaites, *Jesuit Relations*, 59:177.

17. National Oceanic and Atmospheric Administration, accessed May 8, 2021, https://oceanserviced.noaa.gov/facts/gltides.html.

18. Father André in Thwaites, *Jesuit Relations*, 57:299.

19. Marquette in Thwaites, *Jesuit Relations*, 59:177.

20. Marquette in Thwaites, *Jesuit Relations*, 59:187.

21. Marquette in Thwaites, *Jesuit Relations*, 59:187.

22. Marquette in Thwaites, *Jesuit Relations*, 59:187.

23. Zitomersky, *French Americans*, 219. It appears that the Jesuit missionary Druillettes also used the ratio of four nonwarriors to one warrior for the Miami divisions.

24. Allouez in Thwaites, *Jesuit Relations*, 58:21, 57:263–65.

25. Thwaites, *Jesuit Relations*, 55:101, 199; Zitomersky, *French Americans*, 78; Vernon W. Kinietz, *Indians of the Western Great Lakes, 1615–1760*, 161.

26. Thwaites, *Jesuit Relations*, 55:199.

27. We saw in chapter 5 that the Peoria and Moingwena were living west of the Mississippi, out of the reach of Haudenosaunee war parties. We will see that refugees from Haudenosaunee attacks gathered in a common defense inside the village palisades at the Mascouten village at Berlin, Wisconsin. An Haudenosaunee incursion of the Illinois Country occurred in September 1680. See "Tonty's Memoir," in Kellogg, *Early Narratives*, 291–94.

28. Dablon in Thwaites, *Jesuit Relations*, 59:189.

29. *Dictionary of Canadian Biography*, s.v. "Cholenec, Pierre," by Henri Béchard, accessed May 9, 2021, http://www.biographi.ca/en/bio/cholenec_pierre_2E.html.

30. McCafferty, "Jacques Largillier," 191; Mark Walczynski, *The History of Starved Rock*, 81.

Chapter 10. La Salle, Allouez, and Kaskaskia

1. *Dictionary of Canadian Biography*, s.v. "Jolliet, Louis," by André Vachon, accessed August 31, 2017, http://www.biographi.ca/en/bio/jolliet_louis_1E.html.

2. Extraite d'une lettre de Colbert à M. Du Chesneau in Margry, *Découvertes*, 1 :329.

3. *Dictionary of Canadian Biography*, s.v. "Jolliet, Louis," by Vachon.

4. Walczynski, "Jolliet and Marquette," 139–40; *Dictionary of Canadian Biography*, s.v. "Jolliet, Louis," by Vachon.

5. Campeau, "Les cartes relatives," 78.

6. Delanglez, *Life and Voyages of Louis Jolliet*, 136.

7. M. Anderson, *Relation of La Salle*, 15.

8. See the August 1, 1674, conversation between Louis Jolliet and Jesuit superior Claude Dablon in Thwaites, *Jesuit Relations*, 60:91–107 (emphasis added).

9. Accault had previously traded with trans-Mississippi tribes for La Salle out of the explorer's seigniory at Fort Frontenac. Mildred Mott Wedel, "Peering at the Ioway Indians through the Mist of Time, 1650 circa 1700," 30–32; Mark Walczynski, *"Inquietus": La Salle in the Illinois Country*, 16, 30–32.

10. Pierson in Thwaites, *Jesuit Relations*, 60:17–19.

11. André in Thwaites, *Jesuit Relations*, 60:199. It appears that the Menominee who burned the cabin was angry at André because the baptism the priest performed on the Menominee's child did not protect him from a murderer.

12. André in Thwaites, *Jesuit Relations*, 60:199.

13. Silvy in Thwaites, *Jesuit Relations*, 60:205.

14. Allouez in Thwaites, *Jesuit Relations*, 60:149.

15. Thwaites, *Jesuit Relations*, 60:149–51.

16. Thwaites, *Jesuit Relations*, 60:151, 153.

17. Thwaites, *Jesuit Relations*, 60:319n24.

18. Thwaites, *Jesuit Relations*, 60:157.

19. Thwaites, *Jesuit Relations*, 58:47.

20. Thwaites, *Jesuit Relations*, 60:161.

21. Margaret Kimball Brown, *The Zimmerman Site*, 73.

22. Emerson, *Archaeology of the Grand Village of the Illinois*, 183.

23. Allouez in Thwaites, *Jesuit Relations*, 60:159.

24. Allouez in Thwaites, *Jesuit Relations*, 60:157. Allouez was mistaken when he wrote that one year earlier, the village was composed of only Kaskaskia. In 1673 only the Kaskaskia lived at the site, while a year and a half later, as we saw in the proceeding chapter, the village had grown from approximately 1,480 people to about 6,000.

25. Allouez in Thwaites, *Jesuit Relations*, 60:157.

26. M. Anderson, *Relation of La Salle*, 117.

27. M. Anderson, *Relation of La Salle*, 15.

28. Henry Chadwick, *The Early Church*, 45.

29. Jonathan L. Reed, *The Visual Guide to the New Testament*, 7.

30. In chapter 2 of the New Testament book of Galatians, the Apostle Paul tells the Christians that they are no longer bound by the restrictions of Jewish law.

31. Tracy Neal Leavelle, *The Catholic Calumet*, 101; and Allouez in Thwaites, *Jesuit Relations*, 57:267–69.

32. "The Pater," entry in Sébastien Râles, *Illinois Prayerbook*, trans. Michael McCafferty, personal communication, April 27, 2022. See also Leavelle, *The Catholic Calumet*, trans. McCafferty, 114, figure 7.

33. Densmore, *Chippewa Customs*, 108.

34. Bruce G. Trigger, *The Children of Aataentsic, a History of the Huron People to 1600*, 78–79.

35. Jesuit Louis André in Thwaites, *Jesuit Relations*, 58:273 Leavelle, *The Catholic Calumet*, 137.

36. R. David Edmunds and Joseph L. Peyser, *The Fox Wars: The Mesquakie Challenge to New France*, 11–14.

37. Allouez in Thwaites, *Jesuit Relations*, 60:163.

Chapter 11. Hudson Bay, La Salle in the Illinois, and the Recollects

1. Dablon in Thwaites, *Jesuit Relations*, 59:203.

2. Father Pierson had charge of the Wendat mission. Thwaites, *Jesuit Relations*, 61:101.

3. Thwaites, *Jesuit Relations*, 61:69, 101.

4. Delanglez, *Life and Voyages of Louis Jolliet*, 146.

5. *Dictionary of Canadian Biography*, s.v. "Jolliet, Louis," by André Vachon, accessed August 31, 2017, http://www.biographi.ca/en/bio/jolliet_louis_1E.html.

6. When first established, the Ferme du Domaine du Roy had no set boundaries. See Delanglez, *Life and Voyages of Louis Jolliet*, 147.

7. *Dictionary of Canadian Biography*, s.v. "Jolliet, Louis," by Vachon.

8. Dablon in Thwaites, *Jesuit Relations*, 61:93.

9. Dablon in Thwaites, *Jesuit Relations*, 61:153.

10. McCafferty, *Native American Place-Names of Indiana*, 56.

11. M. Anderson, *Relation of La Salle*, 79.

12. La Salle in "Letters of Cavelier de La Salle and Correspondence Relative to His Undertakings (1678–1685)," Miami Tribal History Document Series, Great Lakes—Ohio Valley Ethnohistory Collection, Erminie Wheeler-Voegelin Archives, Indiana University, Bloomington.

13. Dablon in Thwaites, *Jesuit Relations*, 63:105.

14. Marquette in Thwaites, *Jesuit Relations*, 59:159.

15. Anderson, *Relation of La Salle*, 85.

16. Hennepin, *New Discovery of a Vast Country in America*, 1:99.

17. *Dictionary of Canadian Biography*, s.v. "Dolbeau, Jean," by Frédéric Gingras, accessed January 31, 2021, http://www.biographi.ca/en/bio/dolbeau_jean_1E.html. The *Catholic Encyclopedia* suggests that Jamet (Jamey) performed the first Catholic Mass in the colony. See *Catholic Encyclopedia*, s.v. "Denis Jamay," catholic.org/encyclopedia/view.php?id=6247.

18. Viel was the first Franciscan Martyr in Canada. It appears he was killed by his Wendat canoe men while returning to Quebec from Wendat country. See *Dictionary of Canadian Biography*, "Viel, Nicolas," by G.-M. Dumas, accessed February 1, 2021, http://www.biographi .ca/en/bio/viel_nicolas_1E.html.

19. Eccles, *French in North America*, 80.

20. *Dictionary of Canadian Biography*, s.v. "Hennepin, Louis," by Jean-Roch Rioux, accessed January 31, 2021, http://www.biographi.ca/en/bio/hennepin_louis_2E.html.

21. *Dictionary of Canadian Biography*, s.v. "Membré, Zénobe," by Frédéric Gingras, accessed January 31, 2021, http://www.biographi.ca/en/bio/membre_zenobe_1E.html.

22. Hennepin, *New Discovery of a Vast Country in America*, 1:178.

23. *Dictionary of Canadian Biography*, s.v. "La Ribourde, Gabriel de," by Léopold Lamontagne, accessed January 31, 2021, http://www.biographi.ca/en/bio/la_ribourde_gabriel _de_1E.html.

24. Hennepin, *New Discovery of a Vast Country in America*, 1:33–34.

25. Walczynski, *"Inquietus,"* 49; "Memoir on the French Colonies in North America," in *Documents Relating to the Colonial History of New York*, ed. O'Callaghan, 10:229.

26. Moonswa, "The Deer" in Miami-Illinois, has been changed by writers to "Monso" and "Monseau." Michael McCafferty, linguist, personal communication, June 27, 2021.

27. M. Anderson, *Relation of La Salle*, 97–99; Pease and Werner, *French Foundations*, 11–13. La Salle wrote that Allouez "had retired to a village composed partly of Mascouten and Wea [a Miami subtribe]," a location that best described St. Jacques on the Fox in Wisconsin.

28. "La Salle to a Friend," in Margry, *Découvertes*, 2:295–99; M. Anderson, *Relation of La Salle*, 289.

29. Margry, *Découvertes*, 3:502.

30. According to Hennepin, he suffered from a gum "defluxion," and he felt that he was unable to participate in the mission. See Hennepin, *New Discovery of a Vast Country in America*, 177–78; and Walczynski, *"Inquietus,"* 32–33.

31. Franke, *French Peoria and the Illinois Country*, 18.

32. Balesi, *Time of the French in the Heart of North America*, 130.

33. *Dictionary of Canadian Biography*, s.v. "Tonti, Henri," by E. B. Osler, http://www .biographi.ca/en/bio/tonty_henri_2E.html.

34. The peace established between the French and the Haudenosaunee in 1666 was still respected by the Haudenosaunee.

Chapter 12. La Salle, the Illinois Country, and the Gulf

1. La Salle in Margry, *Découvertes*, 2:148; M. Anderson, *Relation of La Salle*, 271.

2. La Salle in Anderson, *Relation of La Salle*, 271.

3. La Salle in Anderson, *Relation of La Salle*, 293.

4. *Dictionary of Canadian Biography*, s.v. "Le Febvre de La Barre, Joseph-Antoine," by R. La Roque de Roquebrune, accessed April 3, 2021, http://www.biographi.ca/en/bio/le _febvre_de_la_barre_joseph_antoine_1E.html.

5. For a more comprehensive rendering of La Salle's meeting with the Miami and the tribe's flight to the Illinois Country, see Walczynski, *"Inquietus,"* 74–77. See also "Letters of Cavelier de La Salle and Correspondence Relative to his Undertakings (1678–1685)," Miami Tribal History Document Series, Great Lakes—Ohio Valley Ethnohistory Collection, Erminie Wheeler-Voegelin Archives, Indiana University, Bloomington.

6. Walczynski, *"Inquietus,"* 76–77.

7. *Dictionary of Canadian Biography*, s.v. "Le Febvre de La Barre, Joseph-Antoine," by La Roque de Roquebrune.

8. La Salle in Margry, *Découvertes*, 2 :317.

9. "Robert Cavalier, Sieur de La Salle, Addressed to Monseigneur de Seignelay, in the Discoveries Made by Him by Order of His Majesty Louis XIV, King of France." See B. F. French, "Robert Cavalier, Sieur de La Salle, Addressed to Monseigneur Seignelay on the Discoveries Made by Him by Order of His Majesty Louis XIV, King of France," Historical Collections of Louisiana and Florida, 2nd ser. (New York: Albert Mason, 1875), 4, accessed August 27, 2016, https://books.google.com.

10. Baugy tried to coax men under Tonti to join with him by offering them land grants. D'Autray's grant was issued in April 1683, while a month still remained on La Salle's patent. Prudhomme's grant was made in August 1683, three months after it had expired. See Pease and Werner, *French Foundations*, 19–36; and *Dictionary of Canadian Biography*, s.v. "Louis-Henri de Baugy," by Jean Hamelin, accessed April 4, 2021, http://www.biographi.ca/en /bio/baugy_louis_henri_de_2E.html.

11. For a full discussion of the problems associated with the Franquelin map, see Walczynski, *"Inquietus,"* 78–85.

12. Robert S. Weddle, Mary Christine Morkovsky, and Patricia Galloway, eds., *La Salle, the Mississippi, and the Gulf: Three Primary Documents*, 43.

13. Marquette's map and *relation* made it abundantly clear that the Mississippi flows south, not west. The missionary wrote, "We had gone down to near the 33rd degree of latitude having proceeded nearly all the time in a southerly direction, when we perceived a village on The water's edge called Mitchigamea." Thwaites, *Jesuit Relations*, 59:149. The 1675 Franquelin-

Jolliet *La Frontenacie* map also shows the Mississippi River coursing in a southerly direction, on an approximate angle of two degrees to the west between the confluence of the Ohio and the Mississippi and the juncture of the Arkansas and Mississippi.

14. "Robert Cavalier, Sieur de La Salle, Addressed to Monseigneur de Seignelay, in the Discoveries Made by Him by Order of His Majesty Louis XIV, King of France."

15. Beginning in the late fall of 1680, the French in the Illinois Country used small, shallow draft vessels to navigate the streams of northeastern Illinois. The canoe convoy captured by the Haudenosaunee on the Kankakee consisted of fourteen men in seven canoes. Trade contracts written for voyageurs who traveled between Montreal and Le Rocher between 1685 and the 1690s reveal that the men traveled in small two-man canoes. For example, see Walczynski, *History of Starved Rock*, 77–78; M. Anderson, *Relation of La Salle*, 73; "Instructions from Monsieur de La Barre to Monsieur de Salvaye," in *Documents Relating to the Colonial History of New York*, edited by O'Callaghan, 3:450–51; and "Account of a Journey in the Country of the Islinois by M. M. Beauvais, Provost, des Rosiers, 1683–1684," in *Découvertes*, ed. Margry, 2:338–44. Margry translation found in Miami Tribal History Document Series, Great Lakes—Ohio Valley Ethnohistory Collection. Engagements to Dumay, Barette, Rouillard and Froment, Morin, Beaujean, fin *French Foundations*, ed. Pease and Werner, 126, 127, 148, 151, 154.

16. Walczynski, *"Inquietus,"* 75.

17. Henri Joutel, *The La Salle Expedition to Texas: The Journal of Henri Joutel*, 49. The missionaries included La Salle's brother Jean Cavelier, Anastase Douay, and Zénobe Membré.

18. Bruseth and Turner, *From a Watery Grave*, 20–21.

19. Joutel, *La Salle Expedition to Texas*, 151, 153. La Salle had made several exploratory treks, searching for the Mississippi, between 1685 and 1687.

20. Walczynski, *History of Starved Rock*, 88.

Epilogue

1. *Dictionary of Canadian Biography*, s.v. "Gravier, Jacques," by Charles E. O'Neill, accessed April 6, 2021, http://www.biographi.ca/en/bio/gravier_jacques_2E.html; *Catholic Encyclopedia*, s.v. "Jacques Gravier," by Lionel Lindsay, accessed April 6, 2021, http://www.newadvent.org/cathen/06732b.htm.

2. Mary Borgias Palm, "Jesuit Missions of the Illinois Country, 1673–1763," 22.

3. Linguist Michael McCafferty, personal communication, January 22, 2018.

4. Walczynski, *History of Starved Rock*, 104; McCafferty, "Jacques Largillier," 191.

5. Franke, *French Peoria and the Illinois Country*, 32.

6. *Dictionary of Canadian Biography*, s.v. "Tonti, Henri," by E. B. Osler, accessed April 6, 2021, http://www.biographi.ca/en/bio/tonty_henri_2E.html.

7. Joutel, *La Salle Expedition to Texas*, 26.

8. *Encyclopedia Britannica*, s.v. "Pierre Le Moyne d'Iberville," by Jay Higginbotham, accessed April 6, 2021, https://www.britannica.com/biography/Pierre-Le-Moyne-dIberville.

9. Palm, "Jesuit Missions of the Illinois Country," 38.

10. *Dictionary of Canadian Biography*, s.v. "Gravier, Jacques," by O'Neill; Thwaites, *Jesuit Relations*, 65:99.

11. Gravier in Thwaites, *Jesuit Relations*, 65:101.

12. Gravier in Thwaites, *Jesuit Relations*, 65:103.

13. Gilbert Garraghan, S.J., "New Light on Old Cahokia," 109–10.

14. Garraghan, "New Light on Old Cahokia," 104.

15. Garraghan, "New Light on Old Cahokia," 101.

16. Clarence Walworth Alvord, *The Illinois Country, 1673–1818*, 115.

17. Garraghan, "New Light on Old Cahokia," 114.

18. Illinois State Museum, accessed May 21, 2021, https://www.museum.state.il.us /RiverWeb/landings/Ambot/Archives/fwp/EarlyHistory.html.

19. Gravier in Thwaites, *Jesuit Relations*, 65:105, 109, 111, 115, 157, 121.

20. Gravier in Thwaites, *Jesuit Relations*, 65:109, 111, 135, 155, 173.

21. Gravier in Thwaites, *Jesuit Relations*, 65:161.

22. Prior to his assuming command at the post upon the death of commandant Ensign Sauvole, Bienville explored the Red and Ouachita Rivers. See *Dictionary of Canadian Biography*, s.v. "Le Moyne De Bienville, Jean-Baptiste," by C. E. O'Neill, accessed May 20, 2021, http://www.biographi.ca/en/bio/le_moyne_de_bienville_jean_baptiste_3E.html.

23. Gravier in Thwaites, *Jesuit Relations*, 65:159.

24. Jean Delanglez, "Tonti Letters," 215.

25. Gravier in Thwaites, *Jesuit Relations*, 65:171.

26. Gravier in Thwaites, *Jesuit Relations*, 65:177.

27. Delanglez, "Tonti Letters," 223–32.

28. *Dictionary of Canadian Biography*, s.v. "Le Moyne De Bienville, Jean-Baptiste," by O'Neill.

29. *Dictionary of Canadian Biography*, s.v. "Laumet, de Lamothe Cadillac, Antoine," by Yves F. Zoltvany, accessed April 12, 2021, http://www.biographi.ca/en/bio/laumet_antoine_2E .html.

30. "Louisiana: European Explorations and the Louisiana Purchase, a Special Presentation from the Geography and Map Division of the Library of Congress," accessed April 12, 2012, https://www.loc.gov/static/collections/louisiana-european-explorations-and-the -louisiana-purchase/images/lapurchase.pdf.

31. Jon Moen, "John Law and the Mississippi Bubble."

32. Alvord, *Illinois Country*, 150–51.

33. Moen, "John Law and the Mississippi Bubble."

34. Moen, "John Law and the Mississippi Bubble."

35. "Louisiana: European Explorations and the Louisiana Purchase."

36. *Dictionary of Canadian Biography*, s.v. "Juchereau, de Saint-Denys, Charles," by John Fortier, accessed April 7, 2021, http://www.biographi.ca/en/bio/juchereau_de_saint _denys_charles_2E.html.

37. Daniel Hechenberger, "Jesuits—History and Impact: From Their Origins prior to the Baroque Crisis to Their Role in the Illinois Country," 97.

38. Palm, "Jesuit Missions of the Illinois Country," 42.

39. Natalia Maree Belting, *Kaskaskia under the French Regime*, 12.

40. Belting, *Kaskaskia under the French Regime*, 12.

41. Zitomersky, *French Americans*, 373.

42. Belting, *Kaskaskia under the French Regime*, 13.

43. Palm, "Jesuit Missions of the Illinois Country," 51.

44. Father Mermet in Thwaites, *Jesuit Relations*, 66:49.

45. Schoolcraft, "Travels in the Central Portions of the Mississippi Valley," 109.

46. Emerson, *Archaeology of the Grand Village of the Illinois*, 32.

47. Army Corps of Engineers surveyed the same stretch of the river in 1867 and in 1883. The results of the 1899 and 1900 surveys became the Woermann Maps.

48. Emerson, *Archaeology of the Grand Village of the Illinois*, 3, 6–7.

49. Hauser, "Ethnohistory of the Illinois Indian Tribe," 356–70; Walczynski, *Massacre, 1769*, 37.

50. Eric Hemenway, Little Traverse Bay Bands of Odawa Indians, "Indian Children Forced to Assimilate at White Boarding Schools," National Park Service, last modified April 18, 2019, https://www.nps.gov/articles/boarding-schools.htm.

51. "Recent Legislation: Truth and Healing Commission on Indian Boarding School Policy Act," *Harvard Law Review* (blog), November 21, 2020, https://blog.harvardlawreview.org/recent-legislation-truth-and-healing-commission-on-indian-boarding-school-policy-act/.

52. "751 Bodies Found Buried at Indigenous School in Canada, Leaders Say," *Huffington Post*, June 24, 2021, https://www.huffpost.com/entry/751-bodies-found-buried-at-indigenous-school-in-canada-leaders-say_n_60d4ac37e4b052e474ff5ad8.

53. National Public Radio, "The Remains of 215 Indigenous Children Have Been Found at a Former School in Canada," May 29, 2021, https://www.npr.org/2021/05/29/1001566509/the-remains-of-215-indigenous-children-have-been-found-at-a-former-school-in-can.

54. Temple, *Indian Villages of the Illinois Country*, 52, 54. By 1801 there were between fifteen and twenty Kaskaskia men.

55. "Minutes of Mr. Hamburgh's Journal, 1763," 359–64.

56. *Mississippi Encyclopedia*, s.v. "Chickasaw War," by David S. Newhall, accessed on April 14, 2021, http://mississippiencyclopedia.org/entries/chickasaw-war/.

57. Claiborne A. Skinner, *Upper Country*, 131–35.

58. *Mississippi Encyclopedia*, s.v. "Chickasaw War," by Newhall.

59. Kelly L. Schmidt, Ayan Ali, and Jeff Harrison, "Jesuit Slaveholding in Colonial Era Kaskaskia," Slavery, History, Memory, and Reconciliation Project, 2020, accessed April 19, 2021, https://www.jesuits.org/our-work/shmr/what-we-have-learned/kaskaskia.

60. B. F. French, ed., *Historical Collections of Louisiana*, 89–95.

61. Nicole Atwill, senior foreign law specialist, "Slavery in the French Colonies: Le Code Noir (the Black Code) of 1685," January 13, 2011, https://blogs.loc.gov/law/2011/01/slavery-in-the-french-colonies/.

62. Scottie Andrew, "Jesuits to Commit $100 Million to the Descendants of People the Order Once Enslaved," CNN, March 16, 2021, https://www.cnn.com/2021/03/16/us/georgetown-slavery-descendants-jesuits-100-million-trnd/index.html.

63. Hechenberger, "Jesuits—History and Impact," 99.

64. Clarence Walworth Alvord and Clarence Edwin Carter, "The Critical Period," 62, 67–68.

65. *Dictionary of Canadian Biography*, s.v. "Jolliet, Louis," by André Vachon, accessed August 31, 2017, http://www.biographi.ca/en/bio/jolliet_louis_1E.html.

66. Walczynski, " Jolliet and Marquette," 139–40.

67. Pease and Werner, *French Foundations*, 2–4; Mark Walczynski, "La Salle vs. Jolliet: A Rivalry for Trade and Colonization in the Illinois Country," 7–8.

68. Walczynski, *"Inquietus,"* 49–50.

69. Schoolcraft, "Travels in the Central Portions of the Mississippi Valley," 118.

70. Walczynski, "Jolliet vs. La Salle," 9.

71. Schoolcraft, "Travels in the Central Portions of the Mississippi Valley," 117, 119.

72. Walczynski, "Jolliet vs. La Salle," 9.

73. Justine Christianson, HAER Historian, Historic American Engineering Record Illinois Waterway HAER No. IL-164, U.S. Army Corps of Engineers, Rock Island District IL-164, Rock Island, Illinois, 2008, 1, https://docslib.org/doc/12932179/illinois-waterway-haer-il-164-u-s-army-corps-of-engineers-rock-island-district-il-164-rock-island-rock-island-illinois.

74. John Hilliard, *Photographic Sketch Book of Old Ottawa, Illinois and Vicinity, 1850s–1930*, 44–45.

75. Hilliard, *Photographic Sketch Book*, 16, 17.

76. "Louisiana: European Explorations and the Louisiana Purchase."

77. *Mississippi Encyclopedia*, s.v. "The Third Treaty of San Ildefonso," by James P. Pate, accessed May 27, 2021, https://mississippiencyclopedia.org/entries/san-ildefonso-third-treaty-of/.

Bibliography

Primary Sources

Alvord, Clarence Walworth, and Clarence Edwin Carter. "The Critical Period." Collections of the Illinois State Historical Library. Vol. 10. British series, vol. 1. Springfield: Illinois State Historical Library, 1915.

Anderson, Melville B., trans. *Relation of Henri de Tonty Concerning the Explorations of LaSalle from 1678 to 1683*. Chicago: Caxton Club, 1898.

———, trans. *Relation of the Discoveries and Voyages of Cavelier de La Salle from 1679 to 1681, the Official Narrative*. Chicago: Caxton Club, 1901.

Blair, Emma Helen, ed. *Indian Tribes of the Upper Mississippi Valley and Region of the Great Lakes*. 2 vols. 1911. Reprint, Lincoln: University of Nebraska Press, 1996.

Charlevoix, Pierre-Francis Xavier de. *Journal of a Voyage to North America*. 2 vols. Ann Arbor: University Microfilms, 1966.

Cox, Isaac Joslin, ed. *The Journeys of Rene Robert Cavelier, Sieur de La Salle*. 2 vols. New York: Allerton, 1906.

———, ed. "Joutel's Historic Journal of Monsieur de La Salle's Last Voyage to Discover the River Mississippi." In *The Journeys of Rene Robert Cavelier, Sieur de La Salle*. 2 vols. New York: Allerton, 1906.

French, B. F., ed. *Historical Collections of Louisiana*. Pt. 3. New York: D. Appleton, 1851.

Hennepin, Louis. *The French Regime in Wisconsin*. Vol. 1, *1634–1727*. Edited by Reuben Gold Thwaites. Collections of the State Historical Society of Wisconsin, vol. 16. Madison: State Historical Society of Wisconsin, 1902.

———. *The French Regime in Wisconsin*. Vol. 2, *1727–1748*. Edited by Reuben Gold Thwaites. Collections of the State Historical Society of Wisconsin, vol. 17. Madison: State Historical Society of Wisconsin, 1906.

———. *A New Discovery of a Vast Country in America*. Vol. 1. Edited by Reuben Gold Thwaites. Toronto: Coles, 1903.

Heward, Hugh. *Hugh Heward's Journal from Detroit to the Illinois: 1790*. http://archive.lib .msu.edu/MMM/JA/09/a/JA09a001p008.pdf.

Imlay, Gilbert, ed. "Mr. Patrick Kennedy's Journal Up the Illinois River." In *A Topographical Description of the Western Territory of North America*. London: printed for J. Debrett, 1797.

Joutel, Henri. *The La Salle Expedition to Texas: The Journal of Henri Joutel*. Edited by William C. Foster. Austin: Texas State Historical Society, 1998.

Kellogg, Louise Phelps, ed. *Early Narratives of the Northwest, 1634–1699*. 1917. Reprint, New York: Scribner's Sons, 2001.

Margry, Pierre, ed. *Découvertes et établissements des Français dans l'ouest et dans le sud de l'Amérique septentrionale, 1614–1754*. 6 vols. Paris: Maisonneuve, 1875. Miami Tribal History Document Series, Great Lakes—Ohio Valley Ethnohistory Collection, Erminie Wheeler-Voegelin Archives. Indiana University, Bloomington.

"Minutes of Mr. Hamburgh's Journal, 1763." In *Travels in the American Colonies*, edited by Newton D. Mereness. New York: Macmillan, 1916.

O'Callaghan, Edmund Bailey, ed. *Documents Relating to the Colonial History of New York*. 15 vols. on CD. Saugerties, NY: Hope Farm Press, 2001.

Pease, Theodore Calvin, and Raymond C. Werner, eds. *French Foundations*. Collections of the Illinois State Historical Library. Vol. 23. French series, vol. 1. Springfield: Trustees of the Illinois State Historical Library, 1934.

Schoolcraft, Henry Rowe. "Travels in the Central Portions of the Mississippi Valley: Comprising Observations on Its Mineral Geography, Internal Resources, and Aboriginal Population." In *Pictures of Illinois, One Hundred Years Ago*, edited by Milo Milton Quaife. Chicago: Lakeside Press, 1918.

Stearns, Raymond Phineas. "Joseph Kellogg: Observations on Senex's Map of North America (1710)." *Mississippi Valley Historical Review* 23, no. 3 (1936): 353. Miami Tribal History Document Series, Great Lakes—Ohio Valley Ethnohistory Collection, Erminie Wheeler-Voegelin Archives, Indiana University, Bloomington.

Thwaites, Reuben Gold, ed. *Collections of the State Historical Society of Wisconsin*. Vol. 16, *1634–1727*. Madison: State Historical Society, 1902.

———, ed. *Jesuit Relations and Allied Documents, 1610–1791*. 73 vols. Cleveland: Burrows, 1901.

Weddle, Robert S., Mary Christine Morkovsky, and Patricia Galloway, eds. *La Salle, the Mississippi, and the Gulf: Three Primary Documents*. College Station: Texas A&M University, 1987.

Williams, Mentor, L., ed. *Schoolcraft's Narrative Journal of Travels*. East Lansing: Michigan State University Press, 1992.

Other Sources

Alvord, Clarence Walworth. *The Illinois Country, 1673–1818*. Urbana: University of Illinois Press, 1920.

Anderson, Gary Clayton. *Kinsmen of Another Kind*. St. Paul: Minnesota Historical Society Press, 1997.

Balesi, Charles J. *The Time of the French in the Heart of North America, 1673–1818*. Chicago: Alliance Francaise, 1991.

Behm, Jeffery A. "The Meskwaki in Eastern Wisconsin: Ethnohistory and Archaeology." *Wisconsin Archaeologist* 89, nos. 1–2 (2008).

Belting, Natalia Maree. *Kaskaskia under the French Regime*. 1948. Reprint, Carbondale: Southern Illinois University Press, 2003.

———. "The Piasa—It Isn't a Bird!" *Journal of the Illinois State Historical Society* 66, no. 3 (1973).

Blasingham, Emily Jane. "The Illinois Indians, 1634–1800: A Study in Depopulation." PhD diss., Indiana University, 1956.

Brown, Margaret Kimball. *The Zimmerman Site*. Illinois State Museum Reports of Investigations, no. 32. Springfield: Illinois State Museum, 1975.

Bruseth, James, and Toni Turner. *From a Watery Grave: The Discovery and Excavation of La Salle's Shipwreck "La Belle."* College Station: Texas A&M University Press, 2005.

Buisseret, David, and Carl Kupfer. "Validating the 1673 'Marquette Map.'" *Journal of Illinois History* 14, no. 4 (2011).

Campeau, Lucien. "Les cartes relatives à la découverte du Missisipi [*sic*] parle le Père Jacques Marquette et Louis Jolliet." Translated by Michael McCafferty. *Les Cahiers des Dix* (1992).

———. "Regard critique sur la narration du P. Jacques Marquette." *Les Cahiers des Dix* (1991).

Caton, John Dean. "The Last of the Illinois: And a Sketch of the Pottawatomies." In *Miscellanies*. Chicago: Rand McNally, 1870.

Chadwick, Henry. *The Early Church*. Penguin History of the Church. Rev. ed. London: Penguin Books, 1993.

Costa, David J. "Illinois." *Society for the Study of the Indigenous Languages of the Americas Newsletter* 25, no. 4 (2007): 9–12.

Delâge, Denys. "French and English Colonial Models in North America." In *Le pays des Illinois: Selections from "Le Journal," 1983–2005*. Extended Publication Series, no. 6. Naperville, IL: Center for French Colonial Studies, 2006.

Delanglez, Jean, S.J. "Calendar of La Salle Travels." In *Jean Delanglez, S.J., Anthology*. New York and London: Garland, 1985.

———. "Jolliet Early Years." *Mid-America, an Historical Review* 27, no. 1 (1945).

———. *Life and Voyages of Louis Jolliet (1645–1700)*. Chicago: Institute of Jesuit History, 1948.

———. "Tonti Letters." In *Jean Delanglez, S.J., Anthology*. New York: Garland, 1985.

Densmore, Frances. *Chippewa Customs*. Minnesota Historical Society reprint of the 1929 Smithsonian Institution *Bureau of American Ethnology Bulletin 86*. St. Paul: Minnesota Historical Society Press, 1979.

Donnelly, Joseph E., S.J. *Jacques Marquette*. Chicago: Loyola University Press, 1968.

Douville, Raymond, S.R.C. "Jacques Largillier dit 'le castor,' coureur des bois et 'frère donné.'" *Les Cahiers des Dix*, no. 29 (1964).

———. "Life and Death of Adrien Jolliet—a Short, Honest and Very Full Life." Translated by Michael McCafferty. *Les Cahiers des Dix* (August 1979).

Eccles, William J. *The Canadian Frontier, 1534–1760*. Rev. ed. Albuquerque: University of New Mexico Press, 2003.

———. *The French in North America, 1500–1783*. East Lansing: Michigan State University Press, 1998.

Edmunds, R. David. *The Potawatomis: Keepers of the Fire.* Norman: University of Oklahoma Press, 1978.

Edmunds, R. David, and Joseph L. Peyser. *The Fox Wars: The Mesquakie Challenge to New France.* Norman: University of Oklahoma Press, 1993.

Eifert, Virginia S. *Louis Jolliet, Explorers of Rivers.* New York: Dodd, Mead, 1961.

Ekberg, Carl J. *Stealing Indian Women: Native Slavery in the Illinois Country.* Urbana: University of Illinois Press, 2007.

Emerson, Thomas E., ed. *The Archaeology of the Grand Village of the Illinois, Report of the Grand Village Research Project, 1991–1996: Grand Village of the Illinois State Historic Site (11-LS-13), La Salle County, Illinois.* Urbana-Champaign: Board of Trustees of the University of Illinois, 1998.

Esarey, Duane. "Seasonal Occupation Patterns in Illinois History: A Case Study in the Lower Illinois River Valley." *Illinois Archaeology* 9, nos. 1–2 (1997).

Esarey, Duane, and Kjersti E. Emerson, eds. *Palos Village, an Early Seventeenth-Century Ancestral Ho-Chunk Occupation in the Chicago Area.* Studies in Archaeology, no. 14. Champaign: Illinois Archaeological Survey, 2022.

Faye, Stanley, ed. "The Journal of Legardeur Delisle, 1722." *Journal of the Illinois State Historical Society* (March 1945).

Franke, Judith A. *French Peoria and the Illinois Country, 1673–1846.* Illinois State Museum Popular Science Series, vol. 12. Springfield: Illinois State Museum, 1995.

Garraghan, Gilbert J., S.J. "La Salle's Jesuit Days." *Mid-America, an Historical Review* 19 (1937).

———. "New Light on Old Cahokia." *Illinois Catholic Historical Review* 11, no. 11 (1928).

———. "Some Hitherto Unpublished Marquettiana." *Mid-America, an Historical Review,* n.s., 18 (1936).

Goddard, Ives. "Mississippi." *Society for the Study of the Indigenous Languages of the Americas* 25, no. 4 (2007).

———. "The West-to-East Cline in Algonquian Dialectology." In *Papers of the 25th Algonquian Conference,* edited by William Cowan, 187–211. Ottawa: Carlton University, 1994.

Grantham, Larry. "The Illini Village of the Jolliet and Marquette Voyage of 1673." *Missouri Archaeologist* 54 (December 1993).

Hagen, Richard. "Starved Rock: An Illinois Time Capsule." *Outdoor Illinois* (Illinois Department of Conservation) 3, no. 1 [year unknown].

Hamilton, Raphael N., S.J. *Father Marquette.* Grand Rapids, MI: Eerdmans, 1970.

———. *Marquette's Explorations: The Narratives Reexamined.* Madison: University of Wisconsin Press, 1970.

Hauser, Raymond E. "Ethnohistory of the Illinois Indian Tribe, 1673–1832." PhD diss., Northern Illinois University, 1973.

Hechenberger, Daniel. "Jesuits—History and Impact: From Their Origins prior to the Baroque Crisis to Their Role in the Illinois Country." *Journal of the Illinois State Historical Society* 100, no. 2 (2007).

Hilliard, John. *Photographic Sketch Book of Old Ottawa, Illinois and Vicinity, 1850s–1930.* N.p.: n.p., 2000.

Hubbard, Gurdon Saltonstall. *The Autobiography of Gurdon Saltonstall Hubbard.* New York: Citadel Press, 1969.

Illinois Department of Natural Resources. *Forest Trees of Illinois*. [Springfield, IL]: Division of Forestry, 2006.

Kinietz, Vernon W. *Indians of the Western Great Lakes, 1615–1760*. Ann Arbor: University of Michigan Press, 1965.

Leavelle, Tracy Neal. *The Catholic Calumet*. Philadelphia: University of Pennsylvania Press, 2012.

Matson, Nehemiah. *French and Indians of the Illinois River*. 1874. Carbondale: Southern Illinois University Press, 2001.

Mazrim, Robert. *Protohistory at the Grand Village of the Kaskaskia: The Illinois Country on the Eve of Colony*. Studies in Archaeology, no. 10, Illinois State Archaeological Survey. Urbana: University of Illinois, 2015.

McCafferty, Michael. "The Illinois Place Name Pimiéoui." *Journal of the Illinois State Historical Society* 102, no. 2 (2009).

———. "Jacques Largillier: French Trader, Jesuit Brother, and Jesuit Scribe 'par Excellence.'" *Journal of the Illinois State Historical Society* 104, no. 3 (2011).

———. *Native American Place-Names of Indiana*. Urbana: University of Illinois Press, 2008.

———. "Peoria." *Le Journal* (Center for French Colonial Studies) (Fall 2011).

———. "Where Did Jean Nicollet Meet the Winnebago in 1634: A Critique of Robert L. Hall's 'Rethinking Jean Nicollet's Route to the Ho-Chunks in 1634.'" *Ontario History* 96, no. 2 (2004): 170–82.

———. "While Cleaning Up a Tribal Name." *Michigan's Habitant Heritage* (French-Canadian Heritage Society of Michigan) 41, no. 4 (2020).

McDonnell, Michael A. *Masters of Empire: Great Lakes Indians and the Making of America*. New York: Hill and Wang, 2015.

Meyer, Roy W. *History of the Santee Sioux: United States Indian Policy on Trial*. Lincoln: University of Nebraska Press, 1993.

Moen, Jon. "John Law and the Mississippi Bubble." *Mississippi History Now, an Online Publication of the Mississippi Historical Society* (October 2001).

Morrissey, Robert Michael. *Empire by Collaboration*. Philadelphia: University of Pennsylvania Press, 2015.

———. "The Power of the Ecotone: Bison, Slavery, and the Rise and Fall of the Grand Village of the Kaskaskia." *Journal of American History* 102, no. 3 (2015): 667–92. https://doi.org/10.1093/jahist/jav514692. https://doi.org/10.1093/jahist/jav514.

Norman, Janell (Belisle *dit* Germain). "The Amazing Louis Jolliet." *Michigan's Habitant Heritage* 38, no. 1 (2017).

Palm, Mary Borgias. "The Jesuit Missions of the Illinois Country, 1673–1763." PhD diss., St. Louis University, 1931.

Reed, Jonathan L. *The Visual Guide to the New Testament*. New York: HarperCollins, 2007.

Rusch, Lynn A. "The Springview Site: A Possible Late Seventeenth-Century Mascouten Village." *Wisconsin Archaeologist* 66, no. 2 (1985).

Shackleford, Alan G. "The Frontier in Pre-Columbian Illinois." *Journal of the Illinois State Historical Society* 100, no. 3 (2007).

Skinner, Claiborne A. *The Upper Country: French Enterprise in the Colonial Great Lakes*. Baltimore: John Hopkins University Press, 2008.

Spooner, Harry. *Indians of Northern Illinois*. Tiskilwa: Tiskilwa Chief, 1941.

Steck, Francis Borgia. *The Jolliet Marquette Expedition, 1673*. Quincy, IL: Franciscan Fathers, 1928.

Steckley, John. "The Early Map 'Nouvelle France,' a Linguistic Analysis." *Ontario Archaeology* 51 (1990).

Storm, Coulton. "Lieutenant John Armstrong's Map of the Illinois River, 1790." *Journal of the Illinois State Historical Society* 32 (March 1944).

Temple, Wayne C. *Indian Villages of the Illinois Country*. Illinois State Museum Scientific Papers, vol. 2, pt. 2. Springfield: Illinois State Museum, 1977.

Thwaites, Reuben G. *France in America, 1497–1763*. New York: Harper and Brothers, 1905.

Titus, W. A. "Historic Spots in Wisconsin: The Lost Village of the Mascouten." *Wisconsin Magazine of History* 5, no. 4 (1922): 382–88.

Trigger, Bruce G. *The Children of Aataentsic, a History of the Huron People to 1600*. Carlton Library Series 195. Montreal: McGill–Queen's University Press, 1976.

———, ed. *Handbook of North American Indians*. Vol. 15. Washington, DC: Smithsonian Institution, 1978.

Walczynski, Mark. "Claude Dablon and Louis Jolliet, Constructing a Narrative from Presuppositions." *Michigan's Habitant Heritage* (French-Canadian Heritage Society of Michigan) 40, no. 2 (2019).

———. *The History of Starved Rock*. Ithaca, NY: Northern Illinois University Press, 2020.

———. *"Inquietus": La Salle in the Illinois Country*. William Potter Publication Series. Plano, TX: Center for French Colonial Studies, 2019.

———. "La Salle vs. Jolliet: A Rivalry for Trade and Colonization in the Illinois Country." *Le Journal* (Center for French Colonial Studies) 32, no. 2 (2016).

———. "Louis Jolliet and Jacques Marquette: Consistencies, Contradictions, and Misconceptions." *Michigan's Habitant Heritage* (French-Canadian Heritage Society of Michigan) 38, no. 3 (2017).

———. *Massacre, 1768: The Search for the Origin of the Legend of Starved Rock*. William Potter Publication Series. St. Louis: Center for French Colonial Studies, 2013.

Wallace, Isabel. *The Life and Letters of General W. H. L. Wallace*. Chicago: R. R. Donnelly, 1909.

Walthall, John. "Aboriginal Pottery and the Eighteenth-century Illini." In *Calumet and Fleur-De-Lys*, ed. John A. Walthall and Thomas E. Emerson. Washington, DC: Smithsonian Institution Press, 1992.

Warren, William W. *History of the Ojibway People*. 1885. Reprint, St. Paul: Minnesota Historical Society Press, 1984.

Wedel, Mildred Mott. "Peering at the Ioway Indians through the Mist of Time, 1650 circa 1700." *Journal of the Iowa Archaeological Society* 33 (1986).

Weiss, Daniel. "When the Inuit Met the Basques." *Archaeology, a Publication of the Archaeological Institute of America* (September–October 2018): 39–40.

Wiggers, Raymond. *Geology Underfoot in Illinois*. Missoula, MT: Mountain Press, 1997.

Wood, John J. "The Mascouten Village." Paper read before the X-Ray Club in Berlin, Wisconsin, February 9, 1907. *Berlin Journal* (1907).

Zitomersky, Joseph. *French Americans: Native Americans in Eighteenth Century French Colonial Louisiana*. Lund, Sweden: Lund University Press, 1995.

Index

Accault, Michel, 136, 203; sent with Hennepin, 184; trades with Des Moines River tribes, 161, 167–68, 202, 264n9

Ackia (village), 217

Albanel, Charles, 63, 66, 162, 188, 235

Algonquian (language), x, 15, 23, 29–32, 36, 77, 91, 95, 97, 228, 245n25, 245n29, 248n27, 250n50, 255n22

Algonquin Indians, 3–4, 7, 25, 244n21, 262n36

Algonquin-Ojibwe (language), 30, 44, 78, 90, 142

Allouez, Claude-Jean, viii–x, 22–23, 44–45, 51–55, 62, 64, 75–79, 89, 102, 136, 142, 144, 158, 162, 173, 176–79, 187, 189, 201, 204, 226, 248n30, 258n55, 262n24; among the Mesquakie, 46–47, 70–71; arrives at Le Rocher,197, 199; arrives in Canada, 23; copper, 33–34; death of, 200; with Dablon, 52–53; enemy of La Salle, 183; establishes St. Marc's, 47; establishes St. Michael's, 50; establishes St. Xavier's, 39; in France, 23, 228, 230–33, 235, 237; on Green Bay, 50; at Kaskaskia, 164–72; at La Pointe, 23–24, 26–32, 34–36; learns of the Mississippi, 31, 45, 65; maps Lake Superior with Marquette, 36–38; at Mascouten village, 47–50, 70–71, 156; at pageant, 57, 61; promoted, 63; at Quebec, 34–35, 39; sends Moonswa

to Illinois, 182, 266n26; travels to Kaskaskia, 163–64

American Bottoms, 94, 206

André, Louis, ix, 51; arrives in Canada, 51; attends pageant, 61–62; with Menominee fishermen, 171; observes true tides, 154; in Wisconsin, 63–64, 70–71, 74–75, 136, 162–63, 183, 188, 232–33, 264n11

aniššina·pe·k Indians, 7–11, 32, 215, 239; land treaties at Chicago, 216, 221, 240; on Manitoulin Island, 57; once a single tribe, 7, 244

Anticosti Island, x, 219, 238; granted to Jolliet, 175, 235–36; Jolliet's map of 145

Aramoni (Vermilion River), x, 113–15, 119, 186, 192, 221

Arius of Alexandria, 170

Arkansas (state), 195

Arkansas country, 206, 216, 237

Arkansas Indians, 99, 102, 104, 199, 256

Arkansas post, 109

Arkansas River, 17, 92, 98, 128, 190, 199, 202, 215, 233, 237

Arkansas village, 98, 100, 131, 206

Armstrong, John, 115, 130

Artaguette, Pierre d', 217, 239

Assiniboine Indians, 44

Atchatchakangouek (Miami subtribe), 192

Aubert de La Chesnaye, Charles, 38

Bacon, Francis, 27

Bailloquet, Pierre, 43, 137, 139, 175

Baugy, Louis Henri de, 192–94, 196, 236, 267n10

Bayly, Charles, 175

Beaujeu, Taneguy Le Gallois de, 197–98

Beaver Wars, 85

Bergier, Marc, 204–6

Big Bend (of the Illinois River), 82, 112–13, 121, 192

Bineteau, Julien, 202

bison, 8, 30, 40, 80, 82, 85, 87, 95, 103, 108–9, 117–18, 136, 151, 155–56, 166, 177, 185, 203, 255n5; migrate to Illinois, 13; parts utilized, 6, 89, 96, 99, 119, 152, 160–61, 167–68, 181–82, 184

Bissot, Claire-Françoise, 159, 234

Bissot, François, 159

Black Hawk, 83, 215, 255n25

Boisseau, Josias, 175–76

Bond (British captain), 207

Boré, Jean, 203

Bouteroue d'Aubigny, Claude de, 38

Brandy Parliament, 160

Bréhant de Galinée, René de, 41–44, 66, 231

Buade, Louis de Comte de Frontenac et de Palluau (Frontenac), 120, 142–46, 160, 181, 190–91, 194, 219–20, 222, 233–36; appoints Franquelin, 139; consults notables, 160; king's instructions, 68–69; recalled, 190; supports exploration, 145

Buffalo Rock, 120–21, 192, 197

Buisson de St. Cosme, Jean François, ix, 205; at demon cove, 94; describes Mississippi, 101; on Des Plaines, 123–24; at Lake Michigan, 204; reaches Mississippi, 92

Buisson de St. Cosme, Michel, 204

Butte des Morts, 76

Cadillac. *See* Laumet de Lamothe Cadillac, Antoine

Cahokia (ancient village), 93

Cahokia (settlement and mission), 12, 93, 97, 168, 204–6, 210, 215

Cahokia Indians (Illinois subtribe), 97, 168, 204–5, 210, 258n31

Cap de la Madeleine, 32–33, 43, 62, 66, 141, 158, 231

Carignan-Salières Regiment, 16, 19, 230

Carte de la Louisiane ou des voyages du Sr. De La Salle, 10, 157, 168, 194, 267n13

Cartier, Jacques, 2, 40, 227

Cass, Louis, 33, 80, 82, 211, 221, 240

Cataraqui River, 69, 137

Cavelier, Jean, 199

Cavelier, René-Robert Sieur de La Salle, viii, x, 10, 18, 40–42, 50–51, 63, 66, 95, 103, 111–14, 120, 124, 130–31, 145, 153, 168, 185, 187, 190–92, 197, 199, 201–3, 206–7, 212, 215–16, 220–22, 226, 232, 237, 239, 268n14; arrives in Canada, 35, 231; born in Rouen, 229, attends Jesuit school, 25–26, 231; builds Fort de Crèvecoeur, 111, 184, 236; builds Fort St. Louis, 115, 191; death of 198, 237; dispatched to Onontagué, 69, 233; finds copper, 121; first expedition, 40–43, 231; at Fort Prudhomme, 96, 206; granted Fort Frontenac and title of nobility, 70, 233; grants land in Arkansas country, 98; grants land to Recollects, 179; Gulf expedition, 176–84, 235; hires men, 136, 160, 233; Illinois land grants, 113–14, 193; Jolliet and Dablon's testimony, 161–62; at Kaskaskia, 178–79, 236; at Lake Peoria, 111, 182–83; La Salle's colony, 192, 236; learns of the Ohio River, 40; leaves Illinois; locates Gulf of Mexico, 189, 225; in Montreal, 65; petitions court for Gulf patent, 193–96, 207, 236; sails on the *Griffon*, 102; second Gulf expedition, 197–98, 236; separates from Dollier and Galinée; on the St. Joseph River, 188–89, 235–36

Cayuga Indians (Haudenosaunee subtribe), 3

Chabanel, Noel, 32

Chachagouessioua, 150, 152, 263n6

Champlain, Samuel de, 3, 11, 40, 180, 227–28

Charlevoix, Pierre-François Xavier de, 97, 108, 112, 115, 121–22, 130, 201, 256n40

charms, 171–72

Chequamegon Bay, 8–10, 12, 23, 33, 44

Chicago Portage, 124–26, 130–31, 141, 145, 151–56, 161, 166, 178, 189, 197, 220–22

Chicago River, 120, 124, 126, 131, 141, 154, 161, 164, 189, 220; reversal of, xi, 103, 212

Chickasaw Indians, viii, 216–17, 239

Choctaw Indians, 216–17

Chouart des Groseilliers, Médard, 15, 81, 230

Christianizing (Gallicizing) Native peoples, 22, 213–14
Clark, James, 212
Code Noir, 218, 239
Coiracoentanon Indians (Illinois subtribe), 168
Colbert, Jean-Baptiste, 16, 38, 40, 50, 66, 68, 142, 145, 159–60, 190, 194, 219, 234; denies Jolliet's request, 159, 235; on Gallicizing the Indians, 22; on locating the Gulf, 63
Compagnie des Cent-Associés (Company of One Hundred Associates), 14, 159, 228–30,
Compagnie d'Occident (Mississippi Company), 208, 211, 217
Compagnie du Canada, 209
copper, 22, 50, 65; found at Lake Superior, 33–34, 39–40, 43, 50, 56, 60, 62, 66–67, 226, 230–32, 240; found by La Salle, 114, 121, 177; found by Allouez in Illinois, 167
Courcelles, Daniel de Rémy de, 16, 39, 41, 60, 68–69, 230, 232–33; arrives in Canada, 20; campaigns against Haudenosaunee, 21
Coureurs des bois, 46, 52, 73, 182–83, 193
Couture, Jean, 98, 199, 237
creeds, 169–71
Crozat, Antoine, 207–8, 238

D'Abancourt, Marie, 138
Dablon, Claude, 36–38, 51, 60–61, 64, 68, 75, 78, 128, 135, 146–47, 156–57, 160, 172, 174–76, 183, 236, 262n24; arrives at Sault, 37; edits Marquette's report, 128–30, 133, 155, 234; Jesuit superior of Canada, 63; in Mackinac, 53–54; meets with Jolliet, 139–42, 160–62, 178, 220, 232, 251n10; meets with Marquette, 51, 232; at pageant, 61–63; superior of western missions, 36; travels with Allouez, 51–54, 232
Daumont sieur de Saint-Lusson, Simon François, 60, 62–63, 79; arrives in Canada, 56; heads to Sault, 51, 56, 59, 62, 251n9; at Quebec, 60; Sault pageant, 57, 61, 70, 153, 232; sent to find copper, 50, 232
D'Autray, Jacques Bourdon, 114, 124, 136, 193–94, 267n10
Davion, Antoine, 92, 205
De Lalande, Jacques, 159, 175, 219, 234–35
Delaunay, Louis, 98, 199, 237
Delbridge Island, 116

Delisle, Legardeur, 108, 111, 115, 130
De Meulles, Jacques, 190, 236
Des Moines River, 12, 83, 86–87, 116, 120, 128, 133, 142, 146, 156, 161–62, 167–68, 184, 186; distance from Illinois village, 254
Des Plaines River, x, xi, 119–20, 122–25, 129–31, 135, 140–41, 154, 161, 164, 176–77, 189, 192, 215, 220–22, 224
Detroit, 9–10, 42–43, 49, 226
D'Iberville. *See* Le Moyne, Pierre d'Iberville
disease, 2, 4, 7, 29, 47, 118, 128, 214, 228
Dodier-Normandin, Jeanne, 138, 233, 261n8
Dolbeau, Jean, 179–80, 228
Dollier de Casson, François, 41–44, 66, 231
Door County Peninsula, 5, 50, 74, 126, 129, 133, 229
Door County (Sturgeon Bay) portage, 127, 133, 149, 163, 197, 260n42
Druillettes, Gabriel, 32, 51, 63, 137, 174, 183, 231–32, 234; tribal population estimates, 264n23
Duchesneau, de la Doussinière et d'Ambault, Jacques, 68, 160, 175, 194, 219, 234–35
Du Plessis, Armand Jean, Richelieu, 2, 3, 21
Dutch (traders), 3, 4, 5, 41–42,

Emerson, Thomas, 213
Emiquon, 109–10
Enjalran, Jean, 174, 187, 235
Erie Indians, 5, 7, 10, 15, 229–30

Ferme du Domaine du Roy, 175, 265n6
fish camps, 2, 226
Forks, the (of the Des Plaines and the Kankakee), 119, 122, 176–77, 192, 215, 239
Fort Armstrong, 82
Fort Bilocchi (Biloxi), 207
Fort Chambly (originally Fort St. Louis), 21
Fort Clark, 111
Fort Dearborn, 211, 221
Fort De Chartres, 93, 210, 215–17, 219, 239
Fort Frontenac, 136–37, 145, 161–62, 179–81, 192–93, 233–34; council at, 69–70
Fort La Boulaye (aka "Mississippi Fort"), 203, 207, 238
Fort Rosalie, 216
Fort St. Jean Baptiste des Natchitoches, 216
Fort St. Louis (Le Rocher), 104, 115, 183, 191–94, 198, 236–37, 258n32

Fort St. Louis (Peoria), 111
Fort St. Louis (Texas), 236
Fort St. Louis de Caddodoches, 216
Fort St. Pierre, 216
Fort Toulouse, 216
Fox Indians. *See* Mesquakie Indians
Fox River (Pestekouy), 10, 119, 121, 154, 192, 223
Fox River (Wisconsin), 9, 12, 47, 49, 75, 78, 120, 154, 168, 181, 197, 233, 236
Fox-Wisconsin portage, 79–80, 107, 120
Franquelin, Jean-Baptiste Louis, 10, 160–61; arrives in Canada, 139; *Carte de la Louisiane*, 168, 192, 194–95; draws maps of 1673 voyage, 142–44, 234, 267n11; General Map of Northern [New] France, 160, 235; sails to France, 193
French military districts in Louisiana, 211

Garcitas Creek, 198
Garnier, Charles, 7
Garreau, Léonard, 15, 229
Georgian Bay, 4, 5, 7, 56, 229
Grand Kankakee Marsh, 11, 176
Grandmaison, Eléonore de (Demoiselle de la Tesserie), 148–49, 234
Gravier, Jacques, ix, x, 90, 158, 202, 204, 255n17; arrives at Kaskaskia, 201, 237; journey down the Mississippi, 206–7, 238; mortally wounded, 89, 211, 238; moves to Rivière des Pères, 203; relationship with Société des Missions Étrangères, 206;
Green Bay (Baie des Puants, La Baie), 9, 11, 39, 50–55, 57, 63, 70, 75, 126–29, 136, 142, 158, 162–63, 168, 171, 226, 232–33, 236, 257n21
Griffon (bark), 43, 102, 168, 181, 185, 235
Gulf of Mexico, viii, 50–51, 79, 95–100, 103, 124, 129, 140–41, 145–46, 153, 160–62, 176, 180, 83–84, 188–99, 202–7, 216, 220, 223, 225–26, 232, 235–38
Gulf of St. Lawrence, 2, 64, 145, 175, 219, 227

Haas site, 84
Hagerman site, 84
Haudenosaunee (Iroquois, Five Nations), viii, 3, 6, 11, 15–16, 23, 32, 34, 36, 40–42, 51–52, 56, 65–66, 70, 162, 171, 173, 185, 188, 190, 193, 200, 229, 244n11, 264n27, 267n34; attack French, 14, 15, 67, 268n15; besiege

Fort St. Louis, 196, 237; council with Frontenac, 69–70, 233; French-Haudenosaunee campaigns, 19–21, 230; influence, 3; intertribal warfare, 4, 8, 10, 15, 46–48, 54, 78, 158, 182, 18–91, 228–30; invade Huronia, 5, 7; meet with Cavelier, 40; name, 243n6; prisoners, 39–40, 42–43, 231–32; warfare with Illinois, 85, 157, 168–69, 172, 182, 186–88, 190, 192, 236
Hennepin (village), 82, 112–13, 192, 197
Hennepin, Louis, 143, 179–81, 266n30; arrives in Canada, 180, 234; captured by Nadouessi, 184; at Kaskaskia, 179; names Lake St. Claire, 102
Henry IV (king), 2
Ho-Chunk (Winnebago), 163, 215, 246n41; in Illinois, 11, 88; name, 250; near Lake Superior, 11; in Wisconsin, 11, 50, 80, 232
Hubbard, Gurdon S., 123–25, 221
Hudson Bay, x, 63, 66, 175–76, 219, 235
Huronia (region), 7, 14, 19, 32, 85, 180, 228
Huronia tribes, viii, 4, 6–7, 30, 32, 228, 244n15

Ice Age (Pleistocene Epoch), 103, 113, 119, 121
Ice Age, Little, 12–13, 64, 229, 246n47
Île d'Orléans, 5, 15, 32
Illiniwek State Historical Site, 84
Illinois (state), 5, 8, 10–11, 13, 17, 93–94, 113–15, 122, 126, 129, 158, 177, 188, 192, 195, 199–200, 206, 213
Illinois and Michigan Canal, 113, 123, 220, 222–23, 240
Illinois Country, vii–xi, 18, 62, 66, 71, 75, 111, 115, 121, 140, 147, 152–54, 158–59, 161–62, 166, 182–88, 191–94, 197, 201–3, 210, 213, 216–19, 232, 234–35, 237, 239
Illinois Indians (*Inohka*), viii, x–xi, 6, 48, 51, 58, 62, 64, 66, 75, 78. 85–89, 98–99, 146, 149–54, 163, 188–89, 202, 206, 210, 230, 232–33, 240; communication between groups, 117, 152, 157; Conduct slave trade, 45, 87–88; demeanor, 30, 33, 53, 84, 86–87, 119–20, 155, 164–65, 172; expulsion from Illinois, 215–16; intertribal warfare, 50–51, 85, 168–69, 172, 185–87, 196; language, 29–31, 44–45, 72, 78–79, 83, 91, 94–95, 97–98, 111–12, 114, 117–18, 123, 142, 158, 170–71, 180, 201–2; name, 90, 246n43, 255n22; population, 89, 120, 132–33, 155–56, 167, 192,

195, 270n54; precontact homelands, 118; subsistence, 30, 53, 86, 118–19, 155–56, 164, 185; trade, 44, 87–88, 98–99, 124, 149, 152, 156–58, 168, 181, 193, 209

Illinois River, viii, x–xi, 6, 8, 18, 82, 90–92, 100–116, 118–22, 128–31, 133, 147, 161, 167, 169, 181, 203, 212, 235–37, 239, 240–41, 245n26; altering channel for commercial navigation, 220–24; maps of 143, 145; water levels (summer pool), 115, 120, 130–31, 140

Illinois River dams, xi, 103, 110, 118, 212, 221, 223–24

Immaculate Conception (mission), 157

Indian boarding schools, 213–15

Irondequoit River, 41

Iroquois. *See* Haudenosaunee

Isle à la Cache, 123–24

Jamet, Denis, 179–80, 228

Jesuits, ix, 6, 18, 24–26, 28, 32, 40, 60, 68, 162, 217, 228; arrive in Canada, 180; attempt to Gallicize Indians, 213; banished from Louisiana, 218–19, 239; beginnings, 27; combat trader influence, 210; enemies of La Salle, 179, 182; killed, 7, 15, 211; learn about the lands and people, 16; learn indigenous languages, 78, 88, 158, 164, 166, 169, 172, 201–2; perceived spiritual powers of, 89, 169; power and influence of, 4, 40, 180, 182–83, 232; slave owners, 217–18; work alongside the Société des Missions Étrangères, 204–6

Jolliet, Adrien, ix, 58–59, 63; at Cap de la Madeleine, 43–44, 66–67; death of, 44, 67, 231; escorts prisoner, 39–40; learns Great Lakes route, 42, 66; searches for copper, 39; at Tinawatawa, 42–43, 249n23; voyageur, 33, 66, 231; wife sues brother Louis, 138–39, 149, 261n7, 261n9

Jolliet, Louis, 58–64, 73, 127–35, 146–47, 153, 156, 167, 181, 190, 206–7, 219, 234–37; buys trade goods from his uncle, 38; canoe wreck, 138, 146, 233; confused with brother Adrien, 66–67; death of, 219, 238; early life, 26, 31–32, 229; explores Hudson Bay, 175–76, 235; in France, 35, 38, 231; journal of, 137–38; linguistic abilities, 78–79, 262; 142; maps, 142–45, 158, 160, 177, 219, 234–35; marriage, 160, 234; meets Marquette,

71–72; meets with Dablon, 139–42, 158, 161–62, 220–22, 224–26, 233; partnerships (1672), 70; at Sault, 57–63, 129–30, 137, 232–33; selected for 1673 voyage, 65–68; summoned to court, 138–39, 148–49, 233

Jolliet-Marquette expedition, vii, x–xii, 1, 13, 17–18, 50, 63, 68, 71, 131, 133, 190, 207, 225–26; among the Illinois, 83–90; among the Menominee, 75; among the Michigamea, 96–97; at the Arkansas, 98–100; at the Chicago portage, 124–26; collect specimens, 76–77; enter the Illinois River, 101–2; at Kaskaskia, 116–20; at the Mascouten village, 77–79; on the Mississippi, 81; at the MONS8PELEA village, 95–96; prepare for the voyage, 72, 74; reaches Green Bay, 126–27, 233; reaches Lake Peoria, 111–12; reaches the Des Plaines, 122; reach the Ohio River, 94–95; reach the Wisconsin portage, 80; return north, 100, 102; the 1673 voyage, 73–135

Jolliet, Zacharie, 70, 137–38, 149

Joutel, Henri, 109, 121, 126, 130, arrive at Fort St. Louis, 199 chronicles La Salle expedition, 104, 183, 203, 206, 250–51n2

Juchereau St. Denys, Charles de, 209, 238

Kankakee Portage, 176–77, 235

Kankakee River (Teakiki), 10, 119, 122, 156, 176–77, 192, 196, 215, 235, 268n15

Kaskaskia (southern Illinois), 93–94, 206, 210, 215, 217, 220–21, 239

Kaskaskia (village), 11, 18, 121, 128–33, 142, 147, 157–58, 162, 168–69, 172, 173, 185–87, 196–97, 201, 259n2, 261n55, 263n12; abandoned, 116, 202, 211, 239; archaeological investigations at, 118, 166, 241; battle to save from developers, 213, 241; captured by Haudenosaunee, 186–90, 236; description of, 116, 118–20, 167, 179, 181–82; during early American period, 211–12, 240; Jolliet and Marquette visit, 116–20; located at portage, 116, 130, 178; Miami-Illinois name, 118; part of La Salle's colony, 192, 236; population, 120, 155–56, 167, 179, 234, 236

Kaskaskia Indians (Illinois subtribe), 48, 89, 97; Escorts French, 122–23, 126; population decline, 215, 265n24, 270n54; settle near the Mississippi, 202–5, 209–10, 215, 238

Kaskaskia River, 97, 209, 238
Keinouché (Odawa subtribe), 44, 51
Kellogg, Joseph, 101
Kennedy, Patrick, 106–9, 115, 130
Kickapoo Indians, 8, 50, 70, 78, 106, 232–33, 256n33; kill de Ribourde, 121, 186, 236
Kilatica Indians (Miami subtribe), 192
Kiskakon Indians, 29, 44–45, 51, 137, 174; exhume Marquette's remains, 173, 235

La Baie. *See* Green Bay
La Belle (frigate), 197–98
La Colbertie (map), 142–44, 160, 234
La Forest, François Dauphin de, 136, 193–94, 199, 202, 234
La Frontenacie (map), 142–44, *144* 160, 168, 234, 267–68n13
L'Aimable (supply ship), 197–98
Lake Erie, 11, 42, 118, 140, 143, 146, 161–62, 181, 220, 249n24
Lake Huron, 39, 42, 54, 56, 73, 140, 143, 245n34
Lake Michigan (*Lac des Ilinois*), 9–11, 39, 74, 88, 100, 119–20, 129, 131, 135, 140, 147, 149–50, 154, 158, 161, 163, 168, 181, 185, 189, 196, 199, 221–25, 232, 235, 245n34, 250–51n2, 253n7, 257n21; name, 250n50, 257n8
Lake Nipissing, 33
Lake Ontario, 4, 40, 43, 69, 140, 143, 145–46, 179, 249n24
Lake Peoria, 12, 18 116, 182, 187, 236; description, 111–12, 124; fort and village, 132, 202–4, 237–38; mission, 89, 202, 205–6, 211
Lake Superior, xi, 9, 11, 15, 23, 32, 43, 60, 87, 142–43, 230; copper located at, 33–34, 240; named for lieutenant-general Tracy, 31, 142; surveyed by Jesuits, 36–38, 231
Lake Winnebago, 9, 76, 83
Lalande, Jacques, 159, 175, 219, 234–35
Lalemant, Gabriel, 7
Landings Development Limited Partnership, 213
La Pointe, viii, 10, 23–34, 35–39, 44–45, 48, 51–52, 54, 57, 62, 72, 87, 136, 163, 165, 173, 226, 230–32; French meet the Peoria, 248n30
La Pointe (mission). *See* St. Esprit
La Potherie, Claude-Charles le Roy de, 46, 59, 107, 257n21

Largillier, Jacques, ix, 129, 146; with Allouez, 163, 197, 201, 235; contract with Jolliet, 70; death of, 210; Jesuit *donne*, 158, 252n37; joins Gravier, 201–2, 211, 237; language skills 201, 79, 147; lay helper, 63, 79; with Marquette, 147, 149–55, 158, 234; 1673 voyage, 72; voyageur, 33, 67
La Salle, Sieur de. *See* Cavelier, René-Robert Sieur de La Salle
La Salle's Indian colony, 192, 202, 236
Laumet de Lamothe Cadillac, Antoine, 208
Laval, Francois, 34, 58–59, 138, 146, 205
Law, John, 208–9, 239
Le Boullenger, Jean-Antoine Robert, 90,
Le Caron, Joseph, 179–80, 228
Le Febvre de La Barre, Joseph-Antoine, 236; arrives in Canada, 190; enemy of La Salle, 191–94, 194; king's instructions, 190
Le Gallois, Taneguy de Beaujeu, 197–98
Le Jeune, Paul, 14
Le Joly (battleship escort), 197
Le Mercier François-Joseph, 21, 31, 34, 36–37, 183, 231
Le Moyne, Jean-Baptiste de Bienville, 207, 210, 217
Le Moyne, Pierre d'Iberville, 198, 203, 207, 238
Le Rocher (Starved Rock), 18, 104, 115–16, 118–23, 126, 183, 185, 191–99, 201–2, 206, 210–15, 221–22, 236–37, 239, 258n31
Limoges, Joseph de, 204
Little Rock site, 114
Livingston, Robert R., 225
Louis XIII (king), 2
Louis XIV (king), 15, 218, 230
Louisiana (colony of), ix, 94, 197–98, 207–10, 216, 218–19, 226, 238–39
Louisiana military districts, 211
Louisiana Purchase, 18, 198, 226, 240

Mackinac Island, 5, 39, 53–54, 229
Mackinac mission. *See* St. Ignace
Mahican Indians, 3, 228
Manitoulin Island, 52, 54, 57, 59, 61, 232, 251n9
Manitoumie maps, 133, *134*
Marest, Pierre-Gabriel, 201–4, 206, 210–11, 238, 245n26
Markman site, 46

Marquette, Jacques, 25–26, 36, 58–62, 64, 73, 131–32, 163–69, 176–78, 182, 187, 200, 204, 212, 225, 256n28; arrives in Canada, 24; cartographer, 38, 82, 132–33, 135, 137, 142–46, 156, 267n13; death of, 158; early years and education, 24, 67; follows tribes to Mackinac, 57–58, 61–62; founds mission of Immaculate Conception, 157, 213; grave located, 173; at Kaskaskia, 155–56; keeps copy of 140, 147; language skills, 44, 72, 78–79, 90, 97, 142; at La Pointe, 44, 52,; learns indigenous language and culture, 32, 35; learns of Mississippi, 45; Marquette's second voyage to Kaskaskia, 131, 146, 149; meets with Dablon at Sault, 51; names Illinois mission, 263n10; recites final vows, 62; relation of, 1, 126–30, 137–38, 206, 256n28, 262n24, 263n36; remains returned to St. Ignace, 174; selected for 1673 voyage, 68; at St. Ignace, 64, 71; at St. Xavier's, 127–29, 146–48; surveys Lake Superior, 36; winters at Chicago, 150–54

Mascouten Indians, 40, 68, 106, 151, 182

Mascouten village (St. Jacques), 48–53, 70–71, 77–79, 135, 142, 156, 163, 176, 232–33, 253n6, 264n27, 266n27

Matagorda Bay, 198, 236

Mazarin, Jules, 15, 230

Membré Zénobe, 179, 181, 185, 193–94, 234; arrives in Canada, 180

Menominee Indians (*folle avoine*), 63, 71, 75, 99, 128, 163, 171, 232–33, 264n11; name of, 250n50

Menominee River, 50, 74, 129

Menominee village, 50, 74

Mesquakie Grand Village (Bell site), 76

Mesquakie Indians (Fox, Renards, Outa-gami), 6, 8, 29–30, 40, 70, 81–82, 85, 136, 166, 170–71, 176, 233, 258; first historical reference to, 229; forced out of Illinois, 215, 240, 255; ill-treated by French, 54–55, 232; at La Point, 9–10, 29–30; migrate to Wisconsin, 9–10, 188; on the Mississippi, 82; name, 9, 262

Mesquakie village (Markman site), 46–47, 54–55, 70–71, 75, 102, 171–72, 232, 253n6

Miami-Illinois (language), 29–31, 44–45, 72, 78–79, 84, 90–91, 97–98, 111, 114, 117, 123, 142, 147, 158, 168, 180, 185, 188; translating, 158, 170–71, 201–2, 232, 255nn22–23

Miami Indians (*myaamia*), 11, 94, 176–77, 204–5; defend Fort St. Louis, 196; determining population, 155, 264n23; hostilities with the Illinois, 153, 182, 188–89, 202; merge with the Peoria, 215; name, 246n43; in Wisconsin, 47–48, 52–53, 70, 78–79, 153, 155–56, 163, 182–83, 196–97, 232–33

Miami post (St. Joseph fort), 184, 188–89, 235–36

Miami villages, 12, 120–21, 188–92, 197, 200, 237, 266n27

Michilimackinac, 53, 58, 62, 120, 136, 141, 173, 181, 196, 203, 217, 250n2

Mihsoora, 119,

Mississippi (state), 207

Mississippi Company. *See* Compagnie d'Occident

Mississippi River, viii, ix, x, 1, 8, 12–18, 29, 60–72, 78–79, 83, 85, 87, 90, 98–100, 101–4, 116, 120, 128–31, 135, 137–41, 146, 161–62, 167, 169, 181–87, 189–90, 194–99, 202, 205–7, 210, 215–16, 225–26, 230, 236–37, 254n30; ancient channel of, 82, 113; artificially manipulated, 103; British regime on 219; Chickasaw and Natchez attack French on, 216; connecting with Great Lakes, 221–22; de Soto at, 1, 227; French learn of, 30, 33–34, 45, 48, 53; juncture with the Illinois, 91, 101; La Salle's altered map of, 195; mapped, 38, 133, 142–43, 145, 168, 267–68n13; at the Missouri, 91–92; mouth of located by d'Iberville, 203, 238; at the Ohio, 94–95, 209; water clarity, 92–93

Missouri (state), 8, 11–12, 78, 83–84, 90, 94–95, 99, 168, 195, 215, 248n29

Missouri Indians, 204

Missouri River, 91–93, 100, 102–3, 131, 133, 146, 168, 205, 209

Mobile, 184, 207, 211, 226

Mohawk Indians (Haudenosaunee subtribe), 3–4, 16, 21, 228; name, 243n8

Mohegan Indians (Loups), 70, 189, 192, 206; defend Fort St. Louis, 196

Moingwena Indians (Illinois subtribe), 85, 156, 167–68, 202–4, 238, 264n27

Monroe, James, 226

Montagnais Indians, 3–4, 7

Montagnais language, 32, 78, 262n20
Montigny, François Jolliet de, 92, 98, 205
Moonswa ("The Deer"), 182–83, 185, 266n26
Moreau, Pierre (*dit* La Toupine), 70, 152–53, 234
Morel, Sieur de La Durantaye, Olivier, 192, 196–97, 236
Mount Jolliet, 123–24
Mud Lake. *See* Chicago Portage

Nadouessi Indians (Sioux), viii, 8, 30, 44–45, 47–48, 51, 88, 204; capture French on Mississippi, 184, 203; hostilities with La Pointe tribes, 23, 35, 52, 62, 75, 232; on the Illinois River, 245n26; killed by Kiskakon at Sault, 137; name, 245n25; warfare with Mesquakie, 70, 171–72
Natchez (city), 216, 226
Natchez Indians, 6, 216–17
Neutral Indians, 5, 15, 229
New Orleans, 203, 211, 216–17, 219–21, 225–26
Niagara, 141, 145, 161, 181, 220, 235
Niagara escarpment, 74
Niagara portage, 162
Nicolas, Louis, ix, 24–25, 32, 137, 173, 230; at La Pointe, 34–36, 231; leaves Jesuits, 36
Nipissing Indians, 34, 38, 229, 244
Normandin, Jeanne Dodier, 138–39, 233, 261n8
Nouvel, Henri, 32, 63, 137, 146, 158, 162, 173–74, 188, 234

Odawa Country, 9
Odawa Indians, x, 7–8, 19, 29, 31, 39, 43–44, 137, 174, 232; attend Indian boarding schools, 214, 240–41; at Buffalo Rock, 121; flee La Pointe, 58, 60–62; in Illinois Country, 215; at La Pointe, 52, 57, 232; name, 244
Odawa language, 31, 44–45
Ogoula Tchetoka (village), 217
Ohio River, 40–42, 94–95, 100, 114, 137, 168, 181, 209, 231, 238–39, 267–68n13; Miami-Illinois name, 97
Ojibwe Indians, 7–9, 19, 39, 77, 137, 171; in Illinois Country, 215; language 44–45, 78–79, 90, 142, 245n29, 250n50, 262n36; name, 244n22
Oliva, J. P., 24–26, 230–31
Oneida Indians (Haudenosaunee subtribe), 3

Onondaga Indians (Haudenosaunee subtribe), 3, 69
Onontagué, 69, 233
Otoe Indians, 86, 161, 184, 192, 236
Ottawa country, 23, 33, 40, 64, 138, 148–49, 205, 231
Ottawa-French River route, 34, 56

Parkman, Francis, 212–13
Patoulet, Jean-Baptiste, 38, 43, 249n21
Peerish (Potawatomi chief), 211–12
Peoria Indians (Illinois subtribe), 255n17, 258n31; at La Pointe, 248n30
Pepikokia Indians (Miami subtribe), 192
Péré, Jean, 39–40, 43, 63, 66–67, 231
Perrot, Nicolas, 11, 23, 39, 59, 77; pageant, 55–57, 61–62
Petun Indians, 5–7, 29–30, 229
Phélypeaux, Louis comte de Pontchartrain, 203
Piankashaw Indians (Miami subtribe), 192, 215, 241
Piasa, 91, 256
Pierson, Philippe, 137, 158, 162, 173, 234–35, 260n48
Pinet, Pierre-François, 202–6
Pirogues, 119
Pontchartrain. *See* Phélypeaux, Louis comte de Pontchartrain
Portage of the Oaks. *See* Chicago Portage
Porteret, Pierre, 146–47, 149–51, 153–55, 158, 234
Potawatomi Indians, 7–8, 150, 262; near Green Bay, 45–46, 50, 63–64, 70–71, 74–75, 149, 163, 232–33; in the Illinois, 111, 152, 211, 215, 239; at La Pointe, 29–31; name, 244
Pratt, Richard, 214
prayer, 44, 70–71, 75, 121, 163–64, 166, 172, 186, 210; at Marquette's grave, 174; taught to Illinois converts, 169–71
Prouville, Alexander de Tracy, 21, 23; appointed lieutenant-general, 16, 230; arrives in Canada, 19; background of, 19–20; leaves Canada, 35, 231
Prudhomme, Pierre, 96; fort named for, 96, 206; land grant, 113, 193–94, 267n10

Quapaw Indians. *See* Arkansas Indians
Quebec (town), 5, 13, 21–24, 32, 34, 35–36, 39, 43, 60–70, 121, 126, 128, 133, 135, 136–47, 149,

158–59, 175–76, 180–81, 184, 190, 193–94, 199, 201, 205, 216, 220, 229, 231–34, 237, 252n25, 256n28, 262n24, 266n18; captured by Kirkes, 2, 7, 228; established, 6, 227; Jesuit *collège*, 26, 144–45

Radisson, Pierre-Esprit, 15, 81, 230
Recollects (Catholic order), 102, 121, 181, 228, 234, 236; arrive in Canada, 6, 228; check on Jesuits, 69, 232; history in Canada, 179–80; in the Illinois, 179, 187
Rector, William, 212
red maples, 122
Red River, 216
Rémy de Courcelles, Daniel de, 39, 41, 60, 69, 230, 232; arrives in Canada, 20; Haudeno-saunee campaign, 20–21; leaves Canada, 68, 233
Ribourde, Gabriel de la, 179–81, 185, 232; killed by Kickapoo, 186, 236
Richelieu, Cardinal, 2–3
Rivière des Pères, 203–4, 209, 238
Rock River, 83

Sagard, Gabriel, 6, 180, 228, 244n17, 247n21
Saffray de Mézy, Augustin de, 16
Sangamon River, 108
Sauk Indians, 8, 81, 85; defend territory from encroachment, 91; forced west of Mis-sissippi, 215, 240; at Green Bay, 45; at La Pointe, 29–30, 245n33; migrate to Wiscon-sin, 9; name, 9, 245n29; at Saukenuk, 83; sign 1804 Treaty, 255
Sault Ste. Marie, xi, 32, 36–39, 44, 48–52, 57–63, 67, 78, 137, 146, 162, 172, 174, 201, 231–34, 251n9; Marquette's remains interred at, 173–74; site of Jolliet's trading post, 57, 59, 67, 127, 129, 137, 141, 143, 149, 233
Sault Ste. Marie (pageant), 57, 59–61, 63, 70, 79, 153, 232
Schoolcraft, Henry, 130; ascends Illinois River, 104–6, 109–10, 112, 115; at Kaskaskia, 211–12, 240; on Lake Superior, 33, 240; line of distinction, 124; on the Mississippi, 83; proposes canal, 221–22; in Wisconsin, 80
scientific method, 27
Seneca (Illinois), 121
Seneca Indians (Haudenosaunee subtribe), 3, 5, 10, 40, 42; name of, 249n13; visit Cavelier, 40–41

Sept-Îsles, 159, 175, 219, 235
shamans, 88, 162, 165, 170, 176, 211; confronts Allouez, 28–29; missionaries believed to be, 7
Shawnee Indians, 40, 97, 132; defend Fort St. Louis, 196; at Kaskaskia, 186; at La Salle's Miami post, 188, 236; name, 249n14; part of La Salle's colony, 192, 236; search for La Salle, 199, 237; travel Aramoni River, 114
Silvy, Antoine, 182, 188, 234; arrives in Can-ada, 136; in Wisconsin, 162–63, 176
Sinagaux (Odawa subtribe), 44, 51, 64
Sioux Indians. *See* Nadouessi Indians
slave boy (Native boy, guide), 87; drowns in St. Lawrence, 138; guide, 107, 116, 120, 232, 259n10
slavery (African), 208, 216; Jesuits and slav-ery, 217–18, 240–41; laws of Code Noir, 218
slavery (Native American), 24, 45, 87, 169, 209, 217
Société des Missions Étrangères, ix, 92, 202, 204–6, 237
Sovereign Council, 16, 69, 230
Spanish, 1–2, 17, 184–85, 195, 207, 227; on the lower Mississippi, 98–99, 137, 195, 198, 210, 225
Springview site, 50
Starved Rock. *See* Le Rocher
Starved Rock Lock and Dam, 212, 224
Ste. Genevieve (Missouri), 94
St. Esprit (mission), xi, 9, 24, 33, 36, 44–45, 51, 61, 71, 230–31; abandoned, 52, 57–58
St. François (ketch), 197–98
St. Ignace, vii–viii, 39, 53, 58, 62–63, 71, 130, 141–42, 158, 162, 173–74, 226, 232–33, 235, 251n23
Stirling, Thomas, 18, 239
St. Jacques (mission), 70, 163, 253n6, 266n27
St. Joseph River, 12, 162, 176–77, 185, 189, 191, 197, 199, 201, 235, 237, 257n21
St. Joseph River fort, 184, 188, 235
St. Lawrence River, x, 2, 13, 16, 21–22, 32, 34, 43, 50, 56, 63, 66, 136–40, 146, 180, 190, 193, 216, 219, 256n28
St. Lawrence Valley, 4, 14, 87
St. Marc's (mission), 47
St. Marie (mission). *See* Sault Ste. Marie
St. Michael (mission), 50
St. Xavier (mission), 46, 64, 70, 75, 102, 127–29, 146–47, 154, 162–63, 197, 233–35; established, 39

Sulfur Springs Hotel, 212, 213

Sulpicians, 35, 69, 199, 231

Talon, Jean, 31, 43, 65, 69, 145, 159, 252n40, 252n49; accomplishments of first term, 38; appointed intendent, 16, 230; background, 21–22; chooses Louis Jolliet for the 1673 voyage, 65–67, 233; conducts census, 31, 231; confuses Louis with Adrien, 66–67, 142; dispatches La Salle west, 50–51, 190, 232; dispatches Péré and Adrien Jolliet west, 40; hopes to Gallicize Indians, 22; instructed to locate South Sea, 63–64; instructions to St. Lusson, 50, 60, 190, 232; locating mines, 22, 34, 39, 63, 190; sails to France, 38, 68, 231; second term as intendent, 56, 232–33

Tamaroa Indians (Illinois subtribe), 156, 204–6

Tamaroa village, 93, 97, 168, 204–6, 256n43

Tapouaro Indians (Illinois subtribe), 168

Texas Survivors, 109, 199

Tinawatawa, 42–43, 231

Titus, W. A., 49

Tonti, Henri, 120, 124, 130–31, 185, 202, 207; Arkansas seigniory, 98, 190, 199, 237; at Fort de Crèvecoeur, 184–85; guides missionaries to the Mississippi, 92, 202–3, 237; leads Illinois against Haudenosaunee, 186; at Le Rocher, 193–94, 199, 237, 267n10

trade concessions, 2, 16, 36–37, 159, 175, 219, 235; in the Illinois Country, 131, 199, 202, 209; in Louisiana, 207–8

Treaty of Castor Hill, 215

Treaty of Chicago, 216, 240

Treaty of Edwardsville, 215, 240

Treaty of Fontainebleau, 225

Treaty of Saint-Germain-en-Laye, 7, 228

Treaty of San Ildefonso, 225

Treaty of Vincennes, 215, 240

Trois Rivieres, 4, 15, 19, 23, 25, 32, 35, 62, 141, 180

Vermilion River. See *Aramoni*

Viel, Nicolas, 6, 180, 228, 266n18

Vitelleschi, Mutius, 7

Voltaire (François-Marie Arouet), 218

Voyer d'Argenson, Pierre de, 15

Washington Island, 168

Wea Indians (Miami subtribe), 70, 192, 215, 233, 241, 266n27

Wendat country, 7, 180, 228

Wendat Indians (Huron), 3, 23, 32, 142, 265n2; ally with Champlain, 3, 228; attacked by Haudenosaunee, 4–5, 8, 15, 229, 244n11; agricultural villages, 6, 30; expelled from Huronia, 15, 19, 85; fish spirits, 247; flee La Pointe, 57–58, 60–61; kill missionary, 266n18; name, 243n6; spar with Nadouessi, 52, 232; at St. Ignace, 62, 64, 162, 174, 251n23; trade networks, 244n15; utilize charms, 171;

wild rice (*Zizania aquatica*), 75, 123–25

Winnebago Indians. *See* Ho-Chunk

Wisconsin (state), 5, 8–12, 39, 46–53, 58, 63, 70, 74–82, 87, 95, 99, 102, 118–19, 121, 126, 158, 162, 176, 187, 197, 200, 229, 233

Wisconsin River, 17, 79–80, 137, 162, 181

Wittry, Warren L., 49

Woermann Maps, xi, 107, 241, 270n47

Wolf River, 9–10, 39, 46, 70–71, 75–76, 166, 172, 232–33

Wood, John J., 49

Zimmerman site, 88, 166

MARK WALCZYNSKI is a retired faculty member at Illinois Valley Community College and the Park Historian for the Starved Rock Foundation. He is the author of *The History of Starved Rock*.

The University of Illinois Press
is a founding member of the
Association of University Presses.

———————————————————

Composed in 11/14.5 Arno Pro
by Kirsten Dennison
at the University of Illinois Press
Manufactured by Sheridan Books, Inc.

University of Illinois Press
1325 South Oak Street
Champaign, IL 61820-6903
www.press.uillinois.edu